THE LANGUAGE OF LITERATURE

THE InterActive READER™

Reading Consultants, *The InterActive Reader*™

Sharon Sicinski-Skeans, Ph.D. Assistant Professor of Reading, University of Houston-Clear Lake; former K–12 Language Arts Program Director, Spring Independent School District, Houston, Texas.
Olga Bautista Reading Coordinator, Will C. Wood Middle School, Sacramento, California.

Senior Consultants, *The Language of Literature*

Arthur N. Applebee Professor of Education, State University of New York at Albany; Director, National Research Center on English Learning and Achievements; Senior Fellow, Center for Writing and Literacy.
Andrea B. Bermúdez Professor of Studies in Language and Culture; Director, Research Center for Language and Culture; Chair, Foundations and Professional Studies, University of Houston-Clear Lake.
Sheridan Blau Senior Lecturer in English and Education and former Director of Composition, University of California at Santa Barbara; Director, South Coast Writing Project; Director, Literature Institute for Teachers; Past President, National Council of Teachers of English.
Rebekah Caplan Coordinator, English Language Arts K–12, Oakland Unified School District, Oakland, California; Teacher-Consultant, Bay Area Writing Project, University of California at Berkeley; served on the California State English Assessment Development Team for Language Arts.
Peter Elbow Professor of English, University of Massachusetts at Amherst; Fellow, Bard Center for Writing and Thinking.
Susan Hynds Professor and Director of English Education, Syracuse University, Syracuse, New York.
Judith A. Langer Professor of Education, State University of New York at Albany; Director, National Research Center on English Learning and Achievements; Director, Albany Institute for Research on Education.
James Marshall Professor of English and English Education, University of Iowa, Iowa City.

Acknowledgments

Penguin Books: Excerpts from *The Epic of Gilgamesh,* translated by N. K. Sandars (Penguin Classics, 1960; Third Edition, 1972). Copyright © 1960, 1964, 1972 by N. K. Sandars. Reproduced by permission of Penguin Books Ltd.

Viking Penguin: "Rama and Ravana in Battle," from *The Ramayana* by R. K. Narayan. Copyright © 1972 by R. K. Narayan. Used by permission of Viking Penguin, a division of Penguin Putnam Inc.

Continued on page 451.

ISBN 0-618-23202-8

1 2 3 4 5 6 7 8 9–PBO–08 07 06 05 04 03 02

THE InterActive READER™

Table of Contents

Introducing *The InterActive Reader*™

***The InterActive Reader*™** is a new kind of literature book. As you will see, this book helps you become an active reader. It is a book to mark on, to write in, and to make your own. You can use it in class *and* take it home.

An Easy-to-Carry Literature Text

This book won't weigh you down—it can fit as comfortably in your hand as it can in your backpack. Yet it contains works by such important authors as . . .

Homer whose epic poem the *Iliad* tells the story of the Trojan War and the heroes who fought in it.

Miguel de Cervantes whose famous story *Don Quixote* describes the adventures of a strange and amusing character who lives in a world of fantasy.

Leo Tolstoy whose story "What Men Live By" explores human nature and human values.

You will read these selections and other great literature—plays, poems, stories, and nonfiction. You will also learn how to understand the texts you use in classes, on tests, and in the real world.

Help for Reading

Many works of literature are challenging the first time you read them. *The InterActive Reader*™ helps you understand these works. Here's how.

Before-You-Read Activities The page before each literary work helps you connect a selection to your everyday life and gives you a key to understanding the selection.

Preview A preview of every selection tells you what to expect.

Reading Tips Useful, specific reading tips are provided at points where language is difficult.

Focus Each longer piece is broken into smaller "bites" or sections. A focus at the beginning of each section tells you what to look for.

Pause and Reflect At the end of each section, a quick question or two helps you check your understanding.

Read Aloud Specific passages are marked for you to read aloud. You will use your voice and ears to interpret literature.

Reread This feature directs you to passages where a lot of action, change, or meaning is packed in a few lines.

Mark It Up This feature invites you to mark your own notes and questions right on the page.

Vocabulary Support

Words to Know Important new words are underlined. Their definitions appear in a Words to Know section at the bottom of any page where they occur in the selection. You will work with these words in the Words to Know SkillBuilder pages.

Personal Word List As you read, you will want to add some words from the selections to your own vocabulary. Write these words in your Personal Word List on page 444.

SkillBuilder Pages

After each literary selection, you will find these SkillBuilder pages:

Active Reading SkillBuilder

Literary Analysis SkillBuilder

Words to Know SkillBuilder (for most selections)

These pages will help you practice and apply important skills.

Academic and Informational Reading

Here is a special collection of real world examples to help you read every kind of informational material, from textbooks to technical directions. The strategies you learn will help you on tests, in other classes, and in the world outside of school. You will find strategies for the following:

Analyzing Text Features This section explains how titles, subtitles, lists, graphics, and special features work in magazines and textbooks.

Understanding Visuals You will learn how to read charts, maps, graphs, and diagrams.

Recognizing Text Structures You will understand the different ways information can be organized, such as cause and effect and comparison and contrast.

Reading in the Content Areas You will learn strategies for reading social studies, science, and mathematics texts.

Reading Beyond the Classroom You will learn about applications, schedules, technical directions, Web pages, and other readings you encounter in the world outside of school.

Links to *The Language of Literature*

If you are using McDougal Littell's *The Language of Literature*, you will find *The InterActive Reader*™ to be the perfect companion. The literary selections in the reader can all be found in that book. *The InterActive Reader*™ helps you read certain core selections from *The Language of Literature* more slowly and in greater depth.

Read on to learn more!

User's Guide

***The InterActive Reader*™ has an easy-to-follow organization, as illustrated by these sample pages from "What Men Live By."**

Connect to Your Life

These activities help you see connections between your own life and what happens in the selection.

Key to the Selection

This section provides a "key" to help you unlock the selection so that you can understand and enjoy it. One of these four kinds of keys will appear:

- **What You Need to Know**—important background information.
- **What's the Big Idea?**—an introduction to key words or concepts in the selection.
- **What Do You Think?**—a preview of an important quotation from the selection.

Before You Read

Connect to Your Life

Think about a time when you came upon a stranger in need. Or imagine a time in the future when you might meet a needy person. Use the concept web below to describe your feelings and actions.

I noticed ____________

I felt ____________

STRANGER IN NEED

I thought about ____________

I decided to ____________

Key to the Story

WHAT'S THE BIG IDEA? The Bible says that a man does not live by bread alone. This statement is key to the theme of the story you are about to read. What do you think this statement means?

Besides bread, a person needs ____________

258

Fiction

What Men Live By

by Leo Tolstoy

Translated by
Louise and Aylmer Maude

PREVIEW Leo Tolstoy's stories often have a moral, a lesson about life and how to live it. This story is about a poor peasant and a stranger he meets one day. Can a person with nothing help someone else in need?

259

PREVIEW

This feature tells you what the selection is about. It may also raise a question that helps you set a purpose for reading.

And there's more!

User's Guide *continued*

1 Focus

Every selection is broken down into parts. A Focus introduces each part and tells you what to look for as you read.

2 MARK IT UP

This feature may appear in the Focus or in the side column next to a boxed passage. It asks you to underline or circle key details in the text.

3 MARK IT UP KEEP TRACK

This easy-to-use marking system helps you track your understanding. Turn to page xii to see a model of how the system can be used.

NOTES

3 MARK IT UP KEEP TRACK As you read, you can use these marks to keep track of your understanding.

* This is important.
? I have a question about this.
! This is a surprise.

260 The InterActive Reader

1 FOCUS

It is winter in Russia, a long time ago. Read to find out about the problems a poor peasant faces as he tries to provide for his family.

2 MARK IT UP As you read, circle details that tell you about his problems. An example is highlighted.

I

A shoemaker named Simon, who had neither house nor land of his own, lived with his wife and children in a peasant's hut and earned his living by his work. Work was cheap but bread was dear, and what he earned he spent for food. The man and his wife had but one sheep-skin coat between them for winter wear, and even that was worn to tatters, and this was the second year he had been wanting to buy sheep-skins for a new coat. Before winter Simon saved up a little money: a three-ruble note lay hidden in his wife's box, and five rubles and twenty kopeks[1] were owed him by customers in the village.

So one morning he prepared to go to the village to buy the sheep-skins. He put on over his shirt his wife's wadded nankeen[2] jacket, and over that he put his own cloth coat. He took the three-ruble note in his pocket, cut himself a stick to serve as a staff, and started off after breakfast. "I'll collect the five rubles that are due to me," thought he, "add the three I have got, and that will be enough to buy sheep-skins for the winter coat."

He came to the village and called at a peasant's hut, but the man was not at home. The peasant's wife promised that the money should be paid next week, but she would not pay it herself. Then Simon called on another peasant, but this one swore he had no money, and would only pay twenty kopeks which he owed for a pair of boots Simon had mended. Simon then tried to buy the sheep-skins on credit, but the dealer would not trust him.

1. **kopeks** (kō′pĕks): A kopek is one hundredth of a ruble.
2. **nankeen:** a sturdy cotton cloth.

"Bring your money," said he, "then you may have your pick of the skins. We know what debt-collecting is like."

So all the business the shoemaker did was to get the twenty kopeks for boots he had mended and to take a pair of felt boots a peasant gave him to sole with leather.

Simon felt downhearted. He spent the twenty kopeks on vodka and started homewards without having bought any skins. In the morning he had felt the frost; but now, after drinking the vodka, he felt warm even without a sheep-skin coat. He trudged along, striking his stick on the frozen earth with one hand, swinging the felt boots with the other, and talking to himself.

"I'm quite warm," said he, "though I have no sheep-skin coat. I've had a drop and it runs through my veins. I need no sheep-skins. I go along and don't worry about anything. That's the sort of man I am! What do I care? I can live without sheep-skins. I don't need them. My wife will fret, to be sure. And, true enough, it is a shame; one works all day long and then does not get paid. Stop a bit! If you don't bring that money along, sure enough I'll skin you, blessed if I don't. How's that? He pays twenty kopeks at a time! What can I do with twenty kopeks? Drink it—that's all one can do! Hard up, he says he is! So he may be—but what about me? You have house, and cattle, and everything; I've only what I stand up in! You have corn of your own growing, I have to buy every grain. Do what I will, I must spend three rubles every week for bread alone. I come home and find the bread all used up and I have to work out another ruble and a half. So just you pay up what you owe, and no nonsense about it!"

4 Pause & Reflect

Pause & Reflect

Review the details you circled. Given the problems Simon faces, do you think he'll be able to solve them? **(Predict)**

YES/NO because

What Men Live By 261

4 Pause & Reflect

Whenever you see these words in the selection, stop reading. Go to the side column and answer the questions. Then move ahead to the next Focus and continue your reading.

Pause-and-Reflect questions at the end of every section follow up the Focus activity at the beginning of each section. They give you a quick check of your understanding.

And there's more!

Student Model

These pages show you how one student made use of *The InterActive Reader*™ for the selection "What Men Live By."

Note how this student used the following symbols:

- ***** marks a place where something is important—a main idea, topic sentence, or important detail.
- **?** marks a place where something is unclear or confusing.
- **!** marks a surprising or critical fact, or a turning point in the action—not just a main idea, but a major event or theme.

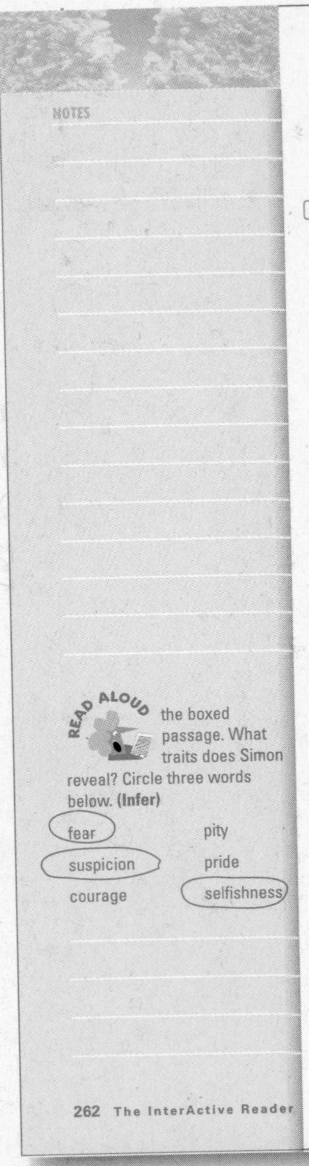

NOTES

READ ALOUD the boxed passage. What traits does Simon reveal? Circle three words below. **(Infer)**

fear	pity
suspicion	pride
courage	selfishness

262 The InterActive Reader

FOCUS

Returning home from the village, Simon notices a stranger behind a shrine.

MARK IT UP As you read, circle details that tell you about Simon's reaction to the stranger.

By this time he had nearly reached the shrine[3] at the bend of the road. Looking up, he saw something whitish behind the shrine. The daylight was fading, and the shoemaker peered at the thing without being able to make out what it was. "There was no white stone here before. Can it be an ox? It's not like an ox. It has a head like a man, but it's too white; and what could a man be doing there?"

He came closer, so that it was clearly visible. To his surprise it really was a man, alive or dead, sitting naked, leaning motionless against the shrine. Terror seized the shoemaker, and he thought, "Some one has killed him, stripped him, and left him here. If I meddle I shall surely get into trouble."

So the shoemaker went on. He passed in front of the shrine so that he could not see the man. When he had gone some way he looked back, and saw that the man was no longer leaning against the shrine but was moving as if looking towards him. The shoemaker felt more frightened than before, and thought, "Shall I go back to him or shall I go on? If I go near him something dreadful may happen. Who knows who the fellow is? He has not come here for any good. If I go near him he may jump up and throttle me, and there will be no getting away. Or if not, he'd still be a burden on one's hands. What could I do with a naked man? I couldn't give him my last clothes. Heaven only help me to get away!"

So the shoemaker hurried on, leaving the shrine behind him—when suddenly his conscience smote him and he stopped in the road.

3. **shrine:** a place at which devotion is paid to God or a holy person.

"What are you doing, Simon?" said he to himself. "The man may be dying of want, and you slip past afraid. Have you grown so rich as to be afraid of robbers? Ah, Simon, shame on you!"

So he turned back and went up to the man.

Pause & Reflect

II

FOCUS

Read to find out how Simon treats the stranger when he returns to the shrine.

Simon approached the stranger, looked at him and saw that he was a young man, fit, with no bruises on his body, but evidently freezing and frightened, and he sat there leaning back without looking up at Simon, as if too faint to lift his eyes. Simon went close to him and then the man seemed to wake up. Turning his head, he opened his eyes and looked into Simon's face. That one look was enough to make Simon fond of the man. He threw the felt boots on the ground, undid his sash, laid it on the boots, and took off his cloth coat.

"It's not a time for talking," said he. "Come, put this coat on at once!" And Simon took the man by the elbows and helped him to rise. As he stood there, Simon saw that his body was clean and in good condition, his hands and feet shapely, and his face good and kind. He threw his coat over the man's shoulders, but the latter could not find the sleeves. Simon guided his arms into them, and drawing the coat on well, wrapped it closely about him, tying the sash round the man's waist.

Simon even took off his cap to put it on the man's head, but then his own head felt cold and he thought: "I'm quite bald, while he has long curly hair." So he put his cap on his

Pause & Reflect

1. Look back at the details you circled. How does Simon react to the stranger when he first sees him? How do Simon's feelings change? Complete the sentences below. **(Compare and Contrast)**

At first, he is afraid of him. He doesn't want to go near him.

But later, he thinks he's being selfish and goes up to him.

2. What does this change tell you about Simon? **(Draw Conclusions)**

Though he thought only about himself at first, he turns out to have a good heart. Most people wouldn't turn back

Before You Read

Connect to Your Life

In this story, a king named Gilgamesh faces a loss he finds hard to accept. Think of a major disappointment or loss that you or someone you know has faced. How difficult was it to accept the situation? Why? Write your ideas below.

Disappointment or Loss	Why It Was Difficult to Accept
A couple years ago, my best friend's Father died (whom I was close to).	It was very difficult to accept because at First it didn't seem real, then it hurt so much that I wanted it to not be real.

Key to the Epic

WHAT YOU NEED TO KNOW *The Epic of Gilgamesh* may be the oldest quest story ever recorded. In a quest story, a hero goes on a long journey and tries to achieve a difficult goal. Historians believe that Gilgamesh was a real Sumerian king who ruled the city-state of Uruk in about 2700 B.C. In the centuries after his death, stories were told and retold about him. Gilgamesh developed into a legendary figure. Two-parts god and one-part human, Gilgamesh has exceptional powers and extraordinary flaws. He represents both the best and worst a person can be.

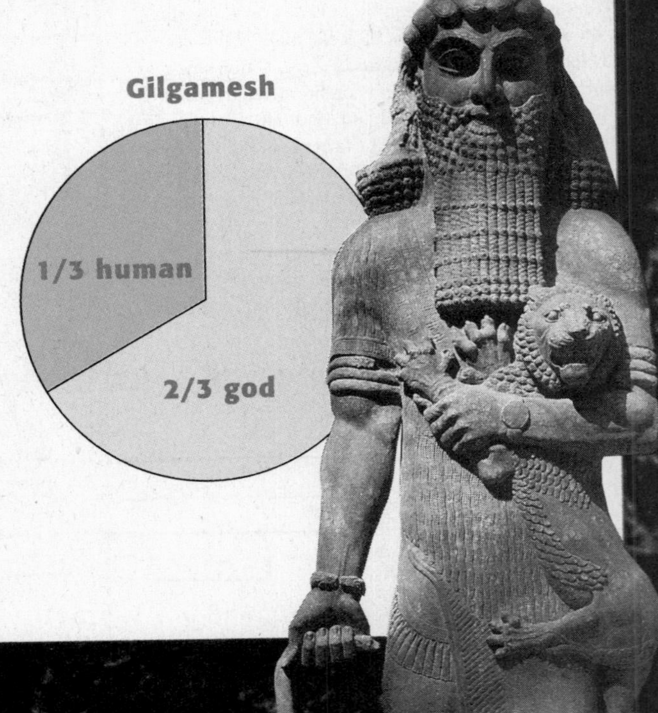

from THE EPIC OF GILGAMESH

Translated by N. K. Sandars

PREVIEW Gilgamesh is a superhuman ruler who has let his power go to his head. Rather than take care of his subjects, he has begun to take advantage of them. Try as they might, the gods are unable to change him. Gilgamesh and his best friend, Enkidu, have caused so much trouble, the gods decide that one of them must die. Since Gilgamesh is part-god, the gods choose Enkidu, who is entirely mortal.

• CHARACTERS AND PLACES IN THE EPIC •

Anu (ā′nōō): Father of the gods, who had an important temple in Uruk.

Anunnaki (ä-nōō-nä′kē): gods who judge the dead and control destinies.

Belit-Sheri (bĕl′ēt shĕr′ē): Scribe and recorder of the underworld gods.

Dilmun (dĭl′mən): A paradise in the world of the gods.

Ea (ā′ä): God of waters and of wisdom, and one of the creators of mankind, toward whom he is usually well-disposed.

Enkidu (ĕn′kē-dōō): Gilgamesh's friend; molded by Aruru, goddess of creation, out of clay, he is wild or natural man.

Enlil (ĕn′lĭl): God of earth, wind, and spirit; carries out tasks for Anu.

Ereshkigal (ĕ-rĕsh′kē′gäl): The queen of the underworld.

Gilgamesh (gĭl′gə-mĕsh′): The king of Uruk and the hero of the epic.

Irkalla (ĭr-kä′lə): Another name for Ereshkigal, the queen of the underworld.

Ishtar (ĭsh′tär): Goddess of love, fertility, and war, called the Queen of Heaven.

Nergal (nĕr′gäl): husband of Ereshkigal and co-ruler of the underworld.

Ninurta (nə-nĕr′tə): A warrior and god of war, wells, and irrigation.

Shamash (shä′mäsh): The sun god, judge and giver of laws.

Siduri (sə-dōō′rē): The divine winemaker and brewer, who lives on the shore of the sea in the garden of the sun.

Urshanabi (ûr′shə-nä-bē): The boatman of Utnapishtim who ferries daily across the waters of death that divide the garden of the sun from the paradise where Utnapishtim lives.

Uruk (ōō′ro͝ok′): Biblical Erech, modern Warka, in southern Babylonia between Fara and Ur. Shown by excavation to have been an important city from very early times, with great temples to the gods Anu and Ishtar.

Utnapishtim (ōōt′nə-pēsh′təm): Friend of the god Ea, with whose help he survives the flood, together with his family and with "the seed of all living creatures." He and his wife are the only mortals to be granted the gift of eternal life.

THE DEATH OF ENKIDU

Before Enkidu dies, he tells Gilgamesh about a dream in which he sees what will happen to him in the afterlife.

FOCUS

Enkidu tells Gilgamesh about a dream he has. Find out what effect this has on Gilgamesh.

MARK IT UP Circle details that help you understand what Enkidu's glimpse of the afterlife is like.

As Enkidu slept alone in his sickness, in bitterness of spirit he poured out his heart to his friend. "It was I who cut down the cedar, I who leveled the forest, I who slew Humbaba and now see what has become of me. Listen, my friend, this is the dream I dreamed last night. The heavens roared, and earth rumbled back an answer; between them stood I before an awful being, the somber-faced man-bird; he had directed on me his purpose. His was a vampire face, his foot was a lion's foot, his hand was an eagle's talon. He fell on me and his claws were in my hair, he held me fast and I smothered; then he transformed me so that my arms became wings covered with feathers. He turned his stare towards me, and led me away to the palace of Irkalla, the Queen of Darkness, to the house from which none who enters ever returns, down the road from which there is no coming back.

"There is the house whose people sit in darkness; dust is their food and clay their meat. They are clothed like birds with wings for covering, they see no light, they sit in darkness. I entered the house of dust and I saw the kings of the earth, their crowns put away for ever; rulers and princes, all those who once wore kingly crowns and ruled the world in the days of old. They who had stood in the place of the gods like Anu and Enlil, stood now like servants to fetch baked meats in the house of dust, to carry cooked meat and cold water from the water-skin. In the house of dust which I entered were high priests and acolytes,[1] priests of the

1. **acolytes** (ăk′ə-līts′): assistants at religious services.

This story contains many character and place names that may be unfamiliar and difficult to pronounce. As you come across these names, look back at the list on page 4 to determine who or what they are. Then make notes in the margin to help you remember who is who.

NOTES

incantation and of ecstasy; there were servers of the temple, and there was Etana, that king of Kish whom the eagle carried to heaven in the days of old. I saw also Samuqan, god of cattle, and there was Ereshkigal the Queen of the Underworld; and Belit-Sheri squatted in front of her, she who is recorder of the gods and keeps the book of death. She held a tablet from which she read. She raised her head, she saw me and spoke: 'Who has brought this one here?' Then I awoke like a man drained of blood who wanders alone in a waste of rushes; like one whom the bailiff has seized and his heart pounds with terror."

Gilgamesh had peeled off his clothes, he listened to his words and wept quick tears, Gilgamesh listened and his tears flowed. He opened his mouth and spoke to Enkidu: "Who is there in strong-walled Uruk who has wisdom like this? Strange things have been spoken, why does your heart speak strangely? The dream was marvelous but the terror was great; we must treasure the dream whatever the terror; for the dream has shown that misery comes at last to the healthy man, the end of life is sorrow." And Gilgamesh lamented, "Now I will pray to the great gods, for my friend had an ominous dream."

This day on which Enkidu dreamed came to an end and he lay stricken with sickness. One whole day he lay on his bed and his suffering increased. He said to Gilgamesh, the friend on whose account he had left the wilderness, "Once I ran for you, for the water of life, and I now have nothing." A second day he lay on his bed and Gilgamesh watched over him but the sickness increased. A third day he lay on his bed, he called out to Gilgamesh, rousing him up. Now he was weak and his eyes were blind with weeping. Ten days he lay and his suffering increased, eleven and twelve days he lay on his bed of pain. Then he called to Gilgamesh, "My friend, the great goddess cursed me and I must die in shame.

WORDS TO KNOW

incantation (ĭn'kăn-tā'shən) *n.* set of words chanted or sung as part of a religious ritual

lament (lə-mĕnt') *v.* to express grief or sorrow

ominous (ŏm'ə-nəs) *adj.* threatening; signaling evil to come

NOTES

MARK IT UP **KEEP TRACK**

As you read, you can use these marks to keep track of your understanding.

- * This is important.
- ? I have a question about this.
- ! This is a surprise.

I shall not die like a man fallen in battle; I feared to fall, but happy is the man who falls in the battle, for I must die in shame." And Gilgamesh wept over Enkidu. . . .

Pause & Reflect

THE SEARCH FOR EVERLASTING LIFE

Enkidu dies. For the first time, Gilgamesh is faced with a situation he cannot control. He also experiences for the first time the human emotions of grief and fear.

> **FOCUS**
>
> Enkidu's death causes Gilgamesh to begin a quest. Find out what he searches for.
>
> **MARK IT UP** Underline the animals, creatures, and gods Gilgamesh meets.

Bitterly Gilgamesh wept for his friend Enkidu; he wandered over the wilderness as a hunter, he roamed over the plains; in his bitterness he cried, "How can I rest, how can I be at peace? Despair is in my heart. What my brother is now, that shall I be when I am dead. Because I am afraid of death I will go as best I can to find Utnapishtim whom they call the Faraway, for he has entered the assembly of the gods." So Gilgamesh traveled over the wilderness, he wandered over the grasslands, a long journey, in search of Utnapishtim, whom the gods took after the deluge;[2] and they set him to live in the land of Dilmun, in the garden of the sun; and to him alone of men they gave everlasting life.

At night when he came to the mountain passes Gilgamesh prayed: "In these mountain passes long ago I saw lions, I was afraid and I lifted my eyes to the moon; I prayed and my prayers went up to the gods, so now, O moon god Sin, protect me." When he had prayed he lay down to sleep, until he was woken from out of a dream. He saw the lions round him glorying in life; then he took his

2. **deluge** (dĕl'yo͞oj): an unusually heavy, destructive flood.

Pause & Reflect

1. **MARK IT UP** Review the details you circled. Then cross out the word below that does *not* go with the images of the afterlife in Enkidu's dream. **(Clarify)**

   dark — dusty — terrifying

2. What does Gilgamesh think about death after hearing his friend's dream? **(Infer)**

   He Fear it, he is afraid he will go to the same place as Enkido.

In this story the setting changes often. You may want to underline each new setting when it is first mentioned. The shaded phrases are examples.

NOTES

REREAD the boxed passage. What do you think is "the common lot of man" that Gilgamesh mentions? **(Analyze)**

axe in his hand, he drew his sword from his belt, and he fell upon them like an arrow from the string, and struck and destroyed and scattered them.

So at length Gilgamesh came to Mashu, the great mountains about which he had heard many things, which guard the rising and the setting sun. Its twin peaks are as high as the wall of heaven and its paps reach down to the underworld. At its gate the Scorpions stand guard, half man and half dragon; their glory is terrifying, their stare strikes death into men, their shimmering halo sweeps the mountains that guard the rising sun. When Gilgamesh saw them he shielded his eyes for the length of a moment only; then he took courage and approached. When they saw him so undismayed the Man-Scorpion called to his mate, "This one who comes to us now is flesh of the gods." The mate of the Man-Scorpion answered, "Two thirds is god but one third is man."

Then he called to the man Gilgamesh, he called to the child of the gods: "Why have you come so great a journey; for what have you traveled so far, crossing the dangerous waters; tell me the reason for your coming?" Gilgamesh answered, "For Enkidu; I loved him dearly, together we endured all kinds of hardships; on his account I have come, for the common lot of man has taken him. I have wept for him day and night, I would not give up his body for burial, I thought my friend would come back because of my weeping. Since he went, my life is nothing; that is why I have traveled here in search of Utnapishtim my father; for men say he has entered the assembly of the gods, and has found everlasting life. I have a desire to question him concerning the living and the dead." The Man-Scorpion opened his mouth and said, speaking to Gilgamesh, "No man born of woman has done what you have asked, no mortal man has gone into the mountain; the length of it is twelve leagues[3] of darkness; in it there is no light, but the heart is oppressed with darkness. From the rising of the sun

3. **twelve leagues:** roughly thirty-six miles.

to the setting of the sun there is no light." Gilgamesh said, "Although I should go in sorrow and in pain, with sighing and with weeping, still I must go. Open the gate of the mountain." And the Man-Scorpion said, "Go, Gilgamesh, I permit you to pass through the mountain of Mashu and through the high ranges; may your feet carry you safely home. The gate of the mountain is open." . . .

Gilgamesh must walk 12 leagues in total darkness to pass through the mountain. But at last he reaches a wonderful world no mortal has seen.

There was the garden of the gods; all round him stood bushes bearing gems. Seeing it he went down at once, for there was fruit of carnelian[4] with the vine hanging from it, beautiful to look at; lapis lazuli leaves hung thick with fruit, sweet to see. For thorns and thistles there were haematite and rare stones, agate, and pearls from out of the sea. While Gilgamesh walked in the garden by the edge of the sea Shamash saw him, and he saw that he was dressed in the skins of animals and ate their flesh. He was distressed, and he spoke and said, "No mortal man has gone this way before, nor will, as long as the winds drive over the sea." And to Gilgamesh he said, "You will never find the life for which you are searching." Gilgamesh said to glorious Shamash, "Now that I have toiled and strayed so far over the wilderness, am I to sleep, and let the earth cover my head for ever? Let my eyes see the sun until they are dazzled with looking. Although I am no better than a dead man, still let me see the light of the sun."

Pause & Reflect

4. **carnelian** (kär-nēl′yən), **lapis lazuli** (lăp′ĭs lăz′ə-lē), **haematite** (hē′mə-tīt′), **agate** (ăg′ĭt): gemstones of various colors. Carnelian is red or reddish-brown, lapis lazuli is deep blue, haematite is a dull metal shade, and agate is often multi-colored stripes.

Pause & Reflect

1. Who does Gilgamesh go off in search of? Why? **(Cause and Effect)**

Utnapishtim, to question life and death

2. What personal trait do you think is most helpful to Gilgamesh in overcoming obstacles on his journey? Explain. **(Evaluate)**

His determination several times he has been faced with situations no one else could handle, but he defeated them and kept on going.

FOCUS

Next, Gilgamesh meets Siduri, a goddess who lives by the sea that lies between the garden of the gods and paradise.

MARK IT UP Circle the passage in which Siduri gives Gilgamesh advice and the passage in which he responds.

Beside the sea she lives, the woman of the vine, the maker of wine; Siduri sits in the garden at the edge of the sea, with the golden bowl and the golden vats that the gods gave her. She is covered with a veil; and where she sits she sees Gilgamesh coming towards her, wearing skins, the flesh of the gods in his body, but despair in his heart, and his face like the face of one who has made a long journey. She looked, and as she scanned the distance she said in her own heart, "Surely this is some felon; where is he going now?" And she barred her gate against him with the cross-bar and shot home the bolt. But Gilgamesh, hearing the sound of the bolt, threw up his head and lodged his foot in the gate; he called to her, "Young woman, maker of wine, why do you bolt your door; what did you see that made you bar your gate? I will break in your door and burst in your gate, for I am Gilgamesh who seized and killed the Bull of Heaven, I killed the watchman of the cedar forest, I overthrew Humbaba who lived in the forest, and I killed the lions in the passes of the mountain."

Then Siduri said to him, "If you are that Gilgamesh who seized and killed the Bull of Heaven, who killed the watchman of the cedar forest, who overthrew Humbaba that lived in the forest, and killed the lions in the passes of the mountain, why are your cheeks so starved and why is your face so drawn? Why is despair in your heart and your face like the face of one who has made a long journey? Yes, why is your face burned from heat and cold, and why do you come here wandering over the pastures in search of the wind?"

Gilgamesh answered her, "And why should not my cheeks be starved and my face drawn? Despair is in my heart and my face is the face of one who has made a long journey, it was burned with heat and with cold. Why

NOTES

This story contains some long and complex sentences. Don't let the length of a sentence confuse you. Look for the most important ideas in the sentence. For example, the boxed text contains one long sentence. The shaded text shows the most important ideas in that sentence.

should I not wander over the pastures in search of the wind? My friend, my younger brother, he who hunted the wild ass of the wilderness and the panther of the plains, my friend, my younger brother who seized and killed the Bull of Heaven and overthrew Humbaba in the cedar forest, my friend who was very dear to me and who endured dangers beside me, Enkidu my brother, whom I loved, the end of mortality has overtaken him. I wept for him seven days and nights till the worm fastened on him. Because of my brother I am afraid of death, because of my brother I stray through the wilderness and cannot rest. But now, young woman, maker of wine, since I have seen your face do not let me see the face of death which I dread so much."

She answered, "Gilgamesh, where are you hurrying to? You will never find that life for which you are looking. When the gods created man they allotted to him death, but life they retained in their own keeping. As for you, Gilgamesh, fill your belly with good things; day and night, night and day, dance and be merry, feast and rejoice. Let your clothes be fresh, bathe yourself in water, cherish the little child that holds your hand, and make your wife happy in your embrace; for this too is the lot of man."

But Gilgamesh said to Siduri, the young woman, "How can I be silent, how can I rest, when Enkidu whom I love is dust, and I too shall die and be laid in the earth. You live by the sea-shore and look into the heart of it; young woman, tell me now, which is the way to Utnapishtim, the son of Ubara-Tutu? What directions are there for the passage; give me, oh, give me directions. I will cross the Ocean if it is possible; if it is not I will wander still farther in the wilderness." . . .

Siduri tells Gilgamesh that he must cross the ocean with the boatman Urshanabi. When she hints that Urshanabi might refuse to take him, Gilgamesh loses his temper. He smashes Urshanabi's sacred stones and the tackle and mast

WORDS TO KNOW
allot (ə-lŏt') *v.* to give as a share or portion

NOTES

MARK IT UP
WORD POWER Mark words that you'd like to add to your **Personal Word List.** After reading, you can record the words and their meanings beginning on page 444.

of his boat. Urshanabi explains that Gilgamesh has destroyed the very things that would protect them both from the waters of death. To make up for his actions, Gilgamesh must cut poles and push the boat himself. Eventually, he has to use his own body and clothing for a sail.

So Urshanabi the ferryman brought Gilgamesh to Utnapishtim, whom they call the Faraway, who lives in Dilmun at the place of the sun's transit, eastward of the mountain. To him alone of men the gods had given everlasting life.

Now Utnapishtim, where he lay at ease, looked into the distance and he said in his heart, musing to himself, "Why does the boat sail here without tackle and mast; why are the sacred stones destroyed, and why does the master not sail the boat? That man who comes is none of mine; where I look I see a man whose body is covered with skins of beasts. Who is this who walks up the shore behind Urshanabi, for surely he is no man of mine?" So Utnapishtim looked at him and said, "What is your name, you who come here wearing the skins of beasts, with your cheeks starved and your face drawn? Where are you hurrying to now? For what reason have you made this great journey, crossing the seas whose passage is difficult? Tell me the reason for your coming."

He replied, "Gilgamesh is my name. I am from Uruk, from the house of Anu." Then Utnapishtim said to him, "If you are Gilgamesh, why are your cheeks so starved and your face drawn? Why is despair in your heart and your face like the face of one who has made a long journey? Yes, why is your face burned with heat and cold; and why do you come here, wandering over the wilderness in search of the wind?" . . .

Gilgamesh explains that he is grieving over the death of his friend and afraid of dying himself. He has come to Utnapishtim to learn the secret of everlasting life.

WORDS TO KNOW

transit (trăn'sĭt) *n.* passage

musing (myōō'zĭng) *adj.* thoughtfully questioning or meditating **muse** *v.*

NOTES I think he will tell Gilgamesh

REREAD the boxed passage. What do you think Gilgamesh will learn from Utnapishtim? **(Predict)**

to enjoy what he has, to be content, for he has been blessed, and he cannot achieve everlasting life.

REREAD the boxed passage on the following page. Why do you think Utnapishtim says what he does to Gilgamesh? **(Draw Conclusions)**

- ☐ to scare Gilgamesh into leaving
- ☒ to convince Gilgamesh that he cannot live forever
- ☐ to tell Gilgamesh that it is time for him to die

Utnapishtim said, "There is no permanence. Do we build a house to stand for ever, do we seal a contract to hold for all time? Do brothers divide an inheritance to keep for ever, does the flood-time of rivers endure? It is only the nymph of the dragon-fly who sheds her larva and sees the sun in his glory. From the days of old there is no permanence. The sleeping and the dead, how alike they are, they are like a painted death. What is there between the master and the servant when both have fulfilled their doom? When the Anunnaki, the judges, come together, and Mammetun the mother of destinies, together they decree the fates of men. Life and death they allot but the day of death they do not disclose."

Then Gilgamesh said to Utnapishtim the Faraway, "I look at you now, Utnapishtim, and your appearance is no different from mine; there is nothing strange in your features. I thought I should find you like a hero prepared for battle, but you lie here taking your ease on your back. Tell me truly, how was it that you came to enter the company of the gods and to possess everlasting life?" Utnapishtim said to Gilgamesh, "I will reveal to you a mystery, I will tell you a secret of the gods."

Pause & Reflect

FOCUS

Utnapishtim is about to reveal the story of how he was granted eternal life. Find out how this gift was granted.

"You know the city Shurrupak, it stands on the banks of Euphrates? That city grew old and the gods that were in it were old. There was Anu, lord of the firmament,[5] their father, and warrior Enlil their counselor, Ninurta the helper,

5. **firmament:** the vault of the heavens; the sky.

Pause & Reflect

1. MARK IT UP Reread the sentences you circled. Sum up the conversation between Gilgamesh and Siduri. **(Paraphrase)**

Siduri's Advice:

To go home and enjoy his life

Gilgamesh's Response:

He want everlasting life

2. Circle three things Gilgamesh does in this part of the story. **(Clarify)**

finds eternal life

meets Utnapishtim

crosses an ocean

wrecks a boat

kills some lions

NOTES

REREAD the boxed passage. What two lies does Ea instruct Utnapishtim to tell the people? **(Clarify)**

Lie #1:

Lie #2:

What else does Ea tell him to do? **(Main Idea)**

and Ennugi watcher over canals; and with them also was Ea. In those days the world teemed, the people multiplied, the world bellowed like a wild bull, and the great god was aroused by the clamor. Enlil heard the clamor and he said to the gods in council, 'The uproar of mankind is intolerable and sleep is no longer possible by reason of the babel.'[6] So the gods agreed to exterminate mankind. Enlil did this, but Ea because of his oath warned me in a dream. He whispered their words to my house of reeds, 'Reed-house, reed-house! Wall, O wall, hearken reed-house, wall reflect; O man of Shurrupak, son of Ubara-Tutu; tear down your house and build a boat, abandon possessions and look for life, despise worldly goods and save your soul alive. Tear down your house, I say, and build a boat. These are the measurements of the barque as you shall build her: let her beam[7] equal her length, let her deck be roofed like the vault that covers the abyss;[8] then take up into the boat the seed of all living creatures.'

"When I had understood I said to my lord, 'Behold, what you have commanded I will honor and perform, but how shall I answer the people, the city, the elders?' Then Ea opened his mouth and said to me, his servant, 'Tell them this: I have learned that Enlil is wrathful against me, I dare no longer walk in his land nor live in his city; I will go down to the Gulf to dwell with Ea my lord. But on you he will rain down abundance, rare fish and shy wild-fowl, a rich harvest-tide. In the evening the rider of the storm will bring you wheat in torrents.'

"In the first light of dawn all my household gathered round me, the children brought pitch and the men whatever was necessary. On the fifth day I laid the keel and the ribs,

---

6. **babel:** loud, unpleasant noise.

7. **beam:** the widest part of a ship.

8. **vault that covers the abyss:** the sky as it stretches across the depths below.

WORDS TO KNOW

teem (tēm) *v.* to be filled to overflowing

then I made fast the planking. The ground-space was one acre, each side of the deck measured one hundred and twenty cubits,[9] making a square. I built six decks below, seven in all, I divided them into nine sections with bulkheads between. I drove in wedges where needed, I saw to the punt-poles,[10] and laid in supplies. The carriers brought oil in baskets, I poured pitch into the furnace and asphalt and oil; more oil was consumed in caulking, and more again the master of the boat took into his stores. I slaughtered bullocks for the people and every day I killed sheep. I gave the shipwrights wine to drink as though it were river water, raw wine and red wine and oil and white wine. There was feasting then as there is at the time of the New Year's festival; I myself anointed my head. On the seventh day the boat was complete.

"Then was the launching full of difficulty; there was shifting of ballast[11] above and below till two thirds was submerged. I loaded into her all that I had of gold and of living things, my family, my kin, the beast of the field both wild and tame, and all the craftsmen. I sent them on board, for the time that Shamash had ordained was already fulfilled when he said, 'In the evening, when the rider of the storm sends down the destroying rain, enter the boat and batten her down.' The time was fulfilled, the evening came, the rider of the storm sent down the rain. I looked out at the weather and it was terrible, so I too boarded the boat and battened her down. All was now complete, the battening and the caulking; so I handed the tiller to Puzur-

9. **cubits:** ancient units of measure, originally equal to the length of the forearm from the elbow to the tip of the middle finger. Length ranges from 17 to 22 inches.

10. **punt-poles:** poles that propel a boat by pushing against the water's bottom.

11. **ballast** (băl′əst): heavy material placed into the bottom of a boat to enhance stability.

WORDS TO KNOW
ordain (ôr-dān′) *v.* to establish by decree or law

NOTES

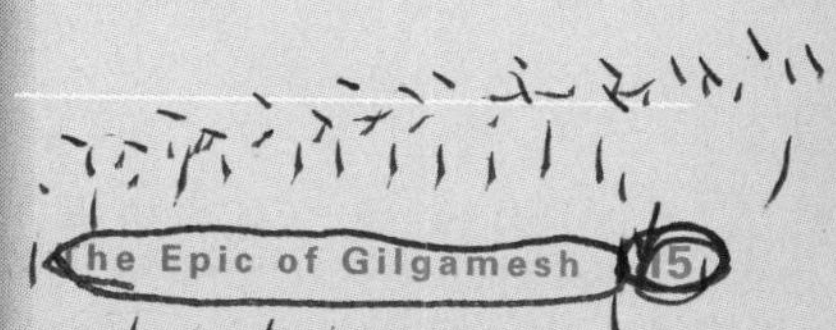

NOTES

Amurri the steersman, with the navigation and the care of the whole boat.

"With the first light of dawn a black cloud came from the horizon; it thundered within where Adad, lord of the storm was riding. In front over hill and plain Shullat and Hanish, heralds of the storm, led on. Then the gods of the abyss rose up; Nergal pulled out the dams of the nether[12] waters, Ninurta the war-lord threw down the dikes, and the seven judges of hell, the Anunnaki, raised their torches, lighting the land with their livid flame. A stupor of despair went up to heaven when the god of the storm turned daylight to darkness, when he smashed the land like a cup. One whole day the tempest raged, gathering fury as it went, it poured over the people like the tides of battle; a man could not see his brother nor the people be seen from heaven. Even the gods were terrified at the flood, they fled to the highest heaven, the firmament of Anu; they crouched against the walls, cowering like curs. Then Ishtar the sweet-voiced Queen of Heaven cried out like a woman in travail:[13] 'Alas the days of old are turned to dust because I commanded evil; why did I command this evil in the council of all the gods? I commanded wars to destroy the people, but are they not my people, for I brought them forth? Now like the spawn of fish they float in the ocean.' The great gods of heaven and of hell wept, they covered their mouths.

"For six days and six nights the winds blew, torrent and tempest and flood overwhelmed the world, tempest and flood raged together like warring hosts. When the seventh day dawned the storm from the south subsided, the sea grew calm, the flood was stilled; I looked at the face of the world and there was silence, all mankind was turned to clay.

---

12. **nether:** lower.

13. **travail** (trə-vāl'): the pain of childbirth.

WORDS TO KNOW

stupor (sto͞o'pər) *n.* a dazed condition, almost without sense or feeling

The surface of the sea stretched as flat as a roof-top; I opened a hatch and the light fell on my face. Then I bowed low, I sat down and I wept, the tears streamed down my face, for on every side was the waste of water. I looked for land in vain, but fourteen leagues distant there appeared a mountain, and there the boat grounded; on the mountain of Nisir the boat held fast, she held fast and did not budge. One day she held, and a second day on the mountain of Nisir she held fast and did not budge. A third day, and a fourth day she held fast on the mountain and did not budge; a fifth day and a sixth day she held fast on the mountain. When the seventh day dawned I loosed a dove and let her go. She flew away, but finding no resting-place she returned. Then I loosed a swallow, and she flew away but finding no resting-place she returned. I loosed a raven, she saw that the waters had retreated, she ate, she flew around, she cawed, and she did not come back. Then I threw everything open to the four winds, I made a sacrifice and poured out a libation[14] on the mountain top. Seven and again seven cauldrons I set up on their stands, I heaped up wood and cane and cedar and myrtle. When the gods smelled the sweet savor, they gathered like flies over the sacrifice. Then, at last, Ishtar also came, she lifted her necklace with the jewels of heaven that once Anu had made to please her. 'O you gods here present, by the lapis lazuli round my neck I shall remember these days as I remember the jewels of my throat; these last days I shall not forget. Let all the gods gather round the sacrifice, except Enlil. He shall not approach this offering, for without reflection he brought the flood; he consigned my people to destruction.'

"When Enlil had come, when he saw the boat, he was wroth and swelled with anger at the gods, the host of heaven, 'Has any of these mortals escaped? Not one was to have survived the destruction.' Then the god of the wells and canals Ninurta opened his mouth and said to the

14. libation: liquid given as an offering to a god.

MARK IT UP Reread the boxed text. Circle words such as *then, next, first, second* that help you follow the sequence of events. Then write the numbers 1–4 in the blanks below to show the order of the events. **(Sequence)**

___ Utnapishtim makes a sacrifice.

___ The boat gets stuck on a mountain.

___ A loosed raven doesn't return.

___ Utnapishtim opens the hatch.

NOTES

the boxed text. Then check the sentence below that best paraphrases it. **(Analyze)**

- [x] Punish only those who have done something wrong, but do not punish too harshly.
- [ ] Punish humans when they break loose, because the sin of one applies to all.

What do you think Ea is saying in the rest of his speech? **(Paraphrase)**

Pause & Reflect

1. How does Utnapishtim become immortal? **(Clarify)**

2. What do you think will happen now that Gilgamesh knows how Utnapishtim achieved everlasting life? **(Predict)**

warrior Enlil, 'Who is there of the gods that can devise[15] without Ea? It is Ea alone who knows all things.' Then Ea opened his mouth and spoke to warrior Enlil, 'Wisest of gods, hero Enlil, how could you so senselessly bring down the flood?

Lay upon the sinner his sin,
Lay upon the transgressor[16] his transgression,
Punish him a little when he breaks loose,
Do not drive him too hard or he perishes;
Would that a lion had ravaged mankind
Rather than the flood,
Would that a wolf had ravaged mankind
Rather than the flood,
Would that famine had wasted the world
Rather than the flood,
Would that pestilence had wasted mankind
Rather than the flood.

It was not I that revealed the secret of the gods; the wise man learned it in a dream. Now take your counsel what shall be done with him.'

"Then Enlil went up into the boat, he took me by the hand and my wife and made us enter the boat and kneel down on either side, he standing between us. He touched our foreheads to bless us saying, 'In time past Utnapishtim was a mortal man; henceforth he and his wife shall live in the distance at the mouth of the rivers.' Thus it was that the gods took me and placed me here to live in the distance, at the mouth of the rivers."

Pause & Reflect

15. **devise** (dĭ-vīz): to plan or think things out.
16. **transgressor:** a person who breaks a command or law.

THE RETURN

FOCUS

Gilgamesh still wants everlasting life. Utnapishtim gives him a test to pass and a secret to take home with him. Find out what they are.

MARK IT UP Put a check mark next to the test and a star next to the secret.

Utnapishtim said, "As for you, Gilgamesh, who will assemble the gods for your sake, so that you may find that life for which you are searching? But if you wish, come and put it to the test: only prevail against sleep for six days and seven nights." But while Gilgamesh sat there resting on his haunches, a mist of sleep like soft wool teased from the fleece drifted over him, and Utnapishtim said to his wife, "Look at him now, the strong man who would have everlasting life, even now the mists of sleep are drifting over him." His wife replied, "Touch the man to wake him, so that he may return to his own land in peace, going back through the gate by which he came." Utnapishtim said to his wife, "All men are deceivers, even you he will attempt to deceive; therefore bake loaves of bread, each day one loaf, and put it beside his head; and make a mark on the wall to number the days he has slept."

So she baked loaves of bread, each day one loaf, and put it beside his head, and she marked on the wall the days that he slept; and there came a day when the first loaf was hard, the second loaf was like leather, the third was soggy, the crust of the fourth had mold, the fifth was mildewed, the sixth was fresh, and the seventh was still on the embers. Then Utnapishtim touched him and he woke. Gilgamesh said to Utnapishtim the Faraway, "I hardly slept when you touched and roused me." But Utnapishtim said, "Count these loaves and learn how many days you slept, for your first is hard, your second like leather, your third is soggy, the crust of your fourth has mold, your fifth is mildewed, your

WORDS TO KNOW
prevail (prĭ-vāl′) *v.* to hold out against; triumph over

NOTES

the boxed passage. Then reread the passages on pages 9–11 in which Gilgamesh spoke to Shamash (lines 151–155) and Siduri (lines 173–179, 190–206). How has Gilgamesh's attitude changed about his quest? Circle the phrases that best complete these sentences. **(Compare and Contrast)**

At first, Gilgamesh felt

excited
determined
furious
confused

Now he feels

resigned
vengeful
determined
optimistic

Gilgamesh is resigned to the fact he is mortal, so Urshanabi gives him new clothes (and a bath) and send him home, but his wife thinks he should give Gilgamesh something. he gives him a secret

sixth is fresh and your seventh was still over the glowing embers when I touched and woke you." Gilgamesh said, "What shall I do, O Utnapishtim, where shall I go? Already the thief in the night has hold of my limbs, death inhabits my room; wherever my foot rests, there I find death."

Then Utnapishtim spoke to Urshanabi the ferryman: "Woe to you Urshanabi, now and for ever more you have become hateful to this harborage; it is not for you, nor for you are the crossings of this sea. Go now, banished from the shore. But this man before whom you walked, bringing him here, whose body is covered with foulness and the grace of whose limbs has been spoiled by wild skins, take him to the washing-place. There he shall wash his long hair clean as snow in the water, he shall throw off his skins and let the sea carry them away, and the beauty of his body shall be shown, the fillet[17] on his forehead shall be renewed, and he shall be given clothes to cover his nakedness. Till he reaches his own city and his journey is accomplished, these clothes will show no sign of age, they will wear like a new garment." So Urshanabi took Gilgamesh and led him to the washing-place, he washed his long hair as clean as snow in the water, he threw off his skins, which the sea carried away, and showed the beauty of his body. He renewed the fillet on his forehead, and to cover his nakedness gave him clothes which would show no sign of age, but would wear like a new garment till he reached his own city, and his journey was accomplished.

Then Gilgamesh and Urshanabi launched the boat on to the water and boarded it, and they made ready to sail away; but the wife of Utnapishtim the Faraway said to him, "Gilgamesh came here wearied out, he is worn out; what will you give him to carry him back to his own country?" So Utnapishtim spoke, and Gilgamesh took a pole and brought the boat in to the bank. "Gilgamesh, you came here a man wearied out, you have worn yourself out; what shall I give

17. **fillet** (fĭl′ĭt): narrow cloth or ribbon worn as a headband

you to carry you back to your own country? Gilgamesh, I shall reveal a secret thing, it is a mystery of the gods that I am telling you. There is a plant that grows under the water, it has a prickle like a thorn, like a rose; it will wound your hands, but if you succeed in taking it, then your hands will hold that which restores his lost youth to a man."

Pause & Reflect

FOCUS

Find out how Gilgamesh's adventure comes to an end.

When Gilgamesh heard this he opened the sluices so that a sweet-water current might carry him out to the deepest channel; he tied heavy stones to his feet and they dragged him down to the water-bed. There he saw the plant growing; although it pricked him he took it in his hands; then he cut the heavy stones from his feet, and the sea carried him and threw him on to the shore. Gilgamesh said to Urshanabi the ferryman, "Come here, and see this marvelous plant. By its virtue a man may win back all his former strength. I will take it to Uruk of the strong walls; there I will give it to the old men to eat. Its name shall be 'The Old Men Are Young Again'; and at last I shall eat it myself and have back all my lost youth." So Gilgamesh returned by the gate through which he had come, Gilgamesh and Urshanabi went together. They traveled their twenty leagues and then they broke their fast; after thirty leagues they stopped for the night.

Gilgamesh saw a well of cool water and he went down and bathed; but deep in the pool there was lying a serpent, and the serpent sensed the sweetness of the flower. It rose out of the water and snatched it away, and immediately it sloughed[18] its skin and returned to the well. Then Gilgamesh sat down and wept, the tears ran down his face, and he took the hand of Urshanabi; "O Urshanabi, was it for this that I toiled with my hands, is it for this I have

18. sloughed (slŭfd): cast off; shed.

Pause & Reflect

1. MARK IT UP What test does Utnapishtim give Gilgamesh? What secret does he tell him? **(Summarize)**

The Test: To not sleep for 6 days; 7 nights

The Result: He fails

The Secret: A plant that restores youth

2. Do you think Utnapishtim treats Gilgamesh fairly? **(Make Judgments)**

☒ Yes ☐ No

My reason:

He gives Gilgamesh a chance at imortality, and even though he fails he gives him another chance to reach his goal.

wrung out my heart's blood? For myself I have gained nothing; not I, but the beast of the earth has joy of it now. Already the stream has carried it twenty leagues back to the channels where I found it. I found a sign and now I have lost it. Let us leave the boat on the bank and go."

After twenty leagues they broke their fast, after thirty leagues they stopped for the night; in three days they had walked as much as a journey of a month and fifteen days. When the journey was accomplished they arrived at Uruk, the strong-walled city. Gilgamesh spoke to him, to Urshanabi the ferryman, "Urshanabi, climb up on to the wall of Uruk, inspect its foundation terrace, and examine well the brickwork; see if it is not of burnt bricks; and did not the seven wise men lay these foundations? One third of the whole is city, one third is garden, and one third is field, with the precinct of the goddess Ishtar. These parts and the precinct are all Uruk."

This too was the work of Gilgamesh, the king, who knew the countries of the world. He was wise, he saw mysteries and knew secret things, he brought us a tale of the days before the flood. He went a long journey, was weary, worn out with labor, and returning engraved on a stone the whole story. ❖

Pause & Reflect

Pause & Reflect

1. MARK IT UP What is the outcome of Gilgamesh's quest for immortality? How does he feel about it? **(Clarify)**

2. How would you describe the overall effect of this journey on Gilgamesh? **(Cause and Effect)**

CHALLENGE Reread the Preview to this selection. Think of what it tells you about Gilgamesh as a ruler. Then reread the last two paragraphs of this selection. How has Gilgamesh changed as a ruler? **(Analyze)**

Active Reading SkillBuilder

Cause and Effect

Events in a story are often related by **cause and effect,** which means that one event in the story can cause another event to happen. The first event is the cause; the resulting event is the effect. Some stories have a chain of causes and effects in which one event causes another, which in turn causes another, and so on. As you read the excerpt from *The Epic of Gilgamesh,* keep track of the relationships between events by using the cause-and-effect chart below. Be on the lookout for effects that cause other events. Remember that you may need to record some events twice—first as an effect and then again as a cause.

Causes	Effects
Enkidu relates the details of his terrible dream to Gilgamesh.	➜ *Gilgamesh is afraid to die.*
Gilgamesh is afraid to die	➜ He goes looking for answers & eternal life
His journey	➜ makes him weary, tired, starved, buraed
Because of his appearance	➜ Everyone he meets at first doubts who he is
Asked Urshanabi for eternal life	➜ Given a test to not sleep for 6 days & nights
Fails the test	➜ Urshanabi tells him of the under water plant
Wants to give some of the plant to others	➜ loses it to a snake in a well
Failed test & lost plant	➜ no eternal life

Literary Analysis SkillBuilder

The Quest Story

A **quest story** is a particular kind of story in which the main character goes on a long journey in order to achieve a goal. The main character of a quest story is called a **quest hero.** A quest hero is both human and superhuman. In some ways, his words and actions are like those of any human. In other ways, he is extraordinary. For example, he may be fantastically strong and brave. He also may get help from the gods. Use the chart below to help you analyze the character of Gilgamesh as a quest hero. In the chart, record details that show Gilgamesh's human and superhuman characteristics.

Human Characteristics	Superhuman Characteristics
Gilgamesh has a best friend.	*Gilgamesh is two-thirds god.*
expresses emotion of grief over Enkidu's death	defeats the lions
Fear that he will die	stands face to face with scorpion
Fear of the lions	defys both Simuri & Shamash
anger at the boatman	made it through Mashu & the ocean to Urshanabi
tired (sleep) for 7 days (couldn't stay awake)	very strong & brave
disappointment over failed mission	made it to the bottom of the sea for the plant

Words to Know SkillBuilder

Words to Know

allot	lamented	ominous	prevail	teem
incantation	musing	ordained	stupor	transit

A. Think about the meaning of each underlined word. Then fill in each blank with the letter of the correct definition.

1. Big cities like Chicago and New York teem with people and automobiles. C
2. "With all this noise, I will never sleep again," lamented Alex when she first moved to the city. G
3. Alex was in a stupor because she hadn't slept in two days. I
4. The barge's transit down the Mississippi River began in Davenport, Iowa. D
5. Jeffery was musing over the strange comment his sister had made to him. E
6. Carly's parents will allot her some space in the basement where she can keep her bug collection. B
7. The minister began the service with a prayer and an incantation. F
8. Dark, ominous clouds were the first sign that a terrible storm was about to hit. A
9. Judge Mayfield ordained that the boys spend all day Saturday picking up trash in the park. H
10. My father always says, "In order to reach a difficult goal, you must prevail against negative thinking." J

A. threatening; signaling evil to come
B. to give as a share or portion
C. to be filled to overflowing
D. passage
E. thoughtfully questioning or meditating
F. a set of words chanted or sung as part of a religious ritual
G. expressed grief or sorrow
H. established by decree or law
I. a dazed condition, almost without sense or feeling
J. to hold out against; triumph over

B. Write a letter of advice to Gilgamesh, helping him accept the loss of his friend. Use at **least** five Words to Know in your letter.

Before You Read

Connect to Your Life

Recall a battle between good and evil, perhaps one that you saw in a movie, TV show, comic book, or novel. Who was the hero and who was the villain? What did they fight over? What powers or weapons were used? Who won? Make some notes in the chart below.

Hero:	Villain:	Winner:

Why they fought:
Powers or weapons used:

Key to the Epic

WHAT YOU NEED TO KNOW The *Ramayana* is one of India's greatest epics. In this ancient story, Prince Rama must rescue his beloved wife, Sita. She has been kidnapped by the evil Ravana, a powerful demon with ten heads and twenty arms. An army of monkeys helps Rama build a bridge to Ravana's island kingdom, and the fierce battle begins.

In India, the *Ramayana* is not just an entertaining story, but a guide for living. Rama is viewed as a great hero—the ideal man and ruler. On the line below, write the name of a real or make-believe hero you think sets a good example for people to follow.

____

from the

RAMAYANA

Retold by R. K. Narayan

PREVIEW The hero Rama is battling hordes of demons with the help of an army of monkeys. Now the great demon Ravana emerges from his castle to fight Rama himself. The hero and the demon will do battle with powerful magic weapons. Which will win the fight, the forces of good or the forces of evil?

You may find some hard words and expressions in this story. The most important words have footnotes. Others may be less important. Don't worry if you don't understand every word. Keep reading, and enjoy the adventure!

MARK IT UP ➤ **KEEP TRACK**
Remember to use these marks to keep track of your understanding.

- * This is important.
- ? I have a question about this.
- ! This is a surprise.

FOCUS

Ravana is watching his army lose the battle to Prince Rama and an army of monkeys. Find out how the gory scene affects him.

MARK IT UP ➤ Underline the details that help you understand what Ravana thinks and feels as he watches the battle rage.

Every moment, news came to Ravana of fresh disasters in his camp. One by one, most of his commanders were lost. No one who went forth with battle cries was heard of again. Cries and shouts and the wailings of the widows of warriors came over the chants and songs of triumph that his courtiers arranged to keep up at a loud pitch in his assembly hall. Ravana became restless and abruptly left the hall and went up on a tower, from which he could obtain a full view of the city. He surveyed the scene below but could not stand it. One who had spent a lifetime in destruction, now found the gory spectacle intolerable. Groans and wailings reached his ears with deadly clarity; and he noticed how the monkey hordes reveled in their bloody handiwork. This was too much for him. He felt a terrific rage rising within him, mixed with some admiration for Rama's valour. He told himself, "The time has come for me to act by myself again."

He hurried down the steps of the tower, returned to his chamber, and prepared himself for the battle. He had a ritual bath and performed special prayers to gain the benediction of Shiva;[1] donned his battle dress, matchless armor, armlets, and crowns. He had on a protective armour for every inch of his body. He girt his sword-belt and attached to his body his accouterments[2] for protection and decoration.

When he emerged from his chamber, his heroic appearance was breathtaking. He summoned his chariot, which could be drawn by horses or move on its own if the horses were hurt or killed. People stood aside when he came out of the

---

1. **Shiva** (shē′və): an important Hindu god.
2. **accouterments** (ə-ko͞o′tər-mənts): military equipment other than uniforms and weapons.

WORDS TO KNOW
benediction (bĕn′ĭ-dĭk′shən) *n.* blessing

palace and entered his chariot. "This is my resolve," he said to himself: "Either that woman Sita,[3] or my wife Mandodari,[4] will soon have cause to cry and roll in the dust in grief. Surely, before this day is done, one of them will be a widow."

Pause & Reflect

FOCUS

In this section, you will meet the hero Rama for the first time. Find out how he prepares to fight Ravana.

MARK IT UP Underline details that show how Rama acts in the face of danger.

The gods in heaven noticed Ravana's determined move and felt that Rama would need all the support they could muster. They requested Indra[5] to send down his special chariot for Rama's use. When the chariot appeared at his camp, Rama was deeply impressed with the magnitude and brilliance of the vehicle. "How has this come to be here?" he asked.

"Sir," the charioteer answered, "my name is Matali.[6] I have the honor of being the charioteer of Indra. Brahma, the four-faced god and the creator of the Universe, and Shiva, whose power has emboldened Ravana now to challenge you, have commanded me to bring it here for your use. It can fly swifter than air over all obstacles, over any mountain, sea, or sky, and will help you to emerge victorious in this battle."

Rama reflected aloud, "It may be that the rakshasas[7] have created this illusion for me. It may be a trap. I don't know how to view it." Whereupon Matali spoke convincingly to dispel the doubt in Rama's mind. Rama, still hesitant, though partially convinced, looked at Hanuman[8]

3. **Sita** (sē′tä): Rama's wife.
4. **Mandodari** (mən-dō′də-rē).
5. **Indra** (ĭn′drə): a warrior god, the lord of rain and thunder.
6. **Matali** (mä′tə-lē).
7. **rakshasas** (räk′shə-səz): demons.
8. **Hanuman** (hŭn′o͝o-mən): a monkey ally of Rama's.

Pause & Reflect

1. **MARK IT UP** Complete the following sentence. **(Summarize)**

As he watches the battle,

Ravana feels

so he decides to

2. How does Ravana get ready for the battle? Check three phrases below. **(Summarize)**
   - ❑ does exercises
   - ❑ takes a bath
   - ❑ says prayers
   - ❑ sharpens his sword
   - ❑ puts on armor
   - ❑ sings a song of triumph

3. What does Ravana plan to do? **(Infer)**

the boxed paragraph. How does Rama's behavior contrast with the atmosphere all around him? **(Compare and Contrast)**

The atmosphere on the battlefield is

Rama acts

NOTES

and Lakshmana[9] and asked, "What do you think of it?" Both answered, "We feel no doubt that this chariot is Indra's; it is not an illusory creation."

Rama fastened his sword, slung two quivers full of rare arrows over his shoulders, and climbed into the chariot.

The beat of war drums, the challenging cries of soldiers, the trumpets, and the rolling chariots speeding along to confront each other, created a deafening mixture of noise. While Ravana had instructed his charioteer to speed ahead, Rama very gently ordered his chariot-driver, "Ravana is in a rage; let him perform all the antics he desires and exhaust himself. Until then be calm; we don't have to hurry forward. Move slowly and calmly, and you must strictly follow my instructions; I will tell you when to drive faster."

Ravana's assistant and one of his staunchest supporters, Mahodara[10]—the giant among giants in his physical appearance—begged Ravana, "Let me not be a mere spectator when you confront Rama. Let me have the honour of grappling with him. Permit me to attack Rama."

"Rama is my sole concern," Ravana replied. "If you wish to engage yourself in a fight, you may fight his brother Lakshmana."

Noticing Mahodara's purpose, Rama steered his chariot across his path in order to prevent Mahodara from reaching Lakshmana. Whereupon Mahodara ordered his chariot-driver, "Now dash straight ahead, directly into Rama's chariot."

The charioteer, more practical-minded, advised him, "I would not go near Rama. Let us keep away." But Mahodara, obstinate and intoxicated with war fever, made straight for Rama. He wanted to have the honour of a direct encounter with Rama himself in spite of Ravana's advice; and for this honour he paid a heavy price, as it was a moment's work for Rama to destroy him, and leave him lifeless and shapeless on the field. Noticing this, Ravana's anger mounted further.

---

9. **Lakshmana** (lŭk'shmə-nə): Rama's brother.

10. **Mahodara** (mə-hō'də-rə).

He commanded his driver, "You will not slacken now. Go." Many ominous signs were seen now—his bow-strings suddenly snapped; the mountains shook; thunders rumbled in the skies; tears flowed from the horses' eyes; elephants with decorated foreheads moved along dejectedly. Ravana, noticing them, hesitated only for a second, saying, "I don't care. This mere mortal Rama is of no account, and these omens do not concern me at all." Meanwhile, Rama paused for a moment to consider his next step; and suddenly turned towards the armies supporting Ravana, which stretched away to the horizon, and destroyed them. He felt that this might be one way of saving Ravana. With his armies gone, it was possible that Ravana might have a change of heart. But it had only the effect of spurring Ravana on; he plunged forward and kept coming nearer Rama and his own doom.

Pause & Reflect

FOCUS

In this section, the one-on-one fight between Rama and Ravana begins. Read to find out how the two will fight each other.

MARK IT UP As you read, put an X next to each main event in the battle.

Rama's army cleared and made way for Ravana's chariot, unable to stand the force of his approach. Ravana blew his conch[11] and its shrill challenge reverberated through space. Following it another conch, called "Panchajanya,"[12] which belonged to Mahavishnu[13] (Rama's original form before his present incarnation), sounded of its own accord in answer to the challenge,

11. **conch** (kŏngk): a large spiral seashell, sometimes used as a trumpet.

12. **Panchajanya** (pän′chə-jŭn′yə).

13. **Mahavishnu** (mə-hä′vĭsh′no͞o): Hinduism's supreme god, who divides himself into the trinity of Brahma, Vishnu, and Shiva.

WORDS TO KNOW

dejectedly (dĭ-jĕk′tĭd-lē) *adv.* sadly; in a depressed way

incarnation (ĭn′kär-nā′shən) *n.* a bodily form taken on by a spirit

Pause & Reflect

1. **MARK IT UP** How does Rama act in battle, compared to Ravana? Write two descriptive words under each warrior's name. **(Classifying Characters)**

Rama	Ravana

2. What quality does Mahodara show that leads to his death? **(Analyze)**

NOTES

agitating the universe with its vibrations. And then Matali picked up another conch, which was Indra's, and blew it. This was the signal indicating the commencement of the actual battle. Presently Ravana sent a shower of arrows on Rama; and Rama's followers, unable to bear the sight of his body being studded with arrows, averted their heads. Then the chariot horses of Ravana and Rama glared at each other in hostility, and the flags topping the chariots—Ravana's ensign of the Veena[14] and Rama's with the whole universe on it—clashed, and one heard the stringing and twanging of bow-strings on both sides, overpowering in volume all other sound. Then followed a shower of arrows from Rama's own bow. Ravana stood gazing at the chariot sent by Indra and swore, "These gods, instead of supporting me, have gone to the support of this petty human being. I will teach them a lesson. He is not fit to be killed with my arrows but I shall seize him and his chariot together and fling them into high heaven and dash them to destruction." Despite his oath, he still strung his bow and sent a shower of arrows at Rama, raining in thousands, but they were all invariably shattered and neutralized by the arrows from Rama's bow, which met arrow for arrow. Ultimately Ravana, instead of using one bow, used ten with his twenty arms, multiplying his attack tenfold; but Rama stood unhurt.

Ravana suddenly realized that he should change his tactics and ordered his charioteer to fly the chariot up in the skies. From there he attacked and destroyed a great many of the monkey army supporting Rama. Rama ordered Matali, "Go up in the air. Our young soldiers are being attacked from the sky. Follow Ravana, and don't slacken."

There followed an aerial pursuit at dizzying speed across the dome of the sky and rim of the earth. Ravana's arrows came down like rain; he was bent upon destroying everything in the world. But Rama's arrows diverted, broke, or neutralized Ravana's. Terror-stricken, the gods watched this pursuit. Presently Ravana's arrows struck Rama's horses

REREAD the boxed paragraph. If you were a movie director, what special effects might you use to show the action in this scene? **(Visualize)**

14. ensign of the Veena (vē′nə): a flag depicting a stringed musical instrument.

and pierced the heart of Matali himself. The charioteer fell. Rama paused for a while in grief, undecided as to his next step. Then he recovered and resumed his offensive. At that moment the divine eagle Garuda was seen perched on Rama's flagpost, and the gods who were watching felt that this could be an auspicious sign.

Pause & Reflect

FOCUS

The battle continues. Read on to find out what other magical weapons Rama and Ravana will use.

MARK IT UP As you read, circle the name of each weapon and underline what it can do.

After circling the globe several times, the duelling chariots returned, and the fight continued over Lanka. It was impossible to be very clear about the location of the battleground as the fight occurred here, there, and everywhere. Rama's arrows pierced Ravana's armour and made him wince. Ravana was so insensible to pain and impervious to attack that for him to wince was a good sign, and the gods hoped that this was a turn for the better. But at this moment, Ravana suddenly changed his tactics. Instead of merely shooting his arrows, which were powerful in themselves, he also invoked several supernatural forces to create strange effects: He was an adept in the use of various asthras[15] which could be made dynamic with special incantations. At this point, the fight became one of attack with supernatural powers, and parrying of such an attack with other supernatural powers.

Ravana realized that the mere aiming of shafts with ten or twenty of his arms would be of no avail because the mortal whom he had so contemptuously thought of

15. **asthras** (ŭs′thrəz): arrows or other weapons powered by supernatural forces.

WORDS TO KNOW

impervious (ĭm-pûr′vē-əs) *adj.* unable to be affected

parrying (păr′ē-ĭng) *n.* a warding off or turning aside **parry** *v.*

Pause & Reflect

1. What is unusual about the way in which Rama and Ravana fight? **(Analyze)**

2. **MARK IT UP** Underline each special power displayed by Rama and Ravana. **(Clarify)**

3. Who do you think will win the battle? Why? **(Predict)**

Pause & Reflect

1. MARK IT UP Draw a line matching each cause with its effect. **(Cause and Effect)**

CAUSE	EFFECT
Ravana winces.	The armies disappear.
Ravana uses the weapon called "Maya."	The gods become hopeful.
Rama uses the weapon called "Gnana."	The dead armies seem to rise.

2. If you could create a magical weapon to fight Ravana, what would you name it and what would it do? **(Connect)**

destroying with a slight effort was proving formidable, and his arrows were beginning to pierce and cause pain. Among the asthras sent by Ravana was one called "Danda," a special gift from Shiva, capable of pursuing and pulverizing its target. When it came flaming along, the gods were struck with fear. But Rama's arrow neutralized it.

Now Ravana said to himself, "These are all petty weapons. I should really get down to proper business." And he invoked the one called "Maya" —a weapon which created illusions and confused the enemy.

With proper incantations and worship, he sent off this weapon and it created an illusion of reviving all the armies and its leaders—Kumbakarna[16] and Indrajit[17] and the others—and bringing them back to the battlefield. Presently Rama found all those who, he thought, were no more, coming on with battle cries and surrounding him. Every man in the enemy's army was again up in arms. They seemed to fall on Rama with victorious cries. This was very confusing and Rama asked Matali, whom he had by now revived, "What is happening now? How are all these coming back? They were dead." Matali explained, "In your original identity you are the creator of illusions in this universe. Please know that Ravana has created phantoms to confuse you. If you make up your mind, you can dispel them immediately." Matali's explanation was a great help. Rama at once invoked a weapon called "Gnana"[18]—which means "wisdom" or "perception." This was a very rare weapon, and he sent it forth. And all the terrifying armies who seemed to have come on in such a great mass suddenly evaporated into thin air.

Pause & Reflect

---

16. **Kumbakarna** (kŏŏm′bə-kûr′nə): Ravana's brother.
17. **Indrajit** (ĭn′-drə-jēt): Ravana's son.
18. **Gnana** (gnä′nə).

WORDS TO KNOW
formidable (fôr′mĭ-də-bəl) *adj.* hard to overcome

FOCUS

In this section, Ravana attacks with his deadliest weapon. Find out how Rama fights back.

MARK IT UP As you read, underline details that show how Ravana fights. Circle details that show how Rama fights.

Ravana then shot an asthra called "Thama," whose nature was to create total darkness in all the worlds. The arrows came with heads exposing frightening eyes and fangs, and fiery tongues. End to end the earth was enveloped in total darkness and the whole of creation was paralyzed. This asthra also created a deluge of rain on one side, a rain of stones on the other, a hailstorm showering down intermittently, and a tornado sweeping the earth. Ravana was sure that this would arrest Rama's enterprise. But Rama was able to meet it with what was named "Shivasthra."[19] He understood the nature of the phenomenon and the cause of it and chose the appropriate asthra for counteracting it.

Ravana now shot off what he considered his deadliest weapon—a trident[20] endowed with extraordinary destructive power, once gifted to Ravana by the gods. When it started on its journey there was real panic all round. It came on flaming toward Rama, its speed or course unaffected by the arrows he flung at it.

When Rama noticed his arrows falling down ineffectively while the trident sailed towards him, for a moment he lost heart. When it came quite near, he uttered a certain mantra[21] from the depth of his being and while he was breathing out that incantation, an esoteric syllable in perfect timing, the trident collapsed. Ravana, who had been so certain of vanquishing Rama with his trident, was astonished to see it fall down within an inch of him, and for a

---

19. Shivasthra (shĭ-vŭs′thrə).

20. trident (trīd′nt): a spear with three prongs.

21. mantra (măn′trə): a word, sound, or phrase used as a prayer or spell.

WORDS TO KNOW

intermittently (ĭn′tər-mĭt′nt-lē) *adv.* with stops and starts; on and off

NOTES

minute wondered if his adversary might not after all be a divine being although he looked like a mortal. Ravana thought to himself, "This is, perhaps, the highest God. Who could he be? Not Shiva, for Shiva is my supporter; he could not be Brahma, who is four faced; could not be Vishnu, because of my immunity from the weapons of the whole trinity. Perhaps this man is the primordial being, the cause behind the whole universe. But whoever he may be, I will not stop my fight until I defeat and crush him or at least take him prisoner."

With this resolve, Ravana next sent a weapon which issued forth monstrous serpents vomiting fire and venom, with enormous fangs and red eyes. They came darting in from all directions.

Pause & Reflect

FOCUS

Ravana is getting weaker. Read to find out whether he will make a comeback.

MARK IT UP As you read, underline details that tell you who might win the battle.

Rama now selected an asthra called "Garuda" (which meant "eagle"). Very soon thousands of eagles were aloft, and they picked off the serpents with their claws and beaks and destroyed them. Seeing this also fail, Ravana's anger was roused to a mad pitch and he blindly emptied a quiver full of arrows in Rama's direction. Rama's arrows met them half way and turned them round so that they went back and their sharp points embedded themselves in Ravana's own chest.

Ravana was weakening in spirit. He realized that he was at the end of his resources. All his learning and equipment in weaponry were of no avail and he had practically come to the end of his special gifts of destruction. While he

WORDS TO KNOW
primordial (prī-môr′dē-əl) *adj.* first-existing; original

Pause & Reflect

1. **MARK IT UP** Review the details you marked. Write *Ravana* or *Rama* next to each action below to show who uses what actions in the battle. **(Clarify)**

brings darkness __________

understands the enemy's weapons __________

sends snakes __________

throws a trident __________

speaks mantras __________

2. Why does Ravana begin to think Rama must be a god? **(Cause and Effect)**

was going down thus, Rama's own spirit was soaring up. The combatants were now near enough to grapple with each other and Rama realized that this was the best moment to cut off Ravana's heads. He sent a crescent-shaped arrow which sliced off one of Ravana's heads and flung it far into the sea, and this process continued; but every time a head was cut off, Ravana had the benediction of having another one grown in its place. Rama's crescent-shaped weapon was continuously busy as Ravana's heads kept cropping up. Rama lopped off his arms but they grew again and every lopped-off arm hit Matali and the chariot and tried to cause destruction by itself, and the tongue in a new head wagged, uttered challenges, and cursed Rama. On the cast-off heads of Ravana, devils and minor demons, who had all along been in terror of Ravana and had obeyed and pleased him, executed a dance of death and feasted on the flesh.

Ravana was now desperate. Rama's arrows embedded themselves in a hundred places on his body and weakened him. Presently he collapsed in a faint on the floor of his chariot. Noticing his state, his charioteer pulled back and drew the chariot aside. Matali whispered to Rama, "This is the time to finish off that demon. He is in a faint. Go on. Go on."

But Rama put away his bow and said, "It is not fair warfare to attack a man who is in a faint. I will wait. Let him recover," and waited.

When Ravana revived, he was angry with his charioteer for withdrawing, and took out his sword, crying, "You have disgraced me. Those who look on will think I have retreated." But his charioteer explained how Rama suspended the fight and forbore to attack when he was in a faint. Somehow, Ravana appreciated his explanation and patted his back and resumed his attacks. Having exhausted his special weapons, in desperation Ravana began to throw on Rama all sorts of things such as staves, cast-iron balls,

NOTES

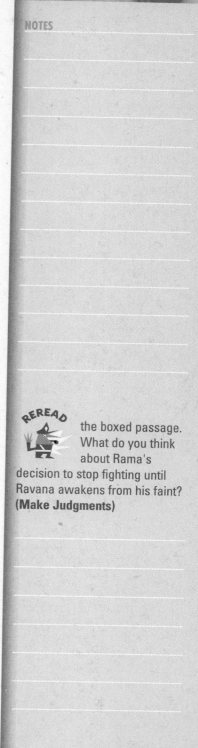

REREAD the boxed passage. What do you think about Rama's decision to stop fighting until Ravana awakens from his faint? **(Make Judgments)**

heavy rocks, and oddments he could lay hands on. None of them touched Rama, but glanced off and fell ineffectually. Rama went on shooting his arrows. There seemed to be no end of this struggle in sight.

Pause & Reflect

FOCUS

In this section, the epic battle ends. Do you think the more honorable warrior will succeed in the end?

MARK IT UP As you read, underline actions that show honor or kindness.

Now Rama had to pause to consider what final measure he should take to bring this campaign to an end. After much thought, he decided to use "Brahmasthra,"[22] a weapon specially designed by the Creator Brahma on a former occasion, when he had to provide one for Shiva to destroy Tripura,[23] the old monster who assumed the forms of flying mountains and settled down on habitations and cities, seeking to destroy the world. The Brahmasthra was a special gift to be used only when all other means had failed. Now Rama, with prayers and worship, invoked its fullest power and sent it in Ravana's direction, aiming at his heart rather than his head; Ravana being vulnerable at heart. While he had prayed for indestructibility of his several heads and arms, he had forgotten to strengthen his heart, where the Brahmasthra entered and ended his career.

Rama watched him fall headlong from his chariot face down onto the earth, and that was the end of the

---

22. **Brahmasthra** (brə-mŭs'thrə).

23. **Tripura** (trĭ-po͞o'rə).

WORDS TO KNOW
ineffectually (ĭn'ĭ-fĕk'cho͞o-əl-ē) *adv.* in a useless manner

Pause & Reflect

1. **MARK IT UP** Check the three sentences below that show Ravana is losing the battle. **(Infer)**
   - ❑ Ravana is weakening in spirit.
   - ❑ Ravana keeps growing new heads.
   - ❑ Ravana is out of magical weapons.
   - ❑ Ravana collapses in his chariot.
   - ❑ Ravana's cut-off arms attack Rama.

2. The characters in this story are superhuman, and their weapons are supernatural. Do you find this battle more or less exciting than a realistic battle? Why? **(Make Judgments)**

great campaign. Now one noticed Ravana's face aglow with a new quality. Rama's arrows had burnt off the layers of dross,[24] the anger, conceit, cruelty, lust, and egotism which had encrusted his real self, and now his personality came through in its pristine form—of one who was devout and capable of tremendous attainments. His constant meditation on Rama, although as an adversary, now seemed to bear fruit, as his face shone with serenity and peace. Rama noticed it from his chariot above and commanded Matali, "Set me down on the ground." When the chariot descended and came to rest on its wheels, Rama got down and commanded Matali, "I am grateful for your services to me. You may now take the chariot back to Indra."

Surrounded by his brother Lakshmana and Hanuman and all his other war chiefs, Rama approached Ravana's body, and stood gazing on it. He noted his crowns and jewelry scattered piecemeal on the ground. The decorations and the extraordinary workmanship of the armour on his chest were blood-covered. Rama sighed as if to say, "What might he not have achieved but for the evil stirring within him!"

At this moment, as they readjusted Ravana's blood-stained body, Rama noticed to his great shock a scar on Ravana's back and said with a smile, "Perhaps this is not an episode of glory for me as I seem to have killed an enemy who was turning his back and retreating. Perhaps I was wrong in shooting the Brahmasthra into him." He looked so concerned at this supposed lapse on his part that Vibishana,[25] Ravana's brother, came forward to explain. "What you have achieved is unique. I say so although it meant the death of my brother."

"But I have attacked a man who had turned his back," Rama said. "See that scar."

---

24. dross (drŏs): waste matter; impurities.

25. Vibishana (vĭ-bē′ shə-nə).

WORDS TO KNOW
pristine (prĭs′tēn′) *adj.* pure; uncorrupted

the boxed passage and circle phrases that say good things about Ravana. How do you think Rama will react to Ravana's death? **(Predict)**

Pause & Reflect

1. How does Rama feel when he sees the scar on Ravana's back? **(Clarify)**

2. What does this reaction tell you about his character? **(Evaluate)**

Hindus in India and other countries view Rama as an example of the ideal person. Using details from the story, write a paragraph on another sheet of paper telling what lessons Rama teaches through his actions and words. **(Analyze)**

Vibishana explained, "It is an old scar. In ancient days, when he paraded his strength around the globe, once he tried to attack the divine elephants that guard the four directions. When he tried to catch them, he was gored in the back by one of the tuskers and that is the scar you see now; it is not a fresh one though fresh blood is flowing on it."

Rama accepted the explanation. "Honour him and cherish his memory so that his spirit may go to heaven, where he has his place. And now I will leave you to attend to his funeral arrangements, befitting his grandeur." ❖

Pause & Reflect

Active Reading SkillBuilder

Classifying Characters

Epics often feature complicated scenes and unusual settings. Many have numerous characters that the reader needs to keep track of to understand the story. As you read the excerpt from the *Ramayana,* use the chart below to **classify the characters.** Provide details about the characters. Give details about their personalities, what they look like, or the role they play in the epic.

Characters on Ravana's Side		Characters on Rama's Side	
Character	**Details**	**Character**	**Details**
Mandodari	Ravana's wife	Sita	Rama's wife

Literary Analysis SkillBuilder

Conflict in an Epic

As you know, the conflict in a story is the struggle between opposing forces that moves a plot forward. In an **epic,** the **conflict** is on a grand scale. The combatants are usually two superhumans who have extraordinary powers. They may be helped by the gods. In addition, supernatural elements are a common feature of the conflict in an epic. As you read about the conflict between Ravana and Rama in the excerpt from the *Ramayana,* look for elements of the battle that make it an epic conflict. Note these elements in the chart below.

Elements of an Epic Conflict
1. The scale of the battle is very large. It involves whole armies, Rama's and Ravana's wives, and an entire city.
2.
3.
4.
5.
6.
7.
8.
9.
10.

Words to Know SkillBuilder

Words to Know

benediction	formidable	incarnation	intermittently	primordial
dejectedly	impervious	ineffectually	parry	pristine

A. Circle the word in each group that is closest in meaning to the boldfaced word.

1. **formidable**	weak	wicked	powerful	confused
2. **pristine**	pure	polluted	spoiled	mild
3. **benediction**	curse	poem	saying	blessing
4. **impervious**	full	unaffected	leaky	closed
5. **dejectedly**	quickly	neatly	sadly	perfectly
6. **primordial**	final	late	first	last
7. **ineffectually**	uselessly	creatively	forcefully	purposefully

B. Fill in the blank in each sentence with the correct Word to Know.

1. Dino watched a movie about the ______________________ of a spirit in the form of a dog.
2. The roof kept leaking as Mr. Crossman tried ______________________ to patch it.
3. The rain fell ______________________ all day long, but Aunt Jane took a short walk between rain showers.
4. Lisa managed to ______________________ the snowballs thrown at her by her brother.
5. The water from the spring is cold and ______________________, so feel free to drink it.
6. The audience made fun of the comedian, but he just smiled and seemed ______________________ to the insults.
7. The soccer players walked ______________________ back to the locker room after they lost the championship game.
8. Lydia thought she would easily win a game of tennis against her father, but he turned out to be a ______________________ player.

C. Write an obituary for Ravana. Use at least **five** of the Words to Know in your obituary.

Connect to Your Life

How do you think leaders should treat the people they lead? How should people treat their leaders? Write your ideas in the chart below.

How leaders should treat followers	How followers should treat leaders

Key to the Epic Poem

WHAT'S THE BIG IDEA? You are about to read an excerpt from the *Iliad* that describes a conflict between a leader and his greatest follower. The *Iliad* is an epic poem that dates back to the time of the ancient Greeks. Many scholars believe Homer created the poem in the 700s B.C. In it, he described a terrible war between the Greeks and the people of Troy. The ancient Greeks believed that supernatural characters—gods and goddesses—played an important role in this war. The chart at the right lists the gods and goddesses you will meet in this excerpt.

Gods and Goddesses	Side favored
Zeus	neither side
Hera	Greeks
Athena	Greeks
Thetis	Greeks
Apollo	Trojans

FROM THE ILIAD

BY HOMER

TRANSLATED BY ROBERT FAGLES

PREVIEW For almost ten years, the Greeks repeatedly have attacked the city of Troy. They have captured treasures and even Trojan women as war prizes. Still, the city stands. The war drags on and seems as though it will never end. The Greek and Trojan leaders and their followers are on edge. What will the gods do to bring events to a crisis?

As the poem opens, the Greek army is suffering from a deadly plague. Apollo has sent the plague to punish the Greeks. The god is angry because Agamemnon has taken the daughter of Chryses, Apollo's priest, as a war prize. When a prophet reveals the cause of Apollo's anger, Agamemnon reluctantly agrees to give her up. He insists, however, on being given Achilles' war prize as compensation. Achilles feels insulted and in his fury threatens to kill Agamemnon. The wise Nestor tries to make peace, with only partial success.

FOCUS

A Trojan named Chryses begs Agamemnon to release his daughter. Find out how Agamemnon responds to this request.

MARK IT UP Underline words and phrases that help you understand Agamemnon's response. An example is highlighted on page 48.

Rage—Goddess, sing the rage of Peleus' son Achilles,
murderous, doomed, that cost the Achaeans countless losses,
hurling down to the House of Death so many sturdy souls,
great fighters' souls, but made their bodies carrion,
feasts for the dogs and birds,
and the will of Zeus was moving toward its end.
Begin, Muse, when the two first broke and clashed,
Agamemnon lord of men and brilliant Achilles.

What god drove them to fight with such a fury?
Apollo the son of Zeus and Leto. Incensed at the king
he swept a fatal plague through the army—men were dying
and all because Agamemnon spurned Apollo's priest.
Yes, Chryses approached the Achaeans' fast ships
to win his daughter back, bringing a priceless ransom
and bearing high in hand, wound on a golden staff,
the wreaths of the god, the distant deadly Archer.
He begged the whole Achaean army but most of all
the two supreme commanders, Atreus' two sons,
"Agamemnon, Menelaus—all Argives geared for war!
May the gods who hold the halls of Olympus give you
Priam's city to plunder, then safe passage home.
Just set my daughter free, my dear one . . . here,
accept these gifts, this ransom. Honor the god
who strikes from worlds away—the son of Zeus, Apollo!"

MARK IT UP **KEEP TRACK**

As you read, you can use these marks to keep track of your understanding.

- * This is important.
- ? I have a question about this.
- ! This is a surprise.

WORDS TO KNOW

spurn (spûrn) *v.* to reject in a scornful way

GUIDE FOR READING

Use this guide for help with unfamiliar words and difficult passages.

1 Goddess: a Muse (goddess of poetry and music) whom the poet calls upon for inspiration.

2 Achaeans (ə-kē'ənz)**:** Greeks.

4 carrion: decaying flesh.

10 Leto (lē'tō)**:** a goddess; **incensed:** enraged.

13 Chryses (krī'sēz)**.**

16 Archer: Apollo, who was thought to be able to cause diseases by shooting people with his arrows.

18 Atreus' (ā'tro͞os')**.**

19 Argives (är'jīvz')**:** Greeks.

20 Olympus (ə-lĭm'pəs)**:** the highest mountain in Greece, believed to be the home of the gods.

21 Priam's city: Troy.

This poem contains some Greek names you may be unfamiliar with. In addition, some characters and groups are called by more than one name. For example, the Greeks are also called the Achaeans, the Argives, and the Danaans. The sidenotes in the **Guide for Reading** will help you pronounce the names and understand who is who.

the boxed text on page 46. Then check the phrase below that best completes the following sentence.

The poet calls upon a goddess to help him tell the story of ________. **(Clarify)**

- ❑ the fall of Troy
- ❑ the start of the Trojan War
- ❑ the fight between Achilles and Agamemnon

And all ranks of Achaeans cried out their assent:
"Respect the priest, accept the shining ransom!"
But it brought no joy to the heart of Agamemnon.
The king dismissed the priest with a brutal order
ringing in his ears: "Never again, old man,
let me catch sight of you by the hollow ships!
Not loitering now, not slinking back tomorrow.
The staff and the wreaths of god will never save you then.
The girl—I won't give up the girl. Long before that,
old age will overtake her in my house, in Argos,
far from her fatherland, slaving back and forth
at the loom, forced to share my bed!
Now go,
don't tempt my wrath—and you may depart alive."

Pause & Reflect

FOCUS

Apollo takes revenge for Agamemnon's cruel treatment of Chryses. Find out how Apollo punishes the Greeks.

MARK IT UP As you read, circle words and phrases that describe Apollo's punishment. Put a star next to the passage that tells what the Greeks must do to appease Apollo.

The old man was terrified. He obeyed the order,
turning, trailing away in silence down the shore
where the roaring battle lines of breakers crash and drag.
And moving off to a safe distance, over and over
the old priest prayed to the son of sleek-haired Leto,
lord Apollo, "Hear me, Apollo! God of the silver bow
who strides the walls of Chryse and Cilla sacrosanct—
lord in power of Tenedos—Smintheus, god of the plague!
If I ever roofed a shrine to please your heart,
ever burned the long rich bones of bulls and goats
on your holy altar, now, now bring my prayer to pass.
Pay the Danaans back—your arrows for my tears!"

His prayer went up and Phoebus Apollo heard him.
Down he strode from Olympus' peaks, storming at heart
with his bow and hooded quiver slung across his shoulders.
The arrows clanged at his back as the god quaked with rage,

WORDS TO KNOW
assent (ə-sĕnt') *n.* agreement

36 **loom:** a device used for weaving cloth, a principal job of women in ancient Greek households.

37 **wrath:** anger.

44 **Chryse** (krī'sē)**:** Chryses' hometown, site of a temple of Apollo; **Cilla** (sĭl'ə)**:** another Trojan town; **sacrosanct** (săk'rō-sangt')**:** regarded as sacred and safe from attack.

45 **Tenedos** (tĕn'ə-dŏs)**:** a small island off the Trojan coast; **Smintheus** (smĭn'tho͞os)**:** a title of Apollo.

49 **Danaans** (də-nā'əns)**:** Greeks.

50 **Phoebus** (fē'bəs)**:** a title of Apollo in his role as god of the sun.

Pause & Reflect

1. Look back at the words and phrases you underlined. Then put a check mark next to each statement below that tells about the encounter between Agamemnon and Chryses. **(Clarify)**

- ❑ Chryses offers a ransom for his daughter.
- ❑ Agamemnon agrees to accept the wreaths of the gods.
- ❑ Agamemnon's soldiers ask him to give the girl back.
- ❑ Agamemnon refuses to give up the girl and insults Chryses.

2. Look again at the words and phrases you underlined. What kind of a person does Agamemnon seem to be? Check four traits. **(Evaluate)**

- ❑ reasonable
- ❑ selfish
- ❑ cruel
- ❑ hot-tempered
- ❑ kind
- ❑ calm
- ❑ proud
- ❑ brave

the god himself on the march and down he came like night.
Over against the ships he dropped to a knee, let fly a shaft
and a terrifying clash rang out from the great silver bow.
First he went for the mules and circling dogs but then,
launching a piercing shaft at the men themselves,
he cut them down in droves—
and the corpse-fires burned on, night and day, no end in
sight.
Nine days the arrows of god swept through the army.
On the tenth Achilles called all ranks to muster—
the impulse seized him, sent by white-armed Hera
grieving to see Achaean fighters drop and die.
Once they'd gathered, crowding the meeting grounds,
the swift runner Achilles rose and spoke among them:
"Son of Atreus, now we are beaten back, I fear,
the long campaign is lost. So home we sail . . .
if we can escape our death—if war and plague
are joining forces now to crush the Argives.
But wait: let us question a holy man,
a prophet, even a man skilled with dreams—
dreams as well can come our way from Zeus—
come, someone to tell us why Apollo rages so,
whether he blames us for a vow we failed, or sacrifice.
If only the god would share the smoky savor of lambs
and full-grown goats, Apollo might be willing, still,
somehow, to save us from this plague."
So he proposed
and down he sat again as Calchas rose among them,
Thestor's son, the clearest by far of all the seers
who scan the flight of birds. He knew all things that are,
all things that are past and all that are to come,
the seer who had led the Argive ships to Troy
with the second sight that god Apollo gave him.
For the armies' good the seer began to speak:
"Achilles, dear to Zeus . . .
you order me to explain Apollo's anger,
the distant deadly Archer? I will tell it all.

57 mules and circling dogs: the animals that are the first to be affected by the plague.

59 he cut them down in droves: Apollo sent a terrible disease that killed many Greek soldiers.

63 Hera (hîr′ə)**:** queen of the gods and wife of Zeus.

67 Son of Atreus: Agamemnon.

76–77 If only . . . full-grown goats: If Apollo would accept an animal sacrifice from the Greek forces.

79 Calchas (kăl′kəs)**:** a priest and prophet.

80 seers: prophets.

81 scan the flight of birds: In ancient Greece, the behavior of birds was thought to provide signs of future events.

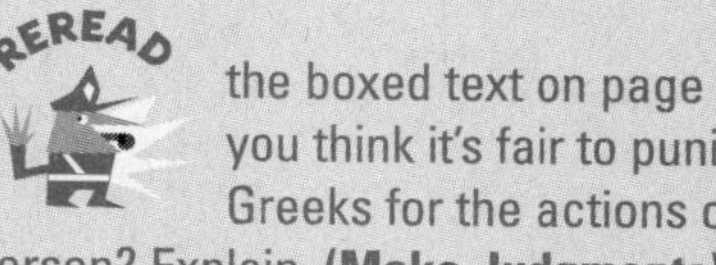

the boxed text on page 50. Do you think it's fair to punish all the Greeks for the actions of one person? Explain. **(Make Judgments)**

MARK IT UP **WORD POWER**

Mark words that you'd like to add to your **Personal Word List.** After reading, you can record the words and their meanings beginning on page 444.

But strike a pact with me, swear you will defend me
with all your heart, with words and strength of hand.
For there is a man I will enrage—I see it now—
a powerful man who lords it over all the Argives,
one the Achaeans must obey . . . A mighty king,
raging against an inferior, is too strong.
Even if he can swallow down his wrath today,
still he will nurse the burning in his chest
until, sooner or later, he sends it bursting forth.
Consider it closely, Achilles. Will you save me?"

And the matchless runner reassured him: "Courage!
Out with it now, Calchas. Reveal the will of god,
whatever you may know. And I swear by Apollo
dear to Zeus, the power you pray to, Calchas,
when you reveal god's will to the Argives—no one,
not while I am alive and see the light on earth, no one
will lay his heavy hands on you by the hollow ships.
None among all the armies. Not even if you mean
Agamemnon here who now claims to be, by far,
the best of the Achaeans."
The seer took heart
and this time he spoke out, bravely: "Beware—
he casts no blame for a vow we failed, a sacrifice.
The god's enraged because Agamemnon spurned his priest,
he refused to free his daughter, he refused the ransom.
That's why the Archer sends us pains and he will
send us more
and never drive this shameful destruction from the Argives,
not till we give back the girl with sparkling eyes
to her loving father—no price, no ransom paid—
and carry a sacred hundred bulls to Chryse town.
Then we can calm the god, and only then appease him."

95–97 Even if . . . forth: Even if Agamemnon can remain calm today, inside he will still be angry, and sooner or later his anger will erupt.

111 spurned: rejected.

118 appease: satisfy.

Pause & Reflect

1. MARK IT UP Look back at the words and phrases you circled as you read. Then complete the following sentences: **(Summarize)**

Apollo punishes the Greeks by

To appease Apollo, the Greeks must

and

2. How do you think Agamemnon will respond to Calchas' words? Why? **(Predict)**

FOCUS

The feud between Achilles and Agamemnon begins. Evaluate the cause of the conflict. Who do you think is more to blame?

So he declared and sat down. But among them rose
the fighting son of Atreus, lord of the far-flung kingdoms,
Agamemnon—furious, his dark heart filled to the brim,
blazing with anger now, his eyes like searing fire.
With a sudden, killing look he wheeled on Calchas first:
"Seer of misery! Never a word that works to my advantage!
Always misery warms your heart, your prophecies—
never a word of profit said or brought to pass.
Now, again, you divine god's will for the armies,
bruit it out, as fact, why the deadly Archer
multiplies our pains: because I, I refused
that glittering price for the young girl Chryseis.
Indeed, I prefer her by far, the girl herself,
I want her mine in my own house! I rank her higher
than Clytemnestra, my wedded wife—she's nothing less
in build or breeding, in mind or works of hand.
But I am willing to give her back, even so,
if that is best for all. What I really want
is to keep my people safe, not see them dying.
But fetch me another prize, and straight off too,
else I alone of the Argives go without my honor.
That would be a disgrace. You are all witness,
look—my prize is snatched away!"
But the swift runner
Achilles answered him at once, "Just how, Agamemnon,
great field marshal . . . most grasping man alive,
how can the generous Argives give you prizes now?
I know of no troves of treasure, piled, lying idle,
anywhere. Whatever we dragged from towns we plundered,
all's been portioned out. But collect it, call it back
from the rank and file? That would be the disgrace.
So return the girl to the god, at least for now.
We Achaeans will pay you back, three, four times over,
if Zeus will grant us the gift, somehow, someday,
to raze Troy's massive ramparts to the ground."

But King Agamemnon countered, "Not so quickly,
brave as you are, godlike Achilles—trying to cheat me.

128 bruit it out: report it.

130 Chryseis (krī-sē′ĭs)**:** Chryses′ daughter.

133 Clytemnestra (klī′təm-nĕs′trə)**.**

146–149 I know . . . disgrace: I know of no treasures just lying around. All the treasures won in battle have been given out, and taking them back from the soldiers would be a shameful thing to do. The word ***troves*** in line 146 means "collections."

153 raze: demolish; **ramparts:** defensive walls.

NOTES

READ ALOUD the boxed text on page 54. Circle the sentence that shows Agamemnon's generous side. Underline the sentence that shows his selfish side. Do you think Agamemnon is basically generous or selfish? Explain. **(Analyze)**

Oh no, you won't get past me, take me in that way!
What do you want? To cling to your own prize
while I sit calmly by—empty-handed here?
Is that why you order me to give her back?
No—if our generous Argives will give me a prize,
a match for my desires, equal to what I've lost,
well and good. But if they give me nothing
I will take a prize myself—your own, or Ajax'
or Odysseus' prize—I'll commandeer her myself
and let that man I go to visit choke with rage!
Enough. We'll deal with all this later, in due time.
Now come, we haul a black ship down to the bright sea,
gather a decent number of oarsmen along her locks
and put aboard a sacrifice, and Chryseis herself,
in all her beauty . . . we embark her too.
Let one of the leading captains take command.
Ajax, Idomeneus, trusty Odysseus or you, Achilles,
you—the most violent man alive—so you can perform
the rites for us and calm the god yourself."
A dark glance
and the headstrong runner answered him in kind:
"Shameless—
armored in shamelessness—always shrewd with greed!
How could any Argive soldier obey your orders,
freely and gladly do your sailing for you
or fight your enemies, full force? Not I, no.
It wasn't Trojan spearmen who brought me here to fight.
The Trojans never did *me* damage, not in the least,
they never stole my cattle or my horses, never
in Phthia where the rich soil breeds strong men
did they lay waste my crops. How could they?
Look at the endless miles that lie between us . . .
shadowy mountain ranges, seas that surge and thunder.
No, you colossal, shameless—we all followed you,
to please you, to fight for you, to win your honor
back from the Trojans—Menelaus and you, you dog-face!
What do you care? Nothing. You don't look right or left.
And now you threaten to strip me of my prize in person—
the one I fought for long and hard, and sons of Achaea

163 Ajax (ā′jăks′)**:** the strongest Greek warrior next to Achilles—known as the Greater Ajax to distinguish him from another warrior of the same name.

164 commandeer (kŏm′ən-dîr′)**:** seize by force.

172 Idomeneus (ī-dŏm′ə-no͞os′)**:** the ruler of the island of Crete.

175 the headstrong runner: Achilles.

183 Phthia (fthī′ə)**:** Achilles' homeland.

189 Menelaus (mĕn′ə-lā′əs)**:** the King of Sparta, whose wife, Helen, ran off to Troy with the Trojan prince Paris—the event that triggered the Trojan War.

NOTES

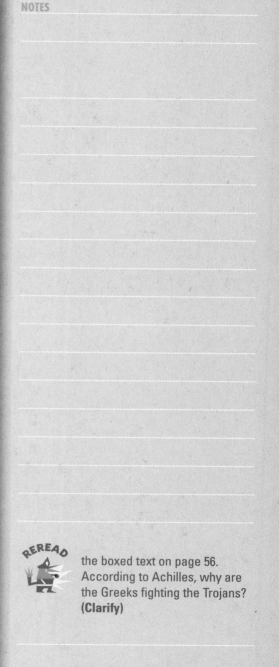

the boxed text on page 56. According to Achilles, why are the Greeks fighting the Trojans? **(Clarify)**

handed her to me.
My honors never equal yours,
whenever we sack some wealthy Trojan stronghold—
my arms bear the brunt of the raw, savage fighting,
true, but when it comes to dividing up the plunder
the lion's share is yours, and back I go to my ships,
clutching some scrap, some pittance that I love,
when I have fought to exhaustion.
No more now—
back I go to Phthia. Better that way by far,
to journey home in the beaked ships of war.
I have no mind to linger here disgraced,
brimming your cup and piling up your plunder."
But the lord of men Agamemnon shot back,
"Desert, by all means—if the spirit drives you home!
I will never beg you to stay, not on my account.
Never—others will take my side and do me honor,
Zeus above all, whose wisdom rules the world.
You—I hate you most of all the warlords
loved by the gods. Always dear to your heart,
strife, yes, and battles, the bloody grind of war.
What if you are a great soldier? That's just a gift of god.
Go home with your ships and comrades, lord it over your
Myrmidons!
You are nothing to me—you and your overweening anger!
But let this be my warning on your way:
since Apollo insists on taking my Chryseis,
I'll send her back in my own ships with my crew.
But I, I will be there in person at your tents
to take Briseis in all her beauty, your own prize—
so you can learn just how much greater I am than you
and the next man up may shrink from matching words
with me,
from hoping to rival Agamemnon strength for strength!"

WORDS TO KNOW
pittance (pĭt'ns) *n.* a small reward; tiny amount

194 sack: capture and loot.

213 Myrmidons (mûr′mə-dŏnz′)**:** Achilles' people.

214 overweening: too proud.

219 Briseis (brī-sē′ĭs)**:** a captive Trojan woman who was given to Achilles.

Pause & Reflect

1. Why are Achilles and Agamemnon angry with each other? Who do you think is more to blame for the conflict? Write your ideas below. **(Evaluate)**

Achilles' reasons for being angry:	Agamemnon's reasons for being angry:

❑ Achilles

❑ Agamemnon

is more to blame because

2. Reread the boxed passage on page 58. What has Agamemnon decided to do? Why? **(Clarify)**

3. If you were Achilles, would you keep on fighting for Agamemnon? **(Connect)**

YES / NO, because

FOCUS

The anger of Achilles—"the most violent man alive"—is always dangerous. Read to find out how various characters, both humans and gods, respond to his anger.

He broke off and anguish gripped Achilles.
The heart in his rugged chest was pounding, torn . . .
Should he draw the long sharp sword slung at his hip,
thrust through the ranks and kill Agamemnon now?—
or check his rage and beat his fury down?
As his racing spirit veered back and forth,
just as he drew his huge blade from its sheath,
down from the vaulting heavens swept Athena,
the white-armed goddess Hera sped her down:
Hera loved both men and cared for both alike.
Rearing behind him Pallas seized his fiery hair—
only Achilles saw her, none of the other fighters—
struck with wonder he spun around, he knew her at once,
Pallas Athena! the terrible blazing of those eyes,
and his winged words went flying: "Why, why now?
Child of Zeus with the shield of thunder, why come now?
To witness the outrage Agamemnon just committed?
I tell you this, and so help me it's the truth—
he'll soon pay for his arrogance with his life!"

Her gray eyes clear, the goddess Athena answered,
"Down from the skies I come to check your rage
if only you will yield.
The white-armed goddess Hera sped me down:
she loves you both, she cares for you both alike.
Stop this fighting, now. Don't lay hand to sword.
Lash him with threats of the price that he will face.
And I tell you this—and I know it is the truth—
one day glittering gifts will lie before you,
three times over to pay for all his outrage.
Hold back now. Obey us both."
So she urged
and the swift runner complied at once: "I must—
when the two of you hand down commands, Goddess,
a man submits though his heart breaks with fury.
Better for him by far. If a man obeys the gods
they're quick to hear his prayers."

WORDS TO KNOW
comply (kəm-plī′) *v.* to agree to a request or carry out an order; obey

233 **Pallas** (păl′əs)**:** a title of Athena.

241 **arrogance** (ăr′ə-gəns)**:** too much pride in oneself.

251 **outrage:** an act or a remark that deeply hurts or angers a person.

NOTES

REREAD the boxed text on page 60. Picture in your mind Athena as she grips Achilles by the hair. Draw them the way you think they would look.

And with that
Achilles stayed his burly hand on the silver hilt
and slid the huge blade back in its sheath.
He would not fight the orders of Athena.
Soaring home to Olympus, she rejoined the gods
aloft in the halls of Zeus whose shield is thunder.

But Achilles rounded on Agamemnon once again,
lashing out at him, not relaxing his anger for a moment:
"Staggering drunk, with your dog's eyes, your fawn's heart!
Never once did you arm with the troops and go to battle
or risk an ambush packed with Achaea's picked men—
you lack the courage, you can see death coming.
Safer by far, you find, to foray all through camp,
commandeering the prize of any man who speaks against
you.
King who devours his people! Worthless husks, the men
you rule—
if not, Atrides, this outrage would have been your last.
I tell you this, and I swear a mighty oath upon it . . .
by this, this scepter, look,
that never again will put forth crown and branches,
now it's left its stump on the mountain ridge forever,
nor will it sprout new green again, now the brazen ax
has stripped its bark and leaves, and now the sons of Achaea
pass it back and forth as they hand their judgments down,
upholding the honored customs whenever Zeus commands—
This scepter will be the mighty force behind my oath:
someday, I swear, a yearning for Achilles will strike
Achaea's sons and all your armies! But then, Atrides,
harrowed as you will be, nothing you do can save you—
not when your hordes of fighters drop and die,
cut down by the hands of man-killing Hector! Then—
then you will tear your heart out, desperate, raging
that you disgraced the best of the Achaeans!"
Down on the ground
he dashed the scepter studded bright with golden nails,

258 **burly:** big and strong; **hilt:** the handle of a sword.

263 **rounded on:** attacked with words.

269 **foray:** raid.

272 **Atrides** (ā-trī′dēz′)**:** "son of Atreus"—that is, Agamemnon.

273–281 Achilles is telling the assembly that the scepter (rod) he now holds, which is usually seen as a symbol of authority, is nothing more than a dead piece of wood—this reflects Achilles' loss of respect for Agamemnon.

274 **scepter:** a rod symbolizing authority, handed in turn to each speaker in the warriors' assembly.

284 **harrowed:** distressed.

286 **Hector:** the greatest warrior of the Trojan army.

NOTES

READ ALOUD the boxed passage. What two flaws does Achilles see in Agamemnon? Check two words below. **(Draw Conclusions)**

- ❑ cowardice
- ❑ violent nature
- ❑ greed
- ❑ stupidity

then took his seat again. The son of Atreus smoldered,
glaring across at him, but Nestor rose between them,
the man of winning words, the clear speaker of Pylos . . .
Sweeter than honey from his tongue the voice flowed on
and on.
Two generations of mortal men he had seen go down by
now,
those who were born and bred with him in the old days,
in Pylos' holy realm, and now he ruled the third.
He pleaded with both kings, with clear good will,
"No more—or enormous sorrow comes to all Achaea!
How they would exult, Priam and Priam's sons
and all the Trojans. Oh they'd leap for joy
to hear the two of you battling on this way,
you who excel us all, first in Achaean councils,
first in the ways of war.
Stop. Please.
Listen to Nestor. You are both younger than I,
and in my time I struck up with better men than you,
even you, but never once did they make light of me.
I've never seen such men, I never will again . . .
men like Pirithous, Dryas, that fine captain,
Caeneus and Exadius, and Polyphemus, royal prince,
and Theseus, Aegeus' boy, a match for the immortals.
They were the strongest mortals ever bred on earth,
the strongest, and they fought against the strongest too,
shaggy Centaurs, wild brutes of the mountains—
they hacked them down, terrible, deadly work.
And I was in their ranks, fresh out of Pylos,
far away from home—they enlisted me themselves
and I fought on my own, a free lance, single-handed.
And none of the men who walk the earth these days
could battle with those fighters, none, but they,
they took to heart my counsels, marked my words.
So now you listen too. Yielding is far better . . .
Don't seize the girl, Agamemnon, powerful as you are—

290 smoldered: felt anger or hate but kept it under control.

292 Pylos (pī'lŏs').

299 exult: rejoice; **Priam** (prī'əm): the King of Troy and the father of Hector and Paris.

308–313 Pirithous (pī-rith'ō-əs), **Dryas** (drī'əs) . . . **Caeneus** (sē'no͞os) **and Exadius** (ĭg-zăd'ē-əs) . . . **Polyphemus** (pŏl'ə-fē'məs) . . . **Theseus** (thē'syo͞os), **Aegeus'** (ē'jo͞os') **boy:** heroes of the legendary war fought by the Lapiths against the **Centaurs** (a monstrous race with bodies half human and half horse).

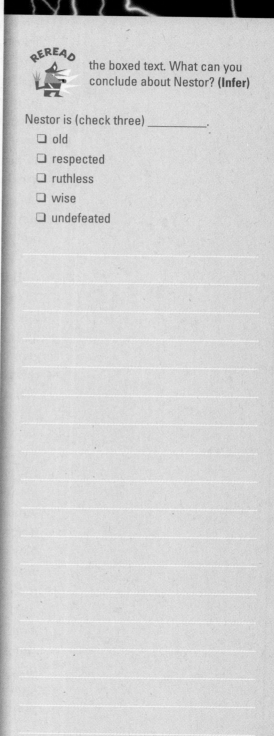

REREAD the boxed text. What can you conclude about Nestor? **(Infer)**

Nestor is (check three) __________.

- ❑ old
- ❑ respected
- ❑ ruthless
- ❑ wise
- ❑ undefeated

leave her, just as the sons of Achaea gave her,
his prize from the very first.
And you, Achilles, never hope to fight it out
with your king, pitting force against his force:
no one can match the honors dealt a king, you know,
a sceptered king to whom great Zeus gives glory.
Strong as you are—a goddess was your mother—
he has more power because he rules more men.
Atrides, end your anger—look, it's Nestor!
I beg you, cool your fury against Achilles.
Here the man stands over all Achaea's armies,
our rugged bulwark braced for shocks of war."

But King Agamemnon answered him in haste,
"True, old man—all you say is fit and proper—
but this soldier wants to tower over the armies,
he wants to rule over all, to lord it over all,
give out orders to every man in sight. Well,
there's one, I trust, who will never yield to him!
What if the everlasting gods have made a spearman of him?
Have they entitled him to hurl abuse at me?"

"Yes!"—blazing Achilles broke in quickly—
"What a worthless, burnt-out coward I'd be called
if I would submit to you and all your orders,
whatever you blurt out. Fling them at others,
don't give me commands!
Never again, I trust, will Achilles yield to you.
And I tell you this—take it to heart, I warn you—
my hands will never do battle for that girl,
neither with you, King, nor any man alive.
You Achaeans gave her, now you've snatched her back.
But all the rest I possess beside my fast black ship—
not one bit of it can you seize against my will, Atrides.
Come, try it! So the men can see, that instant,
your black blood gush and spurt around my spear!"

Pause & Reflect

334 bulwark: defensive barrier.

350–356 my hands . . . my spear!: I won't fight you or anyone else to keep Briseis, the war prize you intend to take back from me. But if you try to take anything else that is mine, I will kill you.

Pause & Reflect

1. How would you describe the outcome of the feud between Achilles and Agamemnon? **(Draw Conclusions)**

2. If you were a Greek soldier, what might you say to Achilles and Agamemnon to persuade them to make peace? **(Connect)**

I would tell Achilles:

I would tell Agamemnon:

Do the Greek fighters regard women as mere objects to be won and lost, or do they value them as people? Discuss this question with a classmate. Find passages that support your argument. **(Analyze)**

Moving On

If you are using ***The Language of Literature,*** go to page 195 to continue reading the *Iliad.* As you do so, continue to be an active reader. Ask yourself the kinds of questions you found in this excerpt from Book One.

Glossary

Gods and Goddesses
(Also known as the **Immortals**)

Apollo: The god of healing, music, poetry, and prophecy; epithets: "the distant deadly Archer," "god of the plague," "God of the silver bow," "Smintheus," "son of Zeus"

Athena: The goddess of wisdom and warfare; epithets: "Child of Zeus," "immortal Athena"

Hera: The queen of the gods, sister and wife of Zeus; epithet: "white-armed Hera"

Thetis: A sea goddess; mother of Achilles; epithet: "the Old Man of the Sea's daughter"

Zeus: The king of the gods; epithets: "Father Zeus," "king of the black cloud," "Lord of the lightning"

Greeks
(Also known as **Achaeans, Argives, Danaans, Dorians, and Myrmidons**)

Achilles: The mightiest Greek warrior; epithets: "brilliant Achilles," "godlike Achilles," "the headstrong runner," "the matchless runner," "Peleus' princely son," "swift runner Achilles"

Agamemnon: The king of Mycenae; epithets: "fighting son of Atreus, " "great field marshal," "lord of the far-flung kingdoms"

Calchas: A priest and prophet; epithets: "the seer," "Thestor's son"

Helen: The wife of Menelaus, daughter of Zeus and Leda

Menelaus: The king of Sparta, whose wife, Helen, was carried off to Troy by Paris

Odysseus: King of Ithaca

Nestor: The king of Pylos, oldest and wisest of the Greek leaders; epithets: "the clear speaker of Pylos," "the man of winning words"

Trojans
(Also known as **Phyrgians, Teucrians**)

Chryses: A priest of Apollo; epithet: "old man"

Hector: The leader and greatest warrior of the Trojan army; epithets: "breaker of horses," "glorious Hector," "man-killing Hector," "noble Hector," "the gallant captain"

Hecuba: The queen of Troy, mother of Hector and Paris

Paris: The Trojan prince whose abduction of Helen was the cause of the Trojan War

Priam: The king of Troy, father of Hector and Paris; epithets: "old and noble Priam," "the majestic king of Troy"

Active Reading SkillBuilder

Evaluating Characters and Events

As you read this excerpt from the *Iliad,* you should examine why important **characters,** such as Agamemnon and Achilles, act the way they do. You should also look for the causes of major **events,** such as the plague and the feud between Agamemnon and Achilles. Finally, you should **evaluate,** or form your own opinions about, the poem's characters and events. Use the chart below to record motives, causes, and your evaluations. Examples have been provided.

Character or Event	Motive or Cause	My Evaluation
Lines 9–12 Apollo sends a plague upon the Greeks.	*To punish Agamemnon for taking the daughter of his priest as a war prize*	*Apollo is a proud god who seeks revenge.*
Lines 135–139, 159–164 Agamemnon offers to return the priest's daughter in exchange for Achilles' prize, Briseis.		
Lines 186–192 Achilles bitterly criticizes Agamemnon for wanting to take Briseis.		
Lines 229–251 Athena visits Achilles.		
Lines 289–333 Nestor tries to reason with Agamemnon and Achilles.		
Lines 343–350 Achilles threatens to leave Agamemnon and the Greek army.		

Literary Analysis SkillBuilder

Epic Hero

An **epic hero** is the larger-than-life figure whose actions are central to an epic poem. Usually male, the epic hero participates in dangerous adventures and accomplishes great deeds that require courage and strength. Often, he is assisted in his pursuits by supernatural forces.

Use the chart to evaluate the extent to which Achilles acts like an epic hero in this excerpt from the *Iliad.* In the first column, list Achilles' larger-than-life qualities and actions. In the second column, list Achilles' human weaknesses and unwise actions.

Heroic Qualities of Achilles	Weaknesses of Achilles
Achilles is a great warrior, admired by the Greeks and feared by the Trojans. He is also the son of a goddess.	*He is sometimes blinded by violent emotions.*

Follow Up: In what ways do you think Achilles' character needs improvement?

Words to Know SkillBuilder

Words to Know

assent comply pittance spurn

A. Decide which word from the list above is described by each clue. Write the word on the blank line next to the clue.

1. This word is a verb that means "to reject in a scornful way." Its origins can be traced back to an Old English verb that means "to kick, or to strike." ______________

2. In the Middle Ages, this word was used to describe the allowance of food given to a monk or a poor person. Today, this word means "a small reward, or a tiny amount." ______________

3. This word means "to do what is asked or demanded." It stems from the Latin word *complēre*. ______________

4. This word means "to say 'yes.'" It stems from the Latin words *ad,* which means "toward," and *sentīre,* which means "to feel." ______________

B. Circle the word in each group that has a similar meaning to the **boldfaced** word.

1. **assent**	request	agreement	warning	command
2. **comply**	disobey	reject	fulfill	oppose
3. **pittance**	minimum	maximum	abundance	excess
4. **spurn**	welcome	refuse	accept	praise

C. Write a brief summary of the events described in this excerpt from the *Iliad.* Use the four Words to Know in your summary.

Before You Read

Connect to Your Life

Do you think it's better to know the truth about the past, even if the truth is very painful? Check your opinion below, and then write the reason why you think as you do.

❑ Better to know ❑ Better not to know

My reason:

____

____

____

____

____

____

Key to the Drama

WHAT YOU NEED TO KNOW This play is based on the Greek legend of Oedipus. As a baby, Oedipus was taken from his real parents, King Laius and Queen Jocasta of Thebes. Oedipus was raised by Polybus and Merope, the king and queen of Corinth, and grew up believing that he was their son. As a young adult, Oedipus left Corinth and came across King Laius at a crossroad. They quarreled about who had the right of way. Unaware that Laius was his real father, Oedipus killed him in a fit of rage. Eventually, Oedipus made his way to Thebes, freed the city from terror by solving the riddle of the Sphinx, and became the city's king. He then took Laius' widow as his wife, not realizing that he was marrying his own mother.

OEDIPUS *the* KING

— BY SOPHOCLES —

Translated by Robert Fagles

PREVIEW For many years Oedipus has ruled Thebes in peace. Suddenly, the city again is faced with a crisis. Can Oedipus save the city for the second time?

***Time and Scene:** The royal house of Thebes. Double doors dominate the façade; a stone altar stands at the center of the stage.*

Many years have passed since Oedipus *solved the riddle of the Sphinx and ascended the throne of Thebes, and now a plague has struck the city. A procession of priests enters; suppliants, broken and despondent, they carry branches wound in wool and lay them on the altar.*

The doors open. Guards assemble. Oedipus *comes forward, majestic but for a telltale limp, and slowly views the condition of his people.*

FOCUS

The priest describes how the people are suffering. Find out how Oedipus responds to his pleas for help.

MARK IT UP As you read, underline details that help you form an impression of Oedipus as a leader. An example is highlighted on this page.

Oedipus. Oh my children, the new blood of ancient Thebes,
why are you here? Huddling at my altar,
praying before me, your branches wound in wool.
Our city reeks with the smoke of burning incense,
rings with cries for the Healer and wailing for the dead.
I thought it wrong, my children, to hear the truth
from others, messengers. Here I am myself—
you all know me, the world knows my fame:
I am Oedipus.
(helping a Priest to his feet)
Speak up, old man. Your years,
your dignity—you should speak for the others.
Why here and kneeling, what preys upon you so?
Some sudden fear? some strong desire?
You can trust me. I am ready to help,
I'll do anything. I would be blind to misery
not to pity my people kneeling at my feet.

Priest. Oh Oedipus, king of the land, our greatest power!
You see us before you now, men of all ages
clinging to your altars. Here are boys,
still too weak to fly from the nest,
and here the old, bowed down with the years,
the holy ones—a priest of Zeus myself—and here
the picked, unmarried men, the young hope of Thebes.

WORDS TO KNOW
despondent (dĭ-spŏn′dənt) *adj.* sad; depressed

Use this guide for help with unfamiliar words and difficult passages.

3 **branches wound in wool:** tokens placed on altars by people seeking favors from the gods.

5 **the Healer:** the god Apollo, who could both cause and cure plagues.

This story is told in the form of a play. Pay close attention to the stage directions in italic, or slanted, type. They describe the setting, give background information, and tell how the characters move on the stage.

Cast of Characters

Oedipus (ĕd'ə-pəs), king of Thebes

Priests of Thebes

Creon (krē'ŏn'), Oedipus' brother-in-law, brother of Queen Jocasta

Chorus, the people of Thebes

Tiresias (tī-rē'sē-əs), a blind prophet

Leader, a wise citizen of Thebes

Guards and attendants

MARK IT UP **WORD POWER**
Mark words that you'd like to add to your **Personal Word List.** After reading, you can record the words and their meanings beginning on page 444.

And all the rest, your great family gathers now,
branches wreathed, massing in the squares,
kneeling before the two temples of queen Athena
or the river-shrine where the embers glow and die
and Apollo sees the future in the ashes.
Our city—
look around you, see with your own eyes—
our ship pitches wildly, cannot lift her head
from the depths, the red waves of death . . .
Thebes is dying. A blight on the fresh crops
and the rich pastures, cattle sicken and die,
and the women die in labor, children stillborn,
and the plague, the fiery god of fever hurls down
on the city, his lightning slashing through us—
raging plague in all its vengeance, devastating
the house of Cadmus! And black Death luxuriates
in the raw, wailing miseries of Thebes.
Now we pray to you. You cannot equal the gods,
your children know that, bending at your altar.
But we do rate you first of men,
both in the common crises of our lives
and face-to-face encounters with the gods.
You freed us from the Sphinx, you came to Thebes
and cut us loose from the bloody tribute we had paid
that harsh, brutal singer. We taught you nothing,
no skill, no extra knowledge, still you triumphed.
A god was with you, so they say, and we believe it—
you lifted up our lives.
So now again,
Oedipus, king, we bend to you, your power—
we implore you, all of us on our knees:
find us strength, rescue! Perhaps you've heard
the voice of a god or something from other men,
Oedipus . . . what do you know?
The man of experience—you see it every day—
his plans will work in a crisis, his first of all.

26 **river-shrine:** a shrine of Apollo in Thebes, where priests foretold the future by interpreting the way offerings to the god burned.

31 **blight:** a disease that withers plants.

37 **Cadmus** (kăd'məs): the founder of Thebes; **luxuriates** (lŭg-zhŏŏr'ē-āts'): takes pleasure.

44 **Sphinx** (sfĭnks): a monster that terrorized Thebes by devouring citizens who could not answer its riddle. Oedipus solved the riddle and became king.

45 **bloody tribute:** the human lives taken by the Sphinx.

NOTES

the boxed text on page 76. What is happening in Thebes? Circle three sentences below. **(Clarify)**

Earthquakes are shaking the city.

Crops are dying.

Lightning is striking.

Cattle are getting sick.

Women and children are dying.

MARK IT UP **KEEP TRACK**

Remember to use these marks to keep track of your reading:

- * This is important.
- ? I have a question about this.
- ! This is a surprise.

Act now—we beg you, best of men, raise up our city!
Act, defend yourself, your former glory!
Your country calls you savior now
for your zeal, your action years ago.
Never let us remember of your reign:
you helped us stand, only to fall once more.
Oh raise up our city, set us on our feet.
The omens were good that day you brought us joy—
be the same man today!
Rule our land, you know you have the power,
but rule a land of the living, not a wasteland.
Ship and towered city are nothing, stripped of men
alive within it, living all as one.

Oedipus. My children,
I pity you. I see—how could I fail to see
what longings bring you here? Well I know
you are sick to death, all of you,
but sick as you are, not one is sick as I.
Your pain strikes each of you alone, each
in the confines of himself, no other. But my spirit
grieves for the city, for myself and all of you.
I wasn't asleep, dreaming. You haven't wakened me—
I have wept through the nights, you must know that,
groping, laboring over many paths of thought.
After a painful search I found one cure:
I acted at once. I sent Creon,
my wife's own brother, to Delphi—
Apollo the Prophet's oracle—to learn
what I might do or say to save our city.

Today's the day. When I count the days gone by
it torments me . . . what is he doing?
Strange, he's late, he's gone too long.
But once he returns, then, then I'll be a traitor
if I do not do all the god makes clear.

60 your action years ago: Oedipus solved the riddle of the Sphinx years ago.

In this play you will find references to things that were well known in ancient Greece but may be unfamiliar to you. Check the sidenotes found in the **Guide for Reading** for explanations.

READ ALOUD the boxed text on page 78. What action has Oedipus taken to try to stop the plague in Thebes? **(Clarify)**

82 Delphi (dĕl′fī′)**:** the site of a temple where prophecies were made; the oracle at Delphi was dedicated to the god Apollo.

Priest. Timely words. The men over there
are signaling—Creon's just arriving.

Pause & Reflect

FOCUS

Creon returns from Delphi with news from the god Apollo. Read to find out what has caused the plague in Thebes and what the people must do to end it.

Oedipus (*sighting* Creon, *then turning to the altar*).
Lord Apollo,
let him come with a lucky word of rescue,
shining like his eyes!

Priest. Welcome news, I think—he's crowned, look,
and the laurel wreath is bright with berries.

Oedipus. We'll soon see. He's close enough to hear—

(*Enter* Creon *from the side; his face is shaded with a wreath.*)

Creon, prince, my kinsman, what do you bring us?
What message from the god?

Creon. Good news.
I tell you even the hardest things to bear,
if they should turn out well, all would be well.

Oedipus. Of course, but what were the god's words? There's no hope
and nothing to fear in what you've said so far.

Creon. If you want my report in the presence of these people . . .

(*pointing to the priests while drawing* Oedipus *toward the palace*)

I'm ready now, or we might go inside.

Oedipus. Speak out,
speak to us all. I grieve for these, my people,
far more than I fear for my own life.

Creon. Very well,
I will tell you what I heard from the god.
Apollo commands us—he was quite clear—

95 laurel wreath: a crown of leaves worn by those seeking the help of the oracle at Delphi.

97 kinsman: close relative.

Pause & Reflect

1. Review the details you underlined. Then put a T next to each phrase below that is true about Oedipus. Put an F next to each phrase that is not true of him. **(Draw Conclusions)**

   ___ cares about his people

   ___ listens to his people

   ___ dislikes his people

   ___ thinks he is doing what he can to help

   ___ is unfair

2. Look back at the boxed text on page 76. What does the priest compare Thebes to? **(Clarify)**

   ❑ a fiery volcano

   ❑ a ship tossed in a storm

   ❑ an angry god

"Drive the corruption from the land,
don't harbor it any longer, past all cure,
don't nurse it in your soil—root it out!"

Oedipus. How can we cleanse ourselves—what rites?
What's the source of the trouble?

Creon. Banish the man, or pay back blood with blood.
Murder sets the plague-storm on the city.

Oedipus. Whose murder?
Whose fate does Apollo bring to light?

Creon. Our leader,
my lord, was once a man named Laius,
before you came and put us straight on course.

Oedipus. I know—
or so I've heard. I never saw the man myself.

Creon. Well, he was killed, and Apollo commands us now—
he could not be more clear,
"Pay the killers back—whoever is responsible."

Oedipus. Where on earth are they? Where to find it now,
the trail of the ancient guilt so hard to trace?

Creon. "Here in Thebes," he said.
Whatever is sought for can be caught, you know,
whatever is neglected slips away.

Oedipus. But where,
in the palace, the fields or foreign soil,
where did Laius meet his bloody death?

Creon. He went to consult an oracle, Apollo said,
and he set out and never came home again.

Oedipus. No messenger, no fellow-traveler saw what
happened?
Someone to cross-examine?

Creon. No,
they were all killed but one. He escaped,
terrified, he could tell us nothing clearly,
nothing of what he saw—just one thing.

Oedipus. What's that?

109 corruption: pollution; contamination.

117 Laius (lā'əs)**:** the king of Thebes before Oedipus.

123–124 Where . . . trace?: Oedipus wonders how they will be able to find Laius' murderer after so many years have passed since the murder.

NOTES

REREAD the boxed text on page 82. What do we know that Oedipus does not? Check one. **(Analyze)**

- ❑ Laius was once king of Thebes.
- ❑ Laius was murdered.
- ❑ Oedipus killed Laius many years before.

One thing could hold the key to it all,
a small beginning give us grounds for hope.

Creon. He said thieves attacked them—a whole band,
not single-handed, cut King Laius down.

Oedipus. A thief,
so daring, so wild, he'd kill a king? Impossible,
unless conspirators paid him off in Thebes.

Creon. We suspected as much. But with Laius dead
no leader appeared to help us in our troubles.

Oedipus. Trouble? Your king was murdered—royal blood!
What stopped you from tracking down the killer
then and there?

Creon. The singing, riddling Sphinx.
She . . . persuaded us to let the mystery go
and concentrate on what lay at our feet.

Oedipus. No,
I'll start again—I'll bring it all to light myself!
Apollo is right, and so are you, Creon,
to turn our attention back to the murdered man.
Now you have me to fight for you, you'll see:
I am the land's avenger by all rights,
and Apollo's champion too.
But not to assist some distant kinsman, no,
for my own sake I'll rid us of this corruption.
Whoever killed the king may decide to kill me too,
with the same violent hand—by avenging Laius
I defend myself.

(*to the priests*)
Quickly, my children.
Up from the steps, take up your branches now.

(*to the guards*)
One of you summon the city here before us,
tell them I'll do everything. God help us,
we will see our triumph—or our fall.

(Oedipus *and* Creon *enter the palace, followed by the guards.*)

143 **conspirators:** people taking part in a secret plan to do something unlawful.

154 **avenger:** one who punishes wrongdoing.

NOTES

REREAD the first boxed passage on page 84. Do you think Oedipus is really "Apollo's champion"? Why or why not? **(Make Judgments)**

READ ALOUD the second boxed passage. Whom does Oedipus unknowingly refer to when he says "Whoever killed the king . . ."? **(Analyze)**

Priest. Rise, my sons. The kindness we came for
Oedipus volunteers himself.
Apollo has sent his word, his oracle—
Come down, Apollo, save us, stop the plague.

(*The priests rise, remove their branches and exit to the side.*)

Pause & Reflect

FOCUS

The Chorus represents the people of Thebes. It enters and chants a plea to the gods, describing the suffering of Thebes.

MARK IT UP As you read, circle words and phrases that tell you about this suffering.

(*Enter a* Chorus, *the citizens of Thebes, who have not heard the news that* Creon *brings. They march around the altar, chanting.*)

Chorus. Zeus!
Great welcome voice of Zeus, what do you bring?
What word from the gold vaults of Delphi
comes to brilliant Thebes? Racked with terror—
terror shakes my heart
and I cry your wild cries, Apollo, Healer of Delos
I worship you in dread . . . what now, what is your price?
some new sacrifice? some ancient rite from the past
come round again each spring?—
what will you bring to birth?
Tell me, child of golden Hope
warm voice that never dies!

You are the first I call, daughter of Zeus
deathless Athena—I call your sister Artemis,
heart of the market place enthroned in glory,
guardian of our earth—
I call Apollo, Archer astride the thunderheads of heaven—
O triple shield against death, shine before me now!
If ever, once in the past, you stopped some ruin
launched against our walls
you hurled the flame of pain
far, far from Thebes—you gods
come now, come down once more!

173 Delos (dē′lŏs′)**:** the island where Apollo was born.

180–244 In this chant the Chorus prays to various gods—Athena, Artemis, Apollo, Zeus, and Dionysus—for help and protection.

Pause & Reflect

1. What is the cause of the plague in Thebes, and what must the people do to end it? **(Cause and Effect)**

   The cause:

   The cure:

2. Do you think Oedipus can rid Thebes of the plague? Why or why not? **(Predict)**

No, no
the miseries numberless, grief on grief, no end—
too much to bear, we are all dying
O my people . . .
Thebes like a great army dying
and there is no sword of thought to save us, no
and the fruits of our famous earth, they will not ripen
no and the women cannot scream their pangs to birth—
screams for the Healer, children dead in the womb
and life on life goes down
you can watch them go
like seabirds winging west, outracing the day's fire
down the horizon, irresistibly
streaking on to the shores of Evening
Death
so many deaths, numberless deaths on deaths, no end—
Thebes is dying, look, her children
stripped of pity . . .
generations strewn on the ground
unburied, unwept, the dead spreading death
and the young wives and gray-haired mothers with them
cling to the altars, trailing in from all over the city—
Thebes, city of death, one long cortege
and the suffering rises
wails for mercy rise
and the wild hymn for the Healer blazes out
clashing with our sobs our cries of mourning—
O golden daughter of god, send rescue
radiant as the kindness in your eyes!
Drive him back!—the fever, the god of death
that raging god of war
not armored in bronze, not shielded now, he burns me,
battle cries in the onslaught burning on—
O rout him from our borders!
Sail him, blast him out to the Sea-queen's chamber
the black Atlantic gulfs
or the northern harbor, death to all

In Greek drama, the Chorus came onstage between dramatic episodes. It danced, sang, and chanted to music. Don't worry if you can't make perfect sense of every passage presented by the Chorus. Imagine a group of people chanting the lines, and try to enjoy the "music." Try reading aloud some passages—for example, lines 205–215—with a group of classmates.

the boxed text on page 88. What picture does this image create in your mind?

(Visualize)

211 **cortege** (kôr-tĕzh′)**:** funeral procession.

216 **golden daughter of god:** Athena.

222 **rout:** defeat and drive away.

223 **Sea-queen's chamber:** the ocean depths—home of Amphitrite, wife of the sea god Poseidon.

where the Thracian surf comes crashing.
Now what the night spares he comes by day and kills—
the god of death.
O lord of the stormcloud,
you who twirl the lightning, Zeus, Father,
thunder Death to nothing!

Apollo, lord of the light, I beg you—
whip your longbow's golden cord
showering arrows on our enemies—shafts of power
champions strong before us rushing on!

Artemis, Huntress,
torches flaring over the eastern ridges—
ride Death down in pain!

God of the headdress gleaming gold, I cry to you—
your name and ours are one, Dionysus—
come with your face aflame with wine
your raving women's cries
your army on the march! Come with the lightning
come with torches blazing, eyes ablaze with glory!
Burn that god of death that all gods hate!

Pause & Reflect

FOCUS

Now Oedipus speaks to his people. Read to find out what he plans to do to Laius' murderer.

(Oedipus *enters from the palace to address the* Chorus, *as if addressing the entire city of Thebes.*)

Oedipus. You pray to the gods? Let me grant your prayers.
Come, listen to me—do what the plague demands:
you'll find relief and lift your head from the depths.

I will speak out now as a stranger to the story,
a stranger to the crime. If I'd been present then,
there would have been no mystery, no long hunt
without a clue in hand. So now, counted
a native Theban years after the murder,
to all of Thebes I make this proclamation:

226 **Thracian** (thrā'shən) **surf:** the rough waters of the western Black Sea.

239 **your name and ours are one, Dionysus** (dī'ə-nī'səs)**:** Dionysus, god of wine, was born of a Theban woman.

253 **proclamation:** an official announcement.

Pause & Reflect

1. Review the words and phrases you circled. What details helped you visualize Thebes as a city of death? **(Visualize)**

2. What does the Chorus ask the gods and goddesses to do? Check three phrases below. **(Clarify)**
   - ❑ drive back the plague
   - ❑ find the killer of Laius
   - ❑ send rescue to Thebes
   - ❑ defeat the Sphinx
   - ❑ come down to help

if any one of you knows who murdered Laius,
the son of Labdacus, I order him to reveal
the whole truth to me. Nothing to fear,
even if he must denounce himself,
let him speak up
and so escape the brunt of the charge—
he will suffer no unbearable punishment,
nothing worse than exile, totally unharmed.

(Oedipus *pauses, waiting for a reply.*)

Next,
if anyone knows the murderer is a stranger,
a man from alien soil, come, speak up.
I will give him a handsome reward, and lay up
gratitude in my heart for him besides.

(*silence again, no reply*)

But if you keep silent, if anyone panicking,
trying to shield himself or friend or kin,
rejects my offer, then hear what I will do.
I order you, every citizen of the state
where I hold throne and power: banish this man—
whoever he may be—never shelter him, never
speak a word to him, never make him partner
to your prayers, your victims burned to the gods.
Never let the holy water touch his hands.
Drive him out, each of you, from every home.
He is the plague, the heart of our corruption,
as Apollo's oracle has just revealed to me.
So I honor my obligations:
I fight for the god and for the murdered man.

Now my curse on the murderer. Whoever he is,
a lone man unknown in his crime
or one among many, let that man drag out
his life in agony, step by painful step—
I curse myself as well . . . if by any chance
he proves to be an intimate of our house,

WORDS TO KNOW
denounce (dĭ-nouns') *v.* to condemn publicly

255 **Labdacus** (lăb′də-kəs).

261 **exile:** the punishment of being banished from one's own country.

263 **alien:** foreign.

274 **holy water:** water used for purification after a sacrifice to the gods.

285 **intimate:** friend.

NOTES

READ ALOUD the boxed passage on page 92. What does Oedipus not realize as he curses the murderer? **(Infer)**

here at my hearth, with my full knowledge,
may the curse I just called down on him strike me!

These are your orders: perform them to the last.
I command you, for my sake, for Apollo's, for this country
blasted root and branch by the angry heavens.
Even if god had never urged you on to act,
how could you leave the crime uncleansed so long?
A man so noble—your king, brought down in blood—
you should have searched. But I am the king now,
I hold the throne that he held then, possess his bed
and a wife who shares our seed . . . why, our seed
might be the same, children born of the same mother
might have created blood-bonds between us
if his hope of offspring had not met disaster—
but fate swooped at his head and cut him short.
So I will fight for him as if he were my father,
stop at nothing, search the world
to lay my hands on the man who shed his blood,
the son of Labdacus descended of Polydorus,
Cadmus of old and Agenor, founder of the line:
their power and mine are one.
Oh dear gods,
my curse on those who disobey these orders!
Let no crops grow out of the earth for them—
shrivel their women, kill their sons,
burn them to nothing in this plague
that hits us now, or something even worse.
But you, loyal men of Thebes who approve my actions,
may our champion, Justice, may all the gods
be with us, fight beside us to the end!

Leader. In the grip of your curse, my king, I swear
I'm not the murderer, I cannot point him out.
As for the search, Apollo pressed it on us—
he should name the killer.

Oedipus. Quite right,
but to force the gods to act against their will—
no man has the power.

304 **Polydorus** (pŏl′ə-dôr′əs).

305 **Agenor** (ə-jē′nôr′)**:** Cadmus' father.

the boxed text on page 94. Then circle the correct answer that completes the sentence below. **(Clarify)**

Oedipus says that his own children and any children born to Laius would have shared the same __________.

A. mother

B. father

C. aunt

the shaded text on page 94. What is ironic about this line? Check one sentence below. **(Analyze)**

- ❑ Oedipus can't fight anymore.
- ❑ Laius is already dead.
- ❑ Laius is Oedipus' father.

Leader. Then if I might mention
the next best thing . . .

Oedipus. The third best too—
don't hold back, say it.

Leader. I still believe . . .
Lord Tiresias sees with the eyes of Lord Apollo.
Anyone searching for the truth, my king,
might learn it from the prophet, clear as day.

Oedipus. I've not been slow with that. On Creon's cue
I sent the escorts, twice, within the hour.
I'm surprised he isn't here.

Leader. We need him—
without him we have nothing but old, useless rumors.

Oedipus. Which rumors? I'll search out every word.

Leader. Laius was killed, they say, by certain travelers.

Oedipus. I know—but no one can find the murderer.

Leader. If the man has a trace of fear in him
he won't stay silent long,
not with your curses ringing in his ears.

Oedipus. He didn't flinch at murder,
he'll never flinch at words.

Pause & Reflect

FOCUS

The prophet Tiresias and Oedipus quarrel. In anger, Tiresias reveals the identity of Laius' murderer. Read to find out whom Tiresias names.

(*Enter* Tiresias, *the blind prophet, led by a boy with escorts in attendance. He remains at a distance.*)

Leader. Here is the one who will convict him, look,
they bring him on at last, the seer, the man of god.
The truth lives inside him, him alone.

Oedipus. O Tiresias,
master of all the mysteries of our life,
all you teach and all you dare not tell,
signs in the heavens, signs that walk the earth!

323–324 I still believe . . . Apollo: Lord Tiresias is a prophet who can find out what the god Apollo thinks.

339 seer: a prophet; someone who has the power to foretell the future and know what other people do not know.

Pause & Reflect

1. What curse does Oedipus put on the killer of Laius? **(Clarify)**
   - ❑ a long and painful life
   - ❑ a swift and painful death
   - ❑ a life sentence in prison

2. Keep in mind that the original audience who watched this play knew the Oedipus legend. How might they have felt hearing Oedipus curse the murderer of Laius? **(Draw Conclusions)**

Blind as you are, you can feel all the more
what sickness haunts our city. You, my lord,
are the one shield, the one savior we can find.

We asked Apollo—perhaps the messengers
haven't told you—he sent his answer back:
"Relief from the plague can only come one way.
Uncover the murderers of Laius,
put them to death or drive them into exile."
So I beg you, grudge us nothing now, no voice,
no message plucked from the birds, the embers
or the other mantic ways within your grasp.
Rescue yourself, your city, rescue me—
rescue everything infected by the dead.
We are in your hands. For a man to help others
with all his gifts and native strength:
that is the noblest work.

Tiresias. How terrible—to see the truth
when the truth is only pain to him who sees!
I knew it well, but I put it from my mind,
else I never would have come.

Oedipus. What's this? Why so grim, so dire?

Tiresias. Just send me home. You bear your burdens,
I'll bear mine. It's better that way,
please believe me.

Oedipus. Strange response . . . unlawful,
unfriendly too to the state that bred and reared you—
you withhold the word of god.

Tiresias. I fail to see
that your own words are so well-timed.
I'd rather not have the same thing said of me . . .

Oedipus. For the love of god, don't turn away,
not if you know something. We beg you,
all of us on our knees.

Tiresias. None of you knows—
and I will never reveal my dreadful secrets,
not to say your own.

352–354 So I beg you . . . within your grasp: Oedipus is asking Tiresias to tell everything he knows regardless of how he knows the information—from birds, glowing coals, or any other unusual sources a prophet has.

354 mantic: prophetic.

NOTES

READ ALOUD the boxed text on page 98 with a partner. Why do you think Tiresias doesn't want to tell Oedipus the truth? **(Draw Conclusions)**

Oedipus. What? You know and you won't tell?
You're bent on betraying us, destroying Thebes?

Tiresias. I'd rather not cause pain for you or me.
So why this . . . useless interrogation?
You'll get nothing from me.

Oedipus. Nothing! You,
you scum of the earth, you'd enrage a heart of stone!
You won't talk? Nothing moves you?
Out with it, once and for all!

Tiresias. You criticize my temper . . . unaware
of the one you live with, you revile me.

Oedipus. Who could restrain his anger hearing you?
What outrage—you spurn the city!

Tiresias. What will come will come.
Even if I shroud it all in silence.

Oedipus. What will come? You're bound to *tell* me that.

Tiresias. I will say no more. Do as you like, build your anger
to whatever pitch you please, rage your worst—

Oedipus. Oh I'll let loose, I have such fury in me—
now I see it all. You helped hatch the plot,
you did the work, yes, short of killing him
with your own hands—and given eyes I'd say
you did the killing single-handed!

Tiresias. Is that so!
I charge you, then, submit to that decree
you just laid down: from this day onward
speak to no one, not these citizens, not myself.
You are the curse, the corruption of the land!

Oedipus. You, shameless—
aren't you appalled to start up such a story?
You think you can get away with this?

WORDS TO KNOW
revile (rĭ-vīl') *v.* to abuse verbally; criticize harshly
appall (ə-pôl') *v.* to horrify

379 interrogation (ĭn-tĕr′ə-gā′shən): questioning.

387 spurn: reject.

NOTES

the boxed text on page 100. What causes Tiresias to tell Oedipus his secret? Circle one phrase below. **(Cause and Effect)**

fear of Oedipus

sympathy for Oedipus

anger at Oedipus

respect for Oedipus

Tiresias. I have already.
The truth with all its power lives inside me.

Oedipus. Who primed you for this? Not your prophet's trade.

Tiresias. You did, you forced me, twisted it out of me.

Oedipus. What? Say it again—I'll understand it better.

Tiresias. Didn't you understand, just now?
Or are you tempting me to talk?

Oedipus. No, I can't say I grasped your meaning.
Out with it, again!

Tiresias. I say you are the murderer you hunt.

Oedipus. That obscenity, twice—by god, you'll pay.

Tiresias. Shall I say more, so you can really rage?

Oedipus. Much as you want. Your words are nothing—futile.

Tiresias. You cannot imagine . . . I tell you,
you and your loved ones live together in infamy,
you cannot see how far you've gone in guilt.

Oedipus. You think you can keep this up and never suffer?

Tiresias. Indeed, if the truth has any power.

Oedipus. It does
but not for you, old man. You've lost your power,
stone-blind, stone-deaf—senses, eyes blind as stone!

Tiresias. I pity you, flinging at me the very insults
each man here will fling at you so soon.

Oedipus. Blind,
lost in the night, endless night that nursed you!
You can't hurt me or anyone else who sees the light—
you can never touch me.

Tiresias. True, it is not your fate
to fall at my hands. Apollo is quite enough,
and he will take some pains to work this out.

Oedipus. Creon! Is this conspiracy his or yours?

WORDS TO KNOW
futile (fyo͞ot'l) *adj.* useless

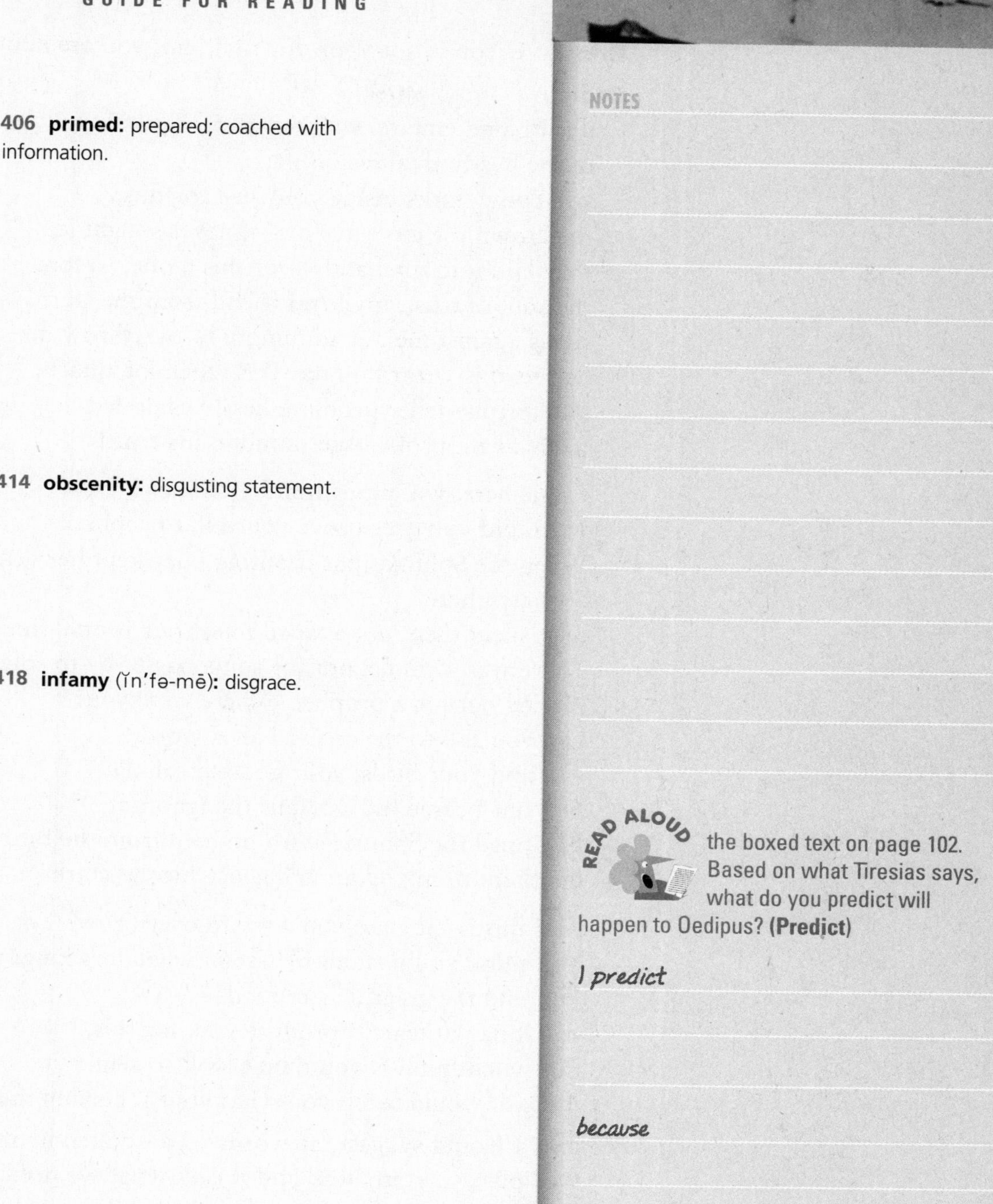

406 primed: prepared; coached with information.

414 obscenity: disgusting statement.

418 infamy (ĭn′fə-mē)**:** disgrace.

NOTES

READ ALOUD the boxed text on page 102. Based on what Tiresias says, what do you predict will happen to Oedipus? **(Predict)**

I predict

because

Tiresias. Creon is not your downfall, no, you are your own.

Oedipus. O power—
wealth and empire, skill outstripping skill
in the heady rivalries of life,
what envy lurks inside you! Just for this,
the crown the city gave me—I never sought it,
they laid it in my hands—for this alone, Creon,
the soul of trust, my loyal friend from the start
steals against me . . . so hungry to overthrow me
he sets this wizard on me, this scheming quack,
this fortune-teller peddling lies, eyes peeled
for his own profit—seer blind in his craft!

Come here, you pious fraud. Tell me,
when did you ever prove yourself a prophet?
When the Sphinx, that chanting Fury kept her death-
watch here,
why silent then, not a word to set our people free?
There was a riddle, not for some passer-by to solve—
it cried out for a prophet. Where were you?
Did you rise to the crisis? Not a word,
you and your birds, your gods—nothing.
No, but I came by, Oedipus the ignorant,
I stopped the Sphinx! With no help from the birds,
the flight of my own intelligence hit the mark.

And this is the man you'd try to overthrow?
You think you'll stand by Creon when he's king?
You and the great mastermind—
you'll pay in tears, I promise you, for this,
this witch-hunt. If you didn't look so senile
the lash would teach you what your scheming means!

Leader. I would suggest his words were spoken in anger,
Oedipus . . . yours too, and it isn't what we need.
The best solution to the oracle, the riddle
posed by god—we should look for that.

Tiresias. You are the king no doubt, but in one respect,
at least, I am your equal: the right to reply.

434 **heady:** violent; passionate.

440 **scheming quack:** a tricky person who pretends to have knowledge or skill.

443 **pious fraud:** one who pretends to be holy and moral.

the boxed text on page 104. What does Oedipus suspect Creon and Tiresias of? Circle one phrase below. **(Clarify)**

stealing his money

casting a spell on him

being fortune tellers

plotting to steal the throne

NOTES

I claim that privilege too.
I am not your slave. I serve Apollo.
I don't need Creon to speak for me in public.
So,
you mock my blindness? Let me tell you this.
You with your precious eyes,
you're blind to the corruption of your life,
to the house you live in, those you live with—
who *are* your parents? Do you know? All unknowing
you are the scourge of your own flesh and blood,
the dead below the earth and the living here above,
and the double lash of your mother and your father's
curse
will whip you from this land one day, their footfall
treading you down in terror, darkness shrouding
your eyes that now can see the light!
Soon, soon
you'll scream aloud—what haven won't reverberate?
What rock of Cithaeron won't scream back in echo?
That day you learn the truth about your marriage,
the wedding-march that sang you into your halls,
the lusty voyage home to the fatal harbor!
And a crowd of other horrors you'd never dream
will level you with yourself and all your children.

There. Now smear us with insults—Creon, myself
and every word I've said. No man will ever
be rooted from the earth as brutally as you.

Oedipus. Enough! Such filth from him? Insufferable—
what, still alive? Get out—
faster, back where you came from—vanish!

Tiresias. I would never have come if you hadn't called me
here.

Oedipus. If I thought you would blurt out such absurdities,
you'd have died waiting before I'd had you summoned.

Tiresias. Absurd, am I! To you, not to your parents:

WORDS TO KNOW
reverberate (rĭ-vûr′bə-rāt′) *v.* to reflect a noise; resound

474 scourge: cause of suffering.

478 shrouding: covering or hiding.

479–484 Soon, soon . . . fatal harbor: Terrible things will happen on the day you learn that you married your mother.

480 haven: place of safety.

481 Cithaeron (sĭ-thîr′ən)**:** a mountain about 12 miles south of Thebes.

490 insufferable: unbearable.

NOTES

The boxed text on page 106. What does Tiresias know about Oedipus that Oedipus does not? Check two sentences below.

- ❑ Oedipus is the son of a beggar.
- ❑ Oedipus killed the king of Thebes.
- ❑ Oedipus married his own mother.

the ones who bore you found me sane enough.

Oedipus. Parents—who? Wait . . . who is my father?

Tiresias. This day will bring your birth and your destruction.

Oedipus. Riddles—all you can say are riddles, murk and darkness.

Tiresias. Ah, but aren't you the best man alive at solving riddles?

Oedipus. Mock me for that, go on, and you'll reveal my greatness.

Tiresias. Your great good fortune, true, it was your ruin.

Oedipus. Not if I saved the city—what do I care?

Tiresias. Well then, I'll be going.

(*to his attendant*)

Take me home, boy.

Oedipus. Yes, take him away. You're a nuisance here.
Out of the way, the irritation's gone.

(*turning his back on* Tiresias, *moving toward the palace*)

Tiresias. I will go,
once I have said what I came here to say.
I will never shrink from the anger in your eyes—
you can't destroy me. Listen to me closely:
the man you've sought so long, proclaiming,
cursing up and down, the murderer of Laius—
he is here. A stranger,
you may think, who lives among you,
he soon will be revealed a native Theban
but he will take no joy in the revelation.
Blind who now has eyes, beggar who now is rich,
he will grope his way toward a foreign soil,
a stick tapping before him step by step.

(Oedipus *enters the palace.*)

Revealed at last, brother and father both
to the children he embraces, to his mother
son and husband both—he sowed the loins
his father sowed, he spilled his father's blood!

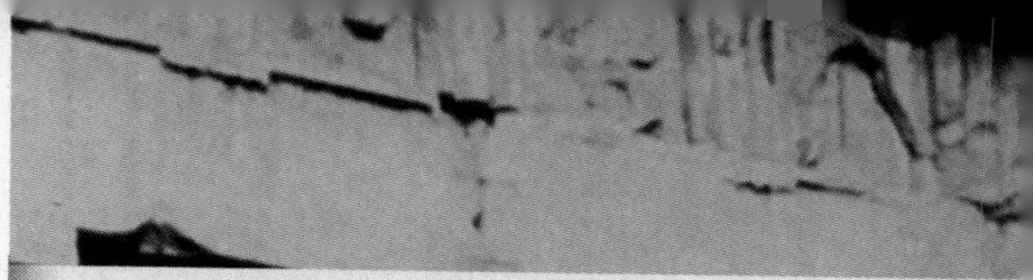

500 murk and darkness: words used to show confusion.

513–516 A stranger . . . revelation: Oedipus thinks he was born to the king and queen of Corinth, but in truth he was born in Thebes. Tiresias tells Oedipus that learning this truth will bring him grief.

520–523 Revealed . . . father's blood: Oedipus killed his father and married his mother, so he is both son and husband to his wife. He is both brother and father to his children.

READ ALOUD the boxed text on page 108. What does Tiresias mean when he tells Oedipus, "Your great good fortune . . . was your ruin"? Complete the chart below. **(Draw Conclusions)**

Oedipus' fortune was . . .	*It was his ruin because . . .*

Go in and reflect on that, solve that.
And if you find I've lied
from this day onward call the prophet blind.

(Tiresias *and the boy exit to the side.*)

Pause & Reflect

FOCUS

The Chorus describes the fate that Laius' murderer faces. It then expresses disbelief that Oedipus might be guilty.

MARK IT UP Circle details that show how the Chorus views Oedipus at this point in the play.

Chorus. Who—
who is the man the voice of god denounces
resounding out of the rocky gorge of Delphi?
The horror too dark to tell,
whose ruthless bloody hands have done the work?
His time has come to fly
to outrace the stallions of the storm
his feet a streak of speed—
Cased in armor, Apollo son of the Father
lunges on him, lightning-bolts afire!
And the grim unerring Furies
closing for the kill.
Look,
the word of god has just come blazing
flashing off Parnassus' snowy heights!
That man who left no trace—
after him, hunt him down with all our strength!
Now under bristling timber
up through rocks and caves he stalks
like the wild mountain bull—
cut off from men, each step an agony, frenzied, racing
blind
but he cannot outrace the dread voices of Delphi
ringing out of the heart of Earth,
the dark wings beating around him shrieking doom
the doom that never dies, the terror—
The skilled prophet scans the birds and shatters me with
terror!

530 ruthless: without feeling.

536 unerring: not turning aside; relentless; **Furies:** terrifying goddesses who pursue and punish criminals.

539 Parnassus' (pär-năs'əs) **snowy heights:** the peaks of the mountain that towers over Delphi.

Pause & Reflect

1. Whom does Tiresias name as the murderer of Laius? **(Clarify)**

2. What character flaws does Oedipus show in his encounter with Tiresias? Check three words below. (Evaluate)

- ❑ dishonesty
- ❑ pride
- ❑ rage
- ❑ distrust
- ❑ cowardliness

I can't accept him, can't deny him, don't know what to
 say,
I'm lost, and the wings of dark foreboding beating—
I cannot see what's come, what's still to come . . .
and what could breed a blood feud between
 Laius' house and the son of Polybus?
I know of nothing, not in the past and not now,
no charge to bring against our king, no cause
to attack his fame that rings throughout Thebes—
 not without proof—not for the ghost of Laius,
 not to avenge a murder gone without a trace.

Zeus and Apollo know, they know, the great masters
 of all the dark and depth of human life.
But whether a mere man can know the truth,
whether a seer can fathom more than I—
there is no test, no certain proof
 though matching skill for skill
a man can outstrip a rival. No, not till I see
these charges proved will I side with his accusers.
We saw him then, when the she-hawk swept against him,
saw with our own eyes his skill, his brilliant triumph—
 there was the test—he was the joy of Thebes!
 Never will I convict my king, never in my heart.

Pause & Reflect

WORDS TO KNOW
foreboding (fôr-bō′dĭng) *n.* a sense of evil or danger to come

555 the son of Polybus (pŏl′ə-bəs): Oedipus, who believes himself to be the son of Polybus, king of Corinth.

564 fathom: understand.

569 she-hawk: the Sphinx.

Pause & Reflect

1. Review the details you circled. How does the Chorus feel about Oedipus at this point in the play? **(Summarize)**

2. How might you feel if a leader you believed in were accused of a terrible crime? **(Connect)**

Oedipus is a tragic hero. He reminds us that though humans have qualities that make them great, they also have flaws that can lead to their ruin. Go back through the text. Put a plus sign (+) next to words or actions that show Oedipus' great qualities. Put a minus sign (-) next to words or actions that show his flaws. Compare your marks with a classmate's. **(Evaluate)**

Moving On

If you are using ***The Language of Literature,*** go to page 285 to continue reading *Oedipus the King.* As you do so, continue to be an active reader. Ask yourself the kinds of questions you found in this excerpt from the play.

Active Reading SkillBuilder

Strategies for Reading Greek Drama

Visualizing is the process through which readers form mental pictures as they read. Good readers use the details supplied by writers to picture characters, settings, and events in their minds. Read pages 74–112 of *Oedipus the King* and use Sophocles' descriptive details to visualize the play's setting, the characters, and the events. Then record your impressions on the chart below.

Impressions		
Setting	**Characters**	**Events**
page 74: I picture the royal house of Thebes as a huge stone palace with many columns.	page 74: I picture Oedipus as a tall and powerful man. The priests look thin, tired, and huddled together miserably.	page 75: The people are begging Oedipus for help. I imagine them reaching up to him with hope in their eyes.

Literary Analysis SkillBuilder

Tragic Hero and Dramatic Irony

A **tragic hero** is a dignified or noble character who is central to a drama. Often, the tragic hero is unaware of some information that readers or viewers are aware of. This situation is called **dramatic irony.** For example, in line 119, Oedipus, speaking of King Laius, says that he "never saw the man." We readers realize—just as Sophocles' original audience did—that Oedipus has seen Laius. In fact, he killed him long ago.

Review the passages that illustrate dramatic irony in *Oedipus the King,* pages 74–112. For each passage, record what the character or characters think and what the reader or audience knows.

Passages	What Character(s) Think	What Reader/Audience Knows
p. 84, lines 140–142	*Oedipus believes that he will find Laius' murderer and rescue Thebes.*	*Oedipus himself killed Laius many years ago. He will bring shame and suffering on his family and city.*
pp. 90–92, lines 248–265		
p. 94, lines 294–306		
p. 100, lines 394–400		

Words to Know SkillBuilder

Words to Know

appall	despondent	futile	revile
denounce	foreboding	reverberate	

A. Fill in the blanks below with the Word to Know that best completes the sentence.

1. As the plague claimed more victims, the people of Thebes grew ________________.

2. The people hoped that their prayers to the gods would be effective, not ________________.

3. Oedipus had a ________________ that the murderer of Laius might try to kill him too.

4. Oedipus was ________________(-ed) when Tiresias named him as Laius' murderer.

5. Tiresias warned Oedipus that one day his screams of horror would ________________ from the caves and mountains.

B. Circle the word in each group that has the opposite meaning to the **boldfaced** word.

1. **denounce**	trick	condemn	praise
2. **despondent**	discouraged	hopeless	joyful
3. **appall**	shock	please	offend
4. **futile**	successful	worthless	busy
5. **revile**	praise	scold	amuse

C. Write a brief character sketch of Oedipus, using at least **four** Words to Know.

NOTES

Connect to Your Life

Think of people whom you regard as good leaders. They may be politicians, teachers, military officers, or even characters from books or movies. In the chart below, list some good leaders and their special qualities.

Person	Leadership Qualities

Key to the Epic Poem

WHAT YOU NEED TO KNOW

The Author: Virgil (70–19 B.C.), favorite poet of ancient Rome

The Poem: The *Aeneid,* ancient Rome's national epic

The Setting: The legendary city of ancient Troy

The Problem: Troy has been at war with Greece for ten years. Worn out from the struggle, the Greeks make one last attempt to conquer Troy. The Trojans are suddenly faced with a battle they cannot win.

The Hero: Aeneas is a Trojan leader and the son of the goddess Venus. He represents the values most admired by the ancient Romans. Legend has it that he is the ancestor of Romulus and Remus, the mythical founders of Rome.

FROM THE AENEID

THE FALL OF TROY ■ BY VIRGIL

TRANSLATED BY
ROBERT FITZGERALD

PREVIEW Aeneas gives an eyewitness account of the fall of Troy. He describes a deadly trick by the Greeks, a fierce battle in the royal palace, and then a tragic personal loss.

FOCUS

After ten long years of war, the Greeks suddenly depart from Troy, leaving behind a huge wooden horse. Read to find out how the Trojans react to the wooden horse.

"Knowing their strength broken in warfare, turned
Back by the fates, and years—so many years—
Already slipped away, the Danaan captains
By the divine handicraft of Pallas built
A horse of timber, tall as a hill,
And sheathed its ribs with planking of cut pine.
This they gave out to be an offering
For a safe return by sea, and the word went round.
But on the sly they shut inside a company
Chosen from their picked soldiery by lot,
Crowding the vaulted caverns in the dark—
The horse's belly—with men fully armed.

Offshore there's a long island, Tenedos,
Famous and rich while Priam's kingdom lasted,
A treacherous anchorage now, and nothing more.
They crossed to this and hid their ships behind it
On the bare shore beyond. We thought they'd gone,
Sailing home to Mycenae before the wind,
So Teucer's town is freed of her long anguish,
Gates thrown wide! And out we go in joy
To see the Dorian campsites, all deserted,
The beach they left behind. Here the Dolopians
Pitched their tents, here cruel Achilles lodged,
There lay the ships, and there, formed up in ranks,
They came inland to fight us. Of our men
One group stood marveling, gaping up to see
The dire gift of the cold unbedded goddess,
The sheer mass of the horse.
Thymoetes shouts
It should be hauled inside the walls and moored
High on the citadel—whether by treason
Or just because Troy's fate went that way now.
Capys opposed him; so did the wiser heads:
'Into the sea with it,' they said, 'or burn it,
Build up a bonfire under it,

MARK IT UP ➤ KEEP TRACK

Remember to use these marks to keep track of your reading:

- * This is important.
- ? I have a question about this.
- ! This is a surprise.

WORDS TO KNOW

gaping (gā′pĭng) *adj.* staring open-mouthed **gape** *v.*

Use this guide for help with unfamiliar words and difficult passages.

3 **Danaan** (də-nā′ən)**:** Greek.

6 **sheathed:** covered.

14 **Priam's kingdom:** the city of Troy, which was ruled by King Priam (prī′əm).

18 **Mycenae** (mī-sē′nē)**:** the city ruled by the Greek commander, Agamemnon.

19 **Teucer's** (to͞o′sərz) **town:** Troy. (Teucer was the first Trojan king.)

21 **Dorian** (dôr′ē-ən)**:** Greek.

22 **Dolopians** (də-lō′pē-ənz)**:** a group of Greek allies.

23 **Achilles** (ə-kĭl′ēz)**:** a fearless Greek warrior.

27 **the cold unbedded goddess:** Pallas, protector of the Greeks; also known as Minerva.

28 **Thymoetes** (thī-mē′tēz′)**.**

30 **citadel** (sĭt′ə-dəl)**:** stronghold.

32 **Capys** (kăp′ĭs)**.**

the boxed passage on page 120. Then check the three phrases below that describe the horse. **(Visualize)**

- ☒ very tall
- ☐ made out of strong steel
- ☒ built out of wood
- ☒ filled with soldiers

they are discussing the pre-battle strategies

READING TIP

In this epic poem, some characters and places have more than one name. For example, the Greeks also are known as Achaeans, Argives, Danaans, Dorians, and Myrmidons. Use the notes in the **Guide for Reading** to help you understand the names and places you come upon. For additional help, refer to the Glossary on page 154.

also discussing what todo with the horse. (I think)

The people of Troy are trying to decide to trust the gift or not

This trick of the Greeks, a gift no one can trust,
Or cut it open, search the hollow belly!'

Contrary notions pulled the crowd apart.
Next thing we knew, in front of everyone,
Laocoön with a great company
Came furiously running from the Height,
And still far off cried out: 'O my poor people,
Men of Troy, what madness has come over you?
Can you believe the enemy truly gone?
A gift from the Danaans, and no ruse?
Is that Ulysses' way, as you have known him?
Achaeans must be hiding in this timber,
Or it was built to butt against our walls,
Peer over them into our houses, pelt
The city from the sky. Some crookedness
Is in this thing. Have no faith in the horse!
Whatever it is, even when Greeks bring gifts
I fear them, gifts and all.'
He broke off then
And rifled his big spear with all his might
Against the horse's flank, the curve of belly.
It stuck there trembling, and the rounded hull
Reverberated groaning at the blow.
If the gods' will had not been sinister,
If our own minds had not been crazed,
He would have made us foul that Argive den
With bloody steel, and Troy would stand today—
O citadel of Priam, towering still!

But now look: hillmen, shepherds of Dardania,
Raising a shout, dragged in before the king
An unknown fellow with hands tied behind—
This all as he himself had planned,
Volunteering, letting them come across him,

WORDS TO KNOW
ruse (ro͞os) *n.* a trick
sinister (sĭn'ĭ-stər) *adj.* having an evil disposition or intent

39 **Laocoön** (lā-ŏk′ō-ŏn)**:** a Trojan nobleman.

45 **Ulysses** (yo͝o-lĭs′ēz)**:** a Greek leader known for his strength, courage, and clever schemes.

46 **Achaeans** (ə-kē′ənz)**:** Greeks.

56 **reverberated:** echoed.

59 **foul that Argive** (är′jīv′) **den:** slash the Greek hiding place.

62 **Dardania** (där-dā′nē-ə)**:** the region surrounding Troy.

NOTES

the boxed passage on page 122. What does Laocoön think the wooden horse is? Check one phrase below. **(Analyze)**

- ❑ a fine gift
- ☒ a trick
- ❑ a peace offering

· Laocoön believes the Horse is a trick
· So he spears it to see if blood will come out
· nothing comes out
· They talk of jeering but I don't understand

So he could open Troy to the Achaeans.
Sure of himself this man was, braced for it
Either way, to work his trick or die.
From every quarter Trojans run to see him,
Ring the prisoner round, and make a game
Of jeering at him. Be instructed now
In Greek deceptive arts: one barefaced deed
Can tell you of them all.

The Greek spy, Sinon, tells a convincing lie about the Trojan horse. He explains that the Greeks built the wooden horse to win back the favor of the goddess Athena. He says that they were planning to sacrifice him to the goddess but he narrowly escaped. Sinon tells the Trojans to treat the statue with respect and to bring it within their city walls. If they do so, they will avoid doom and ensure that the Greeks will meet a terrible fate.

And now another sign, more fearful still,
Broke on our blind miserable people,
Filling us all with dread. Laocoön,
Acting as Neptune's priest that day by lot,
Was on the point of putting to the knife
A massive bull before the appointed altar,
When ah—look there!
From Tenedos, on the calm sea, twin snakes—
I shiver to recall it—endlessly
Coiling, uncoiling, swam abreast for shore,
Their underbellies showing as their crests
Reared red as blood above the swell; behind
They glided with great undulating backs.
Now came the sound of thrashed seawater foaming;
Now they were on dry land, and we could see
Their burning eyes, fiery and suffused with blood,
Their tongues a-flicker out of hissing maws.

WORDS TO KNOW
undulating (ŭn′jə-lā′-tĭng) *adj.* moving with a wavelike motion **undulate** *v.*
suffused (sə-fyo͞ozd′) *adj.* overspread; filled **suffuse** *v.*

The ancient Romans and Greeks believed in many gods and goddesses. As you read, pay attention to the role the gods and goddesses play in the epic poem. Consider how the characters in the poem feel about them.

73 deceptive arts: trickery.

NOTES

• Simon the greek spy convinces the Troy people to take the horse into their city.

• Laocoön is about to slay a bull when a sea serpant rises

78 Neptune (nĕp′to͞on′)**:** the god of the sea.

91 maws: mouths.

We scattered, pale with fright. But straight ahead
They slid until they reached Laocoön.
Each snake enveloped one of his two boys,
Twining about and feeding on the body.
Next they ensnared the man as he ran up
With weapons: coils like cables looped and bound him
Twice round the middle; twice about his throat
They whipped their back-scales, and their heads towered,
While with both hands he fought to break the knots,
Drenched in slime, his head-bands black with venom,
Sending to heaven his appalling cries
Like a slashed bull escaping from an altar,
The fumbled axe shrugged off. The pair of snakes
Now flowed away and made for the highest shrines,
The citadel of pitiless Minerva,
Where coiling they took cover at her feet
Under the rondure of her shield. New terrors
Ran in the shaken crowd: the word went round
Laocoön had paid, and rightfully,
For profanation of the sacred hulk
With his offending spear hurled at its flank.

'The offering must be hauled to its true home,'
They clamored. 'Votive prayers to the goddess
Must be said there!'
So we breached the walls
And laid the city open. Everyone
Pitched in to get the figure underpinned
With rollers, hempen lines around the neck.
Deadly, pregnant with enemies, the horse
Crawled upward to the breach. And boys and girls
Sang hymns around the towrope as for joy
They touched it. Rolling on, it cast a shadow
Over the city's heart. O Fatherland,
O Ilium, home of gods! Defensive wall
Renowned in war for Dardanus's people!
There on the very threshold of the breach

94 boys: sons.

102 appalling: horrifying.

108 rondure: circle.

110–112 Laocoön had paid . . . its flank: Pallas had punished Laocoön for treating the wooden horse with disrespect by throwing his spear at it.

115 breached: broke through.

119 pregnant: filled.

124 Ilium (ĭl′ē-əm)**:** another name for Troy.

NOTES

• the snakes attack Laocoön and his boys they die

the boxed passage on page 126. How does Laocoön's death affect the Trojans?
(Cause and Effect)

They are terrified b/c they think he died b/c he defiled the horse with his sword, so it was his rightful end
• so they let in the horse & praise it

It jarred to a halt four times, four times the arms
In the belly thrown together made a sound—
Yet on we strove unmindful, deaf and blind,
To place the monster on our blessed height.
Then, even then, Cassandra's lips unsealed
The doom to come: lips by a god's command
Never believed or heeded by the Trojans.
So pitiably we, for whom that day
Would be the last, made all our temples green
With leafy festal boughs throughout the city.

As heaven turned, Night from the Ocean stream
Came on, profound in gloom on earth and sky
And Myrmidons in hiding. In their homes
The Teucrians lay silent, wearied out,
And sleep enfolded them. The Argive fleet,
Drawn up in line abreast, left Tenedos
Through the aloof moon's friendly stillnesses
And made for the familiar shore. Flame signals
Shone from the command ship. Sinon, favored
By what the gods unjustly had decreed,
Stole out to tap the pine walls and set free
The Danaans in the belly. Opened wide,
The horse emitted men; gladly they dropped
Out of the cavern, captains first, Thessandrus,
Sthenelus and the man of iron, Ulysses;
Hand over hand upon the rope, Acamas, Thoas,
Neoptolemus and Prince Machaon,
Menelaus and then the master builder,
Epeos, who designed the horse decoy.
Into the darkened city, buried deep
In sleep and wine, they made their way,
Cut the few sentries down,
Let in their fellow soldiers at the gate,
And joined their combat companies as planned.

131 Cassandra (kə-săn′drə)**:** a daughter of Priam, whose predictions always come true but are never believed.

139 Myrmidons (mûr′mə-dŏnz′)**:** Greeks.

140 Teucrians (to͞o′krē-ənz)**:** Trojans.

150–155 Thessandrus (thə-săn′drəs) . . . **Sthenelus** (sthĕn′ə-ləs) . . . **Acamas** (ăk′ə-məs) . . . **Thoas** (thō′əs) . . . **Machaon** (mə-kā′ŏn′). . . **Epeos** (ĕ-pē′əs).

153 Neoptolemus (nē′ŏp-tŏl′ə-məs)**:** a mighty Greek warrior, son of the hero Achilles; also known as Pyrrhus (pĭr′əs).

154 Menelaus (mĕn′ə-lā′əs)**:** a leader of the Greek expedition against Troy; he wants to reclaim his wife, Helen, who ran off with a Trojan prince.

Pause & Reflect

1. What happens after the Trojans bring the wooden horse inside the city? Check one sentence below. **(Sequence)**
   - ❑ The Greeks and the Trojans agree to live in peace.
   - ❑ The Greek soldiers agree to leave Troy forever.
   - ☒ Sinon lets the Greek soldiers out of the horse's belly.

2. **MARK IT UP** What do you think the Greeks will do next? Write a prediction, and then underline the clues in the poem so far that support it. **(Predict)**

   The Greeks are let out and they will go destroy the Trojans.

The ghost of Hector visits Aeneas in his sleep, warning him about the Greek invasion. Hector tells Aeneas to flee the city so that one day he will be able to establish another great city—Rome. Aeneas awakens, puts on his armor, and goes out into the streets of the burning city. He and his comrades defeat a small band of Greek soldiers, take their armor, and put it on to disguise themselves. They continue to fight the invaders. Eventually, the Greeks see through the Trojans' disguise, and many of Aeneas' companions are killed.

FOCUS

Terrible fighting rages outside the palace of Priam, the king of Troy.

MARK IT UP As you read, underline details that help you picture the fighting. An example is highlighted on this page.

Ashes of Ilium!
Flames that consumed my people! Here I swear
That in your downfall I did not avoid
One weapon, one exchange with the Danaans,
And if it had been fated, my own hand
Had earned my death. But we were torn away
From that place—Iphitus and Pelias too,
One slow with age, one wounded by Ulysses,
Called by a clamor at the hall of Priam.
Truly we found here a prodigious fight,
As though there were none elsewhere, not a death
In the whole city: Mars gone berserk, Danaans
In a rush to scale the roof; the gate besieged
By a tortoise shell of overlapping shields.
Ladders clung to the wall, and men strove upward
Before the very doorposts, on the rungs,
Left hand putting the shield up, and the right
Reaching for the cornice. The defenders
Wrenched out upperworks and rooftiles: these
For missiles, as they saw the end, preparing
To fight back even on the edge of death.
And gilded beams, ancestral ornaments,
They rolled down on the heads below. In hall
Others with swords drawn held the entrance way,
Packed there, waiting. Now we plucked up heart
To help the royal house, to give our men

WORDS TO KNOW
prodigious (prə-dĭj'əs) *adj.* impressively great; stupendous

161–166 Ashes . . . death: Aeneas says that he fought hard and would have died to defend Troy and its people. It was his destiny, however, to live.

167 Iphitus (ī′fĭ-təs) **and Pelias** (pĕl′ē-əs)**:** Trojan soldiers.

172 Mars: the god of war; **berserk:** recklessly violent.

173–174 the gate . . . shields: The attacking Greeks enter the gate with their shields overlapping in a pattern that resembles a turtle's shell.

178 cornice (kôr′nĭs)**:** a molding at the top of a wall.

182 gilded: golden.

NOTES ·Aneas the Trojan disguises himself as a Greek to fight.

But his found out and suffers much pain

MARK IT UP **WORD POWER**

Remember to mark words that you'd like to add to your **Personal Word List.** After reading, you can record the words and their meanings beginning on page 444.

A respite, and to add our strength to theirs,
Though all were beaten. And we had for entrance
A rear door, secret, giving on a passage
Between the palace halls; in other days
Andromachë, poor lady, often used it,
Going alone to see her husband's parents
Or taking Astyanax to his grandfather.
I climbed high on the roof, where hopeless men
Were picking up and throwing futile missiles.
Here was a tower like a promontory
Rising toward the stars above the roof:
All Troy, the Danaan ships, the Achaean camp,
Were visible from this. Now close beside it
With crowbars, where the flooring made loose joints,
We pried it from its bed and pushed it over.
Down with a rending crash in sudden ruin
Wide over the Danaan lines it fell;
But fresh troops moved up, and the rain of stones
With every kind of missile never ceased.

Pause & Reflect

FOCUS

The Greek warriors are about to break into the palace. Read to find out whether the Trojans can fight them off.

MARK IT UP As you read, circle details that describe the important events in the battle.

Just at the outer doors of the vestibule
Sprang Pyrrhus, all in bronze and glittering,
As a serpent, hidden swollen underground
By a cold winter, writhes into the light,
On vile grass fed, his old skin cast away,
Renewed and glossy, rolling slippery coils,
With lifted underbelly rearing sunward
And triple tongue a-flicker. Close beside him
Giant Periphas and Automedon,
His armor-bearer, once Achilles' driver,
Besieged the place with all the young of Scyros,

WORDS TO KNOW
respite (rĕs'pĭt) *n.* a rest
writhe (rīth) *v.* to twist about; squirm

191 **Andromachë** (ăn-drŏm′ə-kē), **poor lady:** Andromachë's husband, the Trojan prince Hector, had been killed by Achilles earlier in the war.

193 **Astyanax** (ə-stī′ə-năks′)**:** the son of Hector and Andromachë.

196 **promontory** (prŏm′ən-tôr′ē): a ridge of land extending into a body of water.

206 **vestibule** (vĕs′tə-byo͞ol′)**:** entrance hall.

214 **Periphas** (pə-rī′fəs) . . . **Automedon** (ô-tŏm′ə-dŏn′).

216 **the young of Scyros** (skī′rəs)**:** the followers of Pyrrhus, who lived on the island of Scyros.

Pause & Reflect

Review the details you underlined. What happens during this stage of the battle? Check two sentences below. **(Clarify)**

- [x] The Greeks storm the palace.
- [x] The Trojans push a tower off the palace roof to crush the Greeks.
- [ ] The Trojans start to win the battle.

There is a very desparate tone to this portion of the passage

the boxed passage on page 132. What is Pyrrhus compared to? Check one word below. **(Clarify)**

- [ ] a vulture
- [x] a snake
- [ ] a statue

Hurling their torches at the palace roof.
Pyrrhus shouldering forward with an axe
Broke down the stony threshold, forced apart
Hinges and brazen door-jambs, and chopped through
One panel of the door, splitting the oak,
To make a window, a great breach. And there
Before their eyes the inner halls lay open,
The courts of Priam and the ancient kings,
With men-at-arms ranked in the vestibule.
From the interior came sounds of weeping,
Pitiful commotion, wails of women
High-pitched, rising in the formal chambers
To ring against the silent golden stars;
And, through the palace, mothers wild with fright
Ran to and fro or clung to doors and kissed them.
Pyrrhus with his father's brawn stormed on,
No bolts or bars or men availed to stop him:
Under his battering the double doors
Were torn out of their sockets and fell inward.
Sheer force cleared the way: the Greeks broke through
Into the vestibule, cut down the guards,
And made the wide hall seethe with men-at-arms—
A tumult greater than when dikes are burst
And a foaming river, swirling out in flood,
Whelms every parapet and races on
Through fields and over all the lowland plains,
Bearing off pens and cattle. I myself
Saw Neoptolemus furious with blood
In the entrance way, and saw the two Atridae;
Hecuba I saw, and her hundred daughters,
Priam before the altars, with his blood
Drenching the fires that he himself had blessed.
Those fifty bridal chambers, hope of a line
So flourishing; those doorways high and proud,
Adorned with takings of barbaric gold,
Were all brought low: fire had them, or the Greeks.

NOTES The description of the~~e~~ terror of the women is very detailed and intense

232 **brawn:** muscular strength.

238 **seethe:** boil; surge.

241 **whelms every parapet:** overflows every protective wall.

245 **the two Atridae** (ā-trī′dē)**:** Menelaus and his brother Agamemnon.

246 **Hecuba** (hĕk′yə-bə)**:** the wife of Priam and Queen of Troy.

249–252 **Those fifty . . . the Greeks:** The bridal chambers represent the hope of future generations, a hope that has been destroyed by the downfall of Troy.

the boxed passage on page 134. How are the Greek soldiers similar to a flooding river? **(Compare and Contrast)**

The flowed through the doors covering everywhere & thing inside, like the river covers plains and fields.

What was the fate of Priam, you may ask.
Seeing his city captive, seeing his own
Royal portals rent apart, his enemies
In the inner rooms, the old man uselessly
Put on his shoulders, shaking with old age,
Armor unused for years, belted a sword on,
And made for the massed enemy to die.
Under the open sky in a central court
Stood a big altar; near it, a laurel tree
Of great age, leaning over, in deep shade
Embowered the Penatës. At this altar
Hecuba and her daughters, like white doves
Blown down in a black storm, clung together,
Enfolding holy images in their arms.
Now, seeing Priam in a young man's gear,
She called out:
'My poor husband, what mad thought
Drove you to buckle on these weapons?
Where are you trying to go? The time is past
For help like this, for this kind of defending,
Even if my own Hector could be here.
Come to me now: the altar will protect us,
Or else you'll die with us.'
She drew him close,
Heavy with years, and made a place for him
To rest on the consecrated stone.
Now see
Politës, one of Priam's sons, escaped
From Pyrrhus' butchery and on the run
Through enemies and spears, down colonnades,
Through empty courtyards, wounded. Close behind
Comes Pyrrhus burning for the death-stroke: has him,
Catches him now, and lunges with the spear.
The boy has reached his parents, and before them
Goes down, pouring out his life with blood.
Now Priam, in the very midst of death,
Would neither hold his peace nor spare his anger.

263 embowered the Penatës (pə-nā′tēz)**:** sheltered the images of the household gods.

272 Hector: a Trojan warrior and prince killed by Achilles.

276 consecrated (kŏn′sĭ-krāt′əd)**:** set apart as sacred.

279 colonnades (kŏl′ə-nādz′)**:** rows of columns.

the first boxed passage on page 136. Do you think Priam is heroic or foolish? Explain. **(Make Judgments)**

Both, heoric maybe b/c it give hi's army strength.

the second boxed passage on page 136. Aeneas' description of Hecuba and her daughters creates what emotion? **(Connect)**

I feel sorry for them, because there is nothing they can do to protect themselfs so they wait and hope.

'For what you've done, for what you've dared,' he said,
'If there is care in heaven for atrocity,
May the gods render fitting thanks, reward you
As you deserve. You forced me to look on
At the destruction of my son: defiled
A father's eyes with death. That great Achilles
You claim to be the son of—and you lie—
Was not like you to Priam, his enemy;
To me who threw myself upon his mercy
He showed compunction, gave me back for burial
The bloodless corpse of Hector, and returned me
To my own realm.'
The old man threw his spear
With feeble impact; blocked by the ringing bronze,
It hung there harmless from the jutting boss.
Then Pyrrhus answered:
'You'll report the news
To Pelidës, my father; don't forget
My sad behavior, the degeneracy
Of Neoptolemus. Now die.'
With this,
To the altar step itself he dragged him trembling,
Slipping in the pooled blood of his son,
And took him by the hair with his left hand.
The sword flashed in his right; up to the hilt
He thrust it in his body.
That was the end
Of Priam's age, the doom that took him off,
With Troy in flames before his eyes, his towers
Headlong fallen—he that in other days
Had ruled in pride so many lands and peoples,
The power of Asia.
On the distant shore
The vast trunk headless lies without a name.

288 atrocity (ə-trŏs'ĭ-tē)**:** horrible cruelty.

291 defiled: stained; polluted.

296 compunction: pity.

299 feeble: weak.

300 jutting boss: the raised center of a shield.

302 Pelidës (pē-lī'dēz')**:** "son of Peleus"—that is, Achilles, who was killed earlier in the war.

303 degeneracy: decline into wickedness.

315 the vast trunk: Priam's huge body.

Pause & Reflect

1. What happens to Priam, the King of Troy? **(Summarize)**

He dies in battle

2. Priam compares Pyrrhus with his father, the great warrior Achilles. In the chart below, write the following phrases to show what Priam says about the two warriors. **(Compare and Contrast)**

1 honored his enemies
2 was degenerate
3 showed pity
4 showed cruelty

Achilles	Pyrrhus
1	2
3	4

FOCUS

When Aeneas notices Helen, he gets very angry. He believes that she is to blame for Troy's destruction. Find out how Aeneas deals with her.

For the first time that night, inhuman shuddering
Took me, head to foot. I stood unmanned,
And my dear father's image came to mind
As our king, just his age, mortally wounded,
Gasped his life away before my eyes.
Creusa came to mind, too, left alone;
The house plundered; danger to little Iulus.
I looked around to take stock of my men,
But all had left me, utterly played out,
Giving their beaten bodies to the fire
Or plunging from the roof.
It came to this,
That I stood there alone. And then I saw
Lurking behind the doorsill of the Vesta,
In hiding, silent, in that place reserved,
The daughter of Tyndareus. Glare of fires
Lighted my steps this way and that, my eyes
Glancing over the whole scene, everywhere.
That woman, terrified of the Trojans' hate
For the city overthrown, terrified too
Of Danaan vengeance, her abandoned husband's
Anger after years— Helen, that Fury
Both to her own homeland and Troy, had gone
To earth, a hated thing, before the altars.
Now fires blazed up in my own spirit—
A passion to avenge my fallen town
And punish Helen's whorishness.
'Shall this one
Look untouched on Sparta and Mycenae
After her triumph, going like a queen,
And see her home and husband, kin and children,
With Trojan girls for escort, Phrygian slaves?
Must Priam perish by the sword for this?
Troy burn, for this? Dardania's littoral
Be soaked in blood, so many times, for this?
Not by my leave. I know
No glory comes of punishing a woman,

321 Creusa (krē-o͞o′zə)**:** the wife of Aeneas.

328 the Vesta: the temple of Vesta, goddess of the hearth.

330 the daughter of Tyndareus (tĭn-dăr′ē-əs)**:** Helen. (Tyndareus, although not actually Helen's father, was the husband of her mother, Leda.)

335–336 her abandoned husband's anger: the anger of Menelaus, the husband Helen deserted to run off with Paris.

336 Helen: the wife of the Greek leader Menelaus, who betrayed him by running off with the Trojan prince Paris; Helen's betrayal of her husband triggered the Trojan War.

342 Sparta (spär′tə)**:** the city ruled by Menelaus.

345 Phrygian (frĭj′ē-ən)**:** Trojan.

347 littoral (lĭt′ər-əl)**:** seashore.

NOTES Aeneas has lost many people he was close to in this battle

-

he is trying to decide between revenge and his honor

the boxed passage on page 140. What does Aeneas want to do to Helen of Troy? **(Infer)**

He wants to do something (either kill or kidnap) Helen of Troy b/c ~~they~~ she was a traitor and in revenge for the destruction of her city.

The feat can bring no honor. Still, I'll be
Approved for snuffing out a monstrous life,
For a just sentence carried out. My heart
Will teem with joy in this avenging fire,
And the ashes of my kin will be appeased.'

So ran my thoughts. I turned wildly upon her,
But at that moment, clear, before my eyes—
Never before so clear—in a pure light
Stepping before me, radiant through the night,
My loving mother came: immortal, tall,
And lovely as the lords of heaven know her.
Catching me by the hand, she held me back,
Then with her rose-red mouth reproved me:
'Son,
Why let such suffering goad you on to fury
Past control? Where is your thoughtfulness
For me, for us? Will you not first revisit
The place you left your father, worn and old,
Or find out if your wife, Creusa, lives,
And the young boy, Ascanius—all these
Cut off by Greek troops foraging everywhere?
Had I not cared for them, fire would by now
Have taken them, their blood glutted the sword.
You must not hold the woman of Laconia,
That hated face, the cause of this, nor Paris.
The harsh will of the gods it is, the gods,
That overthrows the splendor of this place
And brings Troy from her height into the dust.
Look over there: I'll tear away the cloud
That curtains you, and films your mortal sight,
The fog around you.—Have no fear of doing
Your mother's will, or balk at obeying her.—
Look: where you see high masonry thrown down,
Stone torn from stone, with billowing smoke and dust,
Neptune is shaking from their beds the walls

WORDS TO KNOW
reprove (rĭ-pro͞ov') *v.* to scold

NOTES Venus is Aeneas' mother, his Father is the King of Troy She comes to give him advice

360 **my loving mother:** Venus, the goddess of love and beauty.

364 **goad:** drive; urge.

370 **foraging:** plundering.

373 **the woman of Laconia** (lə-kō′nē-ə): Helen.

the boxed passage on page 142. What does Venus tell Aeneas? Check three sentences below. **(Clarify)**

- [x] You're out of control.
- [ ] Helen deserves to suffer.
- [x] Don't blame Helen.
- [ ] Your family has been killed.
- [x] Try to find your family.

MARK IT UP Underline the reason Venus gives for the fall of Troy. **(Infer)**

It was the will of the gods for Troy to Fall

That his great trident pried up, undermining,
Toppling the whole city down. And look:
Juno in all her savagery holds
The Scaean Gates, and raging in steel armor
Calls her allied army from the ships.
Up on the citadel—turn, look—Pallas Tritonia
Couched in a stormcloud, lightening, with her Gorgon!
The Father himself empowers the Danaans,
Urges assaulting gods on the defenders.
Away, child; put an end to toiling so.
I shall be near, to see you safely home.'

She hid herself in the deep gloom of night,
And now the dire forms appeared to me
Of great immortals, enemies of Troy.
I knew the end then: Ilium was going down
In fire, the Troy of Neptune going down,
As in high mountains when the countrymen
Have notched an ancient ash, then make their axes
Ring with might and main, chopping away
To fell the tree—ever on the point of falling,
Shaken through all its foliage, and the treetop
Nodding; bit by bit the strokes prevail
Until it gives a final groan at last
And crashes down in ruin from the height.

Now I descended where the goddess guided,
Clear of the flames, and clear of enemies,
For both retired; so gained my father's door,
My ancient home. I looked for him at once,
My first wish being to help him to the mountains;
But with Troy gone he set his face against it,
Not to prolong his life, or suffer exile.

385 **undermining:** digging under the foundations.

387 **Juno** (jo͞o′nō)**:** the queen of the gods.

390 **Tritonia** (trī-tō′nē-ə)**:** a title of Pallas.

391 **Gorgon:** the monstrous Medusa, whose head Pallas bears on her shield.

Pause & Reflect

1. What does Aeneas decide to do? Check one phrase below. **(Infer)**
   - ☐ marry Helen
   - ☐ punish Helen
   - ☒ find his family

2. READ ALOUD the boxed passage on page 144. What does Aeneas compare Troy to? Check one phrase below. **(Clarify)**
   - ☐ a city destroyed by an earthquake
   - ☐ a sailboat sunk by huge waves
   - ☒ an old tree cut down by axes

- He listens to Venus and decides his family is most important
- He leaves Helen alone

Unmoved by the protests of his family, Aeneas' father refuses to leave his home. However, he is finally persuaded by two divine signs. First, a small flame appears on the head of Iulus, Aeneas' son, touching the boy but not burning him. After Aeneas and his wife put out the flame, there comes the second sign—a crack of thunder outside, followed by a falling star.

FOCUS

Aeneas tries to lead his father, wife, and son to safety. Read to find out whether he succeeds.

Now indeed
My father, overcome, addressed the gods,
And rose in worship of the blessed star.

'Now, now, no more delay. I'll follow you.
Where you conduct me, there I'll be.
Gods of my fathers,
Preserve this house, preserve my grandson. Yours
This portent was. Troy's life is in your power.
I yield. I go as your companion, son.'
Then he was still. We heard the blazing town
Crackle more loudly, felt the scorching heat.

'Then come, dear father. Arms around my neck:
I'll take you on my shoulders, no great weight.
Whatever happens, both will face one danger,
Find one safety. Iulus will come with me,
My wife at a good interval behind.
Servants, give your attention to what I say.
At the gate inland there's a funeral mound
And an old shrine of Ceres the Bereft;
Near it an ancient cypress, kept alive
For many years by our fathers' piety.
By various routes we'll come to that one place.
Father, carry our hearthgods, our Penatës.
It would be wrong for me to handle them—
Just come from such hard fighting, bloody work—
Until I wash myself in running water.'

When I had said this, over my breadth of shoulder
And bent neck, I spread out a lion skin

422 **portent:** a sign of future events; omen.

433 **Ceres the Bereft:** the goddess of grain, whose daughter Proserpina was stolen away by Pluto, god of the underworld.

NOTES

· His Father would rather die than desert Troy, but the gods convince him otherwise

· His family splits up and agrees to meet at a certain cypress

· They take their gods with them

For tawny cloak and stooped to take his weight.
Then little Iulus put his hand in mine
And came with shorter steps beside his father.
My wife fell in behind. Through shadowed places
On we went, and I, lately unmoved
By any spears thrown, any squads of Greeks,
Felt terror now at every eddy of wind,
Alarm at every sound, alert and worried
Alike for my companion and my burden.
I had got near the gate, and now I thought
We had made it all the way, when suddenly
A noise of running feet came near at hand,
And peering through the gloom ahead, my father
Cried out:
'Run, boy; here they come; I see
Flame light on shields, bronze shining.'
I took fright,
And some unfriendly power, I know not what,
Stole all my addled wits—for as I turned
Aside from the known way, entering a maze
Of pathless places on the run—
Alas,
Creusa, taken from us by grim fate, did she
Linger, or stray, or sink in weariness?
There is no telling. Never would she be
Restored to us. Never did I look back
Or think to look for her, lost as she was,
Until we reached the funeral mound and shrine
Of venerable Ceres. Here at last
All came together, but she was not there;
She alone failed her friends, her child, her husband.
Out of my mind, whom did I not accuse,
What man or god? What crueler loss had I
Beheld, that night the city fell? Ascanius,
My father, and the Teucrian Penatës,
I left in my friends' charge, and hid them well
In a hollow valley.

459 **addled wits:** confused powers of mind.

the first boxed passage on page 148. How have Aeneas' emotions changed now that he is trying to lead his family to safety? **(Draw Conclusions)**

During the battle, Aeneas felt angry and ready to take on anyone

Now he feels afraid even terrified for the safety of those he is with

the second boxed passage on page 148. What terrible event happens as the family is fleeing? **(Clarify)**

His wife is taken (dies). But they don't know now.

I turned back alone
Into the city, cinching my bright harness.
Nothing for it but to run the risks
Again, go back again, comb all of Troy,
And put my life in danger as before:
First by the town wall, then the gate, all gloom,
Through which I had come out—and so on backward,
Tracing my own footsteps through the night;
And everywhere my heart misgave me: even
Stillness had its terror. Then to our house,
Thinking she might, just might, have wandered there.
Danaans had got in and filled the place,
And at that instant fire they had set,
Consuming it, went roofward in a blast;
Flames leaped and seethed in heat to the night sky.
I pressed on, to see Priam's hall and tower.
In the bare colonnades of Juno's shrine
Two chosen guards, Phoenix and hard Ulysses,
Kept watch over the plunder. Piled up here
Were treasures of old Troy from every quarter,
Torn out of burning temples: altar tables,
Robes, and golden bowls. Drawn up around them,
Boys and frightened mothers stood in line.
I even dared to call out in the night;
I filled the streets with calling; in my grief
Time after time I groaned and called Creusa,
Frantic, in endless quest from door to door.
Then to my vision her sad wraith appeared—
Creusa's ghost, larger than life, before me.
Chilled to the marrow, I could feel the hair
On my head rise, the voice clot in my throat;
But she spoke out to ease me of my fear:

'What's to be gained by giving way to grief
So madly, my sweet husband? Nothing here
Has come to pass except as heaven willed.
You may not take Creusa with you now;
It was not so ordained, nor does the lord

477 cinching: fastening tightly.

484 my heart misgave me: I had feelings of dread.

503 wraith: ghost.

511–513 You may not . . . leave: Creusa's ghost tells Aeneas that he must go on without her because that is the will of the gods.

the first boxed passage on page 150. Aeneas' decision to go back to look for Creusa shows _______. (check two) **(Make Judgments)**

- [ ] foolishness
- [x] love
- [x] courage
- [ ] fear

Though their is little chance he will recover her, his love is so strong it dictates his actions for him.

· he sees Troy in ruins, even his house on fire

the second boxed passage on page 150. Who appears to Aeneas? Check one phrase below. **(Clarify)**

- [ ] Helen's ghost
- [x] Creusa's ghost
- [ ] his father's ghost

Of high Olympus give you leave. For you
Long exile waits, and long sea miles to plow.
You shall make landfall on Hesperia
Where Lydian Tiber flows, with gentle pace,
Between rich farmlands, and the years will bear
Glad peace, a kingdom, and a queen for you.
Dismiss these tears for your beloved Creusa.
I shall not see the proud homelands of Myrmidons
Or of Dolopians, or go to serve
Greek ladies, Dardan lady that I am
And daughter-in-law of Venus the divine.
No: the great mother of the gods detains me
Here on these shores. Farewell now; cherish still
Your son and mine.'
With this she left me weeping,
Wishing that I could say so many things,
And faded on the <u>tenuous</u> air. Three times
I tried to put my arms around her neck,
Three times enfolded nothing, as the wraith
Slipped through my fingers, bodiless as wind,
Or like a flitting dream.
So in the end
As night waned I rejoined my company.
And there to my astonishment I found
New refugees in a great crowd: men and women
Gathered for exile, young—pitiful people
Coming from every quarter, minds made up,
With their belongings, for whatever lands
I'd lead them to by sea.
The morning star
Now rose on Ida's ridges, bringing day.
Greeks had secured the city gates. No help
Or hope of help existed.
So I resigned myself, picked up my father,
And turned my face toward the mountain range."

WORDS TO KNOW
tenuous (tĕn′yo͞o-əs) *adj.* thin or flimsy

515 Hesperia (hĕ-spîr′ē-ə)**:** "western land"—that is, Italy.

516 Lydian Tiber (lĭd′ē-ən tī′bər)**:** the river beside which Rome would be built—called Lydian here because it flowed through the lands of the Etruscans, who originally came from Lydia in Asia Minor.

530–532 Three times . . . a flitting dream: Aeneas says he tried to hug his wife's ghost three times, but each time her spirit slipped through his fingers, leaving him holding nothing but air.

540 Ida's ridges: the crests of a mountain range near Troy.

Pause & Reflect

1. What does Creusa's ghost predict about Aeneas' future? **(Summarize)**

He will live in exile From Troy, but in Peace

2. If you were in Aeneas' position, how would you feel about leading the Trojan refugees to safety? **(Connect)**

I'd Feel it a great burden but would gladly do it for my people

What role do the characters believe the gods and goddesses play in their lives? Find and circle passages in the poem that support your answer. **(Analyze)**

They contributed to the Fall of Troy

Glossary

Gods and Goddesses

Juno: The queen of the gods

Mars: The god of war

Neptune: The god of the sea

Pallas: The goddess of wisdom; also known as **Minerva;** epithet: "the cold unbedded goddess"

Venus: The goddess of love and beauty, mother of Aeneas

Greeks

(Also known as **Achaeans, Argives, Danaans, Dorians,** and **Myrmidons**)

Menelaus: A leader of the expedition of Troy, husband of Helen

Neoptolemus: A mighty warrior, son of the hero Achilles; also known as **Pyrrhus**

Sinon: A warrior sent into Troy as a spy

Ulysses: A leader known for his wily schemes

Trojans

(Also known as **Phrygians, Teucrians**)

Aeneas: The hero of the epic and the son of the Venus and Anchises

Anchises: The father of Aeneas

Cassandra: A daughter of Priam, whose prophecies always come true but are never believed

Creusa: The wife of Aeneas

Hecuba: The wife of Priam and the queen of Troy

Helen: The wife of the Greek leader Menelaus, who betrayed him by running off with the Trojan prince Paris; epithets: "that Fury," "the daughter of Tyndareus," "woman of Laconia"

Iulus: The young son of Aeneas and Creusa; also known as **Ascanius**

Laocoön: A nobleman, brother of Anchises

Priam: The king of Troy; epithet: "the power of Asia"

Politës: A son of Priam

Troy: Also known as **Ilium;** epithets: "citadel of Priam," "Fatherland," "Teucer's town"

Active Reading SkillBuilder

Predicting

Good readers make **predictions,** or reasonable guesses, about what will happen in a story. They consider details about the characters, setting, and events. They also use personal knowledge and experience of human behavior to make predictions.

As you read the *Aeneid,* use the chart below to record your predictions and the clues that led you to them. When you finish reading the *Aeneid,* check your predictions against the actual outcomes. Then write *yes* or *no* in the final column of the chart. An example is shown.

Predictions	Clues	Correct? (Yes/No)
The wooden horse is a trick.	In lines 57-60, Aeneas says that the Trojans should have killed the Greeks hiding in the horse.	Yes

Literary Analysis SkillBuilder

Culture Hero

A **culture hero** is a larger-than-life figure who reflects the values of a specific people. He stands for the ideals of a nation. Use the chart below to evaluate the extent to which Aeneas reflects the values of the ancient Romans. For each value given in the first column, list a way in which Aeneas shows it in the second column. In the third column, cite lines from the text to support your ideas.

Roman Values	Aeneas' Actions	Evidence
Courage	*Aeneas fights to protect the Trojans from the Greeks.*	*"Ashes of Ilium . . . earned my death." (lines 161–166)*
Compassion		
Respect for the Gods		
Loyalty to Family		
Allegiance to Country		

Words to Know SkillBuilder

Words to Know

gaping	reprove	ruse	suffused	undulating
prodigious	respite	sinister	tenuous	writhe

A. Decide which word from the word list is described by each clue. Write the words on the blank line next to the clue.

1. This word comes from a Latin word that means "on the left, unlucky." In current usage, it means "suggesting or threatening evil." ________________
2. This word is a verb that means "to twist, as in pain." Its origins can be traced back to the Old English root *wreit.* ________________
3. This word means a crafty strategem, or trick. It comes from an Old French verb that means "to drive back." ________________
4. This word is often used to describe something great in size, force, or extent. It stems from a Latin word that means "portentious, or monstrous." ________________
5. The Latin root for this word means "small wave." It is often used to describe the slithery, up-and-down movements of snakes. ________________

B. Circle the word in each group that has the same meaning, or a similar meaning, as the **boldfaced** word.

1. **tenuous**	broken	smooth	temporary	flimsy
2. **gaping**	reaching	organizing	destroying	staring
3. **suffused**	decorated	filled	fiery	ruined
4. **respite**	rest	celebration	dream	trap
5. **reprove**	scold	soothe	assist	repeat

C. Write a serious newspaper account of the Fall of Troy. Use at least **three** Words to Know in your work.

Before You Read

Connect to Your Life

In two of the poems you are about to read, the speakers seem to long for loved ones who are far away. In the third, the speaker prefers solitude. Have you ever experienced times of loneliness or enjoyed moments of solitude—or maybe both? Describe your experiences below.

A time of loneliness	A moment of solitude

Key to the Poems

WHAT TO LOOK FOR **Images** are words and phrases that create powerful pictures or feelings for readers. These four phrases are images from "The River-Merchant's Wife: A Letter." Choose one of these phrases and describe or draw the picture it creates in your mind.

"river of swirling eddies"
"The monkeys make sorrowful noise overhead"
"The leaves fall early this autumn"
"The paired butterflies are already yellow with August"

Selected Poems by Li Po

PREVIEW In the following three poems, you will read about a young woman whose husband has left her behind, a person who longs for home, and an adventurer who delights in nature. In each poem, Li Po emphasizes an emotion—loneliness, longing, or wonder.

The River-Merchant's Wife: A Letter

Translated by Ezra Pound

FOCUS

The speaker in this poem is a young woman who has been left behind by her husband. How does she feel about the separation?

MARK IT UP As you read, underline details that help you understand the speaker's feelings.

NOTES

While my hair was still cut straight across my forehead
I played about the front gate, pulling flowers.
You came by on bamboo stilts, playing horse,
You walked about my seat, playing with blue plums.
And we went on living in the village of Chōkan:[1]
Two small people, without dislike or suspicion.

At fourteen I married My Lord you.
I never laughed, being bashful.
Lowering my head, I looked at the wall.
Called to, a thousand times, I never looked back.

At fifteen I stopped scowling,
I desired my dust to be mingled with yours
Forever and forever and forever.
Why should I climb the look out?[2]

At sixteen you departed,
You went into far Ku-tō-en,[3] by the river of swirling eddies,
And you have been gone five months.
The monkeys make sorrowful noise overhead.

---

1. **Chōkan** (chō′kän): a town near Nanking in eastern China, located on the Yangtze River, China's longest.
2. **Why . . . look out?**: a reference to the story of a young wife who spent years in a tower, watching for the return of her departed husband.
3. **Ku-tō-en** (ko͞o′tō-ĕn′): a narrow, dangerous section of the Yangtze, far upriver from Chōkan; **eddies:** whirlpools.

You dragged your feet when you went out.
By the gate now, the moss is grown, the different mosses,
Too deep to clear them away!
The leaves fall early this autumn, in wind.
The paired butterflies are already yellow with August
Over the grass in the West garden;
They hurt me. I grow older.
If you are coming down through the narrows of the river
  Kiang,[4]
Please let me know beforehand,
And I will come out to meet you
              As far as Chō-fū-Sa.[5]

Pause & Reflect

4. **river Kiang** (jyäng): the Yangtze River.

5. **Chō-fū-Sa** (chō'fōō-sä'): "Long Wind Beach," several hundred miles upriver from Chōkan.

Pause & Reflect

1. How do the speaker's feelings toward her husband change? **(Paraphrase)**

At fourteen she feels

At fifteen she feels

2. What do you think the mosses represent for the speaker? Check one. (Imagery)
   - ❑ nature
   - ❑ neglect
   - ❑ autumn

NOTES

Still Night Thoughts

Translated by Burton Watson

FOCUS

The speaker in this poem is alone in a bedroom at night. What keeps him awake?

Moonlight in front of my bed—
I took it for frost on the ground!
I lift my head, gaze at the bright moon,
lower it and dream of home.

Pause & Reflect

Pause & Reflect

1. From the poem, what can you tell about the speaker? Check two. **(Draw Conclusions)**
   - ❑ He is far from home.
   - ❑ He is with his family.
   - ❑ He appreciates the natural world.
2. How does the moon affect the speaker's thoughts and dreams? **(Infer)**

Gazing at the Lu Mountain Waterfall

Translated by David Hinton

FOCUS

A hiker suddenly catches sight of a huge waterfall. Read to find out what effect it has on him.

MARK IT UP As you read, underline the images and details that help you visualize the waterfall.

1

Climbing west toward Incense-Burner Peak,[1]
I look south and see a falls of water, a cascade

hanging there, three thousand feet high,
then seething dozens of miles down canyons.

Sudden as lightning breaking into flight,
its white rainbow of mystery appears. Afraid

at first the celestial Star River[2] is falling,
splitting and dissolving into cloud heavens,

I look up into force churning in strength,
all power, the very workings of Creation.

It keeps ocean winds blowing ceaselessly,
shines a mountain moon back into empty space,

empty space it tumbles and sprays through,
rinsing green cliffs clean on both sides,

sending pearls in flight scattering into mist
and whitewater seething down towering rock.

Here, after wandering among these renowned
mountains, the heart grows rich with repose.[3]

Why talk of cleansing elixirs of immortality?[4]
Here, the world's dust rinsed from my face,

I'll stay close to what I've always loved,
content to leave that peopled world forever.

2

Sunlight on Incense-Burner kindles violet smoke.
Watching the distant falls hang there, river

headwaters plummeting three thousand feet in flight,
I see Star River falling through nine heavens.

Pause & Reflect

1. **Incense-Burner Peak:** a peak of Lu Mountain in China's Kiangsi province. Seeking to escape a war in his home region, Li Po moved to a town near Lu Mountain for a time.
2. **celestial Star River:** the Milky Way.
3. **repose:** rest; calm.
4. **elixirs of immortality:** magic potions with the power to make people live forever.

Pause & Reflect

1. How does the sight of the waterfall make the speaker feel? Check two words below. **(Infer)**
   - ❑ disappointed
   - ❑ awestruck
   - ❑ frightened
   - ❑ peaceful
2. **MARK IT UP** Which word or phrase from this poem is most vivid or memorable to you? Underline it. **(Connect)**

Compare the qualities of nature described in this poem with those described in "The River-Merchant's Wife." **(Compare and Contrast)**

Active Reading SkillBuilder

Visualizing

Visualizing is the act of mentally picturing something you read. Visualizing while reading can help readers understand and appreciate the imagery in poetry. "The River-Merchant's Wife: A Letter" includes times, places, and people. Read the poem and list the details that describe these elements of the poem.

Question	Details	What I Visualize
1. What is the setting of the poem?	*a front gate, garden, at the speakers' home in the village of Chōkan*	*a small yard with a little fence around it in a small town*
2. What does the speaker of the poem look like?		
3. Other than the speaker, who else is mentioned in the poem?		
4. What images describe the season?		
5. What other details trigger mental pictures?		

Literary Analysis SkillBuilder

Imagery

Imagery is the use of words and phrases that create a vivid sensory experience for the reader. Imagery can appeal to all five senses: sight, hearing, smell, touch, and taste. Some images appeal to several senses. On the chart below, list examples of imagery from Li Po's poems and identify the sense or senses the image appeals to.

Image	Poem/Line(s)	Sense(s) Appealed To
"empty space . . . on both sides"	"Gazing at the Lu Mountain Waterfall" lines 13–14	sight, hearing, touch

Before You Read

Connect to Your Life

Have you ever had to prove you could do something when others thought you couldn't? Describe what happened.

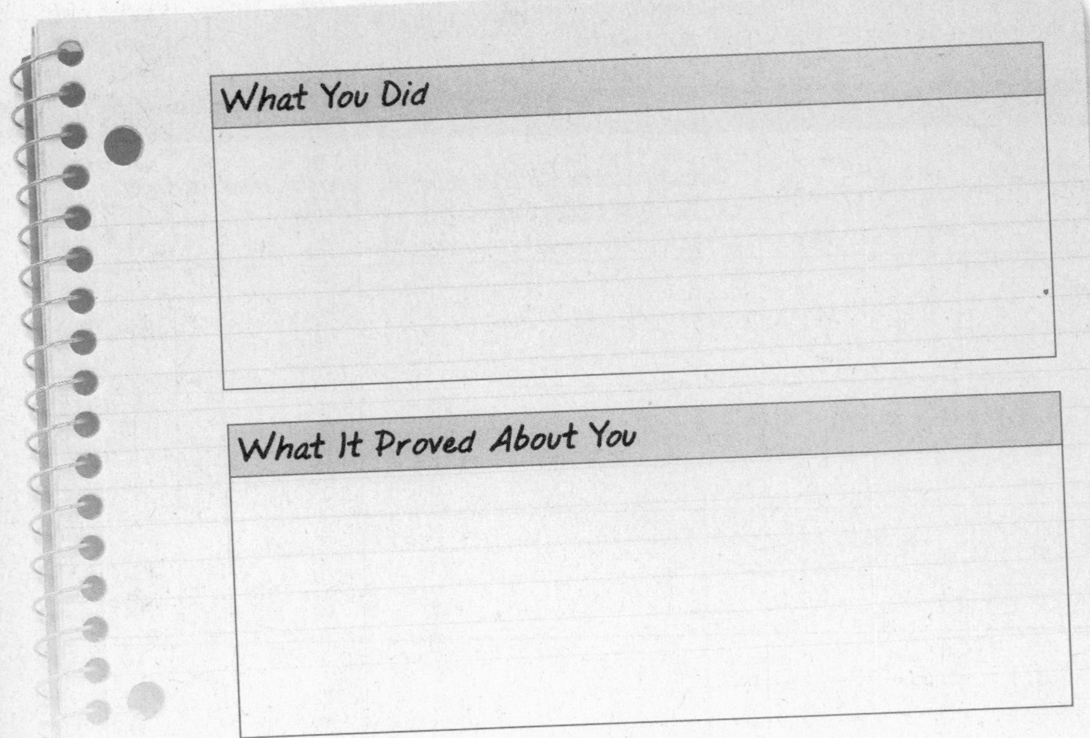

What You Did
What It Proved About You

Key to the Epic

WHAT YOU NEED TO KNOW This story is part of a hero's tale from the African empire of Mali. The epic tells the story of Sundiata Keita, a real leader who founded the Mali empire in about 1235. Over time, Sundiata came to be portrayed as a larger-than-life hero with superhuman abilities. *Sundiata* is an example of an oral epic—a story told and retold by trained storytellers called *griots* (grē-ō'). Even today, versions of *Sundiata* are told in West African villages.

from Sundiata

An Epic of Old Mali

Recorded by D. T. Niane
Translated by G. D. Pickett

PREVIEW Sundiata is the son of King Naré Maghan. His mother, Sogolon Kedjou, is an ugly, hunchbacked "buffalo-woman" whom the king married because of a prophecy that she would give birth to a great ruler. Despite the prophecy, the child Sundiata lags far behind other children and seems destined for failure. Read to find out whether he is able to prove his worthiness as a leader.

This story contains many names that may be difficult to pronounce. In addition, some characters have more than one name. For example, Sundiata is also called Sogolon Djata and Mari Djata. The footnotes tell you how to pronounce the names and also give important information about people and places in the story. More help with these names appears in the Glossary on page 180.

This part of the epic retells a famous incident from Sundiata's childhood. Sassouma Bérété is the king's first wife. She is an ambitious woman who wants her own son, Dankaran, to inherit the throne. She takes pleasure in the fact that Sundiata is so slow to develop, mocking the young boy and his mother.

Childhood

FOCUS

This section tells about the young Sundiata. Read to find out how Sundiata is different from other children his age.

MARK IT UP Underline details that describe Sundiata as a child.

God has his mysteries which none can fathom.[1] You, perhaps, will be a king. You can do nothing about it. You, on the other hand, will be unlucky, but you can do nothing about that either. Each man finds his way already marked out for him and he can change nothing of it.

Sogolon's son[2] had a slow and difficult childhood. At the age of three he still crawled along on all-fours while children of the same age were already walking. He had nothing of the great beauty of his father Naré Maghan.[3] He had a head so big that he seemed unable to support it; he also had large eyes which would open wide whenever anyone entered his mother's house. He was taciturn and used to spend the whole day just sitting in the middle of the house. Whenever his mother went out he would crawl on all-fours to rummage about in the calabashes[4] in search of food, for he was very greedy.

MARK IT UP KEEP TRACK

Remember to use these marks to keep track of your reading:

- * This is important.
- ? I have a question about this.
- ! This is a surprise.

1. **fathom:** to get to the bottom of; to understand.
2. **Sogolon's son:** Sundiata. Sogolon is his mother.
3. **Naré Maghan** (nä-rā′ mä′gäN): king of a large territory in Mali.
4. **calabashes** (kăl′ə-bă′shəz): fruits whose dried shells are used to make dishes, bottles, rattles, pipes, and drums.

WORDS TO KNOW
taciturn (tăs′ĭ-tûrn′) *adj.* not talkative

Malicious tongues began to blab. What three-year-old has not yet taken his first steps? What three-year-old is not the despair of his parents through his whims and shifts of mood? What three-year-old is not the joy of his circle through his backwardness in talking? Sogolon Djata[5] (for it was thus that they called him, prefixing his mother's name to his), Sogolon Djata, then, was very different from others of his own age. He spoke little and his severe face never relaxed into a smile. You would have thought that he was already thinking, and what amused children of his age bored him. Often Sogolon would make some of them come to him to keep him company. These children were already walking and she hoped that Djata, seeing his companions walking, would be tempted to do likewise. But nothing came of it. Besides, Sogolon Djata would brain the poor little things with his already strong arms and none of them would come near him any more.

The king's first wife[6] was the first to rejoice at Sogolon Djata's infirmity.[7] Her own son, Dankaran Touman,[8] was already eleven. He was a fine and lively boy, who spent the day running about the village with those of his own age. He had even begun his initiation in the bush.[9] The king had had a bow made for him and he used to go behind the town to practice archery with his companions. Sassouma was quite happy and snapped her fingers at Sogolon, whose child was still crawling on the ground. Whenever the latter happened to pass by her house, she would say, "Come, my son, walk, jump, leap about. The jinn[10] didn't promise you anything out of the ordinary, but I prefer a son who walks on his two legs to a lion that crawls on the ground."

5. **Sogolon Djata** (sō′gō-lôn′ jä′tä): This, as well as Mari Djata, is an alternate name of Sundiata.

6. **the king's first wife:** Sassouma Bérété (sä′so͞o-mä bā′rā-tā).

7. **infirmity** (ĭn-fûr′mə-tē): lack of power; disability.

8. **Dankaran Touman** (dän-kä′räN to͞o′mäN).

9. **initiation in the bush:** preparation, through learning tribal history, for becoming a full-fledged member of the tribe.

10. **jinn:** spirits that have supernatural influence over people.

WORDS TO KNOW
malicious (mə-lĭsh′əs) *adj.* evil; wicked

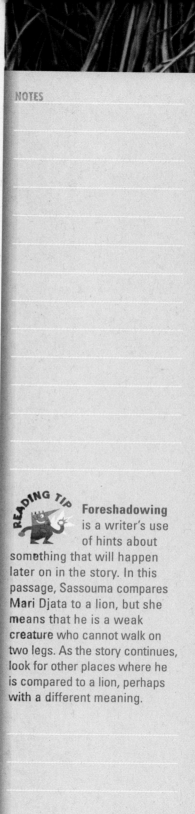

NOTES
READING TIP
Foreshadowing is a writer's use of hints about something that will happen later on in the story. In this passage, Sassouma compares Mari Djata to a lion, but she means that he is a weak creature who cannot walk on two legs. As the story continues, look for other places where he is compared to a lion, perhaps with a different meaning.

Pause & Reflect

1. Why is the young Sundiata such a disappointment? **(Main Idea)**

2. Do you think Sundiata is fit to become a king? Why or why not? **(Make Judgments)**

NOTES

She spoke thus whenever Sogolon went by her door. The <u>innuendo</u> would go straight home and then she would burst into laughter, that diabolical laughter which a jealous woman knows how to use so well.

Her son's infirmity weighed heavily upon Sogolon Kedjou; she had resorted to all her talent as a sorceress to give strength to her son's legs, but the rarest herbs had been useless. The king himself lost hope.

Pause & Reflect

FOCUS

Read to find out what happens to the king's confidence in Sundiata. Pay attention to the reasons why the king feels as he does.

How impatient man is! Naré Maghan became <u>imperceptibly</u> estranged[11] but Gnankouman Doua never ceased reminding him of the hunter's words.[12] Sogolon became pregnant again. The king hoped for a son, but it was a daughter called Kolonkan. She resembled her mother and had nothing of her father's beauty. The disheartened king debarred[13] Sogolon from his house and she lived in semi-disgrace for a while. Naré Maghan married the daughter of one of his allies, the king of the Kamaras.[14] She was called Namandjé[15] and her beauty was legendary. A year later she brought a boy into the world. When the king consulted

11. **estranged:** unsympathetic or indifferent.
12. **Gnankouman Doua** (nyäɴ'ko͞o-mäɴ do͞o'ä) **. . . the hunter's words:** Gnankouman Doua is the king's griot and chief counselor. A hunter had foretold that the king must marry the ugly Sogolon, who would bear him a great son.
13. **debarred:** excluded or shut out.
14. **Kamaras** (kä'mä-räs)**:** a clan related to that of Naré Maghan.
15. **Namandjé** (nä-mäɴ'jā).

WORDS TO KNOW

innuendo (ĭn'yo͞o-ĕn'dō) *n.* an indirect hint or reference, usually negative
imperceptibly (ĭm'pər-sĕp'tə-blē) *adv.* in a barely noticeable way

soothsayers on the destiny of this son he received the reply that Namandjé's child would be the right hand of some mighty king. The king gave the newly-born the name of Boukari. He was to be called Manding Boukari or Manding Bory later on.

Naré Maghan was very perplexed. Could it be that the stiff-jointed son of Sogolon was the one the hunter soothsayer had foretold?

"The Almighty has his mysteries," Gnankouman Doua would say and, taking up the hunter's words, added, "The silk-cotton tree emerges from a tiny seed."

One day Naré Maghan came along to the house of Nounfaïri,[16] the blacksmith seer of Niani. He was an old, blind man. He received the king in the anteroom which served as his workshop. To the king's question he replied, "When the seed germinates growth is not always easy; great trees grow slowly but they plunge their roots deep into the ground."

"But has the seed really germinated?" said the king.

"Of course," replied the blind seer. "Only the growth is not as quick as you would like it; how impatient man is."

This interview and Doua's confidence gave the king some assurance. To the great displeasure of Sassouma Bérété the king restored Sogolon to favor and soon another daughter was born to her. She was given the name of Djamarou.[17]

However, all Niani talked of nothing else but the stiff-legged son of Sogolon. He was now seven and he still crawled to get about. In spite of all the king's affection, Sogolon was in despair. Naré Maghan aged and he felt his time coming to an end. Dankaran Touman, the son of Sassouma Bérété, was now a fine youth.

One day Naré Maghan made Mari Djata come to him and he spoke to the child as one speaks to an adult. "Mari Djata, I am growing old and soon I shall be no more among you, but before death takes me off I am going to

16. Nounfaïri (nōō-fä′rē).

17. Djamarou (jä′-mä-rōō).

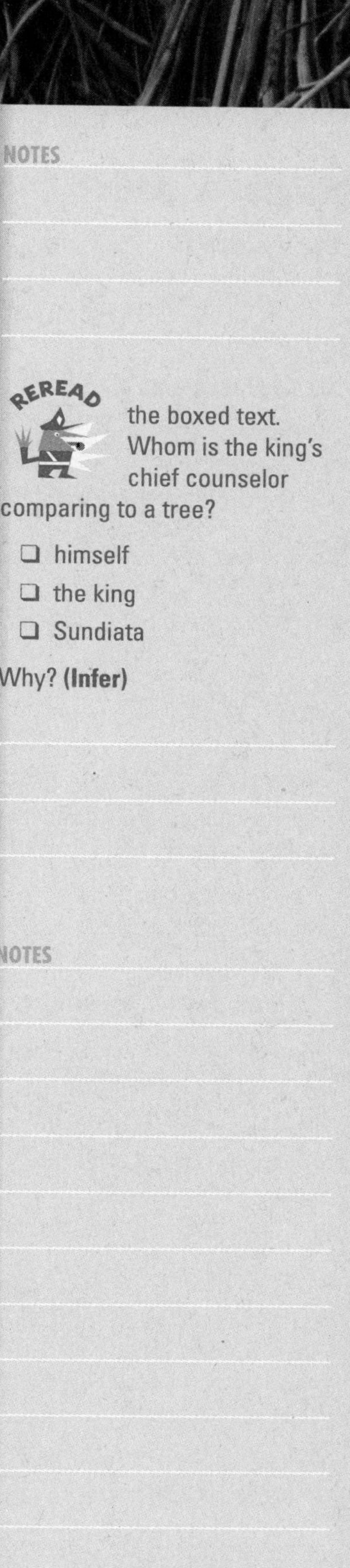

NOTES

REREAD the boxed text. Whom is the king's chief counselor comparing to a tree?

- ❑ himself
- ❑ the king
- ❑ Sundiata

Why? **(Infer)**

NOTES

Pause & Reflect

1. How do the king's feelings toward Sundiata change? Finish these sentences. **(Clarify)**

At first, the king feels

By the end of the section, he feels

2. Circle two reasons why the king's feelings about Sundiata change. **(Cause and Effect)**

Doua reminds him of the hunter's prophecy.

Everyone in Niani talks of Sogolon's stiff-legged son.

The blacksmith seer tells him great trees grow slowly.

Dankaran Touman, son of Sassouma, is not as fine a youth as he appears to be.

give you the present each king gives his successor. In Mali every prince has his own griot.[18] Doua's father was my father's griot, Doua is mine and the son of Doua, Balla Fasséké[19] here, will be your griot. Be inseparable friends from this day forward. From his mouth you will hear the history of your ancestors, you will learn the art of governing Mali according to the principles which our ancestors have bequeathed[20] to us. I have served my term and done my duty too. I have done everything which a king of Mali ought to do. I am handing an enlarged kingdom over to you and I leave you sure allies.[21] May your destiny be accomplished, but never forget that Niani is your capital and Mali the cradle of your ancestors."

The child, as if he had understood the whole meaning of the king's words, beckoned Balla Fasséké to approach. He made room for him on the hide he was sitting on and then said, "Balla, you will be my griot."

"Yes, son of Sogolon, if it pleases God," replied Balla Fasséké.

The king and Doua exchanged glances that radiated confidence.

Pause & Reflect

18. **griot** (grē-ō′): an advisor, oral historian, and praise-singer.
19. **Balla Fasséké** (bä′lä fä-sä-kā′).
20. **bequeathed** (bĭ-kwē*th*d′): passed on or handed down.
21. **allies:** friends; close associates.

The Lion's Awakening

FOCUS

In the next part of the story, the king dies. Find out how Sundiata and his mother are treated now.

MARK IT UP Put an X next to each act of cruelty committed by a character.

A short while after this interview between Naré Maghan and his son the king died. Sogolon's son was no more than seven years old. The council of elders met in the king's palace. It was no use Doua's defending the king's will which reserved the throne for Mari Djata, for the council took no account of Naré Maghan's wish. With the help of Sassouma Bérété's intrigues, Dankaran Touman was proclaimed king and a regency council[22] was formed in which the queen mother was all-powerful. A short time after, Doua died.

As men have short memories, Sogolon's son was spoken of with nothing but irony and scorn. People had seen one-eyed kings, one-armed kings, and lame kings, but a stiff-legged king had never been heard tell of. No matter how great the destiny promised for Mari Djata might be, the throne could not be given to someone who had no power in his legs; if the jinn loved him, let them begin by giving him the use of his legs. Such were the remarks that Sogolon heard every day. The queen mother, Sassouma Bérété, was the source of all this gossip.

Having become all-powerful, Sassouma Bérété persecuted Sogolon because the late Naré Maghan had preferred her. She banished Sogolon and her son to a back yard of the palace. Mari Djata's mother now occupied an old hut which had served as a lumber-room of Sassouma's.

The wicked queen mother allowed free passage to all those inquisitive people who wanted to see the child that still crawled at the age of seven. Nearly all the inhabitants of Niani filed into the palace and the poor Sogolon wept to

22. **regency council:** group chosen to rule in place of a monarch who is too young to assume control.

WORDS TO KNOW
intrigue (ĭn'trēg') *n.* secret scheme; plot

NOTES

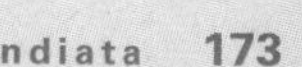

NOTES

Pause & Reflect

1. Look again at the cruel actions you marked. How does Sassouma make life miserable for Sogolon and her family? **(Summarize)**

2. Why do you think Sogolon turns on her son as she does? **(Make Judgments)**

see herself thus given over to public ridicule. Mari Djata took on a ferocious look in front of the crowd of sightseers. Sogolon found a little consolation only in the love of her eldest daughter, Kolonkan. She was four and she could walk. She seemed to understand all her mother's miseries and already she helped her with the housework. Sometimes, when Sogolon was attending to the chores, it was she who stayed beside her sister Djamarou, quite small as yet.

Sogolon Kedjou and her children lived on the queen mother's left-overs, but she kept a little garden in the open ground behind the village. It was there that she passed her brightest moments looking after her onions and gnougous. One day she happened to be short of condiments and went to the queen mother to beg a little baobab leaf.[23]

"Look you," said the malicious Sassouma, "I have a calabash full. Help yourself, you poor woman. As for me, my son knew how to walk at seven and it was he who went and picked these baobab leaves. Take them then, since your son is unequal to mine." Then she laughed derisively with that fierce laughter which cuts through your flesh and penetrates right to the bone.

Sogolon Kedjou was dumbfounded. She had never imagined that hate could be so strong in a human being. With a lump in her throat she left Sassouma's. Outside her hut Mari Djata, sitting on his useless legs, was blandly eating out of a calabash. Unable to contain herself any longer, Sogolon burst into sobs and seizing a piece of wood, hit her son.

"Oh son of misfortune, will you never walk? Through your fault I have just suffered the greatest affront of my life! What have I done, God, for you to punish me in this way?"

Pause & Reflect

23. **gnougous** (nyo͞oʹgo͞oz) . . . **baobab** (bāʹō-băb) **leaf:** Gnougous are African food plants. The baobab is a tree whose leaves are used for seasoning.

WORDS TO KNOW

condiment (kŏnʹdə-mənt) *n.* a spice or other substance used as a seasoning
derisively (dĭ-rīʹsĭv-lē) *adv.* in a mocking or jeering manner
blandly (blăndʹlē) *adv.* in an easygoing, unconcerned way
affront (ə-frŭntʹ) *n.* an open insult

FOCUS

Upset by his mother's unhappiness, Sundiata becomes determined to make things right.

MARK IT UP As you read, underline details which suggest that things are about to change for Sundiata.

Mari Djata seized the piece of wood and, looking at his mother, said, "Mother, what's the matter?"

"Shut up, nothing can ever wash me clean of this insult."

"But what then?"

"Sassouma has just humiliated me over a matter of a baobab leaf. At your age her own son could walk and used to bring his mother baobab leaves."

"Cheer up, Mother, cheer up."

"No. It's too much. I can't."

"Very well then, I am going to walk today," said Mari Djata. "Go and tell my father's smiths to make me the heaviest possible iron rod. Mother, do you want just the leaves of the baobab or would you rather I brought you the whole tree?"

"Ah, my son, to wipe out this insult I want the tree and its roots at my feet outside my hut."

Balla Fasséké, who was present, ran to the master smith, Farakourou,[24] to order an iron rod.

Sogolon had sat down in front of her hut. She was weeping softly and holding her head between her two hands. Mari Djata went calmly back to his calabash of rice and began eating again as if nothing had happened. From time to time he looked up discreetly at his mother who was murmuring in a low voice, "I want the whole tree, in front of my hut, the whole tree."

All of a sudden a voice burst into laughter behind the hut. It was the wicked Sassouma telling one of her serving women about the scene of humiliation and she was laughing loudly so that Sogolon could hear. Sogolon fled into the hut and hid her face under the blankets so as not

NOTES

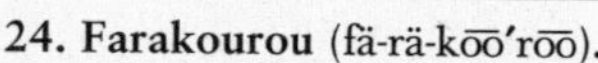

24. Farakourou (fă-rä-kōō′rōō).

to have before her eyes this heedless boy, who was more preoccupied with eating than with anything else. With her head buried in the bed-clothes Sogolon wept and her body shook violently. Her daughter, Sogolon Djamarou, had come and sat down beside her and she said, "Mother, Mother, don't cry. Why are you crying?"

Mari Djata had finished eating and, dragging himself along on his legs, he came and sat under the wall of the hut for the sun was scorching. What was he thinking about? He alone knew.

The royal forges[25] were situated outside the walls and over a hundred smiths worked there. The bows, spears, arrows and shields of Niani's warriors came from there. When Balla Fasséké came to order the iron rod, Farakourou said to him, "The great day has arrived then?"

"Yes. Today is a day like any other, but it will see what no other day has seen."

The master of the forges, Farakourou, was the son of the old Nounfaïri, and he was a soothsayer like his father. In his workshops there was an enormous iron bar wrought by his father Nounfaïri. Everybody wondered what this bar was destined to be used for. Farakourou called six of his apprentices and told them to carry the iron bar to Sogolon's house.

When the smiths put the gigantic iron bar down in front of the hut the noise was so frightening that Sogolon, who was lying down, jumped up with a start. Then Balla Fasséké, son of Gnankouman Doua, spoke.

"Here is the great day, Mari Djata. I am speaking to you, Maghan,[26] son of Sogolon. The waters of the Niger can efface[27] the stain from the body, but they cannot wipe out

25. **forges** (fôr′jəz): furnaces where metals are heated.

26. **Maghan:** name relating Sundiata to his father.

27. **efface** (ĭ-fās′): to rub out; erase.

WORDS TO KNOW
heedless (hēd′lĭs) adj. thoughtless; unmindful

NOTES

the boxed passage. What do the iron workers seem to know that other characters do not know? Check two. **(Infer)**

- ❑ that Sundiata would one day ask for an iron bar
- ❑ that Sundiata is not strong enough to hold the iron bar
- ❑ that the iron bar has an important purpose
- ❑ that Sogolon would be punished for accepting the iron bar

an insult. Arise, young lion, roar, and may the bush know that from henceforth it has a master."

Pause & Reflect

FOCUS

Sundiata is about to show the world what he is capable of. Read to find out what he does.

MARK IT UP As you read, underline people's reactions to the "young lion" who has awakened.

The apprentice smiths were still there, Sogolon had come out and everyone was watching Mari Djata. He crept on all-fours and came to the iron bar. Supporting himself on his knees and one hand, with the other hand he picked up the iron bar without any effort and stood it up vertically. Now he was resting on nothing but his knees and held the bar with both his hands. A deathly silence had gripped all those present. Sogolon Djata closed his eyes, held tight, the muscles in his arms tensed. With a violent jerk he threw his weight on to it and his knees left the ground. Sogolon Kedjou was all eyes and watched her son's legs which were trembling as though from an electric shock. Djata was sweating and the sweat ran from his brow. In a great effort he straightened up and was on his feet at one go—but the great bar of iron was twisted and had taken the form of a bow!

Then Balla Fasséké sang out the "Hymn to the Bow," striking up with his powerful voice:

"Take your bow, Simbon,[28]
Take your bow and let us go.
Take your bow, Sogolon Djata."

When Sogolon saw her son standing she stood dumb for a moment, then suddenly she sang these words of thanks to God who had given her son the use of his legs:

"Oh day, what a beautiful day,
Oh day, day of joy;

28. Simbon: a title used for a great hunter.

Pause & Reflect

1. Why is this a "great day," according to Balla Fasséké? **(Infer)**
   - ❑ It is the day for Sundiata to rise up.
   - ❑ It is the day for making iron bars.
   - ❑ It is the day for Sassouma to die.
2. How do you think Sundiata will use the iron bar? **(Predict)**

Allah Almighty, you never created a finer day.
So my son is going to walk!"

Standing in the position of a soldier at ease, Sogolon Djata, supported by his enormous rod, was sweating great beads of sweat. Balla Fasséké's song had alerted the whole palace and people came running from all over to see what had happened, and each stood bewildered before Sogolon's son. The queen mother had rushed there and when she saw Mari Djata standing up she trembled from head to foot. After recovering his breath Sogolon's son dropped the bar and the crowd stood to one side. His first steps were those of a giant. Balla Fasséké fell into step and pointing his finger at Djata, he cried:

"Room, room, make room!
The lion has walked;
Hide antelopes,
Get out of his way."

Behind Niani there was a young baobab tree and it was there that the children of the town came to pick leaves for their mothers. With all his might the son of Sogolon tore up the tree and put it on his shoulders and went back to his mother. He threw the tree in front of the hut and said, "Mother, here are some baobab leaves for you. From henceforth it will be outside your hut that the women of Niani will come to stock up."

Pause & Reflect

1. How did people react to Sundiata's actions? **(Summarize)**

2. Recall the foreshadowing discussed on page 169. What event in this section was being hinted at on page 169? **(Analyze)**

FOCUS

The talk around Niani changes after Sundiata uproots the baobab. Find out what people say about Sundiata and Sassouma now.

Sogolon Djata walked. From that day forward the queen mother had no more peace of mind. But what can one do against destiny? Nothing. Man, under the influence of certain illusions, thinks he can alter the course which God has mapped out, but everything he does falls into a higher order which he barely understands. That is why Sassouma's efforts were vain against Sogolon's son, everything she did lay in the child's destiny. Scorned the day before and the object of public ridicule, now Sogolon's son was as popular as he had been despised. The multitude loves and fears strength. All Niani talked of nothing but Djata; the mothers urged their sons to become hunting companions of Djata and to share his games, as if they wanted their offspring to profit from the nascent glory of the buffalo-woman's son.[29] The words of Doua on the name-giving day[30] came back to men's minds and Sogolon was now surrounded with much respect; in conversation people were fond of contrasting Sogolon's modesty with the pride and malice of Sassouma Bérété. It was because the former had been an exemplary wife and mother that God had granted strength to her son's legs for, it was said, the more a wife loves and respects her husband and the more she suffers for her child, the more valorous will the child be one day. Each is the child of his mother; the child is worth no more than the mother is worth. It was not astonishing that the king Dankaran Touman was so colorless, for his mother had never shown the slightest respect to her husband and never, in the presence of the late king, did she show that humility which every wife should show before her husband. People recalled her scenes of jealousy and the spiteful remarks she circulated about her co-wife and her child. And people would conclude gravely, "Nobody knows God's mystery. The snake has no legs yet it is as swift as any other animal that has four." ❖

Pause & Reflect

29. **nascent** (năs'ənt) **. . . the buffalo-woman's son:** Sogolon, Sundiata's mother, had a buffalo for a totem. A totem is a family emblem and protector. Nascent means "emerging."

30. **the words of Doua on the name-giving day:** Gnankouman Doua had stated that Sundiata would be the first of a great line of kings.

Pause & Reflect

1. How do Sassouma's insults work against her in the end? **(Analyze)**

2. According to this story, what is the main reason why Sundiata is successful at last? **(Cause and Effect)**
   - ❑ His father wanted him to succeed.
   - ❑ It was his destiny to succeed.
   - ❑ He is good at heart.

The narrator believes that destiny (or fate) plays a huge role in life. Underline passages in the story that talk about destiny or fate. Then answer the questions below. **(Analyze)**

What does the narrator say the role of fate is?

Do you agree? Explain.

Glossary

Balla Fasséké: Sundiata's griot

Boukari: Son of King Naré Maghan and his third wife, Namandjé; also called Manding Boukari and Manding Bory

Dankaran Touman: Son of Naré Maghan and Sassouma Bérété; Sundiata's step-brother

Djata: Another name for Sundiata; he is also called Sogolon Djata, Mari Djata, and Maghan

Farakourou: Master of the forges; a soothsayer like his father Nounfaïri; gives Sundiata an iron bar to help him stand up

Gnankouman Doua: Naré Maghan's griot and counselor; also called Doua

Kolonkan: Daughter of Naré Maghan and Sogolon; Sundiata's younger sister

Maghan: Name used to refer to Sundiata; the name relates Sundiata to his father, Naré Maghan.

Manding Bory: Son of King Naré Maghan and his third wife, Namandjé; also called Boukari and Manding Boukari

Mari Djata: Another name for Sundiata; he is also called Djata, Sogolon Djata, and Maghan.

Namandjé: Third wife of Naré Maghan

Naré Maghan: King of a large territory in Mali; father of Sundiata; husband of Sassouma Bérété, Sogolon Kedjou, and Namandjé

Nounfaïri: Blacksmith and soothsayer; the father of Farakourou

Sassouma Bérété: Naré Maghan's first wife; the mother of Dankaran Touman

Sogolon: Second wife of the king and mother of Sundiata; also called Sogolon Kedjou

Sogolon Djata: Another name for Sundiata; he is also called Djata, Maghan, and Mari Djata.

Sogolon Kedjou: Second wife of King Naré Maghan; mother of Sundiata; also called Sogolon

Sundiata: The hero of the story; son of the king and Sogolon Kedjou; he is also called Sogolon Djata, Mari Djata, Djata, and Maghan

Active Reading SkillBuilder

Predicting

Predicting is the process of using text clues and prior knowledge to make a reasonable guess about what will happen next in a story. As you read, you may recognize foreshadowing or other clues in a story. When you combine these clues with your own experiences and knowledge, you may be able to make accurate predictions. As you read the excerpt from *Sundiata,* pause to make predictions about what will happen next in the story. In the chart below, record your predictions and any information that helped you make them.

Predictions	Clues
I predict that Sundiata will become great.	*A hunter foretold that the king would have a great son. In stories, prophecies usually come true.*

Literary Analysis SkillBuilder

Conflict

Conflict is the struggle between opposing forces. **External conflict** occurs when a character is pitted against an outside force, such as society, nature, or another character. **Internal conflict** takes place within a character's mind. It may occur when a character has to make a difficult decision or deal with opposing feelings. Review the conflicts in the excerpt from *Sundiata.* In the chart below, identify four conflicts and the opposing forces that are involved in each conflict. Indicate whether each conflict is internal or external. Then state how the conflict is resolved, if at all.

Conflict	External or Internal?	Resolution
Sassouma repeatedly humiliates Sogolon.	*External*	*Sundiata finally shows his strength by walking. This frightens Sassouma.*

Words to Know SkillBuilder

Words to Know

affront	condiment	heedless	innuendo	malicious
blandly	derisively	imperceptibly	intrigue	taciturn

A. Think about the meaning of each underlined word. Then fill in each blank with the letter of the correct definition.

_______ 1. In China, giving tips to waiters, cab drivers, and others is rude. In fact, tipping is considered an affront.

_______ 2. Until I was five years old, I was a shy and taciturn child. Then everything changed and I talked all the time.

_______ 3. When Jill said to me, "Nice sweater. My grandmother has one just like it," her innuendo was clear. She was actually saying that my sweater was out of style and old-fashioned.

_______ 4. Jeb teases his little sister, but he is never malicious. He is just having fun with her.

_______ 5. The snail moved imperceptibly across the path. It seemed to take hours to travel just one inch.

_______ 6. Ketchup and mayonnaise are the two condiments I always put on a hamburger.

_______ 7. Every day, the bully stole the little kids' lunch money and laughed derisively when they cried.

_______ 8. The babysitter blandly watched the children make a terrible mess in the house. How could she be so relaxed?

_______ 9. Jack's heedless dog never does what he is told. When Jack tells the dog to sit or stay, the dog doesn't pay any attention to him.

_______ 10. The royal gardener created a plan to overthrow the king. Only a few people knew about the gardener's intrigue.

A. not talkative
B. evil or wicked
C. an indirect hint or reference, usually negative
D. in a barely noticeable way
E. secret scheme or plot
F. a spice or other substance used as a seasoning
G. in a mocking or jeering manner
H. in an easygoing, unconcerned way
I. an open insult
J. thoughtless or unmindful

B. Write a newspaper article telling about the day Sundiata finally walked. Use at least **five** Words to Know in your article.

Before You Read

Connect to Your Life

Think of three acts that you consider wrong—for example, lying, stealing, and murder. Which of these acts do you think is the greatest wrong? In the diagram below, list these acts from least to most serious.

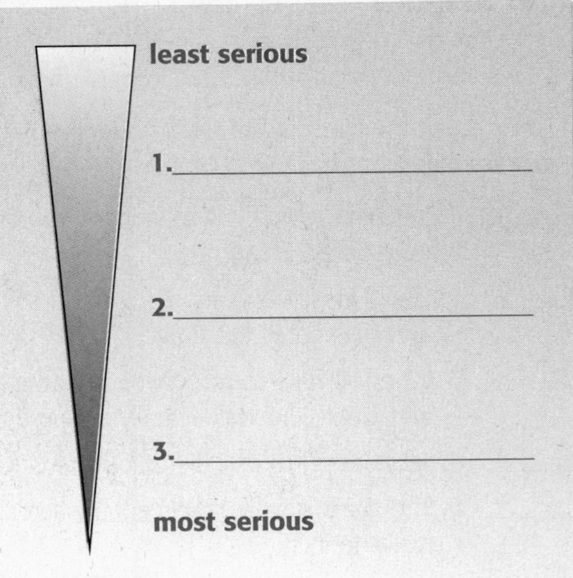

Key to the Poem

WHAT YOU NEED TO KNOW

The author: Dante Alighieri (dän′tā ä′lē-gyĕ′rē), who lived from 1265 to 1321

The poem: The *Inferno* is the first of the three sections of *The Divine Comedy.* Each section is divided into parts called *cantos,* from the Latin word for "song."

The main character: Dante himself, a traveler who stands for all of humanity

The journey: In *The Divine Comedy,* Dante journeys through the afterlife. First he visits Hell, a hideous place where people who sinned terribly in life suffer eternal punishment. He then travels to Purgatory, a place of temporary punishment, and finally to Paradise, where at last he stands before the throne of God.

FROM THE INFERNO

BY DANTE ALIGHIERI

TRANSLATED BY ROBERT PINSKY

PREVIEW Dante recalls a frightening time in his life when he felt that he had lost his way. He then describes the start of his journey through Hell. What will he witness as he travels where no living person has ever gone?

FOCUS

Dante finds himself trapped in a dark forest. Read to find what he meets up with.

MARK IT UP As you read, circle details that tell you about the creatures Dante runs into. An example is highlighted on page 188.

CANTO 1

Midway on our life's journey, I found myself
In dark woods, the right road lost. To tell
About those woods is hard—so tangled and rough

And savage that thinking of it now, I feel
The old fear stirring: death is hardly more bitter.
And yet, to treat the good I found there as well

I'll tell what I saw, though how I came to enter
I cannot well say, being so full of sleep
Whatever moment it was I began to blunder

Off the true path. But when I came to stop
Below a hill that marked one end of the valley
That had pierced my heart with terror, I looked up

Toward the crest and saw its shoulders already
Mantled in rays of that bright planet that shows
The road to everyone, whatever our journey.

Then I could feel the terror begin to ease
That churned in my heart's lake all through the night.
As one still panting, ashore from dangerous seas,

Looks back at the deep he has escaped, my thought
Returned, still fleeing, to regard that grim defile
That never left any alive who stayed in it.

After I had rested my weary body awhile
I started again across the wilderness,
My left foot always lower on the hill,

GUIDE FOR READING

Use this guide for help with unfamiliar words and difficult passages.

1–2 Midway . . . the right road lost: As Canto 1 begins, Dante, who has reached middle age, awakens and finds himself lost in a dark wood.

6–7 And yet . . . what I saw: I'll describe everything I saw in the dark woods because I saw good things there, too.

11–15 a hill . . . journey: The hill, whose top is lit by the sun, contrasts with the dark woods.

13 crest: the top of the hill.

14 that bright planet: the sun, which in Dante's time was believed to be a planet that moved around the earth.

17 my heart's lake: This detail reflects the medieval belief that the heart was a container for blood.

18–21 As one . . . stayed in it: Dante compares himself to someone who has nearly drowned. After reaching land safely, that person looks back at the sea, happy to be alive. So too, Dante looks back at the dark woods.

20 defile: a steep, narrow valley.

This poem contains difficult language and references to people, places, and events that may be unfamiliar to you. Try using the following tips:

- Read for general meaning and keep moving. Pause at the end of a line only if you come upon a mark of punctuation.
- Use the **Guide for Reading** for help with difficult terms and passages.

NOTES

And suddenly—a leopard, near the place
  The way grew steep: lithe, spotted, quick of foot.
  Blocking the path, she stayed before my face

And more than once she made me turn about
  To go back down. It was early morning still,
  The fair sun rising with the stars attending it

As when Divine Love set those beautiful
  Lights into motion at creation's dawn,
  And the time of day and season combined to fill

My heart with hope of that beast with festive skin—
  But not so much that the next sight wasn't fearful:
  A lion came at me, his head high as he ran,

Roaring with hunger so the air appeared to tremble.
  Then, a grim she-wolf—whose leanness seemed to
    compress
  All the world's cravings, that had made miserable

Such multitudes; she put such heaviness
  Into my spirit, I lost hope of the crest.
  Like someone eager to win, who tested by loss

Surrenders to gloom and weeps, so did that beast
  Make me feel, as harrying toward me at a lope
  She forced me back toward where the sun is lost.

25–38 a leopard . . . a lion . . . a grim she-wolf: Dante will come upon three animals that block his path. They are believed by critics to stand for the main forces of evil in the world: the leopard for lust, the lion for pride, and the she-wolf for greed.

31 Divine Love: God.

34 that beast with festive skin: the leopard, whose coat is gaily colored.

38–39 whose leanness . . . cravings: whose thinness seemed to squeeze together all the desires of the world.

44 harrying: moving threateningly; **lope:** long, jumping steps.

Pause & Reflect

1. Look back at the details you circled. What three beasts does Dante meet?

2. What does the she-wolf cause Dante to do? Check two phrases below.
(Cause and Effect)

- ❑ to run up the hill
- ❑ to go back down into the valley
- ❑ to grow confident
- ❑ to lose hope

3. What do you think the following characters and objects stand for? Draw a line to match each one with what it represents.
(Clarify Meaning)

the beasts	hope
the valley	despair
the sun	sins

FOCUS

Dante meets the spirit of Virgil, the long dead Roman poet (70 B.C.–14 B.C.). He will now be Dante's guide.

MARK IT UP As you read, circle details that help you form an impression of Virgil.

While I was ruining myself back down to the deep,
Someone appeared—one who seemed nearly to fade
As though from long silence. I cried to his human shape

In that great wasteland: "Living man or shade,
Have pity and help me, whichever you may be!"
"No living man, though once I was," he replied.

"My parents both were Mantuans from Lombardy,
And I was born *sub Julio,* the latter end.
I lived in good Augustus's Rome, in the day

Of the false gods who lied. A poet, I hymned
Anchises' noble son, who came from Troy
When superb Ilium in its pride was burned.

But you—why go back down to such misery?
Why not ascend the delightful mountain, source
And principle that causes every joy?"

"Then are you Virgil? Are you the font that pours
So overwhelming a river of human speech?"
I answered, shamefaced. "The glory and light are yours,

That poets follow—may the love that made me search
Your book in patient study avail me, Master!
You are my guide and author, whose verses teach

The graceful style whose model has done me honor.
See this beast driving me backward—help me resist,
For she makes all my veins and pulses shudder."

"A different path from this one would be best
For you to find your way from this feral place,"
He answered, seeing how I wept. "This beast,

WORDS TO KNOW
avail (ə-vāl') *v.* to be of use to; help

46 ruining: falling into ruin or disaster.

47–48 Someone appeared . . . long silence: The opening scene, with its mood of nightmare, leads to the miraculous appearance of the spirit of Virgil.

49 shade: a spirit of a dead person.

52 Mantuans from Lombardy: Lombardy, a region in northern Italy, is where the city of Mantua is located.

53 *sub Julio:* during the reign of Julius Caesar.

54 Augustus's Rome: Rome under its first emperor, Augustus, grandnephew of Julius Caesar.

56 Anchises' (ăn-kī'sēz') **noble son:** Aeneas (ĭ-nē'əs), who fled from Troy (Ilium) when it was burned and eventually founded Rome. His story is told in Virgil's *Aeneid* (see pages 118–157).

61–62 Are you the font . . . human speech: Are you the one who has produced such wonderful works of literature?

70 A different path: Dante must choose a longer and harder road if he is to reach his final destination. He must first visit Hell and Purgatory.

71 feral: wild; savage.

Use the quotation marks to help you follow the changes in speakers.

the boxed text on page 190. How does Dante feel about Virgil? **(Draw Conclusions)**

The cause of your complaint, lets no one pass
Her way—but harries all to death. Her nature
Is so malign and vicious she cannot appease

Her voracity, for feeding makes her hungrier.
Many are the beasts she mates: there will be more,
Until the Hound comes who will give this creature

A painful death. Not nourished by earthly fare,
He will be fed by wisdom, goodness and love.
Born between Feltro and Feltro, he shall restore

Low Italy, as Nisus fought to achieve.
And Turnus, Euryalus, Camilla the maiden—
All dead from wounds in war. He will remove

This lean wolf, hunting her through every region
Till he has thrust her back to Hell's abyss
Where Envy first dispatched her on her mission.

Therefore I judge it best that you should choose
To follow me, and I will be your guide
Away from here and through an eternal place:

To hear the cries of despair, and to behold
Ancient tormented spirits as they lament
In chorus the second death they must abide.

Then you shall see those souls who are content
To dwell in fire because they hope some day
To join the blessed: toward whom, if your ascent

Continues, your guide will be one worthier than I—
When I must leave you, you will be with her.
For the Emperor who governs from on high

75 malign (mə-līn'): evil in nature.

75–76 appease her voracity: satisfy her hunger.

78–81 the Hound . . . Feltro and Feltro: The Hound may be Cangrande della Scala, who supported Dante in exile and who was born in Verona, between the cities of Feltre and Montefeltro.

82–83 Nisus . . . Turnus, Euryalus (yo͞o-rī'ə-ləs)**, Camilla the maiden:** These are characters in Virgil's *Aeneid* who die in the war between the Trojans and the Latins.

88–90 Therefore . . . an eternal place: Virgil is suggesting that Dante follow him and travel through Hell.

94–96 souls who are content . . . to join the blessed: souls in purgatory, who know they will someday go to heaven.

97 one worthier than I: Beatrice. Virgil explains that if Dante wants to visit Heaven also, Beatrice must replace him as Dante's guide.

the first boxed passage on page 192. Then complete the sentence below. **(Analyze)**

The she-wolf can never be satisfied because

READ ALOUD the second boxed passage on page 192. If you were in Dante's position, how would you feel about going on such a journey? **(Connect)**

Wills I not enter His city, where none may appear
Who lived like me in rebellion to His law.
His empire is everything and everywhere,

But that is His kingdom, His city, His seat of awe.
Happy is the soul He chooses for that place!"
I: "Poet, please—by the God you did not know—

Help me escape this evil that I face,
And worse. Lead me to witness what you have said,
Saint Peter's gate, and the multitude of woes—"

Then he set out, and I followed where he led.

Pause & Reflect

Virgil tells Dante that Beatrice, the woman Dante loved from afar when she was alive, descended from Heaven in order to ask Virgil to guide Dante on his journey.

CANTO 3

FOCUS

Virgil and Dante arrive at the gate of Hell and read the inscription above the gate. They then enter and notice the souls confined there. Read to find out about these souls.

THROUGH ME YOU ENTER INTO THE CITY OF WOES,
THROUGH ME YOU ENTER INTO ETERNAL PAIN,
THROUGH ME YOU ENTER THE POPULATION OF LOSS.

JUSTICE MOVED MY HIGH MAKER, IN POWER DIVINE,
WISDOM SUPREME, LOVE PRIMAL. NO THINGS WERE
BEFORE ME NOT ETERNAL; ETERNAL I REMAIN.

ABANDON ALL HOPE, YOU WHO ENTER HERE.
These words I saw inscribed in some dark color
Over a portal. "Master," I said, "make clear

100–101 where none may appear. . . His law: Virgil, a pagan Roman, did not worship God and thus cannot enter Heaven. Virgil lived before the time of Jesus Christ.

108 Saint Peter's gate: Peter's gate is in Purgatory. Dante is asking Virgil to accompany him as far as he can; **multitude of woes:** many sorrows.

4–5 JUSTICE . . . LOVE PRIMAL: The "High Maker" is God in the three persons of the Trinity: "Power Divine" is God the Father; "Wisdom Supreme" is God the Son; and "Love Primal" is God the Holy Spirit.

5 primal: original; most important.

7 ABANDON: give up.

9 portal: doorway.

Pause & Reflect

1. What does Virgil tell Dante to do? Check two phrases below. **(Clarify)**

   ___ to pray to God

   ___ to take a different path

   ___ to fight the she-wolf

   ___ to follow him

2. Look back at the details you circled as you read. Do you think Virgil is a good choice to be Dante's guide? **(Evaluate)**

YES / NO, because

Their meaning, which I find too hard to gather."
Then he, as one who understands: "All fear
Must be left here, and cowardice die. Together,

We have arrived where I have told you: here
You will behold the wretched souls who've lost
The good of intellect." Then, with good cheer

In his expression to encourage me, he placed
His hand on mine: so, trusting to my guide,
I followed him among things undisclosed.

The sighs, groans and laments at first were so loud,
Resounding through starless air, I began to weep:
Strange languages, horrible screams, words imbued

With rage or despair, cries as of troubled sleep
Or of a tortured shrillness—they rose in a coil
Of tumult, along with noises like the slap

Of beating hands, all fused in a ceaseless flail
That churns and frenzies that dark and timeless air
Like sand in a whirlwind. And I, my head in a swirl

Of error, cried: "Master, what is this I hear?
What people are these, whom pain has overcome?"
He: "This is the sorrowful state of souls unsure,

Whose lives earned neither honor nor bad fame.
And they are mingled with angels of that base sort
Who, neither rebellious to God nor faithful to Him,

Chose neither side, but kept themselves apart—
Now Heaven expels them, not to mar its splendor,
And Hell rejects them, lest the wicked of heart

Take glory over them." And then I: "Master,

WORDS TO KNOW
imbued (ĭm-byo͞od') *adj.* filled or inspired **imbue** v.

11–12 "All fear . . . cowardice die: You must leave all fear behind.

14–15 souls . . . intellect: those who have lost sight of God.

20 Resounding through starless air: echoing in the darkness.

30–37 souls unsure, . . . glory over them: those souls who in life acted neither for good nor evil but only for themselves. They are unfit for Heaven and not allowed in Hell proper.

NOTES

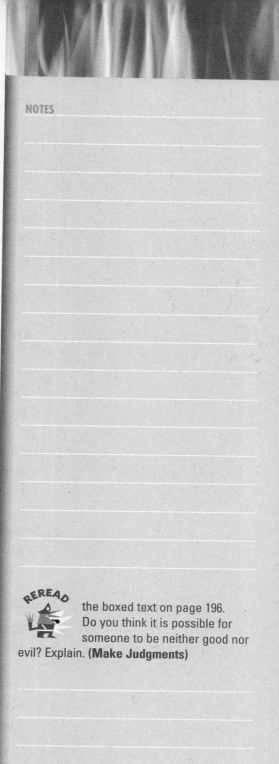

REREAD the boxed text on page 196. Do you think it is possible for someone to be neither good nor evil? Explain. **(Make Judgments)**

What agony is it, that makes them keen their grief
With so much force?" He: "I will make brief answer:

They have no hope of death, but a blind life
So abject, they envy any other fate.
To all memory of them, the world is deaf.

Mercy and justice disdain them. Let us not
Speak of them: look and pass on." I looked again:
A whirling banner sped at such a rate

It seemed it might never stop; behind it a train
Of souls, so long that I would not have thought
Death had undone so many. When more than one

I recognized had passed, I beheld the shade
Of him who made the Great Refusal, impelled
By cowardice: so at once I understood

Beyond all doubt that this was the dreary guild
Repellent both to God and His enemies—
Hapless ones never alive, their bare skin galled

By wasps and flies, blood trickling down the face,
Mingling with tears for harvest underfoot
By writhing maggots. Then, when I turned my eyes

Farther along our course, I could make out
People upon the shore of some great river.
"Master," I said, "it seems by this dim light

That all of these are eager to cross over—
Can you tell me by what law, and who they are?"
He answered, "Those are things you will discover

WORDS TO KNOW

abject (ăb′jĕkt′) *adj.* very low or miserable in condition
disdain (dĭs-dān′) *v.* to look down on or treat with contempt
hapless (hăp′lĭs) *adj.* unfortunate

38 **keen:** to wail with sadness.

42 **To all memory . . . deaf:** Living people have forgotten all about these souls.

49–51 **the shade of him . . . by cowardice:** probably a reference to Pope Celestine V, who gave up his title after only five months due to political pressures on him.

52–53 **the dreary guild repellent . . . enemies:** the unhappy group offensive to both God and demons.

54 **galled:** broken; made sore.

57 **maggots:** the larva of flies, often found in decaying matter.

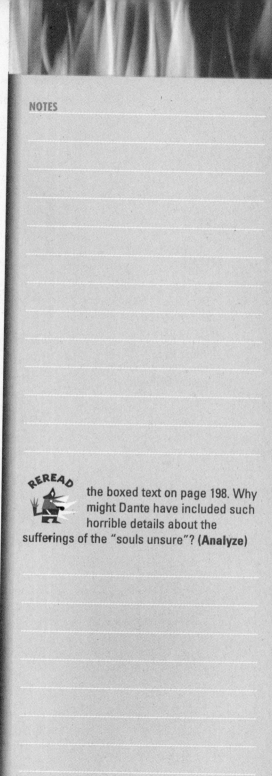

the boxed text on page 198. Why might Dante have included such horrible details about the sufferings of the "souls unsure"? **(Analyze)**

When we have paused at Acheron's dismal shore."
I walked on with my head down after that,
Fearful I had displeased him, and spoke no more.

Pause & Reflect

FOCUS

Dante notices an old man in a boat. Read to find out who he is and what he does.

MARK IT UP As you read, underline details that describe the old man.

Then, at the river—an old man in a boat:
White-haired, as he drew closer shouting at us,
"Woe to you, wicked souls! Give up the thought

Of Heaven! I come to ferry you across
Into eternal dark on the opposite side,
Into fire and ice! And you there—leave this place,

You living soul, stand clear of these who are dead!"
And then, when he saw that I did not obey:
"By other ports, in a lighter boat," he said,

"You will be brought to shore by another way."
My master spoke then, "Charon, do not rage:
Thus is it willed where everything may be

Simply if it is willed. Therefore, oblige,
And ask no more." That silenced the grizzled jaws
Of the gray ferryman of the livid marsh,

Who had red wheels of flame about his eyes.
But at his words the forlorn and naked souls
Were changing color, cursing the human race,

God and their parents. Teeth chattering in their skulls,
They called curses on the seed, the place, the hour
Of their own begetting and their birth. With wails

64 Acheron's (ăk'ə-rŏnz') **dismal shore:** Acheron is the first river Dante comes upon in Hell. This river flows downward to form the frozen lake at the lowest level of Hell.

67–68 an old man . . . white-haired: Charon (kâr'ən), who, in classical mythology, ferries the souls of the dead across the river of death.

74–76 when he saw . . . by another way: Charon realizes that Dante, a living person, does not belong in Hell.

78–79 Thus it is . . . if it is willed: It is the will of God for us to travel to Hell; **oblige:** perform the service.

83–85 the forlorn and naked souls . . . their parents: The souls of the damned are without divine grace and are not permitted to repent; they can only curse.

Pause & Reflect

1. Do you think that the "souls unsure" should be punished so severely? **(Make Judgments)**

YES / NO, because

2. What do you think will happen next? Circle one statement below. **(Predict)**

Dante will return to the dark woods.

Dante will continue the journey alone.

Virgil and Dante will reach the River Acheron.

And tears they gathered on the evil shore
That waits for all who don't fear God. There demon
Charon beckons them, with his eyes of fire;

Crowded in a herd, they obey if he should summon,
And he strikes at any laggards with his oar.
As leaves in quick succession sail down in autumn

Until the bough beholds its entire store
Fallen to the earth, so Adam's evil seed
Swoop from the bank when each is called, as sure

As a trained falcon, to cross to the other side
Of the dark water; and before one throng can land
On the far shore, on this side new souls crowd.

"My son," said the gentle master, "here are joined
The souls of all who die in the wrath of God,
From every country, all of them eager to find

Their way across the water—for the goad
Of Divine Justice spurs them so, their fear
Is transmuted to desire. Souls who are good

Never pass this way; therefore, if you hear
Charon complaining at your presence, consider
What that means." Then, the earth of that grim shore

Began to shake: so violently, I shudder
And sweat recalling it now. A wind burst up
From the tear-soaked ground to erupt red light and batter

My senses—and so I fell, as though seized by sleep.

Pause & Reflect

92 **laggards:** individuals who lag behind.

93–98 **As leaves . . . dark water:** Notice the comparison between the souls being swept away and the leaves falling from a tree.

95 **Adam's evil seed:** descendants of Adam, the first human and the cause of mankind's fall from Paradise.

98 **throng:** large group.

101 **The souls . . . wrath of God:** At the shore the souls of all who died in the state of sin wait to be taken across the river into Hell.

103 **goad:** something that prods.

104–105 **their fear . . . desire:** In life the sinners hardened their hearts against grace. They are now required by Divine Justice to wish for Hell.

Pause & Reflect

1. Look back at the details you underlined. What details helped you the most to imagine what Charon looks like? **(Visualize)**

2. What does Charon do to the souls of the damned? **(Summarize)**

How would you describe Dante's view of life? Mark passages in the poem that support your ideas.

Moving On

If you are using the ***Language of Literature,*** go to page 748 to continue reading the *Inferno.* As you do so, continue to be an active reader. Ask yourself the kinds of questions you found in this excerpt from the *Inferno.* **(Analyze)**

Active Reading SkillBuilder

Clarifying Meaning

The *Inferno* can be read as an allegory, a work with two layers of meaning. You can often **clarify** the meaning by following these steps: Reread difficult passages carefully, and use the sidenotes found in the Guide for Reading for help. Then ask yourself questions about the passages, and try to **paraphrase** them, or state them in your own words. Use these strategies while reading Dante's epic work. Record on the chart below any difficult words and passages, questions about them, and possible meanings for each word or passage.

Difficult Words or Passages	Questions About Words/Passages	Possible Meanings of Words/Passages
page 188: "she put such heaviness / Into my spirit, I lost hope of the crest."	*What does the phrase "lost hope of the crest" mean?*	*It might mean "I lost confidence that I could climb to the top of the hill."*

Literary Analysis SkillBuilder

Allegory

The *Inferno* can be read as an **allegory,** a literary work in which most of the characters, objects, and events represent abstract qualities, such as kindness or greed. An allegory has a second level of meaning in addition to its literal meaning. Use the chart below to analyze allegorical elements within Dante's epic work. Give a possible meaning for the listed elements. An example has been completed for you.

Character, Object, Place, Event	Possible Meaning
1. The dark woods	*The confusion and misery caused by sin*
2. The sunlight on the hill	
3. A whirling banner followed by many souls	
4. The character of Virgil	
5. Acheron's dismal shore	

Words to Know SkillBuilder

Words to Know

abject avail disdain hapless imbued

A. Think about the meaning of each underlined word. Then fill in each blank with the letter of the correct definition.

1. The students who missed the field trip to the amusement park were a <u>hapless</u> bunch. ________
2. At Thanksgiving, Grandma's house was <u>imbued</u> with the aromas of homemade turkey and pumpkin pie. ________
3. The lecturer <u>disdains</u> late arrivals. ________
4. Volunteers changed the <u>abject</u> conditions of the town's gardens by removing litter and planting bushes. ________
5. Good coaching and a challenging schedule will <u>avail</u> the team during the state tournament. ________

Definitions

a. to be of use to; help
b. filled or inspired
c. very low or miserable in condition
d. looks down on or treats with contempt
e. unfortunate

B. Complete each sentence with a Word to Know.

1. Dante hoped that his love of Virgil's writings would ________ him in his time of need.
2. The dark air in Hell was ________ with the groans and shrieks of sinners.
3. Dante saw an old boatman who ________ the sinners, snarling at them and even striking some with his oar.
4. He warned them of the ________ conditions they would endure on the opposite side.
5. Still, those ________ sinners felt a strong desire to cross over the river.

C. Write a brief summary of the events described in this excerpt from the *Inferno.* Use at least **four** Words to Know.

NOTES

Before You Read

Connect to Your Life

The main character in *Don Quixote* is a poor, aging gentleman whose imagination gets the better of him. What is your view of dreaming and imagining? How can imagination be useful? Can it ever be dangerous? Write your ideas below.

Imagination

Can be useful because . . .	Can be dangerous because . . .

Key to the Story

WHAT DO YOU THINK? Read the following dialogue between the main character, Don Quixote, and his assistant, Sancho Panza.

D.Q: Fortune is guiding our affairs better than we could have wished; for see there before you, friend Sancho Panza, some thirty or more lawless giants with whom I mean to do battle . . . "

S.P: "But look, your Grace, those are not giants, but windmills, and what appear to be arms are their wings . . . "

What does this exchange tell you about Don Quixote?

from DON QUIXOTE

by Miguel de Cervantes

A **parody** is a work of literature that imitates or makes fun of another work of literature. *Don Quixote* is a parody of the 16th-century romance, a literary form featuring rambling tales of heroic knights, evil sorcerers, and maidens in distress. The story's main character is a poor country gentleman who becomes so absorbed in these romances that he thinks he is living in one. This situation creates humor throughout the story.

CHAPTER 1 Part 1

READING TIP In this story the author mentions many characters, places, and terms that come from romantic stories and myths of long ago. The footnotes explain many of these words. Don't worry if you can't pronounce each word or understand every reference. Read for overall understanding, and try to enjoy the humor in this unusual adventure story.

MARK IT UP **KEEP TRACK**
As you read, you can use these marks to keep track of your reading:

- * This is important.
- ? I have a question about this.
- ! This is a surprise.

FOCUS

This section introduces the main character and begins to show how he lives his life.

MARK IT UP **As you read, put a check mark** next to the sections that show his favorite activities.

In a village of La Mancha[1] the name of which I have no desire to recall, there lived not so long ago one of those gentlemen who always have a lance in the rack, an ancient buckler,[2] a skinny nag, and a greyhound for the chase. A stew with more beef than mutton in it, chopped meat for his evening meal, scraps for a Saturday, lentils on Friday, and a young pigeon as a special delicacy for Sunday, went to account for three-quarters of his income.

The rest of it he laid out on a broadcloth greatcoat[3] and velvet stockings for feast days, with slippers to match, while the other days of the week he cut a figure in a suit of the finest homespun. Living with him were a housekeeper in her forties, a niece who was not yet twenty, and a lad of the field and market place who saddled his horse for him and wielded the pruning knife.

This gentleman of ours was close on to fifty, of a robust constitution[4] but with little flesh on his bones and a face that was lean and gaunt. He was noted for his early rising, being very fond of the hunt. They will try to tell you that his surname was Quijada or Quesada[5]—there is some difference of opinion among those who have written on the subject—but according to the most likely conjectures we are to

1. **La Mancha:** a high, flat, barren region in central Spain.
2. **buckler:** a small, round shield carried or worn on the arm.
3. **broadcloth greatcoat:** a heavy wool overcoat.
4. **robust constitution:** vigorous, healthy physical nature.
5. **Quijada** (kē-hä'dä) **or Quesada** (kĕ-sä'dä): last names mistakenly given to the main character.

WORDS TO KNOW
conjecture (kən-jĕk'chər) *n.* conclusion based on guesswork

understand that it was really Quejana.[6] But all this means very little so far as our story is concerned, providing that in the telling of it we do not depart one iota[7] from the truth.

You may know, then, that the aforesaid gentleman, on those occasions when he was at leisure, which was most of the year around, was in the habit of reading books of chivalry with such pleasure and devotion as to lead him almost wholly to forget the life of a hunter and even the administration of his estate. So great was his curiosity and infatuation in this regard that he even sold many acres of tillable land in order to be able to buy and read the books that he loved, and he would carry home with him as many of them as he could obtain.

Of all those that he thus devoured none pleased him so well as the ones that had been composed by the famous Feliciano de Silva,[8] whose lucid prose style and involved conceits[9] were as precious to him as pearls; especially when he came to read those tales of love and amorous challenges that are to be met with in many places, such a passage as the following, for example: "The reason of the unreason that afflicts my reason, in such a manner weakens my reason that I with reason lament me of your comeliness."[10] And he was similarly affected when his eyes fell upon such lines as these: ". . . the high Heaven of your divinity divinely fortifies you with the stars and renders you deserving of that desert your greatness doth deserve."

Pause & Reflect

6. **Quejana** (kĕ-hä′nä).
7. **iota** (ī-ō′tə): small bit.
8. **Feliciano de Silva** (fĕ-lē-syä′nô dĕ sēl′vä): Spanish author of fictional books about knights.
9. **conceits:** lengthy, exaggerated comparisons.
10. **comeliness:** beauty.

WORDS TO KNOW
infatuation (ĭn-făch′o͞o-ā′shən) *n.* foolish, unreasonable attraction
lucid (lo͞o′sĭd) *adj.* clear; easily understood

Pause & Reflect

1. What is Don Quixote's favorite thing to do? **(Clarify)**

2. What action does he take in order to pursue this hobby? Do you think this is a good idea? Explain. **(Make Judgments)**

NOTES

MARK IT UP **WORD POWER** Mark words that you'd like to add to your **Personal Word List.** After reading, you can record the words and their meanings beginning on page 444.

FOCUS

Books about knights and their adventures take up more and more of the old man's time and imagination. Find out what this leads to.

MARK IT UP Underline clues that the gentleman has sunk too far into fantasy. The shaded text is an example.

The poor fellow used to lie awake nights in an effort to disentangle the meaning and make sense out of passages such as these, although Aristotle[11] himself would not have been able to understand them, even if he had been resurrected for that sole purpose. He was not at ease in his mind over those wounds that Don Belianís[12] gave and received; for no matter how great the surgeons who treated him, the poor fellow must have been left with his face and his entire body covered with marks and scars. Nevertheless, he was grateful to the author for closing the book with the promise of an interminable adventure to come; many a time he was tempted to take up his pen and literally finish the tale as had been promised, and he undoubtedly would have done so, and would have succeeded at it very well, if his thoughts had not been constantly occupied with other things of greater moment.[13]

He often talked it over with the village curate,[14] who was a learned man, a graduate of Sigüenza,[15] and they would hold long discussions as to who had been the better knight, Palmerin of England or Amadis of Gaul;[16] but Master Nicholas, the barber of the same village, was in the habit of saying that no one could come up to the Knight of Phoebus,[17]

---

11. **Aristotle:** Greek philosopher (384–322 B.C.) widely known for his wisdom.
12. **Don Belianís** (dôn bĕ-lyä-nēs′): hero of a knighthood romance.
13. **moment:** importance.
14. **curate** (kyo͝or′ĭt): priest in charge of a parish.
15. **Sigüenza** (sē-gwĕn′sä): a "minor" university of Spain, whose graduates were often mocked.
16. **Palmerin of England or Amadis** (ä′mə-dĭs) **of Gaul:** two legendary knights known for bravery and unbelievably heroic deeds.
17. **Knight of Phoebus** (fē′bəs): hero of a romance called *Knight of the Sun, Mirror of Princes and Knights.*

WORDS TO KNOW

interminable (ĭn-tûr′mə-nə-bəl) *adj.* unending

and that if anyone could compare with him it was Don Galaor,[18] brother of Amadis of Gaul, for Galaor was ready for anything—he was none of your finical[19] knights, who went around whimpering as his brother did, and in point of valor he did not lag behind him.

In short, our gentleman became so immersed in his reading that he spent whole nights from sundown to sunup and his days from dawn to dusk in poring over his books, until, finally, from so little sleeping and so much reading, his brain dried up and he went completely out of his mind. He had filled his imagination with everything that he had read, with enchantments, knightly encounters, battles, challenges, wounds, with tales of love and its torments, and all sorts of impossible things, and as a result had come to believe that all these fictitious happenings were true; they were more real to him than anything else in the world. He would remark that the Cid Ruy Díaz[20] had been a very good knight, but there was no comparison between him and the Knight of the Flaming Sword,[21] who with a single backward stroke had cut in half two fierce and monstrous giants. He preferred Bernardo del Carpio,[22] who at Roncesvalles had slain Roland despite the charm the latter bore, availing himself of the stratagem which Hercules employed when he strangled Antaeus, the son of Earth, in his arms.

He had much good to say for Morgante[23] who, though he belonged to the haughty, overbearing race of giants, was

NOTES

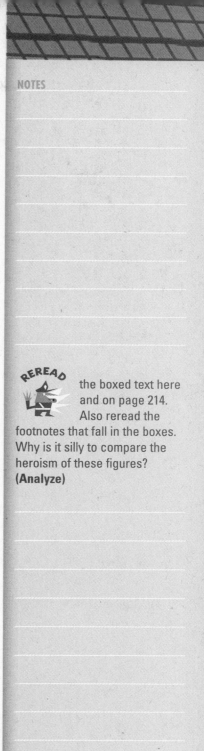

REREAD the boxed text here and on page 214. Also reread the footnotes that fall in the boxes. Why is it silly to compare the heroism of these figures? **(Analyze)**

---

18. **Galaor** (gä-lä-ôr′).

19. **finical:** finicky; picky.

20. **Cid Ruy Díaz** (sēd rwē dē′äs): Rodrigo Díaz, known as the Cid, was an actual Spanish military leader and national hero about whom an epic poem was written.

21. **Knight of the Flaming Sword:** Amadis of Greece, a hero of romances who had a red sword stamped on his shield.

22. **Bernardo del Carpio** was another subject of Spanish epic poetry. The story referred to here puts him at the battle portrayed in the French epic *The Song of Roland* and claims he killed Roland by lifting him up into the air until Roland was dead, as Hercules did to the giant Antaeus.

23. **Morgante** (môr-gän′tĕ): ferocious giant in an Italian romantic poem who later became sweet and loving.

Pause & Reflect

1. What has happened to Don Quixote as the result of so much reading, talking, and thinking about knights? **(Analyze Exposition)**

2. **REREAD** the boxed sentence. What does this sentence lead you to predict he might do next? **(Predict)**

of an affable disposition and well brought up. But, above all, he cherished an admiration for Rinaldo of Montalbán,[24] especially as he beheld him sallying forth from his castle to rob all those that crossed his path, or when he thought of him overseas stealing the image of Mohammed[25] which, so the story has it, was all of gold. And he would have liked very well to have had his fill of kicking that traitor Galalón,[26] a privilege for which he would have given his housekeeper with his niece thrown into the bargain.

Pause & Reflect

FOCUS

The main character is about to adopt a new role in life. Read to find out what it is. As you read, pay attention to how he prepares for his new role.

MARK IT UP Put an asterisk (*) next to each preparation that seems odd.

At last, when his wits were gone beyond repair, he came to conceive the strangest idea that ever occurred to any madman in this world. It now appeared to him fitting and necessary, in order to win a greater amount of honor for himself and serve his country at the same time, to become a knight-errant[27] and roam the world on horseback, in a suit of armor; he would go in quest of adventures, by way of putting into practice all that he had read in his books; he would right every manner of wrong, placing himself in situations of the

24. **Rinaldo of Montalbán** (môn-täl-bän′): hero of a series of French epic poems.

25. **Mohammed:** Arab prophet and founder of Islam.

26. **Galalón** (gä-lä-lôn′): Ganelon, the stepfather and betrayer of Roland, the French epic hero.

27. **knight-errant:** knight who wanders the countryside in search of adventure to prove his chivalry.

WORDS TO KNOW
haughty (hô′tē) *adj.* overly proud; tending to look down on others
affable (ăf′ə-bəl) *adj.* pleasant; agreeable

greatest peril such as would redound[28] to the eternal glory of his name. As a reward for his valor and the might of his arm, the poor fellow could already see himself crowned Emperor of Trebizond[29] at the very least; and so, carried away by the strange pleasure that he found in such thoughts as these, he at once set about putting his plan into effect.

The first thing he did was to burnish up some old pieces of armor, left him by his great-grandfather, which for ages had lain in a corner, moldering and forgotten. He polished and adjusted them as best he could, and then he noticed that one very important thing was lacking: there was no closed helmet, but only a morion, or visorless headpiece, with turned up brim of the kind foot soldiers wore. His ingenuity, however, enabled him to remedy this, and he proceeded to fashion out of cardboard a kind of half-helmet, which, when attached to the morion, gave the appearance of a whole one. True, when he went to see if it was strong enough to withstand a good slashing blow, he was somewhat disappointed; for when he drew his sword and gave it a couple of thrusts, he succeeded only in undoing a whole week's labor. The ease with which he had hewed it to bits disturbed him no little, and he decided to make it over. This time he placed a few strips of iron on the inside, and then, convinced that it was strong enough, refrained from putting it to any further test; instead, he adopted it then and there as the finest helmet ever made.

After this, he went out to have a look at his nag; and although the animal had more *cuartos,* or cracks, in its hoof than there are quarters in a real,[30] and more blemishes than

NOTES

28. redound: to have an effect.

29. Trebizond: a former Greek empire, often referred to in stories of knighthood.

30. quarters in a real (rā-äl′): a real was a coin worth about five cents.

WORDS TO KNOW
ingenuity (ĭn′jə-no͞o′ĭ-tē) *n.* cleverness

Pause & Reflect

1. What role does Don Quixote take on, and how does he prepare for it? **(Summarize)**

2. What is surprising about the name he chooses for his horse? **(Analyze)**

We expect him to pick a name that is

but he picks a name that is

Gonela's steed[31] which *tantum pellis et ossa fuit,*[32] it nonetheless looked to its master like a far better horse than Alexander's Bucephalus or the Babieca of the Cid.[33] He spent all of four days in trying to think up a name for his mount; for—so he told himself—seeing that it belonged to so famous and worthy a knight, there was no reason why it should not have a name of equal renown. The kind of name he wanted was one that would at once indicate what the nag had been before it came to belong to a knight-errant and what its present status was; for it stood to reason that, when the master's worldly condition changed, his horse also ought to have a famous, high-sounding appellation,[34] one suited to the new order of things and the new profession that it was to follow.

After he in his memory and imagination had made up, struck out, and discarded many names, now adding to and now subtracting from the list, he finally hit upon "Rocinante,"[35] a name that impressed him as being sonorous[36] and at the same time indicative of what the steed had been when it was but a hack, whereas now it was nothing other than the first and foremost of all the hacks[37] in the world.

Pause & Reflect

31. **Gonela's steed:** the horse of the Italian court comedian Pietro Gonela which was famous for having gas.

32. ***tantum pellis et ossa fuit:*** Latin phrase meaning "He was only skin and bones."

33. **Alexander's Bucephalus** (byo͞o-sĕf′ə-ləs) **or the Babieca** (bä-byĕ′kä) **of the Cid:** famous horses. Alexander is Alexander the Great, the early conqueror of Asia.

34. **appellation:** name.

35. **Rocinante** (rô-sē-nän′tĕ).

36. **sonorous** (sŏn′ər-əs): having a full, rich sound.

37. **foremost of all the hacks:** *Rocin* means "nag" or "hack" in Spanish; *ante* means "before" or "first." So the name Rocinante indicates that it is the first, or premier, nag.

FOCUS

Don Quixote needs two more things in order to be a real knight. Find out what they are and how he gets them.

Having found a name for his horse that pleased his fancy, he then desired to do as much for himself, and this required another week, and by the end of that period he had made up his mind that he was henceforth to be known as Don Quixote,[38] which, as has been stated, has led the authors of this veracious[39] history to assume that his real name must undoubtedly have been Quijada, and not Quesada as others would have it. But remembering that the valiant Amadis was not content to call himself that and nothing more, but added the name of his kingdom and fatherland that he might make it famous also, and thus came to take the name Amadis of Gaul, so our good knight chose to add his place of origin and become "Don Quixote de la Mancha"; for by this means, as he saw it, he was making very plain his lineage[40] and was conferring honor upon his country by taking its name as his own.

And so, having polished up his armor and made the morion over into a closed helmet, and having given himself and his horse a name, he naturally found but one thing lacking still: he must seek out a lady of whom he could become enamored;[41] for a knight-errant without a ladylove was like a tree without leaves or fruit, a body without a soul.

"If," he said to himself, "as a punishment for my sins or by a stroke of fortune I should come upon some giant hereabouts, a thing that very commonly happens to knights-errant, and if I should slay him in a hand-to-hand encounter or perhaps cut him in two, or, finally, if I should vanquish and subdue him, would it not be well to have someone to whom I may send him as a present, in order that he, if he

Many of the sentences in this story are long and complicated, with words and phrases coming between subjects and verbs. As you read, try to mentally screen out these words and phrases. Instead, look for the subjects and verbs, the most important part of each sentence. The shaded text shows the most important parts of one long sentence. Read the shaded text here and on the next page, ignoring the other words and phrases. Try doing the same thing with other long, complicated sentences.

38. **Quixote** (kë-hō′tĕ)**:** the literal meaning is a piece of armor that protects the thigh.

39. **veracious:** truthful.

40. **lineage:** ancestry.

41. **become enamored:** to be captivated by.

Pause & Reflect

1. What two additional things does Don Quixote need? **(Clarify)**

2. How does he get them? **(Main Idea)**

is living, may come in, fall upon his knees in front of my sweet lady, and say in a humble and submissive tone of voice, 'I, lady, am the giant Caraculiambro,[42] lord of the island Malindrania, who has been overcome in single combat by that knight who never can be praised enough, Don Quixote de la Mancha, the same who sent me to present myself before your Grace that your Highness may dispose of me as you see fit'?"

Oh, how our good knight reveled in this speech, and more than ever when he came to think of the name that he should give his lady! As the story goes, there was a very good-looking farm girl who lived near by, with whom he had once been smitten,[43] although it is generally believed that she never knew or suspected it. Her name was Aldonza Lorenzo,[44] and it seemed to him that she was the one upon whom he should bestow the title of mistress of his thoughts. For her he wished a name that should not be incongruous with his own and that would convey the suggestion of a princess or a great lady; and, accordingly, he resolved to call her "Dulcinea del Toboso,"[45] she being a native of that place. A musical name to his ears, out of the ordinary and significant, like the others he had chosen for himself and his appurtenances.[46]

Pause & Reflect

42. **Caraculiambro** (kä-rä-ko͞o-lyäm′brô).
43. **smitten:** entranced with; in love with.
44. **Aldonza Lorenzo** (äl-dôn′sä lô-rĕn′sô).
45. **Dulcinea del Toboso** (do͞ol-sē-nĕ′ä dĕl tô-bô′sô).
46. **appurtenances:** additions to something; accessories.

WORDS TO KNOW
incongruous (ĭn-kông′gro͞o-əs) *adj.* not appropriate; out of place

FROM

CHAPTER 7 Part 1

After completing his preparations, Don Quixote sets off on his first adventure. During his three days of travel, he persuades an innkeeper to dub him a knight. Then he "rescues" a servant boy from his master's beating, but as soon as "our knight" leaves, the master beats the boy even harder. Don Quixote next mistakes a traveling group of merchants for hostile knights. After insulting the merchants for failing to swear to the beauty of Dulcinea del Toboso, he is badly beaten. A neighbor finds him on the road and carries him home, to the great relief of his family and friends. They blame Don Quixote's mad behavior on his reading habits, so for his own good they decide to burn his books.

FOCUS

After a disastrous setback, Don Quixote decides to get a partner. Find out whether anyone is foolish enough to join him.

. . . That night the housekeeper burned all the books there were in the stable yard and in all the house; and there must have been some that went up in smoke which should have been preserved in everlasting archives,[47] if the one who did the scrutinizing had not been so indolent. Thus we see the truth of the old saying, to the effect that the innocent must sometimes pay for the sins of the guilty.

One of the things that the curate and the barber advised as a remedy for their friend's sickness was to wall up the room where the books had been, so that, when he arose, he would not find them missing—it might be that the cause being removed, the effect would cease—and they could tell

47. **archives:** places where records and other documents are stored.

WORDS TO KNOW

scrutinizing (skro͞ot'n-īz-ĭng) *n.* observing or inspecting with great care
scrutinize *v.*

indolent (ĭn'də-lənt) *adj.* lazy

NOTES

NOTES

READ ALOUD the boxed text. Do you think Don Quixote will believe this story? Why or why not? **(Predict)**

❑ yes ❑ no

because

him that a magician had made away with them, room and all. This they proceeded to do as quickly as possible. Two days later, when Don Quixote rose from his bed, the first thing he did was to go have a look at his library, and, not finding it where he had left it, he went from one part of the house to another searching for it. Going up to where the door had been, he ran his hands over the wall and rolled his eyes in every direction without saying a word; but after some little while he asked the housekeeper where his study was with all his books.

She had been well instructed in what to answer him. "Whatever study is your Grace talking about?" she said. "There is no study, and no books, in this house; the devil took them all away."

"No," said the niece, "it was not the devil but an enchanter who came upon a cloud one night, the day after your Grace left here; dismounting from a serpent that he rode, he entered your study, and I don't know what all he did there, but after a bit he went flying off through the roof, leaving the house full of smoke; and when we went to see what he had done, there was no study and not a book in sight. There is one thing, though, that the housekeeper and I remember very well: at the time that wicked old fellow left, he cried out in a loud voice that it was all on account of a secret enmity that he bore the owner of those books and that study, and that was why he had done the mischief in this house which we would discover. He also said that he was called Muñatón[48] the Magician."

"Frestón, he should have said," remarked Don Quixote.

"I can't say as to that," replied the housekeeper, "whether he was called Frestón or Fritón;[49] all I know is that his name ended in a *tón.*"

---

48. **Muñatón** (mo͞o-nyä-tôn′).

49. **Frestón** (frĕs-tôn′) **or Fritón** (frē-tôn′): Frestón, a magician, was thought to be the author of *History of Belianís of Greece*.

"So it does," said Don Quixote. "He is a wise enchanter, a great enemy of mine, who has a grudge against me because he knows by his arts and learning that in the course of time I am to fight in single combat with a knight whom he favors, and that I am to be the victor and he can do nothing to prevent it. For this reason he seeks to cause me all the trouble that he can, but I am warning him that it will be hard to gainsay or shun that which Heaven has ordained."[50] . . .

In the meanwhile Don Quixote was bringing his powers of persuasion to bear upon a farmer who lived near by, a good man—if this title may be applied to one who is poor—but with very few wits in his head. The short of it is, by pleas and promises, he got the hapless rustic[51] to agree to ride forth with him and serve him as his squire. Among other things, Don Quixote told him that he ought to be more than willing to go, because no telling what adventure might occur which would win them an island, and then he (the farmer) would be left to be the governor of it. As a result of these and other similar assurances, Sancho Panza forsook[52] his wife and children and consented to take upon himself the duties of squire to his neighbor.

Next, Don Quixote set out to raise some money, and by selling this thing and pawning that and getting the worst of the bargain always, he finally scraped together a reasonable amount. He also asked a friend of his for the loan of a buckler[53] and patched up his broken helmet as well as he could. He advised his squire, Sancho, of the day and hour when they were to take the road and told him to see to laying in a supply of those things that were most necessary, and, above all, not to forget the saddlebags. Sancho replied that he would see to all this and added that he was also thinking of taking along with him a very good ass that he had, as he was not much used to going on foot.

50. **to gainsay . . . Heaven has ordained:** to deny or oppose the will of God.

51. **hapless rustic:** unfortunate country bumpkin.

52. **forsook:** gave up, abandoned.

53. **buckler:** a small, round shield.

the boxed text. Why does Don Quixote believe that the magician Frestón is his enemy? **(Clarify)**

Pause & Reflect

1. How does Don Quixote convince Sancho Panza to become his squire? Check two. **(Clarify)**
   - ❑ He pleads with Sancho.
   - ❑ He promises Sancho he can govern an island.
   - ❑ He gets Sancho a new horse.
   - ❑ He dubs Sancho a knight-errant.

2. **MARK IT UP** The narrator says that Sancho Panza has "very few wits in his head." Underline the details on page 221 that show this is true. **(Infer)**

With regard to the ass, Don Quixote had to do a little thinking, trying to recall if any knight-errant had ever had a squire thus asininely[54] mounted. He could not think of any, but nevertheless he decided to take Sancho with the intention of providing him with a nobler steed as soon as occasion offered; he had but to appropriate[55] the horse of the first discourteous knight he met. Having furnished himself with shirts and all the other things that the innkeeper had recommended, he and Panza rode forth one night unseen by anyone and without taking leave of wife and children, housekeeper or niece. They went so far that by the time morning came they were safe from discovery had a hunt been started for them. . . .

Pause & Reflect

FROM

CHAPTER 8 Part 1

FOCUS

Don Quixote mistakes some windmills for "lawless giants." Find out what happens when he tries to fight them.

MARK IT UP As you read, underline the reason Don Quixote gives for fighting the "giants."

At this point they caught sight of thirty or forty windmills which were standing on the plain there, and no sooner had Don Quixote laid eyes upon them than he turned to his squire and said, "Fortune is guiding our affairs better than we could have wished; for you see there before you, friend

54. **asininely:** foolishly; ridiculously. The word is derived from the name of the animal.

55. **appropriate** (ə-prō′prē-āt): take possession of something, usually without permission.

Sancho Panza, some thirty or more lawless giants with whom I mean to do battle. I shall deprive them of their lives, and with the spoils from this encounter we shall begin to enrich ourselves; for this is righteous warfare, and it is a great service to God to remove so accursed a breed from the face of the earth."

"What giants?" said Sancho Panza.

"Those that you see there," replied his master, "those with the long arms some of which are as much as two leagues in length."

"But look, your Grace, those are not giants but windmills, and what appear to be arms are their wings which, when whirled in the breeze, cause the millstone to go."

"It is plain to be seen," said Don Quixote, "that you have had little experience in this matter of adventures. If you are afraid, go off to one side and say your prayers while I am engaging them in fierce, unequal combat."

Saying this, he gave spurs to his steed Rocinante, without paying any heed to Sancho's warning that these were truly windmills and not giants that he was riding forth to attack. Nor even when he was close upon them did he perceive what they really were, but shouted at the top of his lungs, "Do not seek to flee, cowards and vile creatures that you are, for it is but a single knight with whom you have to deal!"

At that moment a little wind came up and the big wings began turning.

"Though you flourish as many arms as did the giant Briareus,"[56] said Don Quixote when he perceived this, "you still shall have to answer to me."

He thereupon commended himself with all his heart to his lady Dulcinea, beseeching her to succor[57] him in this peril; and, being well covered with his shield and with his lance at rest, he bore down upon them at a full gallop and fell upon the first mill that stood in his way, giving a thrust

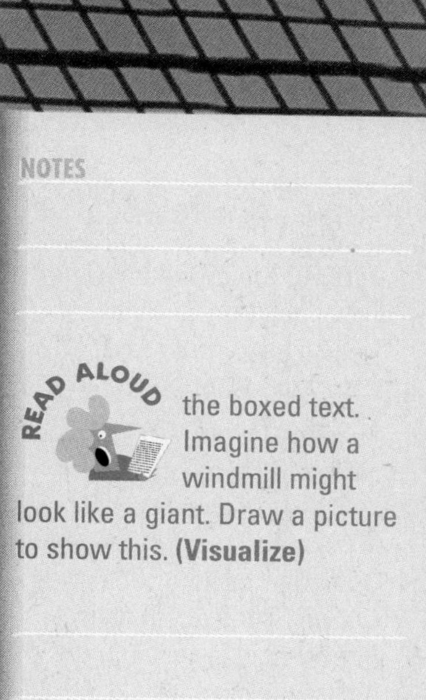

NOTES

READ ALOUD the boxed text. Imagine how a windmill might look like a giant. Draw a picture to show this. **(Visualize)**

56. Briareus (brē-âr′yo͞os): a mythological giant with 100 arms.

57. succor: to provide aid; help.

Pause & Reflect

1. **REREAD** the boxed passage. How does Don Quixote explain his run-in with the windmills? **(Clarify)**

2. What four qualities does Don Quixote show about himself through this misadventure? **(Infer)**

   Don Quixote is

   - ❑ wise
   - ❑ fearless
   - ❑ stubborn
   - ❑ crazy
   - ❑ smart
   - ❑ persistent

3. What advice would you give Sancho Panza? **(Evaluate)**

Remember that *Don Quixote* is a parody of a romance, a type of book popular in the 16th century. It takes the basic elements of a romance—knights, squires, villains, and fair maidens—and presents them in a silly way. What types of books or movies are popular today? Choose one, such as a murder mystery or a science-fiction tale, and consider its basic elements (types of character, conflict, and setting). Then write a short parody of it.

at the wing, which was whirling at such a speed that his lance was broken into bits and both horse and horseman went rolling over the plain, very much battered indeed. Sancho upon his donkey came hurrying to his master's assistance as fast as he could, but when he reached the spot, the knight was unable to move, so great was the shock with which he and Rocinante had hit the ground.

"God help us!" exclaimed Sancho, "did I not tell your Grace to look well,[58] that those were nothing but windmills, a fact which no one could fail to see unless he had other mills of the same sort in his head?"[59]

"Be quiet, friend Sancho," said Don Quixote. "Such are the fortunes of war, which more than any other are subject to constant change. What is more, when I come to think of it, I am sure that this must be the work of that magician Frestón, the one who robbed me of my study and my books, and who has thus changed the giants into windmills in order to deprive me of the glory of overcoming them, so great is the enmity that he bears me; but in the end his evil arts shall not prevail against this trusty sword of mine."

"May God's will be done," was Sancho Panza's response. And with the aid of his squire the knight was once more mounted on Rocinante, who stood there with one shoulder half out of joint. And so, speaking of the adventure that had just befallen them, they continued along the Puerto Lápice highway;[60] for there, Don Quixote said, they could not fail to find many and varied adventures, this being a much traveled thoroughfare. . . . ❖

Pause & Reflect

58. **look well:** be careful.

59. **unless . . . in his head:** unless he was crazy.

60. **Puerto Lápice** (pwĕr′tô lä′pē-sĕ).

Active Reading SkillBuilder

Exposition

Exposition is the stage of the plot that provides background information. The first chapter of *Don Quixote* serves as an exposition that introduces the main character. Using the chart below, record details about Don Quixote. Make sure to indicate why the details are important to the story.

Background Information of Don Quixote	Why Are These Details Important to the Story?
1. His age and physical appearance	*He seems too old and weak to be a knight.*
2. His possessions	
3. His position in life and lifestyle	
4. His passions	
5. His view of himself	

Literary Analysis SkillBuilder

Characterization

Characterization refers to the techniques that writers use to develop characters. Writers can portray a character using four basic methods:

1. words which describe the character's physical appearance
2. the character's own speech, thoughts, feelings, and actions
3. the speech, thoughts, feelings, and actions of other characters
4. words of the narrator

As you read, identify five short passages within the selection that help create a strong impression of Don Quixote. Use the chart below to record your findings. An example has been provided.

Don Quixote Passage	Method of Characterization	Qualities Revealed
1. *"his wits were gone beyond repair"*	*4*	*Don Quixote has become completely absorbed by his reading. Members of his household believe that he has lost his mind.*
2.		
3.		
4.		
5.		

Words to Know SkillBuilder

Words to Know

affable	incongruous	ingenuity	lucid
conjecture	indolent	interminable	scrutinizing
haughty	infatuation		

A. Think about the meaning of each underlined word. Then fill in each blank with the letter of the correct definition.

1. The great heat and humidity forced us to be <u>indolent</u>, rather than active. ________
2. Thomas A. Edison was known for his tremendous <u>ingenuity</u>. ________
3. Katie's striped blouse was <u>incongruous</u> with her plaid skirt. ________
4. Evan's <u>infatuation</u> with baseball causes him to collect cards, caps, t-shirts, and autographs. ________
5. Although the bodyguard looks unfriendly, he's actually quite <u>affable</u>. ________
6. The detective's <u>scrutinizing</u> of the crime scene took several hours. ________
7. Aunt Jane took care to leave <u>lucid</u> instructions with the babysitter. ________
8. The pastor's sermon seemed <u>interminable</u>, causing Hector to look impatiently at his wristwatch. ________
9. Ryan's opinion of the stranger was based on <u>conjecture</u>, not facts. ________
10. The play's director criticized Lucy for her <u>haughty</u> attitude toward the crew. ________

Definitions

a. foolish, unreasonable attraction
b. cleverness
c. pleasant, agreeable
d. not appropriate, out of place
e. lazy
f. guesswork
g. clear; easily understood
h. unending
i. overly proud; tending to look down on others
j. observing or inspecting with great care

B. What is revealed about Don Quixote in the excerpt from Cervantes' novel? Describe the type of man he is, using at least **three** Words to Know.

Before You Read

Connect to Your Life

In this verse drama, a scholar named Faust (foust) is willing to sell his soul to get god-like knowledge and experience. What would you give up to achieve your greatest goal? Health? Love? The respect of others? Write your thoughts in the space below.

My Greatest Goal
In order to achieve my greatest goal, I am willing to sacrifice

Key to the Verse Drama

WHAT YOU NEED TO KNOW The real Faust was a German astrologer and magician, who lived around 1540. Legend has it that he sold his soul to the devil to gain knowledge. Johann Wolfgang von Goethe (yō′hän vôlf′gäng vôn gœ′tə) wrote a drama based on this legend. In his version, Doctor Faust is a learned but unhappy man. After spending his life reading and studying, he has found neither wisdom nor pleasure. He is tempted by the devil, Mephisto (mə-fĭs′tō), who promises to help him discover real knowledge. But Faust must give up his soul in return.

FROM

Faust

BY Johann Wolfgang von Goethe

TRANSLATED BY WALTER KAUFMANN

PREVIEW **In this part of the drama, Mephisto makes two deals—one with the Lord in Heaven and the other with Faust on Earth. The devil is convinced that Faust will agree to trade his soul for knowledge. The Lord believes otherwise.**

Prologue in Heaven

FOCUS

Mephisto visits Heaven and makes a deal with the Lord for the soul of Faust. Read to find out what the Lord thinks of Faust.

MARK IT UP As you read, circle any words or phrases that help you understand how the Lord regards Faust. An example is highlighted on page 232.

Mephisto:

Since you, oh Lord, have once again drawn near,
And ask how we have been, and are so genial,
And since you used to like to see me here,
You see me, too, as if I were a menial.
I cannot speak as nobly as your staff,
Though by this circle here I shall be spurned:
My pathos would be sure to make you laugh,
Were laughing not a habit you've unlearned.
Of suns and worlds I know nothing to say;
I only see how men live in dismay.
The small god of the world will never change his ways
And is as whimsical—as on the first of days.
His life might be a bit more fun,
Had you not given him that spark of heaven's sun;
He calls it reason and employs it, resolute
To be more brutish than is any brute.
He seems to me, if you don't mind, Your Grace,
Like a cicada of the long-legged race,
That always flies, and, flying, springs,
And in the grass the same old ditty sings;
If only it were grass he could repose in!
There is no trash he will not poke his nose in.

The Lord:

Can you not speak but to abuse?
Do you come only to accuse?
Does nothing on the earth seem to you right?

WORDS TO KNOW

genial (jēn'yəl) *adj.* pleasant; agreeable
resolute (rĕz'ə-lo͞ot') *adj.* resolved; determined
repose (rĭ-pōz') *v.* to rest

GUIDE FOR READING

Use this guide for help with unfamiliar words and difficult passages.

4 **menial** (mē′nē-əl)**:** servant.

7 **pathos** (pā′thŏs)**:** quality or situation that arouses pity or sadness.

11 **The small god of the world:** humankind.

13–14 **His life . . . heaven's sun:** Humans would have much more fun if they hadn't been given the power to think.

17–20 **He seems . . . ditty sings:** Humans seem like insects, doing the same silly things over and over.

This play is difficult for even the best readers. The language is poetic and rich in meaning. The following strategies may help:

- Remember that you don't have to understand every word in a passage to get the overall sense. Read for general meaning.
- Read entire sentences at a time, pausing at the end of a line only if you come upon a mark of punctuation.
- Use the information in the **Guide for Reading,** beginning on page 231, to help you with difficult lines and passages. Also try reading these lines and passages aloud.

MARK IT UP **KEEP TRACK**

Remember to use these marks to keep track of your reading.

- ✱ This is important.
- ? I have a question about this.
- ! This is a surprise.

Mephisto:

No, Lord. I find it still a rather sorry sight.
Man moves me to compassion, so wretched is his plight.
I have no wish to cause him further woe.

The Lord:

Do you know Faust?

Mephisto:

The doctor?

The Lord:

Aye, my servant.

Mephisto:

Lo!

He serves you most peculiarly, I think.
Not earthly are the poor fool's meat and drink.
His spirit's ferment drives him far,
And he half knows how foolish is his quest:
From heaven he demands the fairest star,
And from the earth all joys that he thinks best;
And all that's near and all that's far
Cannot soothe the upheaval in his breast.

The Lord:

Though now he serves me but confusedly,
I shall soon lead him where the vapor clears.
The gardener knows, however small the tree,
That bloom and fruit adorn its later years.

Mephisto:

What will you bet? You'll lose him yet to me,
If you will graciously connive
That I may lead him carefully.

The Lord:

As long as he may be alive,
So long you shall not be prevented.
Man errs as long as he will strive.

WORDS TO KNOW
connive (kə-nīv') *v.* to fail to take action; secretly cooperate

27–28 Man moves me . . . further woe: I feel sorry for humans because their lives are so awful; I don't want to cause them more suffering.

31–32 Not earthly . . . drives him far: Faust is not interested in food and drink; he is driven by the unrest in his soul.

36–37 And all that's near . . . his breast: Nothing makes Faust happy or contented.

39 I shall soon . . . where the vapor clears: The Lord will help Faust think clearly.

40–41 The gardener . . . years: This image depicts Faust's situation. The Lord is the gardener, and Faust is the small tree that one day will yield good fruit.

47 Man errs . . . strive: Even while trying to do good, humans make mistakes.

NOTES

READ ALOUD the boxed passage on page 232. According to Mephisto, what is the cause of Faust's suffering? Check two statements below. **(Cause and Effect)**

- ❑ He expects too much from life.
- ❑ He has a terrible disease.
- ❑ He can't enjoy life's little pleasures.
- ❑ He demands too little from life.

Mephisto:

Be thanked for that; I've never been contented
To waste my time upon the dead.
I far prefer full cheeks, a youthful curly-head.
When corpses come, I have just left the house—
I feel as does the cat about the mouse.

The Lord:

Enough—I grant that you may try to clasp him,
Withdraw this spirit from his primal source
And lead him down, if you can grasp him,
Upon your own abysmal course—
And stand abashed when you have to attest:
A good man in his darkling aspiration
Remembers the right road throughout his quest.

Mephisto:

Enough—he will soon reach his station;
About my bet I have no hesitation,
And when I win, concede your stake
And let me triumph with a swelling breast:
Dust he shall eat, and that with zest,
As my relation does, the famous snake.

The Lord:

Appear quite free on that day, too;
I never hated those who were like you:
Of all the spirits that negate,
The knavish jester gives me least to do.
For man's activity can easily abate,
He soon prefers uninterrupted rest;
To give him this companion hence seems best
Who roils and must as Devil help create.
But you, God's rightful sons, give voice
To all the beauty in which you rejoice;
And that which ever works and lives and grows
Enfold you with fair bonds that love has wrought,
And what in wavering apparition flows
That fortify with everlasting thought.
(*The heavens close, the Archangels disperse.*)

WORDS TO KNOW
abate (ə-bāt') *v.* to lessen in intensity

53–56 Enough—I grant . . . abysmal (ə-bĭz′məl) **course:** You have my permission to try to make him follow you on your terrible course to Hell.

54 his primal source: God, or the desire for good.

57 And stand . . . attest: and be ashamed when you must admit.

58 darkling: dim; confused.

64 he: Faust.

65 the famous snake: Satan, who, disguised as a serpent, tempted Eve in the Garden of Eden.

68 negate: deny.

69 knavish jester: foolish joker.

71–72 He soon . . . seems best: People need a challenge to keep them from becoming lazy and satisfied with themselves.

73 roils (roilz)**:** disturbs; vexes.

74 But you, God's rightful sons: The Lord is now addressing the archangels.

76–79 And that which . . . everlasting thought: Let all that is good keep you strong and full of faith.

the boxed text on page 234. What is the Lord saying about Faust? Check two statements below. **(Infer)**

- ❑ Faust has no will of his own.
- ❑ Faust is a good man.
- ❑ Nothing can save Faust now.
- ❑ In the end, Faust will choose what's right.

MARK IT UP WORD POWER
Mark words that you'd like to add to your **Personal Word List.** After reading, you can record the words and their meanings on page 444.

Mephisto (*alone*):

I like to see the Old Man now and then
And try to be not too uncivil.
It's charming in a noble squire when
He speaks humanely with the very Devil.

Pause & Reflect

Frustrated by the limits of human knowledge, Faust uses magic to summon the Spirit of the Earth. The Spirit, however, is too powerful for Faust and vanishes. Trying to escape his earthbound life, Faust is about to take poison when he hears a choir of angels. Their song momentarily recalls him to life, but his sadness quickly returns. Faust seeks to lift his spirits by walking in the countryside. There he sees a strange poodle. The dog follows Faust to his study, where the animal reveals himself to be Mephisto. Faust tries to hold the devil but in vain. Mephisto soon returns, however, and offers a remedy for Faust's unhappiness.

Faust's Study

FOCUS

Read to find out about the deal that Faust makes with Mephisto.

MARK IT UP As you read, underline details that help you understand this deal.

Mephisto:

Stop playing with your melancholy
That, like a vulture, ravages your breast;
The worst of company still cures this folly,
For you are human with the rest.
Yet that is surely not to say
That you should join the herd you hate.
I'm not one of the great,

WORDS TO KNOW
humanely (hyo͞o-mān'lē) *adv.* in a compassionate or sympathetic way

80 the Old Man: the Lord.

84–85 Stop playing . . . breast: Do something to get rid of the sadness that is tearing you apart inside.

89 the herd you hate: other human beings.

Pause & Reflect

1. Look back at the words and phrases you circled. Why does the Lord allow Mephisto to tempt Faust? Check two statements below. **(Cause and Effect)**
   - ❑ The Lord thinks that Faust will resist Mephisto's temptations.
   - ❑ The Lord wants to punish Faust for his sins.
   - ❑ The Lord knows that Faust's soul is doomed.
   - ❑ The Lord believes that Faust needs a challenge.

2. Imagine that you were present at the conversation between Mephisto and the Lord. What would you say to them? **(Connect)**

I would tell Mephisto:

I would tell the Lord:

But if you want to make your way
Through the world with me united,
I should surely be delighted
To be yours, as of now,
Your companion, if you allow;
And if you like the way I behave,
I shall be your servant, or your slave.

Faust:
And in return, what do you hope to take?

Mephisto:
There's so much time—so why insist?

Faust:
No, no! The Devil is an egoist
And would not just for heaven's sake
Turn into a philanthropist.
Make your conditions very clear;
Where such a servant lives, danger is near.

Mephisto:
Here you shall be the master, I be bond,
And at your nod I'll work incessantly;
But when we meet again *beyond,*
Then you shall do the same for me.

Faust:
Of the beyond I have no thought;
When you reduce this world to nought,
The other one may have its turn.
My joys come from this earth, and there,
That sun has burnt on my despair:
Once I have left those, I don't care:
What happens is of no concern.
I do not even wish to hear
Whether beyond they hate and love,
And whether in that other sphere
One realm's below and one above.

WORDS TO KNOW
despair (dĭ-spâr') *n.* complete loss of hope

91–97 But if you . . . or your slave: Mephisto invites Faust to travel through the world with him; he offers to be Faust's servant.

100 egoist (ē′gō-ĭst)**:** a person concerned only with himself or herself.

102 philanthropist (fĭ-lăn′thrə-pĭst)**:** a person who does charitable work.

105 bond: servant or slave.

106 incessantly (ĭn-sĕs′ənt-lē)**:** without stopping.

107 ***beyond:*** in the life after death.

110 nought: nothing.

NOTES

READ ALOUD the boxed passage on page 238. What is Faust's attitude toward life after death? **(Infer)**

Mephisto:

So minded, dare it cheerfully.
Commit yourself and you shall see
My arts with joy. I'll give you more
Than any man has seen before.

Faust:

What would you, wretched Devil, offer?
Was ever a man's spirit in its noble striving
Grasped by your like, devilish scoffer?
But have you food that is not satisfying,
Red gold that rolls off without rest,
Quicksilver-like, over your skin—
A game in which no man can win—
A girl who, lying at my breast,
Ogles already to entice my neighbor,
And honor—that perhaps seems best—
Though like a comet it will turn to vapor?
Show me fruit that, before we pluck them, rot,
And trees whose foliage every day makes new!

Mephisto:

Such a commission scares me not,
With such things I can wait on you.
But, worthy friend, the time comes when we would
Recline in peace and feast on something good.

Faust:

If ever I recline, calmed, on a bed of sloth,
You may destroy me then and there.
If ever flattering you should wile me
That in myself I find delight,
If with enjoyment you beguile me,
Then break on me, eternal night!
This bet I offer.

Mephisto:

I accept it.

WORDS TO KNOW
sloth (slôth) *n.* laziness

126 grasped: understood; **devilish scoffer:** wicked liar.

130–136 A game . . . makes new: Faust tells the devil that the earthly joys and pleasures he is offering give no lasting joy or satisfaction.

137 commission: assigned task.

143 wile me: tempt me through trickery.

144 That in myself I find delight: I become too pleased with myself.

145 beguile me: distract me from my purpose or goal.

NOTES

the boxed text on page 240. What does Faust think of love and honor? **(Infer)**

Faust:

Right.
If to the moment I should say:
Abide, you are so fair—
Put me in fetters on that day,
I *wish* to perish then, I swear.
Then let the death bell ever toll,
Your service done, you shall be free,
The clock may stop, the hand may fall,
As time comes to an end for me.

Mephisto:

Consider it, for we shall not forget it.

Faust:

That is a right you need not waive.
I did not boast, and I shall not regret it.
As I grow stagnant I shall be a slave,
Whether or not to anyone indebted.

Mephisto:

At the doctor's banquet tonight I shall do
My duties as a servant without fail.
But for life's sake, or death's—just one detail:
Could you give me a line or two?

Faust:

You pedant need it black on white?
Are man and a man's word indeed new to your sight?
Is not my spoken word sufficient warrant
When it commits my life eternally?
Does not the world rush on in every torrent,
And a mere promise should hold me?
Yet this illusion our heart inherits,
And who would want to shirk his debt?
Blessed who counts loyalty among his merits.
No sacrifice will he regret.
And yet a parchment, signed and sealed, is an abhorrent
Specter that haunts us, and it makes us fret.

WORDS TO KNOW
waive (wāv) *v.* to voluntarily give up; abandon

150 fetters: chains.

159–160 As I . . . indebted: Faust is saying that if his mind were to stop searching and become content **(As I grow stagnant)**, then he will have lost his freedom—even if he had not made a deal with Mephisto.

161 the doctor's banquet: an awards dinner for professors that Faust would be attending.

165–168 You pedant . . . eternally?: Are you so narrow-minded that you need it in writing? Why isn't it enough that I give you my word?

172 shirk his debt: not keep his promise.

175–176 abhorrent (ăb-hôr′ənt) **specter:** hateful ghost or spirit.

the boxed passage on page 242. Faust says that if he ever experiences a moment that he wishes would never end, then the devil may take his soul. If you were in Faust's position, would you make such a deal? **(Connect)**

YES / NO, because

The word dies when we seize the pen,
And wax and leather lord it then.
What, evil spirit, do you ask?
Paper or parchment, stone or brass?
Should I use chisel, style, or quill?
It is completely up to you.

Mephisto:

Why get so hot and overdo
Your rhetoric? Why must you shrill?
Use any sheet, it is the same;
And with a drop of blood you sign your name.

Faust:

If you are sure you like this game,
Let it be done to humor you.

Mephisto:

Blood is a very special juice.

Pause & Reflect

FOCUS

As you read, think about what types of knowledge and experience Faust hopes to gain.

Faust:

You need not fear that someday I retract.
That all my striving I unloose
Is the whole purpose of the pact.
Oh, I was puffed up all too boldly,
At your rank only is my place.
The lofty spirit spurned me coldly,
And nature hides from me her face.
Torn is the subtle thread of thought,
I loathe the knowledge I once sought.
In sensuality's abysmal land
Let our passions drink their fill!
In magic veils, not pierced by skill,
Let every wonder be at hand!
Plunge into time's whirl that dazes my sense,

181 style: slender, pointed writing instrument once used on wax tablets.

183–184 Why get . . . you shrill?: Why do you have to get angry and start yelling?

190 retract: take back my promise.

191 unloose: unleash; give free rein to.

194 At your rank . . . place: Faust suggests that his pride places him on a level with the devil.

198 loathe (lōth): hate.

Pause & Reflect

1. Review the details you underlined. According to Faust's own terms, under what condition will he lose his soul? **(Clarify)**

2. Read aloud the boxed passage on page 244. Why do you think the devil wants Faust to sign his name in blood? **(Analyze)**

Into the torrent of events!
And let enjoyment, distress,
Annoyance and success
Succeed each other as best they can;
For restless activity proves a man.

Mephisto:

You are not bound by goal or measure.
If you would nibble everything
Or snatch up something on the wing,
You're welcome to what gives you pleasure.
But help yourself and don't be coy!

Faust:

Do you not hear, I have no thought of joy!
The reeling whirl I seek, the most painful excess,
Enamored hate and quickening distress.
Cured from the craving to know all, my mind
Shall not henceforth be closed to any pain,
And what is portioned out to all mankind,
I shall enjoy deep in my self, contain
Within my spirit summit and abyss,
Pile on my breast their agony and bliss,
And thus let my own self grow into theirs, unfettered,
Till as they are, at last I, too, am shattered.

Mephisto:

Believe me who for many a thousand year
Has chewed this cud and never rested,
That from the cradle to the bier
The ancient leaven cannot be digested.
Trust one like me, this whole array
Is for a God—there's no contender:
He dwells in his eternal splendor,
To darkness we had to surrender,
And you need night as well as day.

Faust:

And yet it is my will.

204 **torrent:** rushing stream.

209–213 There is no limit to the earthly pleasures you can enjoy.

213 **coy:** shy in a false way.

215–216 **The reeling whirl . . . distress:** I want to experience all the confusion of life—the mixed emotions and intense sorrow.

221 **summit and abyss:** highest point and lowest point.

223 **unfettered:** not restricted.

227 **bier:** a stand on which a corpse is placed before burial.

228 **The ancient leaven:** all the experience and sensation that the world has to offer.

229–230 **Trust one . . . no contender:** Only God is able to experience all that the world has to offer.

NOTES

the boxed text on page 246. Then circle the two phrases below that tell what Faust hopes to gain from his deal with Mephisto. **(Clarify)**

- only feelings of joy
- a thirst for knowledge
- the greatest sorrows and joys
- a happy afterlife
- every excess known to humans
- religious faith

Mephisto:

It does sound bold.
But I'm afraid, though you are clever,
Time is too brief, though art's forever.
Perhaps you're willing to be told.
Why don't you find yourself a poet,
And let the gentleman ransack his dreams:
And when he finds a noble trait, let him bestow it
Upon your worthy head in reams and reams:
The lion's daring,
The swiftness of the hind,
The northerner's forbearing
And the Italian's fiery mind,
Let him resolve the mystery
How craft can be combined with magnanimity,
Or how a passion-crazed young man
Might fall in love after a plan.
If there were such a man, I'd like to meet him,
As Mr. Microcosm I would greet him.

Faust:

Alas, what am I, if I can
Not reach for mankind's crown which merely mocks
Our senses' craving like a star?

Mephisto:

You're in the end—just what you are!
Put wigs on with a million locks
And put your foot on ell-high socks,
You still remain just what you are.

Faust:

I feel, I gathered up and piled up high
In vain the treasures of the human mind:
When I sit down at last, I cannot find
New strength within—it is all dry.
My stature has not grown a whit,
No closer to the Infinite.

WORDS TO KNOW
stature (stăch'ər) *n.* status or importance gained by growth or achievement

NOTES

239 ransack: to search frantically.

241 reams and reams: very large amounts.

243 hind: deer.

247 How craft . . . magnanimity (măg′nə-nĭm′ĭ-tē): how cunning can be combined with a noble heart.

251 Mr. Microcosm (mī′krə-kŏz′əm): a person who would have all the qualities that Mephisto has named.

257 ell-high socks: An ell is a measurement 45 inches long.

259–264 I feel . . . to the Infinite: I have studied everything I can, and I am no happier or more spiritual.

READ ALOUD the boxed passage on page 248. The phrase "treasures of the human mind" refers to the knowledge found in books. Why does Faust reject this knowledge? **(Infer)**

Mephisto:

Well, my good sir, to put it crudely,
You see matters just as they lie;
We have to look at them more shrewdly,
Or all life's pleasures pass us by.
Your hands and feet—indeed that's trite—
And head and seat are yours alone;
Yet all in which I find delight,
Should they be less my own?
Suppose I buy myself six steeds:
I buy their strength; while I recline
I dash along at whirlwind speeds,
For their two dozen legs are mine.
Come on! Let your reflections rest
And plunge into the world with zest!
I say, the man that speculates
Is like a beast that in the sand,
Led by an evil spirit, round and round gyrates,
And all about lies gorgeous pasture land.

Faust:

How shall we set about it?

Mephisto:

Simply leave. . . .

A student appears outside Faust's study. When Faust exclaims that he doesn't want to see the student, Mephisto dons the doctor's cap and gown. After the soliloquy that appears here, Mephisto will pretend to be Faust while the doctor prepares for their trip.

Some fifteen minutes should be all I need;
Meanwhile get ready for our trip, and speed!

(Faust *exit.*)

Mephisto (*in* Faust's *long robe*):

Have but contempt for reason and for science,
Man's noblest force spurn with defiance,
Subscribe to magic and illusion,
The Lord of Lies aids your confusion,
And, pact or no, I hold you tight.—

267 shrewdly: cleverly, cunningly.

271–272 Yet all . . . less my own?: Shouldn't I possess all the things that give me pleasure?

279 the man that speculates: someone who thinks too much.

281 gyrates (jī'rāts')**:** spins.

282 gorgeous pasture land: all the pleasure people miss by thinking too deeply.

287 spurn with defiance: to reject forcefully.

289 The Lord of Lies: the devil.

NOTES

the boxed passage on page 250. What does Mephisto advise Faust to do? Circle one phrase below. **(Infer)**

to think more deeply

to give up pleasures

to enjoy experiences without thinking

The spirit which he has received from fate
Sweeps ever onward with unbridled might,
Its hasty striving is so great
It leaps over the earth's delights.
Through life I'll drag him at a rate,
Through shallow triviality,
That he shall writhe and suffocate;
And his insatiability,
With greedy lips, shall see the choicest plate
And ask in vain for all that he would cherish—
And were he not the Devil's mate
And had not signed, he still must perish.

Pause & Reflect

292 **unbridled might:** limitless strength.

296 **shallow triviality:** all that is of no importance or consequence.

302 **perish:** die.

Pause & Reflect

1. What kind of knowledge does Faust hope to gain? **(Clarify)**

2. Reread the boxed passage on page 252. How would you compare Mephisto's plans with his promises to Faust? **(Compare and Contrast)**

After long years of study, Faust concludes that only limited knowledge can be found in books. Do you think he's right? On another sheet of paper, write a paragraph or two comparing the knowledge gained from books with that gained from experience. **(Compare and Contrast)**

Active Reading SkillBuilder

Clarifying Meaning

Often, poetry or drama written long ago requires readers to stop from time to time and clarify what they have read so far. As you read this excerpt from Goethe's *Faust,* use the following suggestions and chart to help you clarify meaning in difficult passages.

Read Sidenotes and Words to Know Use the **Guide for Reading** and the Words to Know at the bottom of the pages to learn the meaning of unfamiliar words.
Reorder Words Unusual word order is often used in poetry to maintain meter or a rhyme scheme. Reorder words so the passage sounds more natural and makes sense to you.
Paraphrase Restate in your own words what you think is being said in difficult lines and speeches.
Summarize Clarify the speeches in *Faust* by summarizing the most important idea or ideas being expressed.

Write a difficult passage from *Faust* in the first column. Then, use one of the above strategies. Restate the passage in your own words, expressing the meaning as you understand it.

Passage	Restate in your own words (paraphrase, summarize, or re-order)
1. His life might be a bit more fun, / Had you not given him that spark of heaven's sun; / He calls it reason and employs it, resolute / To be more brutish than is any brute.	Mankind's life on earth might be more fun if the Lord hadn't given Man intelligence. Man calls intelligence "reason." Man uses it to justify wicked acts.

Literary Analysis SkillBuilder

Dialogue

Dialogue is written conversation between two or more characters. In drama, the story is told primarily through dialogue, or the words of the characters. Writers use dialogue as a way of developing characters and revealing their relationships with one another. Choose two or three examples of dialogue from the excerpt of *Faust.* Write a few lines of the dialogue in the chart. Then list the personality traits revealed by the dialogue. Indicate what the dialogue suggests about the relationships between the characters. One example has been done for you.

	Dialogue	Traits revealed about each character	What is revealed about the relationship?
1.	"Mephisto: If only it were grass he could repose in! There is no trash he will not poke his nose in. The Lord: Can you not speak but to abuse? Do you come only to accuse?"	Mephisto is critical of mankind. He thinks humans are lazy and vile. The Lord wants to know if Mephisto has come to Heaven only to complain.	Mephisto is not afraid to tell the Lord what he thinks, and the Lord is not afraid to challenge Mephisto's motives.
2.			
3.			
4.			

Words to Know SkillBuilder

Words to Know

abate	despair	humanely	resolute	stature
connive	genial	repose	sloth	waive

A. Fill in each line with the letter of the correct definition, listed below.

1. The mother smiled and was very genial when she met her daughter's new boyfriend. ____________
2. Because he finished in second place last season, he is resolute to win the race this year. ____________
3. The cat stretches out in repose in the center of the king-sized bed. ____________
4. Behind closed doors, two burglars connive to steal a fortune. ____________
5. When the flood rains abate, farmers will assess their crops for damage. ____________
6. The woman acted humanely when she stopped her car to help a wounded bird. ____________
7. "Do not despair," the teacher told her class. "If you fail this test, you may take it again next week." ____________
8. He tried to overcome his sloth and finish his homework. ____________
9. She may waive her right to remain silent. ____________
10. The former police chief gained stature in the community when he was elected mayor. ____________

Definitions

a. to lessen in intensity
b. secretly cooperate
c. give up hope
d. pleasant; agreeable
e. in a compassionate or sympathetic way
f rest
g. resolved; determined
h. laziness
i. status or importance gained by growth or achievement
j. to give up voluntarily

B. Why do you think Faust made a deal with the Devil? Write a letter that Faust may have written to his students explaining why he made the pact with Mephisto. Use at least **three** Words to Know in your letter.

NOTES

Before You Read

Connect to Your Life

Think about a time when you came upon a stranger in need. Or imagine a time in the future when you might meet a needy person. Use the concept web below to describe your feelings and actions.

I noticed ______________________

I felt ______________________

STRANGER IN NEED

I thought about ______________________

I decided to ______________________

Key to the Story

WHAT'S THE BIG IDEA? The Bible says that a man does not live by bread alone. This statement is key to the theme of the story you are about to read. What do you think this statement means?

Besides bread, a person needs ______________________

What Men Live By

by Leo Tolstoy

Translated by
Louise and Aylmer Maude

PREVIEW Leo Tolstoy's stories often have a moral, a lesson about life and how to live it. This story is about a poor peasant and a stranger he meets one day. Can a person with nothing help someone else in need?

This story takes place in a **setting** very different from the one you live in. To get the true feeling of this time and place, use details in the story to help you **visualize** what the setting is like.

NOTES

MARK IT UP **KEEP TRACK**
As you read, you can use these marks to keep track of your understanding.

- * This is important.
- ? I have a question about this.
- ! This is a surprise.

I

FOCUS

It is winter in Russia, a long time ago. Read to find out about the problems a poor peasant faces as he tries to provide for his family.

MARK IT UP As you read, circle details that tell you about his problems. An example is highlighted.

A shoemaker named Simon, who had neither house nor land of his own, lived with his wife and children in a peasant's hut and earned his living by his work. Work was cheap but bread was dear, and what he earned he spent for food. The man and his wife had but one sheep-skin coat between them for winter wear, and even that was worn to tatters, and this was the second year he had been wanting to buy sheep-skins for a new coat. Before winter Simon saved up a little money: a three-ruble note lay hidden in his wife's box, and five rubles and twenty kopeks[1] were owed him by customers in the village.

So one morning he prepared to go to the village to buy the sheep-skins. He put on over his shirt his wife's wadded nankeen[2] jacket, and over that he put his own cloth coat. He took the three-ruble note in his pocket, cut himself a stick to serve as a staff, and started off after breakfast. "I'll collect the five rubles that are due to me," thought he, "add the three I have got, and that will be enough to buy sheep-skins for the winter coat."

He came to the village and called at a peasant's hut, but the man was not at home. The peasant's wife promised that the money should be paid next week, but she would not pay it herself. Then Simon called on another peasant, but this one swore he had no money, and would only pay twenty kopeks which he owed for a pair of boots Simon had mended. Simon then tried to buy the sheep-skins on credit, but the dealer would not trust him.

1. **kopeks** (kō′pĕks): A kopek is one hundredth of a ruble.
2. **nankeen:** a sturdy cotton cloth.

"Bring your money," said he, "then you may have your pick of the skins. We know what debt-collecting is like."

So all the business the shoemaker did was to get the twenty kopeks for boots he had mended and to take a pair of felt boots a peasant gave him to sole with leather.

Simon felt downhearted. He spent the twenty kopeks on vodka and started homewards without having bought any skins. In the morning he had felt the frost; but now, after drinking the vodka, he felt warm even without a sheep-skin coat. He trudged along, striking his stick on the frozen earth with one hand, swinging the felt boots with the other, and talking to himself.

"I'm quite warm," said he, "though I have no sheep-skin coat. I've had a drop and it runs through my veins. I need no sheep-skins. I go along and don't worry about anything. That's the sort of man I am! What do I care? I can live without sheep-skins. I don't need them. My wife will fret, to be sure. And, true enough, it is a shame; one works all day long and then does not get paid. Stop a bit! If you don't bring that money along, sure enough I'll skin you, blessed if I don't. How's that? He pays twenty kopeks at a time! What can I do with twenty kopeks? Drink it—that's all one can do! Hard up, he says he is! So he may be—but what about me? You have house, and cattle, and everything; I've only what I stand up in! You have corn of your own growing, I have to buy every grain. Do what I will, I must spend three rubles every week for bread alone. I come home and find the bread all used up and I have to work out another ruble and a half. So just you pay up what you owe, and no nonsense about it!"

Pause & Reflect

Pause & Reflect

Review the details you circled. Given the problems Simon faces, do you think he'll be able to solve them? **(Predict)**

YES/NO because

NOTES

the boxed passage. What traits does Simon reveal? Circle three words below. **(Infer)**

fear	pity
suspicion	pride
courage	selfishness

FOCUS

Returning home from the village, Simon notices a stranger behind a shrine.

MARK IT UP As you read, circle details that tell you about Simon's reaction to the stranger.

By this time he had nearly reached the shrine[3] at the bend of the road. Looking up, he saw something whitish behind the shrine. The daylight was fading, and the shoemaker peered at the thing without being able to make out what it was. "There was no white stone here before. Can it be an ox? It's not like an ox. It has a head like a man, but it's too white; and what could a man be doing there?"

He came closer, so that it was clearly visible. To his surprise it really was a man, alive or dead, sitting naked, leaning motionless against the shrine. Terror seized the shoemaker, and he thought, "Some one has killed him, stripped him, and left him here. If I meddle I shall surely get into trouble."

So the shoemaker went on. He passed in front of the shrine so that he could not see the man. When he had gone some way he looked back, and saw that the man was no longer leaning against the shrine but was moving as if looking towards him. The shoemaker felt more frightened than before, and thought, "Shall I go back to him or shall I go on? If I go near him something dreadful may happen. Who knows who the fellow is? He has not come here for any good. If I go near him he may jump up and throttle me, and there will be no getting away. Or if not, he'd still be a burden on one's hands. What could I do with a naked man? I couldn't give him my last clothes. Heaven only help me to get away!"

So the shoemaker hurried on, leaving the shrine behind him—when suddenly his conscience smote him and he stopped in the road.

3. **shrine:** a place at which devotion is paid to God or a holy person.

"What are you doing, Simon?" said he to himself. "The man may be dying of want, and you slip past afraid. Have you grown so rich as to be afraid of robbers? Ah, Simon, shame on you!"

So he turned back and went up to the man.

Pause & Reflect

II

FOCUS

Read to find out how Simon treats the stranger when he returns to the shrine.

Simon approached the stranger, looked at him and saw that he was a young man, fit, with no bruises on his body, but evidently freezing and frightened, and he sat there leaning back without looking up at Simon, as if too faint to lift his eyes. Simon went close to him and then the man seemed to wake up. Turning his head, he opened his eyes and looked into Simon's face. That one look was enough to make Simon fond of the man. He threw the felt boots on the ground, undid his sash, laid it on the boots, and took off his cloth coat.

"It's not a time for talking," said he. "Come, put this coat on at once!" And Simon took the man by the elbows and helped him to rise. As he stood there, Simon saw that his body was clean and in good condition, his hands and feet shapely, and his face good and kind. He threw his coat over the man's shoulders, but the latter could not find the sleeves. Simon guided his arms into them, and drawing the coat on well, wrapped it closely about him, tying the sash round the man's waist.

Simon even took off his cap to put it on the man's head, but then his own head felt cold and he thought: "I'm quite bald, while he has long curly hair." So he put his cap on his

Pause & Reflect

1. Look back at the details you circled. How does Simon react to the stranger when he first sees him? How do Simon's feelings change? Complete the sentences below. **(Compare and Contrast)**

At first,

But later,

2. What does this change tell you about Simon? **(Draw Conclusions)**

NOTES

MARK IT UP
WORD POWER Mark words that you'd like to add to your **Personal Word List**. After reading, you can record the words and their meanings beginning on page 444.

own head again. "It will be better to give him something for his feet," thought he; and he made the man sit down and helped him to put on the felt boots, saying, "There, friend, now move about and warm yourself. Other matters can be settled later on. Can you walk?"

The man stood up and looked kindly at Simon but could not say a word.

"Why don't you speak?" said Simon. "It's too cold to stay here, we must be getting home. There now, take my stick, and if you're feeling weak lean on that. Now step out!"

The man started walking and moved easily, not lagging behind.

As they went along, Simon asked him, "And where do you belong to?"

"I'm not from these parts."

"I thought as much. I know the folks hereabouts. But how did you come to be there by the shrine?"

"I cannot tell."

"Has some one been ill-treating you?"

"No one has ill-treated me. God has punished me."

"Of course God rules all. Still, you'll have to find food and shelter somewhere. Where do you want to go to?"

"It is all the same to me."

Simon was amazed. The man did not look like a rogue,[4] and he spoke gently, but yet he gave no account of himself. Still Simon thought, "Who knows what may have happened?" And he said to the stranger: "Well then, come home with me and at least warm yourself awhile."

So Simon walked towards his home, and the stranger kept up with him, walking at his side. The wind had risen and Simon felt it cold under his shirt. He was getting over his tipsiness[5] by now and began to feel the frost. He went along sniffling and wrapping his wife's coat round him, and he thought to himself: "There now—talk about sheep-skins!

---

4. **rogue** (rōg): a dishonest person.

5. **tipsiness:** slight drunkenness.

I went out for sheep-skins and come home without even a coat to my back, and what is more, I'm bringing a naked man along with me. Matrëna[6] won't be pleased!" And when he thought of his wife he felt sad, but when he looked at the stranger and remembered how he had looked up at him at the shrine, his heart was glad.

Pause & Reflect

III

FOCUS

Simon brings the stranger home to his hut. What will his wife, Matrëna, think when she sees them?

Simon's wife had everything ready early that day. She had cut wood, brought water, fed the children, eaten her own meal, and now she sat thinking. She wondered when she ought to make bread: now or tomorrow? There was still a large piece left.

"If Simon has had some dinner in town," thought she, "and does not eat much for supper, the bread will last out another day."

She weighed the piece of bread in her hand again and again and thought: "I won't make any more today. We have only enough flour left to bake one batch. We can manage to make this last out till Friday."

So Matrëna put away the bread and sat down at the table to patch her husband's shirt. While she worked she thought how her husband was buying skins for a winter coat.

"If only the dealer does not cheat him. My good man is much too simple; he cheats nobody, but any child can take him in. Eight rubles is a lot of money—he should get a good coat at that price. Not tanned skins, but still a proper

6. **Matrëna** (mä-trō′nä).

Pause & Reflect

1. What does Simon learn about the stranger? Check four phrases below. **(Summarize)**
   - ❑ in good condition
   - ❑ injured by bandits
   - ❑ not from the local area
   - ❑ says God is punishing him
   - ❑ doesn't care where he goes

2. Why does Simon give the stranger his coat? **(Infer)**

NOTES

winter coat. How difficult it was last winter to get on without a warm coat. I could neither get down to the river nor go out anywhere. When he went out he put on all we had, and there was nothing left for me. He did not start very early today, but still it's time he was back. I only hope he has not gone on the spree!"[7]

Hardly had Matrëna thought this than steps were heard on the threshold and some one entered. Matrëna stuck her needle into her work and went out into the passage. There she saw two men: Simon, and with him a man without a hat and wearing felt boots.

Matrëna noticed at once that her husband smelt of spirits.[8] "There now, he has been drinking," thought she. And when she saw that he was coatless, had only her jacket on, brought no parcel, stood there silent, and seemed ashamed, her heart was ready to break with disappointment. "He has drunk the money," thought she, "and has been on the spree with some good-for-nothing fellow whom he has brought home with him."

Matrëna let them pass into the hut, followed them in, and saw that the stranger was a young, slight man, wearing her husband's coat. There was no shirt to be seen under it, and he had no hat. Having entered, he stood neither moving nor raising his eyes, and Matrëna thought: "He must be a bad man—he's afraid."

Matrëna frowned, and stood beside the stove looking to see what they would do.

Simon took off his cap and sat down on the bench as if things were all right.

"Come, Matrëna; if supper is ready, let us have some."

Matrëna muttered something to herself and did not move but stayed where she was, by the stove. She looked first at the one and then at the other of them and only shook her head. Simon saw that his wife was annoyed, but tried to

---

7. **on the spree:** on a wild or carefree outing.

8. **spirits:** alcohol.

pass it off. Pretending not to notice anything, he took the stranger by the arm.

"Sit down, friend," said he, "and let us have some supper."

The stranger sat down on the bench.

"Haven't you cooked anything for us?" said Simon.

Matrëna's anger boiled over. "I've cooked, but not for you. It seems to me you have drunk your wits away. You went to buy a sheep-skin coat but come home without so much as the coat you had on and bring a naked vagabond[9] home with you. I have no supper for drunkards like you."

"That's enough, Matrëna. Don't wag your tongue without reason! You had better ask what sort of man—"

"And you tell me what you've done with the money?"

Simon found the pocket of the jacket, drew out the three-ruble note, and unfolded it.

"Here is the money. Trifonov did not pay, but promises to pay soon."

Matrëna got still more angry; he had bought no sheep-skins but had put his only coat on some naked fellow and had even brought him to their house.

She snatched up the note from the table, took it to put away in safety, and said: "I have no supper for you. We can't feed all the naked drunkards in the world."

"There now, Matrëna, hold your tongue a bit. First hear what a man has to say—!"

"Much wisdom I shall hear from a drunken fool. I was right in not wanting to marry you—a drunkard. The linen my mother gave me you drank; and now you've been to buy a coat—and have drunk it too!"

Simon tried to explain to his wife that he had only spent twenty kopeks; tried to tell how he had found the man—but Matrëna would not let him get a word in. She talked nineteen to the dozen[10] and dragged in things that had happened ten years before.

9. **vagabond:** someone who moves from place to place.

10. **nineteen to the dozen:** quickly and excessively.

This part of the story is told mostly through **dialogue**—the words spoken by characters to each other. These words are enclosed in quotation marks. Remember that each time there is a change of speaker, a new paragraph begins.

Pause & Reflect

1. Why does Matrëna get angry with Simon? **(Cause and Effect)**

2. What happens to Matrëna's jacket when she tries to grab it from Simon? **(Clarify)**

Matrëna talked and talked, and at last she flew at Simon and seized him by the sleeve.

"Give me my jacket. It is the only one I have, and you must needs take it from me and wear it yourself. Give it here, you mangy dog, and may the devil take you."

Simon began to pull off the jacket, and turned a sleeve of it inside out; Matrëna seized the jacket and it burst its seams. She snatched it up, threw it over her head, and went to the door. She meant to go out, but stopped undecided—she wanted to work off her anger, but she also wanted to learn what sort of a man the stranger was.

Pause & Reflect

IV

FOCUS

Read to find out how Matrëna's feelings toward the stranger change.

Matrëna stopped and said: "If he were a good man he would not be naked. Why, he hasn't even a shirt on him. If he were all right, you would say where you came across the fellow."

"That's just what I am trying to tell you," said Simon. "As I came to the shrine I saw him sitting all naked and frozen. It isn't quite the weather to sit about naked! God sent me to him or he would have perished. What was I to do? How do we know what may have happened to him? So I took him, clothed him, and brought him along. Don't be so angry, Matrëna. It is a sin. Remember, we must all die one day."

Angry words rose to Matrëna's lips, but she looked at the stranger and was silent. He sat on the edge of the bench, motionless, his hands folded on his knees, his head drooping on his breast, his eyes closed, and his brows knit as if in pain. Matrëna was silent, and Simon said: "Matrëna, have you no love of God?"

Matrëna heard these words, and as she looked at the stranger, suddenly her heart softened towards him. She came back from the door, and going to the stove she got out the supper. Setting a cup on the table, she poured out some kvas.[11] Then she brought out the last piece of bread and set out a knife and spoons.

"Eat, if you want to," said she.

Simon drew the stranger to the table.

"Take your place, young man," said he.

Simon cut the bread, crumbled it into the broth, and they began to eat. Matrëna sat at the corner of the table, resting her head on her hand and looking at the stranger.

And Matrëna was touched with pity for the stranger and began to feel fond of him. And at once the stranger's face lit up; his brows were no longer bent, he raised his eyes and smiled at Matrëna.

When they had finished supper, the woman cleared away the things and began questioning the stranger. "Where are you from?" said she.

"I am not from these parts."

"But how did you come to be on the road?"

"I may not tell."

"Did some one rob you?"

"God punished me."

"And you were lying there naked?"

"Yes, naked and freezing. Simon saw me and had pity on me. He took off his coat, put it on me, and brought me here. And you have fed me, given me drink, and shown pity on me. God will reward you!"

Matrëna rose, took from the window Simon's old shirt she had been patching, and gave it to the stranger. She also brought out a pair of trousers for him.

"There," said she, "I see you have no shirt. Put this on, and lie down where you please, in the loft or on the stove."

---

11. kvas (kväs)**:** a Russian drink, similar to beer, made from fermented grains.

NOTES

READ ALOUD the boxed passage. Why does the stranger smile at Matrëna? **(Infer)**

Pause & Reflect

1. How do Matrëna's feelings toward the stranger change? **(Infer)**

2. Read aloud the boxed passage on this page. Then have a partner read aloud lines 163–166 (And when . . . glad) on page 265. How would you compare Simon's and Matrëna's reactions to the stranger? **(Compare and Contrast)**

The stranger took off the coat, put on the shirt, and lay down in the loft. Matrëna put out the candle, took the coat, and climbed to where her husband lay on the stove.

Matrëna drew the skirts of the coat over her and lay down but could not sleep; she could not get the stranger out of her mind.

When she remembered that he had eaten their last piece of bread and that there was none for tomorrow and thought of the shirt and trousers she had given away, she felt grieved; but when she remembered how he had smiled, her heart was glad.

Long did Matrëna lie awake, and she noticed that Simon also was awake—he drew the coat towards him.

"Simon!"

"Well?"

"You have had the last of the bread and I have not put any to rise. I don't know what we shall do tomorrow. Perhaps I can borrow some of the neighbor Martha."

"If we're alive we shall find something to eat."

The woman lay still awhile, and then said, "He seems a good man, but why does he not tell us who he is?"

"I suppose he has his reasons."

"Simon!"

"Well?"

"We give; but why does nobody give us anything?"

Simon did not know what to say; so he only said, "Let us stop talking" and turned over and went to sleep.

Pause & Reflect

V

FOCUS

Read to find out what happens after Simon and Matrëna take the stranger into their home.

In the morning Simon awoke. The children were still asleep; his wife had gone to the neighbor's to borrow some bread. The stranger alone was sitting on the bench, dressed in the old shirt and trousers, and looking upwards. His face was brighter than it had been the day before.

Simon said to him, "Well, friend; the belly wants bread and the naked body clothes. One has to work for a living. What work do you know?"

"I do not know any."

This surprised Simon, but he said, "Men who want to learn can learn anything."

"Men work and I will work also."

"What is your name?"

"Michael."

"Well, Michael, if you don't wish to talk about yourself, that is your own affair; but you'll have to earn a living for yourself. If you will work as I tell you, I will give you food and shelter."

"May God reward you! I will learn. Show me what to do."

Simon took yarn, put it round his thumb and began to twist it.

"It is easy enough—see!"

Michael watched him, put some yarn round his own thumb in the same way, caught the knack,[12] and twisted the yarn also.

Then Simon showed him how to wax the thread. This also Michael mastered. Next Simon showed him how to twist the bristle in, and how to sew, and this, too, Michael learned at once.

12. knack: the exact way of doing something.

NOTES

READ ALOUD the boxed passage with a partner. What do you predict the stranger will do to earn a living? **(Predict)**

Pause & Reflect

1. What does Michael do in return for room and board? **(Clarify)**

2. What can you tell about Michael from the way he works? Check three boxes below. **(Infer)**
   - ❑ skilled with his hands
   - ❑ awkward and slow
   - ❑ quick to learn
   - ❑ hard-working

Whatever Simon showed him he understood at once, and after three days he worked as if he had sewn boots all his life. He worked without stopping and ate little. When work was over he sat silently, looking upwards. He hardly went into the street, spoke only when necessary, and neither joked nor laughed. They never saw him smile, except that first evening when Matrëna gave him supper.

Pause & Reflect

VI

FOCUS

In this part of the story, a wealthy gentleman visits Simon's hut.

MARK IT UP Underline details that help you form an impression of this man.

Day by day and week by week the year went round. Michael lived and worked with Simon. His fame spread till people said that no one sewed boots so neatly and strongly as Simon's workman, Michael; from all the district round people came to Simon for their boots, and he began to be well off.

One winter day, as Simon and Michael sat working, a carriage on sledge-runners, with three horses and with bells, drove up to the hut. They looked out of the window; the carriage stopped at their door; a fine servant jumped down from the box and opened the door. A gentleman in a fur coat got out and walked up to Simon's hut. Up jumped Matrëna and opened the door wide. The gentleman stooped to enter the hut, and when he drew himself up again his head nearly reached the ceiling and he seemed quite to fill his end of the room.

Simon rose, bowed, and looked at the gentleman with astonishment. He had never seen any one like him. Simon himself was lean, Michael was thin, and Matrëna was dry as a bone, but this man was like some one from another world: red-faced, burly,[13] with a neck like a bull's, and looking altogether as if he were cast in iron.

The gentleman puffed, threw off his fur coat, sat down on the bench, and said, "Which of you is the master bootmaker?"

"I am, your Excellency," said Simon, coming forward.

Then the gentleman shouted to his lad, "Hey, Fédka,[14] bring the leather!"

The servant ran in, bringing a parcel. The gentleman took the parcel and put it on the table.

"Untie it," said he. The lad untied it.

The gentleman pointed to the leather.

"Look here, shoemaker," said he, "do you see this leather?"

"Yes, your honor."

"But do you know what sort of leather it is?"

Simon felt the leather and said, "It is good leather."

"Good, indeed! Why, you fool, you never saw such leather before in your life. It's German and cost twenty rubles."

Simon was frightened and said, "Where should I ever see leather like that?"

"Just so! Now, can you make it into boots for me?"

"Yes, your Excellency, I can."

Then the gentleman shouted at him: "You can, can you? Well, remember whom you are to make them for, and what the leather is. You must make me boots that will wear for a year, neither losing shape nor coming unsewn. If you can do it, take the leather and cut it up; but if you can't, say so. I warn you now, if your boots come unsewn or lose shape within a year I will have you put in prison. If they don't burst or lose shape for a year, I will pay you ten rubles for your work."

---

13. burly: heavy and strong.

14. Fédka (fyĕd′kă).

NOTES

the boxed passage on this page. What does this dialogue between Simon and Michael show? Check one sentence below. **(Infer)**

- ❑ Simon is afraid of Michael.
- ❑ Simon trusts Michael.
- ❑ Simon and Michael dislike the wealthy man.

Don't worry if you don't understand why Michael smiles at this point in the story. You will find out why as you continue to read.

Simon was frightened and did not know what to say. He glanced at Michael and nudging him with his elbow, whispered: "Shall I take the work?"

Michael nodded his head as if to say, "Yes, take it."

Simon did as Michael advised and undertook to make boots that would not lose shape or split for a whole year.

Calling his servant, the gentleman told him to pull the boot off his left leg, which he stretched out.

"Take my measure!" said he.

Simon stitched a paper measure seventeen inches long, smoothed it out, knelt down, wiped his hands well on his apron so as not to soil the gentleman's sock, and began to measure. He measured the sole, and round the instep, and began to measure the calf of the leg, but the paper was too short. The calf of the leg was as thick as a beam.

"Mind you don't make it too tight in the leg."

Simon stitched on another strip of paper. The gentleman twitched his toes about in his sock looking round at those in the hut, and as he did so he noticed Michael.

"Whom have you there?" asked he.

"That is my workman. He will sew the boots."

"Mind," said the gentleman to Michael, "remember to make them so that they will last me a year."

Simon also looked at Michael and saw that Michael was not looking at the gentleman, but was gazing into the corner behind the gentleman, as if he saw some one there. Michael looked and looked, and suddenly he smiled, and his face became brighter.

"What are you grinning at, you fool?" thundered the gentleman. "You had better look to it that the boots are ready in time."

"They shall be ready in good time," said Michael.

"Mind it is so," said the gentleman, and he put on his boots and his fur coat, wrapped the latter round him, and went to the door. But he forgot to stoop, and struck his head against the lintel.[15]

15. lintel: a piece of wood set lengthwise across the top of a door.

He swore and rubbed his head. Then he took his seat in the carriage and drove away.

When he had gone, Simon said: "There's a figure of a man for you! You could not kill him with a mallet.[16] He almost knocked out the lintel, but little harm it did him."

And Matrëna said: "Living as he does, how should he not have grown strong? Death itself can't touch such a rock as that."

Pause & Reflect

VII

FOCUS

Simon and Michael work on the boots. Find out what happens when they complete their work.

Then Simon said to Michael: "Well, we have taken the work, but we must see we don't get into trouble over it. The leather is dear,[17] and the gentleman hot-tempered. We must make no mistakes. Come, your eye is truer and your hands have become nimbler than mine, so you take this measure and cut out the boots. I will finish off the sewing of the vamps."[18]

Michael did as he was told. He took the leather, spread it out on the table, folded it in two, took a knife and began to cut out.

Matrëna came and watched him cutting and was surprised to see how he was doing it. Matrëna was accustomed to seeing boots made, and she looked and saw that Michael was not cutting the leather for boots, but was cutting it round.

She wished to say something, but she thought to herself: "Perhaps I do not understand how gentlemen's boots

16. **mallet:** a wooden hammer.

17. **dear:** costly.

18. **vamps:** upper parts of shoes or boots, covering the instep or the instep and the toes.

Pause & Reflect

1. Review the details you underlined. How does the wealthy man treat Simon? **(Evaluate)**

2. What deal does the wealthy man make with Simon? **(Clarify)**

3. Sometimes a writer gives hints about events that will happen later in the story. This technique is known as **foreshadowing**. Reread the boxed passage on this page. What future event might Simon's and Matrëna's words hint at? **(Predict)**

NOTES

should be made. I suppose Michael knows more about it—and I won't interfere."

When Michael had cut up the leather he took a thread and began to sew not with two ends, as boots are sewn, but with a single end, as for soft slippers.

Again Matrëna wondered, but again she did not interfere. Michael sewed on steadily till noon. Then Simon rose for dinner, looked around, and saw that Michael had made slippers out of the gentleman's leather.

"Ah!" groaned Simon, and he thought, "How is it that Michael, who has been with me a whole year and never made a mistake before, should do such a dreadful thing? The gentleman ordered high boots, welted,[19] with whole fronts, and Michael has made soft slippers with single soles and has wasted the leather. What am I to say to the gentleman? I can never replace leather such as this."

And he said to Michael, "What are you doing, friend? You have ruined me! You know the gentleman ordered high boots, but see what you have made!"

Hardly had he begun to rebuke[20] Michael, when "rat-tat" went the iron ring hung at the door. Some one was knocking. They looked out of the window; a man had come on horseback and was fastening his horse. They opened the door, and the servant who had been with the gentleman came in.

"Good day," said he.

"Good day," replied Simon. "What can we do for you?"

"My mistress has sent me about the boots."

"What about the boots?"

"Why, my master no longer needs them. He is dead."

"Is it possible?"

"He did not live to get home after leaving you but died in the carriage. When we reached home and the servants came to help him alight,[21] he rolled over like a sack. He

19. **welted:** made with a leather strip stitched between the shoe sole and the vamp.

20. **rebuke:** to criticize; express disapproval of.

21. **alight:** step down.

was dead already, and so stiff that he could hardly be got out of the carriage. My mistress sent me here, saying: 'Tell the bootmaker that the gentleman who ordered boots of him and left the leather for them no longer needs the boots, but that he must quickly make soft slippers for the corpse. Wait till they are ready and bring them back with you.' That is why I have come."

Michael gathered up the remnants of the leather; rolled them up, took the soft slippers he had made, slapped them together, wiped them down with his apron, and handed them and the roll of leather to the servant, who took them and said: "Good-bye, masters, and good day to you!"

Pause & Reflect

VIII

FOCUS

Five years later, a woman with two little girls visits Simon's hut.

MARK IT UP As you read, underline details that tell you about Michael's reaction to the visitors.

Another year passed, and another, and Michael was now living his sixth year with Simon. He lived as before. He went nowhere, only spoke when necessary, and had only smiled twice in all those years—one when Matrëna gave him food, and a second time when the gentleman was in their hut. Simon was more than pleased with his workman. He never now asked him where he came from and only feared lest[22] Michael should go away.

They were all at home one day. Matrëna was putting iron pots in the oven; the children were running along the benches and looking out of the window; Simon was sewing at one window and Michael was fastening on a heel at the other.

22. **lest:** that.

Pause & Reflect

1. What unusual events occur in this part of the story? List two below. **(Clarify)**

Event #1

Event #2

2. Based on the events of the story so far, who do you think Michael might turn out to be? **(Predict)**

NOTES

One of the boys ran along the bench to Michael, leant on his shoulder, and looked out of the window.

"Look, Uncle Michael! There is a lady with little girls! She seems to be coming here. And one of the girls is lame."

When the boy said that, Michael dropped his work, turned to the window, and looked out into the street.

Simon was surprised. Michael never used to look out into the street, but now he pressed against the window, staring at something. Simon also looked out and saw that a well-dressed woman was really coming to his hut, leading by the hand two little girls in fur coats and woolen shawls. The girls could hardly be told one from the other, except that one of them was crippled in her left leg and walked with a limp.

The woman stepped into the porch and entered the passage. Feeling about for the entrance she found the latch, which she lifted and opened the door. She let the two girls go in first, and followed them into the hut.

"Good day, good folk!"

"Pray come in," said Simon. "What can we do for you?"

The woman sat down by the table. The two little girls pressed close to her knees, afraid of the people in the hut.

"I want leather shoes made for these two little girls, for spring."

"We can do that. We never have made such small shoes, but we can make them; either welted or turnover shoes,[23] linen lined. My man, Michael, is a master at the work."

Simon glanced at Michael and saw that he had left his work and was sitting with his eyes fixed on the little girls. Simon was surprised. It was true the girls were pretty, with black eyes, plump, and rosy-cheeked, and they wore nice kerchiefs[24] and fur coats, but still Simon could not understand why Michael should look at them like that—

23. **turnover shoes:** shoes made with a piece of leather folded over.

24. **kerchiefs:** scarves worn over the head.

just as if he had known them before. He was puzzled but went on talking with the woman and arranging the price. Having fixed it, he prepared the measure. The woman lifted the lame girl on to her lap and said: "Take two measures from this little girl. Make one shoe for the lame foot and three for the sound one. They both have the same-sized feet. They are twins."

Simon took the measure and, speaking of the lame girl, said: "How did it happen to her? She is such a pretty girl. Was she born so?"

"No, her mother crushed her leg."

Then Matrëna joined in. She wondered who this woman was and whose the children were, so she said: "Are not you their mother, then?"

"No, my good woman; I am neither their mother nor any relation to them. They were quite strangers to me, but I adopted them."

"They are not your children and yet you are so fond of them?"

"How can I help being fond of them? I fed them both at my own breasts. I had a child of my own, but God took him. I was not so fond of him as I now am of these."

"Then whose children are they?"

Pause & Reflect

Pause & Reflect

Review the details you underlined. Then complete these sentences. **(Summarize)**

When Michael first sees the little girls, he

Simon is surprised at Michael's reaction because

NOTES

FOCUS

Read to find out how the woman came to adopt the two little girls.

IX

The woman, having begun talking, told them the whole story.

"It is about six years since their parents died, both in one week: their father was buried on the Tuesday, and their mother died on the Friday. These orphans were born three days after their father's death, and their mother did not live another day. My husband and I were then living as peasants in the village. We were neighbors of theirs, our yard being next to theirs. Their father was a lonely man, a wood-cutter in the forest. When felling[25] trees one day they let one fall on him. It fell across his body and crushed his bowels out. They hardly got him home before his soul went to God; and that same week his wife gave birth to twins—these little girls. She was poor and alone; she had no one, young or old, with her. Alone she gave them birth, and alone she met her death.

"The next morning I went to see her, but when I entered the hut, she, poor thing, was already stark and cold. In dying she had rolled on to this child and crushed her leg. The village folk came to the hut, washed the body, laid her out, made a coffin, and buried her. They were good folk. The babies were left alone. What was to be done with them? I was the only woman there who had a baby at the time. I was nursing my first-born—eight weeks old. So I took them for a time. The peasants came together, and thought and thought what to do with them; and at last they said to me: 'For the present, Mary, you had better keep the girls, and later on we will arrange what to do for them.' So I nursed the sound one at my breast, but at first I did not feed this crippled one. I did not suppose she would live. But then I thought to myself, why should the poor innocent suffer? I pitied her and began to feed her. And so I fed my own boy and these two—the three of them—at my own

READ ALOUD the boxed passage. Based on the woman's actions and words, what kind of person do you think she is? **(Draw Conclusions)**

25. **felling:** cutting down.

breast. I was young and strong and had good food, and God gave me so much milk that at times it even overflowed. I used sometimes to feed two at a time, while the third was waiting. When one had had enough I nursed the third. And God so ordered it that these grew up, while my own was buried before he was two years old. And I had no more children, though we prospered. Now my husband is working for the corn merchant at the mill. The pay is good and we are well off. But I have no children of my own, and how lonely I should be without these little girls! How can I help loving them! They are the joy of my life!"

She pressed the lame little girl to her with one hand, while with the other she wiped the tears from her cheeks.

And Matrëna sighed, and said: "The proverb is true that says, 'One may live without father or mother, but one cannot live without God.'"

So they talked together, when suddenly the whole hut was lighted up as though by summer lightning from the corner where Michael sat. They all looked towards him and saw him sitting, his hands folded on his knees, gazing upwards and smiling.

Pause & Reflect

X

FOCUS

Read to find out who Michael really is and what he had to learn about humans.

The woman went away with the girls. Michael rose from the bench, put down his work, and took off his apron. Then, bowing low to Simon and his wife, he said: "Farewell, masters. God has forgiven me. I ask your forgiveness, too, for anything done amiss."

And they saw that a light shone from Michael. And Simon rose, bowed down to Michael, and said: "I see,

Pause & Reflect

1. How does the woman feel about the girls she adopted? **(Infer)**

2. Reread the boxed passage on this page. Why do you think Tolstoy includes this proverb in the story? **(Author's Purpose)**

3. How does Michael react to the woman's weeping? **(Cause and Effect)**

the boxed sentence at the bottom of the page. Contrast these words spoken by the dying mother with the proverb spoken by Matrëna on page 281. **(Compare and Contrast)**

Michael, that you are no common man, and I can neither keep you nor question you. Only tell me this: how is it that when I found you and brought you home, you were gloomy, and when my wife gave you food you smiled at her and became brighter? Then when the gentleman came to order the boots, you smiled again and became brighter still? And now, when this woman brought the little girls, you smiled a third time and have become as bright as day? Tell me, Michael, why does your face shine so, and why did you smile those three times?"

And Michael answered: "Light shines from me because I have been punished, but now God has pardoned[26] me. And I smiled three times, because God sent me to learn three truths, and I have learnt them. One I learnt when your wife pitied me, and that is why I smiled the first time. The second I learnt when the rich man ordered the boots, and then I smiled again. And now, when I saw those little girls, I learnt the third and last, and I smiled the third time."

And Simon said: "Tell me, Michael, what did God punish you for? and what were the three truths? that I, too, may know them."

And Michael answered: "God punished me for disobeying him. I was an angel in heaven and disobeyed God. God sent me to fetch a woman's soul. I flew to earth and saw a sick woman lying alone who had just given birth to twin girls. They moved feebly[27] at their mother's side but she could not lift them to her breast. When she saw me, she understood that God had sent me for her soul, and she wept and said: 'Angel of God! My husband has just been buried, killed by a falling tree. I have neither sister, nor aunt, nor mother: no one to care for my orphans. Do not take my soul! Let me nurse my babes, feed them, and set them on their feet before I die. Children cannot live without father or mother.' And I

26. **pardoned:** forgiven.

27. **feebly:** weakly.

hearkened[28] to her. I placed one child at her breast and gave the other into her arms, and returned to the Lord in heaven. I flew to the Lord, and said: 'I could not take the soul of the mother. Her husband was killed by a tree; the woman has twins and prays that her soul may not be taken. She says: "Let me nurse and feed my children, and set them on their feet. Children cannot live without father or mother." I have not taken her soul.' And God said: 'Go—take the mother's soul, and learn three truths: Learn What dwells in man, What is not given to man, and What men live by. When thou hast learnt these things, thou shalt return to heaven'. So I flew again to earth and took the mother's soul. The babes dropped from her breasts. Her body rolled over on the bed and crushed one babe, twisting its leg. I rose above the village, wishing to take her soul to God, but a wind seized me and my wings drooped and dropped off. Her soul rose alone to God, while I fell to earth by the roadside."

XI

FOCUS

Read to find out how Michael learned the three truths about humans.

And Simon and Matrëna understood who it was that had lived with them and whom they had clothed and fed. And they wept with awe and with joy. And the angel said: "I was alone in the field, naked. I had never known human needs, cold and hunger, till I became a man. I was famished,[29] frozen, and did not know what to do. I saw, near the field I was in, a shrine built for God, and I went to it hoping to find shelter. But the shrine

28. **hearkened:** paid attention to; listened.

29. **famished:** very, very hungry.

Pause & Reflect

1. Who is Michael, and why has God punished him? **(Clarify)**

2. What must Michael learn about humans? Check three phrases below. **(Clarify)**

- ❑ how they earn a living
- ❑ what dwells inside them
- ❑ what they live by
- ❑ how they get to heaven
- ❑ what is not given to them to know

NOTES

READ ALOUD the boxed passage. What change took place in Simon that Michael recognized as "the presence of God"? **(Infer)**

was locked and I could not enter. So I sat down behind the shrine to shelter myself at least from the wind. Evening drew on, I was hungry, frozen, and in pain. Suddenly I heard a man coming along the road. He carried a pair of boots and was talking to himself. For the first time since I became a man I saw the mortal[30] face of a man, and his face seemed terrible to me and I turned from it. And I heard the man talking to himself of how to cover his body from the cold in winter, and how to feed his wife and children. And I thought: 'I am perishing of cold and hunger and here is a man thinking only of how to clothe himself and his wife, and how to get bread for themselves. He cannot help me.' When the man saw me he frowned and became still more terrible and passed me by on the other side. I despaired;[31] but suddenly I heard him coming back. I looked up and did not recognize the same man: before, I had seen death in his face; but now he was alive and I recognized in him the presence of God. He came up to me, clothed me, took me with him, and brought me to his home. I entered the house; a woman came to meet us and began to speak. The woman was still more terrible than the man had been; the spirit of death came from her mouth; I could not breathe for the stench[32] of death that spread around her. She wished to drive me out into the cold, and I knew that if she did so she would die. Suddenly her husband spoke to her of God, and the woman changed at once. And when she brought me food and looked at me, I glanced at her and saw that death no longer dwelt in her; she had become alive, and in her too I saw God.

"Then I remembered the first lesson God had set me: 'Learn what dwells in man.' And I understood that in man dwells Love! I was glad that God had already begun to show me what He had promised, and I smiled for the first

30. **mortal:** human.

31. **despaired:** lost hope.

32. **stench:** foul smell.

time. But I had not yet learnt all. I did not yet know What is not given to man, and What men live by.

"I lived with you and a year passed. A man came to order boots that should wear for a year without losing shape or cracking. I looked at him, and suddenly, behind his shoulder, I saw my comrade[33]—the angel of death. None but me saw that angel; but I knew him, and knew that before the sun set he would take the rich man's soul. And I thought to myself, 'The man is making preparation for a year and does not know that he will die before evening.' And I remembered God's second saying, 'Learn what is not given to man.'

"What dwells in man I already knew. Now I learnt what is not given him. It is not given to man to know his own needs. And I smiled for the second time. I was glad to have seen my comrade angel—glad also that God had revealed to me the second saying.

"But I still did not know all. I did not know What men live by. And I lived on, waiting till God should reveal to me the last lesson. In the sixth year came the girl-twins with the woman; and I recognized the girls and heard how they had been kept alive. Having heard the story, I thought, 'Their mother besought[34] me for the children's sake, and I believed her when she said that children cannot live without father or mother; but a stranger has nursed them and has brought them up.' And when the woman showed her love for the children that were not her own and wept over them, I saw in her the living God, and understood What men live by. And I knew that God had revealed to me the last lesson and had forgiven my sin. And then I smiled for the third time."

Pause & Reflect

33. **comrade:** friend.

34. **besought:** begged.

Pause & Reflect

Briefly explain each truth that Michael learns about humans. **(Paraphrase)**

What Dwells in Man

What Is Not Given to Man

What Men Live By

NOTES

XII

FOCUS

Read to find out what happens to Michael at the end of the story.

And the angel's body was bared, and he was clothed in light so that eye could not look on him; and his voice grew louder, as though it came not from him but from heaven above. And the angel said: "I have learnt that all men live not by care for themselves, but by love.

"It was not given to the mother to know what her children needed for their life. Nor was it given to the rich man to know what he himself needed. Nor is it given to any man to know whether, when evening comes, he will need boots for his body or slippers for his corpse.

"I remained alive when I was a man, not by care of myself but because love was present in a passer-by and because he and his wife pitied and loved me. The orphans remained alive not because of their mother's care, but because there was love in the heart of a woman, a stranger to them, who pitied and loved them. And all men live not by the thought they spend on their own welfare, but because love exists in man.

"I knew before that God gave life to men and desires that they should live; now I understood more than that.

"I understood that God does not wish men to live apart, and therefore he does not reveal to them what each one needs for himself; but he wishes them to live united, and therefore reveals to each of them what is necessary for all.

"I have now understood that though it seems to men that they live by care for themselves, in truth it is love alone by which they live. He who has love, is in God, and God is in him, for God is love."

And the angel sang praise to God, so that the hut trembled at his voice. The roof opened, and a column of fire rose from earth to heaven. Simon and his wife and children fell to the ground. Wings appeared upon the angel's shoulders and he rose into the heavens.

And when Simon came to himself the hut stood as before, and there was no one in it but his own family. ❖

Pause & Reflect

Pause & Reflect

1. According to Michael, what kept him alive when he was a man? Circle one phrase below. **(Clarify)**

   his love of himself

   the love that others gave to him

2. Read aloud the boxed text. What details help you imagine what happens to Michael at the end of the story? **(Visualize)**

At times in the story, Tolstoy gives clues that suggest that Michael is different from ordinary humans. Go back through the story and underline these clues. **(Analyze)**

Active Reading SkillBuilder

Predicting

A **prediction** is a reasonable guess about what will happen. In literature, when making predictions, people consider the characters, setting, and events of a story. They also consider hints, or **foreshadowing,** that the author gives in a story. "What Men Live By" is full of mysterious events, many of which are examples of foreshadowing. As you read the story, write down questions about these strange events as they occur. Then write a brief **prediction** that might answer each question. The chart has been started for you.

Question	Prediction
Who's the stranger that appears in section 1?	*a messenger from God*

FOR USE WITH **What Men Live By**

Literary Analysis SkillBuilder

Foreshadowing

In a short story, a writer may use hints or clues to suggest events that will occur later. This technique, called **foreshadowing,** creates suspense and prepares readers for what is to come. The use of foreshadowing often points readers to significant developments in the story. Use the chart below to list examples of foreshadowing in "What Men Live By." The chart has been started for you.

Example of Foreshadowing	What it Foreshadows
Matrëna says that death cannot touch the wealthy man.	*The wealthy man dies.*

Before You Read

Connect to Your Life

"As Gregor Samsa awoke one morning from uneasy dreams he found himself transformed in his bed into a gigantic insect." So begins Franz Kafka's unforgettable story "Metamorphosis." Imagine yourself in Gregor's situation. What would you do? What thoughts might go through your mind? How might your family respond? Write your ideas below.

If I woke up as a giant bug . . .

What I would think:	What I would do:	How my family might respond:

Key to the Story

WHAT'S THE BIG IDEA? Kafka's story draws upon the traditions of mythology and folklore, which are filled with stories of metamorphosis. A **metamorphosis** is a transformation from one state to another: a Greek god becomes a swan; a man turns into a donkey. In "Metamorphosis," Kafka blends fantastic elements with detailed descriptions of everyday life to create a convincing, disturbing tale.

Fiction

METAMORPHOSIS

by FRANZ KAFKA

Translated by
Willa and Edwin Muir

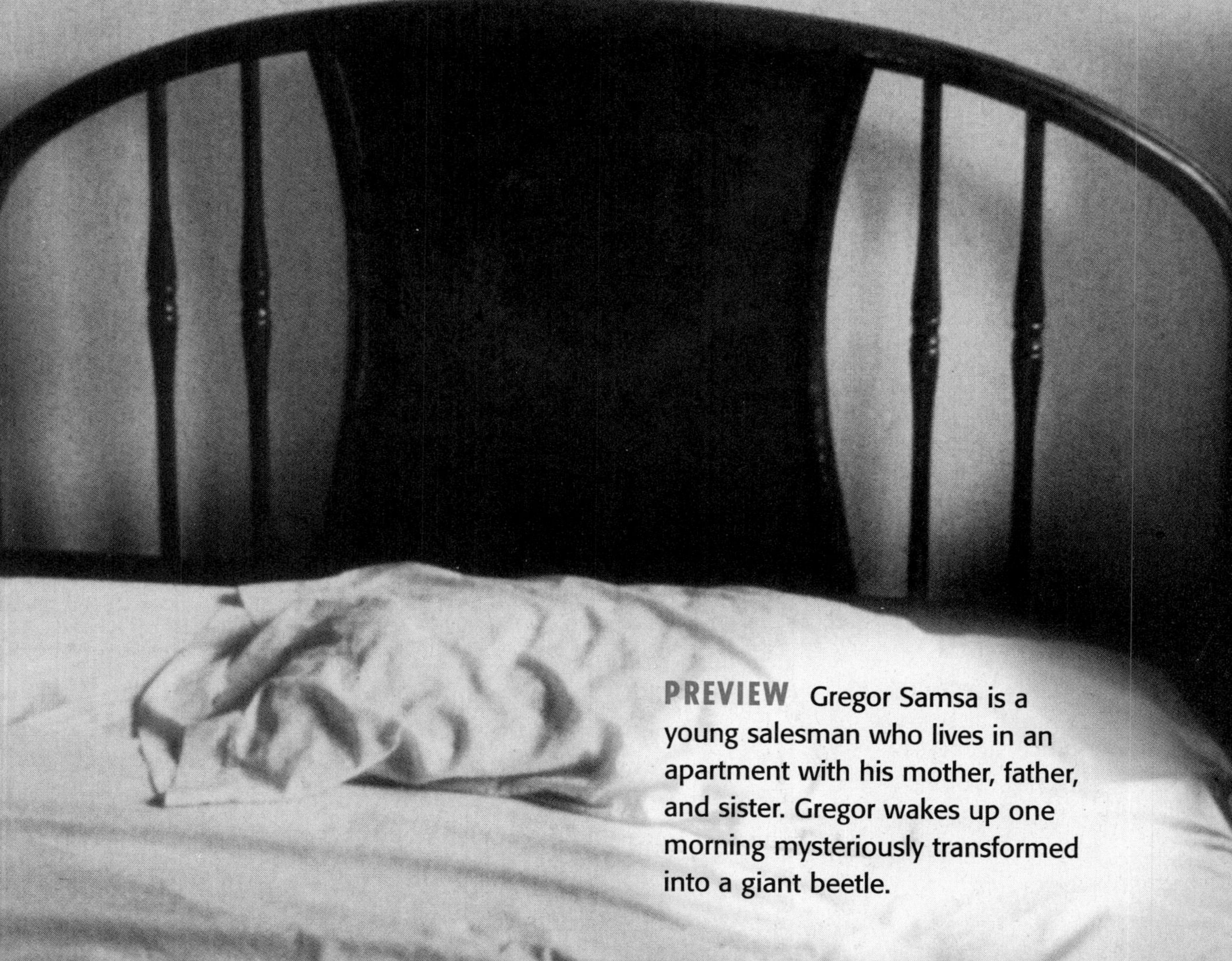

PREVIEW Gregor Samsa is a young salesman who lives in an apartment with his mother, father, and sister. Gregor wakes up one morning mysteriously transformed into a giant beetle.

This story is based on an unrealistic event. As you read, don't worry about whether or not you find it believable. Try to accept it for what it is and pay attention to how this bizarre event affects the characters in the story.

MARK IT UP **KEEP TRACK**
Remember to use these marks to keep track of your reading:

* * This is important.
* ? I have a question about this.
* ! This is a surprise.

I

FOCUS
Read the first part of the story to find out how Gregor reacts at first to his very strange situation.
MARK IT UP Underline the things that Gregor worries about.

As Gregor Samsa awoke one morning from uneasy dreams he found himself transformed in his bed into a gigantic insect. He was lying on his hard, as it were armor-plated, back and when he lifted his head a little he could see his domelike brown belly divided into stiff arched segments on top of which the bed quilt could hardly keep in position and was about to slide off completely. His numerous legs, which were pitifully thin compared to the rest of his bulk, waved helplessly before his eyes.

What has happened to me? he thought. It was no dream. His room, a regular human bedroom, only rather too small, lay quiet between the four familiar walls. Above the table on which a collection of cloth samples was unpacked and spread out—Samsa was a commercial traveler[1]—hung the picture which he had recently cut out of an illustrated magazine and put into a pretty gilt frame. It showed a lady, with a fur cap on and a fur stole, sitting upright and holding out to the spectator a huge fur muff into which the whole of her forearm had vanished!

Gregor's eyes turned next to the window, and the overcast sky—one could hear raindrops beating on the window gutter—made him quite melancholy.[2] What about sleeping a little longer and forgetting all this nonsense, he thought, but it could not be done, for he was accustomed to sleep on his right side and in his present condition he could not turn himself over. However violently he forced himself toward his right side he always rolled onto his back

1. **commercial traveler:** traveling salesperson.
2. **melancholy** (mĕl′ən-kŏl′ē): sad or depressed.

again. He tried it at least a hundred times, shutting his eyes to keep from seeing his struggling legs, and only desisted when he began to feel in his side a faint dull ache he had never experienced before.

Oh God, he thought, what an exhausting job I've picked on! Traveling about day in, day out. It's much more irritating work than doing the actual business in the office, and on top of that there's the trouble of constant traveling, of worrying about train connections, the bed and irregular meals, casual acquaintances that are always new and never become intimate friends. The devil take it all! He felt a slight itching up on his belly; slowly pushed himself on his back nearer to the top of the bed so that he could lift his head more easily; identified the itching place which was surrounded by many small white spots the nature of which he could not understand and made to touch it with a leg, but drew the leg back immediately, for the contact made a cold shiver run through him.

He slid down again into his former position. This getting up early, he thought, makes one quite stupid. A man needs his sleep. Other commercials live like harem women.[3] For instance, when I come back to the hotel of a morning to write up the orders I've got, these others are only sitting down to the breakfast. Let me just try that with my chief; I'd be sacked on the spot. Anyhow, that might be quite a good thing for me, who can tell? If I didn't have to hold my hand[4] because of my parents I'd have given notice long ago, I'd have gone to the chief and told him exactly what I think of him. That would knock him endways from his desk! It's a queer way of doing, too, this sitting on high at a desk and talking down to employees, especially when they have to come quite near because the chief is hard of hearing. Well, there's still hope; once I've saved enough money to pay back my parents' debts to him—that should take another

NOTES
REREAD
the boxed text. What can you tell about Gregor and his boss, the chief? **(Infer)**

3. **Other commercials . . . :** people in other kinds of jobs live a much easier life.

4. **hold my hand:** hold back.

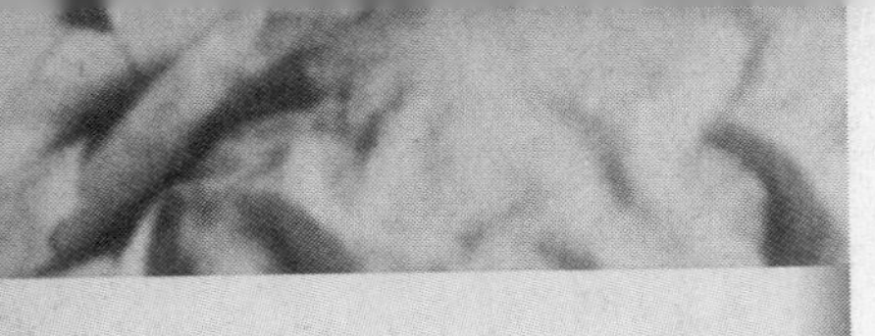

Pause & Reflect

1. What kinds of things does Gregor worry about? **(Summarize)**

2. What is strange or surprising about these things? **(Analyze)**

MARK IT UP

WORD POWER Remember to use words that you'd like to add to your **Personal Word List**. Later, You can record the words and their meanings beginning on page 000.

five or six years—I'll do it without fail. I'll cut myself completely loose then. For the moment, though, I'd better get up, since my train goes at five.

He looked at the alarm clock ticking on the chest. Heavenly Father! he thought. It was half-past six o'clock and the hands were quietly moving on, it was even past the half-hour, it was getting on toward a quarter to seven. Had the alarm clock not gone off? From the bed one could see that it had been properly set for four o'clock; of course it must have gone off. Yes, but was it possible to sleep quietly through that ear-splitting noise? Well, he had not slept quietly, yet apparently all the more soundly for that. But what was he to do now? The next train went at seven o'clock; to catch that he would need to hurry like mad and his samples weren't even packed up, and he himself wasn't feeling particularly fresh and active. And even if he did catch the train he wouldn't avoid a row[5] with the chief, since the firm's porter would have been waiting for the five o'clock train and would have long since reported his failure to turn up. The porter was a creature of the chief's, spineless and stupid. Well, supposing he were to say he was sick? But that would be most unpleasant and would look suspicious, since during his five years' employment he had not been ill once. The chief himself would be sure to come with the sick-insurance doctor, would reproach his parents with their son's laziness, and would cut all excuses short by referring to the insurance doctor, who of course regarded all mankind as perfectly healthy malingerers.[6] And would he be so far wrong on this occasion? Gregor really felt quite well, apart from a drowsiness that was utterly superfluous after such a long sleep, and he was even unusually hungry.

Pause & Reflect

5. **row** (rou): disagreement; fight.
6. **malingerers** (mə-lĭng′gər-ərz): people who pretend to be sick in order to avoid work.

FOCUS

When Gregor's family realizes that he hasn't yet left for work, they come to his door. Find out what he tells them.

As all this was running through his mind at top speed without his being able to decide to leave his bed—the alarm clock had just struck a quarter to seven—there came a cautious tap at the door behind the head of his bed. "Gregor," said a voice—it was his mother's—"it's a quarter to seven. Hadn't you a train to catch?" That gentle voice! Gregor had a shock as he heard his own voice answering hers, unmistakably his own voice, it was true, but with a persistent horrible twittering squeak behind it like an undertone, which left the words in their clear shape only for the first moment and then rose up reverberating around them to destroy their sense, so that one could not be sure one had heard them rightly. Gregor wanted to answer at length and explain everything, but in the circumstances he confined himself to saying: "Yes, yes, thank you, Mother, I'm getting up now." The wooden door between them must have kept the change in his voice from being noticeable outside, for his mother contented herself with this statement and shuffled away. Yet this brief exchange of words had made the other members of the family aware that Gregor was still in the house, as they had not expected, and at one of the side doors his father was already knocking, gently, yet with his fist. "Gregor, Gregor," he called, "What's the matter with you?" And after a little while he called again in a deeper voice: "Gregor! Gregor!" At the other side door his sister was saying in a low, plaintive[7] tone: "Gregor? Aren't you well? Are you needing anything?" He answered them both at once: "I'm just ready," and did his best to make his voice sound as normal as possible by enunciating the words very clearly and leaving long pauses between them. So his father went back to his breakfast, but his sister whispered: "Gregor, open the door, do." However, he was not thinking

READING TIP In this story, a change of speaker is not always signaled by a new paragraph. Instead, single paragraphs often contain many changes in speaker. You may find it helpful to reread the passages that contain dialogue to check that you understand who is speaking.

7. **plaintive** (plān′tĭv): sorrowful; sad.

NOTES

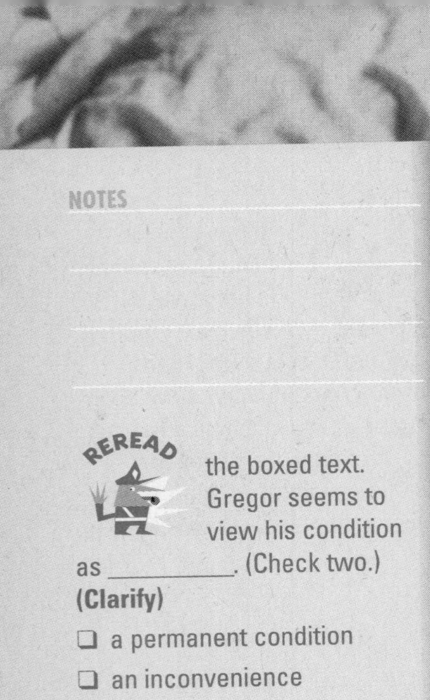

the boxed text. Gregor seems to view his condition as __________. (Check two.) **(Clarify)**

- ❑ a permanent condition
- ❑ an inconvenience
- ❑ a horrifying event
- ❑ a minor illness

of opening the door, and felt thankful for the prudent[8] habit he had acquired in traveling of locking all doors during the night, even at home.

His immediate intention was to get up quietly without being disturbed, to put on his clothes, and above all eat his breakfast, and only then consider what else was to be done, since in bed, he was well aware, his meditations would come to no sensible conclusion. He remembered that often enough in bed he had felt small aches and pains, probably caused by awkward postures, which had proved purely imaginary once he got up, and he looked forward eagerly to seeing this morning's delusions gradually fall away. That the change in his voice was nothing but the precursor[9] of a severe chill, a standing ailment of commercial travelers, he had not the least possible doubt.

To get rid of the quilt was quite easy; he had only to inflate himself a little and it fell off by itself. But the next move was difficult, especially because he was so uncommonly broad. He would have needed arms and hands to hoist himself up; instead he had only the numerous little legs which never stopped waving in all directions and which he could not control in the least. When he tried to bend one of them it was the first to stretch itself straight; and did he succeed at last in making it do what he wanted, all the other legs meanwhile waved the more wildly in a high degree of unpleasant agitation. "But what's the use of lying idle in bed," said Gregor to himself.

He thought that he might get out of bed with the lower part of his body first, but this lower part, which he had not yet seen and of which he could form no clear conception, proved too difficult to move; it shifted so slowly; and when finally, almost wild with annoyance, he gathered his forces together and thrust out recklessly, he had miscalculated the direction and bumped heavily against the lower end of the bed, and the stinging pain he felt informed him that

8. **prudent** (prŭ′dənt): careful.

9. **precursor:** something that comes before; forerunner.

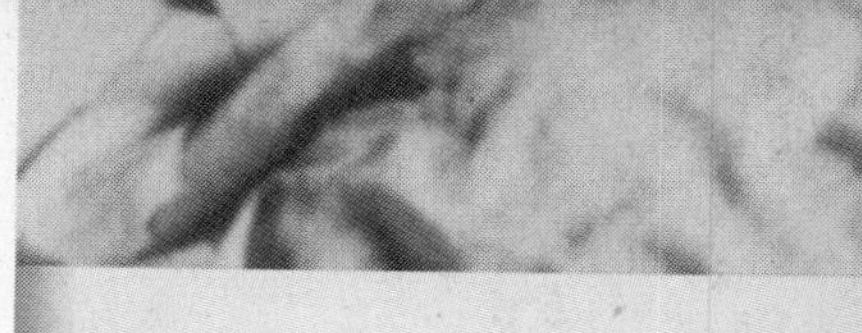

precisely this lower part of his body was at the moment probably the most sensitive.

So he tried to get the top part of himself out first, and cautiously moved his head toward the edge of the bed. That proved easy enough, and despite its breadth and mass the bulk of his body at last slowly followed the movement of his head. Still, when he finally got his head free over the edge of the bed he felt too scared to go on advancing, for after all if he let himself fall in this way it would take a miracle to keep his head from being injured. And at all costs he must not lose consciousness now, precisely now; he would rather stay in bed.

But when after a repetition of the same efforts he lay in his former position again, sighing, and watched his little legs struggling against each other more wildly than ever, if that were possible, and saw no way of bringing any order into this arbitrary confusion, he told himself again that it was impossible to stay in bed and that the most sensible course was to risk everything for the smallest hope of getting away from it. At the same time he did not forget to remind himself occasionally that cool reflection, the coolest possible, was much better than desperate resolves.[10] In such moments he focused his eyes as sharply as possible on the window, but, unfortunately, the prospect of the morning fog, which muffled even the other side of the narrow street, brought him little encouragement and comfort. "Seven o'clock already," he said to himself when the alarm clock chimed again, "seven o'clock already and still such a thick fog." And for a little while he lay quiet, breathing lightly, as if perhaps expecting such complete repose to restore all things to their real and normal condition.

But then he said to himself: "Before it strikes a quarter past seven I must be quite out of this bed, without fail. Anyhow, by that time someone will have come from the office to ask for me, since it opens before seven." And he set himself to rocking his whole body at once in a regular

10. desperate resolves: decisions made while feeling panicked.

NOTES

the boxed text. List the advantages Gregor sees in trying to get out of bed. Then list the advantages he sees in staying there. **(Analyze)**

Advantages of . . .

Getting Up	Staying in Bed

NOTES

the boxed text. If you were Gregor, would you call for help? Why or why not? **(Connect)**

rhythm, with the idea of swinging it out of the bed. If he tipped himself out in that way he could keep his head from injury by lifting it at an acute angle when he fell. His back seemed to be hard and was not likely to suffer from a fall on the carpet. His biggest worry was the loud crash he would not be able to help making, which would probably cause anxiety, if not terror, behind all the doors. Still, he must take the risk.

When he was already half out of the bed—the new method was more a game than an effort, for he needed only to hitch himself across by rocking to and fro—it struck him how simple it would be if he could get help. Two strong people—he thought of his father and the servant girl—would be amply sufficient; they would only have to thrust their arms under his convex[11] back, lever him out of the bed, bend down with their burden, and then be patient enough to let him turn himself right over onto the floor, where it was to be hoped his legs would then find their proper function. Well, ignoring the fact that the doors were all locked, ought he really to call for help? In spite of his misery he could not suppress a smile at the very idea of it.

He had got so far that he could barely keep his equilibrium when he rocked himself strongly, and he would have to nerve himself very soon for the final decision since in five minutes' time it would be quarter past seven—when the front doorbell rang. "That's someone from the office," he said to himself, and grew almost rigid, while his little legs only jigged about all the faster. For a moment everything stayed quiet. "They're not going to open the door," said Gregor to himself, catching at some kind of irrational hope. But then of course the servant girl went as usual to the door with her heavy tread and opened it. Gregor needed only to hear the first good morning of the visitor to know immediately who it was—the chief clerk himself. What a

11. **convex:** curved outward.

WORDS TO KNOW
equilibrium (ē'kwə-lĭb'rē-əm) *n.* a stable or balanced condition

fate, to be condemned to work for a firm where the smallest omission at once gave rise to the gravest suspicion! Were all employees in a body nothing but scoundrels, was there not among them one single loyal devoted man who, had he wasted only an hour or so of the firm's time in a morning, was so tormented by conscience as to be driven out of his mind and actually incapable of leaving his bed? Wouldn't it really have been sufficient to send an apprentice to inquire—if any inquiry were necessary at all—did the chief clerk himself have to come and thus indicate to the entire family, an innocent family, that this suspicious circumstance could be investigated by no one less versed in affairs than himself? And more through the agitation caused by these reflections than through any act of will Gregor swung himself out of bed with all his strength. There was a loud thump, but it was not really a crash. His fall was broken to some extent by the carpet, his back, too, was less stiff than he thought, and so there was merely a dull thud, not so very startling. Only he had not lifted his head carefully enough and had hit it; he turned it and rubbed it on the carpet in pain and irritation.

Pause & Reflect

FOCUS

The chief clerk tries to bully Gregor into opening the door. Find out how Gregor responds to the chief's demands.

MARK IT UP As you read, put a star next to each accusation the chief clerk makes against Gregor.

"That was something falling down in there," said the chief clerk in the next room to the left. Gregor tried to suppose to himself that something like what had happened to him today might someday happen to the chief clerk; one really could not deny that it was possible. But as if in brusque[12] reply to this

12. **brusque:** quick and rather rude.

WORDS TO KNOW
omission (ō-mĭsh′ən) *n.* an act of leaving out, passing over, or neglecting

Pause & Reflect

1. What is Gregor's strategy for dealing with his situation? Check two. **(Analyze)**
   - ❑ Pretend everything is fine.
   - ❑ Tell people the truth.
   - ❑ Hold people off.
   - ❑ Go back to sleep.

2. Who rings the front doorbell? How does Gregor feel about the visitor? **(Infer)**

NOTES

READING TIP A semicolon (;) is used to link independent clauses, which can also stand on their own as complete sentences. In Mrs. Samsa's speech, as many as four sentences are connected by semicolons. In doing this, the author shows readers that Mrs. Samsa is speaking quickly and nervously, giving detail after detail to prove to the chief that Gregor is devoted to his job.

supposition[13] the chief clerk took a couple of firm steps in the next-door room and his patent leather boots creaked. From the right-hand room his sister was whispering to inform him of the situation: "Gregor, the chief clerk's here." "I know," muttered Gregor to himself; but he didn't dare to make his voice loud enough for his sister to hear it.

"Gregor," said his father now from the left-hand room, "the chief clerk has come and wants to know why you didn't catch the early train. We don't know what to say to him. Besides, he wants to talk to you in person. So open the door, please. He will be good enough to excuse the untidiness of your room." "Good morning, Mr. Samsa," the chief clerk was calling amiably meanwhile. "He's not well," said his mother to the visitor, while his father was still speaking through the door, "he's not well, sir, believe me. What else would make him miss a train! The boy thinks about nothing but his work. It makes me almost cross the way he never goes out in the evenings; he's been here the last eight days and has stayed at home every single evening. He just sits there quietly at the table reading a newspaper or looking through railway timetables. The only amusement he gets is doing fretwork.[14] For instance, he spent two or three evenings cutting out a little picture frame; you would be surprised to see how pretty it is; it's hanging in his room; you'll see it in a minute when Gregor opens the door. I must say I'm glad you've come, sir; we should never have got him to unlock the door by ourselves; he's so obstinate; and I'm sure he's unwell, though he wouldn't have it to be so this morning." "I'm just coming," said Gregor slowly and carefully, not moving an inch for fear of losing one word of the conversation. "I can't think of any other explanation, madame," said the chief clerk, "I hope it's nothing serious. Although on the other hand

---

13. **supposition:** assumption.

14. **fretwork:** ornamental woodworking.

WORDS TO KNOW
amiably (ā′mē-ə-blē) *adv.* in a friendly manner; pleasantly

I must say that we men of business—fortunately or unfortunately—very often simply have to ignore any slight indisposition,[15] since business must be attended to."

"Well, can the chief clerk come in now?" asked Gregor's father impatiently, again knocking on the door. "No," said Gregor. In the left-hand room a painful silence followed this refusal, in the right-hand room his sister began to sob.

Why didn't his sister join the others? She was probably newly out of bed and hadn't even begun to put on her clothes yet. Well, why was she crying? Because he wouldn't get up and let the chief clerk in, because he was in danger of losing his job, and because the chief would begin dunning[16] his parents again for the old debts? Surely these were things one didn't need to worry about for the present. Gregor was still at home and not in the least thinking of deserting the family. At the moment, true, he was lying on the carpet and no one who knew the condition he was in could seriously expect him to admit the chief clerk. But for such a small discourtesy, which could plausibly be explained away somehow later on, Gregor could hardly be dismissed on the spot. And it seemed to Gregor that it would be much more sensible to leave him in peace for the present than to trouble him with tears and entreaties.[17] Still, of course, their uncertainty bewildered them all and excused their behavior.

"Mr. Samsa," the chief clerk called now in a louder voice, "what's the matter with you? Here you are, barricading yourself in your room, giving only 'yes' and 'no' for answers, causing your parents a lot of unnecessary trouble and neglecting—I mention this only in passing—neglecting your business duties in an incredible fashion. I am speaking here in the name of your parents and of your chief, and I beg you quite seriously to give me an immediate and precise explanation. You amaze me, you amaze me. I thought you were a quiet, dependable person, and now all at once you

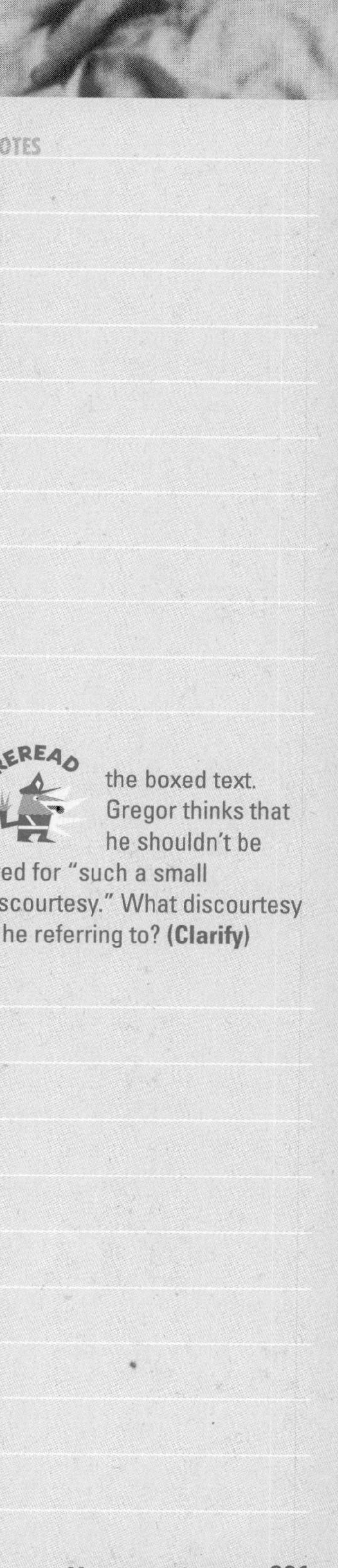

NOTES
REREAD
the boxed text. Gregor thinks that he shouldn't be fired for "such a small discourtesy." What discourtesy is he referring to? **(Clarify)**

15. **indisposition:** minor illness.

16. **dunning:** pestering for payment.

17. **entreaties:** desperate requests.

NOTES

READ ALOUD the boxed text. How would you describe Gregor's speech? **(Analyze)**

seem bent on making a disgraceful exhibition of yourself. The chief did hint to me early this morning a possible explanation for your disappearance—with reference to the cash payments that were entrusted to you recently—but I almost pledged my solemn word of honor that this could not be so. But now that I see how incredibly obstinate you are, I no longer have the slightest desire to take your part at all. And your position in the firm is not so unassailable.[18] I came with the intention of telling you all this in private, but since you are wasting my time so needlessly I don't see why your parents shouldn't hear it too. For some time past your work has been most unsatisfactory; this is not the season of the year for a business boom, of course, we admit that, but a season of the year for doing no business at all, that does not exist, Mr. Samsa, must not exist."

"But, sir," cried Gregor, beside himself and in his agitation forgetting everything else, "I'm just going to open the door this very minute. A slight illness, an attack of giddiness, has kept me from getting up. I'm still lying in bed. But I feel all right again. I'm getting out of bed now. Just give me a moment or two longer! I'm not quite so well as I thought. But I'm all right, really. How a thing like that can suddenly strike me down! Only last night I was quite well, my parents can tell you, or rather I did have a slight presentiment.[19] I must have showed some sign of it. Why didn't I report it at the office! But one always thinks that an indisposition can be got over without staying in the house. Oh sir, do spare my parents! All that you're reproaching me with now has no foundation; no one has ever said a word to me about it. Perhaps you haven't looked at the last orders I sent in. Anyhow, I can still catch the eight o'clock train, I'm much better for my few hours' rest. Don't let me detain you here, sir; I'll be attending to business very soon, and do be good enough to tell the chief so and to make my excuses to him!"

18. unassailable (ŭn′ə-sā′lə-bəl): safe from question or attack.

19. presentiment (prĭ-zĕn′tə-mənt): feeling that something is going to happen.

And while all this was tumbling out pell-mell and Gregor hardly knew what he was saying, he had reached the chest quite easily, perhaps because of the practice he had had in bed, and was now trying to lever himself upright by means of it. He meant actually to open the door, actually to show himself and speak to the chief clerk; he was eager to find out what the others, after all their insistence, would say at the sight of him. If they were horrified then the responsibility was no longer his and he could stay quiet. But if they took it calmly, then he had no reason either to be upset, and could really get to the station for the eight o'clock train if he hurried. At first he slipped down a few times from the polished surface of the chest, but at length with a last heave he stood upright; he paid no more attention to the pains in the lower part of his body, however they smarted. Then he let himself fall against the back of a nearby chair, and clung with his little legs to the edges of it. That brought him into control of himself again and he stopped speaking, for now he could listen to what the chief clerk was saying.

"Did you understand a word of it?" the chief clerk was asking; "surely he can't be trying to make fools of us?" "Oh dear," cried his mother, in tears, "perhaps he's terribly ill and we're tormenting him. Grete! Grete!" she called out then. "Yes Mother?" called his sister from the other side. They were calling to each other across Gregor's room. "You must go this minute for the doctor. Gregor is ill. Go for the doctor, quick. Did you hear how he was speaking?" "That was no human voice," said the chief clerk in a voice noticeably low beside the shrillness of the mother's. "Anna! Anna!" his father was calling through the hall to the kitchen, clapping his hands, "get a locksmith at once!" And the two girls were already running through the hall with a swish of skirts—how could his sister have got dressed so quickly?—and were tearing the front door open. There was no sound of its closing again; they had evidently left it open, as one does in houses where some great misfortune has happened.

Pause & Reflect

Pause & Reflect

1. What has the chief clerk accused Gregor of? Check three. **(Clarify)**

- ❑ having an illness
- ❑ being a disgrace
- ❑ being a bug
- ❑ stealing money
- ❑ ignoring his work

2. When Gregor answers the chief clerk, everyone panics. Why are people so horrified by Gregor's response? **(Draw Conclusions)**

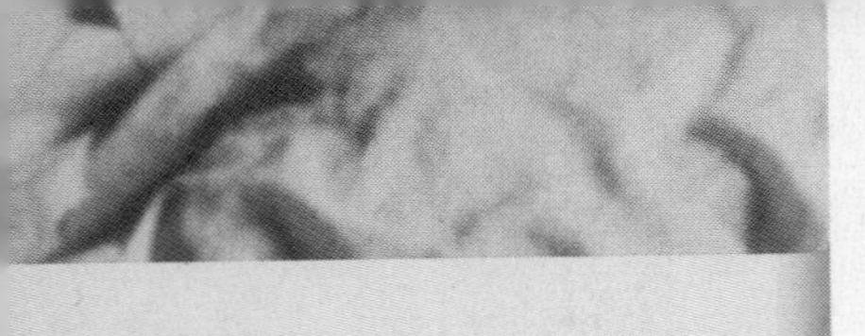

NOTES

FOCUS

Gregor manages to unlock the door and let himself into the hallway. Find out what happens when the others see him.

MARK IT UP Underline the details that help you picture how each person reacts to Gregor's appearance.

But Gregor was now much calmer. The words he uttered were no longer understandable, apparently, although they seemed clear enough to him, even clearer than before, perhaps because his ear had grown accustomed to the sound of them. Yet at any rate people now believed that something was wrong with him, and were ready to help him. The positive certainty with which these first measures had been taken comforted him. He felt himself drawn once more into the human circle and hoped for great and remarkable results from both the doctor and the locksmith, without really distinguishing precisely between them. To make his voice as clear as possible for the decisive conversation that was now imminent he coughed a little, as quietly as he could, of course, since this noise too might not sound like a human cough for all he was able to judge. In the next room meanwhile there was complete silence. Perhaps his parents were sitting at the table with the chief clerk, whispering, perhaps they were all leaning against the door and listening.

Slowly Gregor pushed the chair toward the door, then let go of it, caught hold of the door for support—the soles at the end of his little legs were somewhat sticky—and rested against it for a moment after his efforts. Then he set himself to turning the key in the lock with his mouth. It seemed, unhappily, that he hadn't really any teeth—what could he grip the key with?—but on the other hand his jaws were certainly very strong; with their help he did manage to set the key in motion, heedless of the fact that he was undoubtedly damaging them somewhere, since a brown fluid issued from his mouth, flowed over the key,

WORDS TO KNOW

imminent (ĭm′ə-nənt) *adj.* about to happen

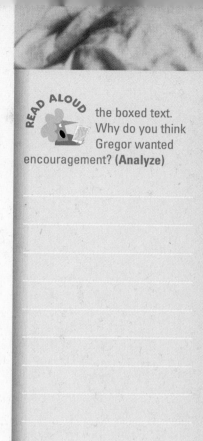

and dripped on the floor. "Just listen to that," said the chief clerk next door; "he's turning the key." That was a great encouragement to Gregor; but they should all have shouted encouragement to him, his father and mother too: "Go on, Gregor," they should have called out, "keep going, hold on to that key!" And in the belief that they were all following his efforts intently, he clenched his jaws recklessly on the key with all the force at his command. As the turning of the key progressed he circled around the lock, holding on now only with his mouth, pushing on the key, as required, or pulling it down again with all the weight of his body. The louder click of the finally yielding lock literally quickened Gregor. With a deep breath of relief he said to himself: "So I didn't need the locksmith," and laid his head on the handle to open the door wide.

Since he had to pull the door toward him, he was still invisible when it was really wide open. He had to edge himself slowly around the near half of the double door, and to do it very carefully if he was not to fall plump upon his back just on the threshold. He was still carrying out this difficult maneuver, with no time to observe anything else, when he heard the chief clerk utter a loud "Oh!"—it seemed like a gust of wind—and now he could see the man, standing as he was nearest to the door, clapping one hand before his open mouth and slowly backing away as if driven by some invisible steady pressure. His mother—in spite of the chief clerk's being there her hair was still undone and sticking up in all directions—first clasped her hands and looked at his father, then took two steps toward Gregor and fell on the floor among her outspread skirts, her face quite hidden on her breast. His father knotted his fist with a fierce expression on his face as if he meant to knock Gregor back into his room, then looked uncertainly around the living room, covered his eyes with his hands, and wept till his great chest heaved.

Gregor did not go now into the living room, but leaned against the inside of the firmly shut wing of the door, so

the boxed text. Why do you think Gregor wanted encouragement? **(Analyze)**

that only half his body was visible and his head above it bending sideways to look at the others. The light had meanwhile strengthened; on the other side of the street one could see clearly a section of the endless long, dark gray building opposite—it was a hospital—abruptly punctuated by its row of regular windows; the rain was still falling, but only in large singly discernible and literally singly splashing drops.[20] The breakfast dishes were set out on the table lavishly, for breakfast was the most important meal of the day to Gregor's father, who lingered it out for hours over various newspapers. Right opposite Gregor on the wall hung a photograph of himself in military service, as a lieutenant, hand on sword, a carefree smile on his face, inviting one to respect his uniform and military bearing.[21] The door leading to the hall was open, and one could see that the front door stood open too, showing the landing beyond and the beginning of the stairs going down.

"Well," said Gregor, knowing perfectly that he was the only one who had retained any composure, "I'll put my clothes on at once, pack up my samples, and start off. Will you only let me go? You see, sir, I'm not obstinate, and I'm willing to work; traveling is a hard life, but I couldn't live without it. Where are you going, sir? To the office? Yes? Will you give a true account of all this? One can be temporarily incapacitated, but that's just the moment for remembering former services and bearing in mind that later on, when the incapacity has been got over, one will certainly work with all the more industry and concentration. I'm loyally bound to serve the chief, you know that very well. Besides, I have to provide for my parents and my sister. I'm in great difficulties, but I'll get out of them again. Don't make things any worse for me than they are. Stand up for me in the firm. Travelers are not popular there, I know. People think they earn sacks

NOTES

READ ALOUD the boxed text. How do you think the chief clerk will respond to Gregor's request? **(Predict)**

---

20. large singly discernible . . . : large, easily visible drops.

21. military bearing: way of standing as a proper soldier does.

WORDS TO KNOW
lavishly (lăv′ĭsh-lē) *adv.* very freely and abundantly

of money and just have a good time. A prejudice there's no particular reason for revising. But you, sir, have a more comprehensive view of affairs than the rest of the staff, yes, let me tell you in confidence, a more comprehensive view of affairs than the chief himself, who, being the owner, lets his judgment easily be swayed against one of his employees. And you know very well that the traveler, who is never seen in the office almost the whole year around, can so easily fall a victim to gossip and ill luck and unfounded complaints, which he mostly knows nothing about, except when he comes back exhausted from his rounds, and only then suffers in person from their evil consequences, which he can no longer trace back to the original causes. Sir, sir, don't go away without a word to me to show that you think me in the right at least to some extent!"

But at Gregor's very first words the chief clerk had already backed away and only stared at him with parted lips over one twitching shoulder. And while Gregor was speaking he did not stand still one moment but stole away toward the door, without taking his eyes off Gregor, yet only an inch at a time, as if obeying some secret injunction to leave the room. He was already at the hall, and the suddenness with which he took his last step out of the living room would have made one believe he had burned the sole of his foot. Once in the hall he stretched his right arm before him toward the staircase, as if some supernatural power were waiting there to deliver him.

Pause & Reflect

FOCUS

Gregor wants to stop the chief clerk from leaving on an unpleasant note. Find out what happens when he tries to communicate.

Gregor perceived that the chief clerk must on no account be allowed to go away in this frame of mind if his position in the firm were not to be endan-

Pause & Reflect

1. All things considered, would you say that Gregor's family and boss responded well to Gregor's new appearance? Explain. **(Make Judgments)**

2. Which statement best summarizes Gregor's reaction to his own transformation? Circle one. **(Infer)**

He is shocked to be a bug and wonders how it happened to him.

He thinks he can go on working despite being a bug.

NOTES

READ ALOUD the boxed text. Gregor believes that his new ability to move might bring "final relief from all his sufferings." What "sufferings" do you think this is referring to? **(Infer)**

gered to the utmost. His parents did not understand this so well; they had convinced themselves in the course of years that Gregor was settled for life in this firm, and besides they were so preoccupied with their immediate troubles that all foresight had forsaken them. Yet Gregor had this foresight. The chief clerk must be detained, soothed, persuaded, and finally won over; the whole future of Gregor and his family depended on it! If only his sister had been there! She was intelligent; she had begun to cry while Gregor was still lying quietly on his back. And no doubt the chief clerk, so partial to[22] ladies, would have been guided by her; she would have shut the door of the flat and in the hall talked him out of his horror. But she was not there, and Gregor would have to handle the situation himself. And without remembering that he was still unaware what powers of movement he possessed, without even remembering that his words in all possibility, indeed in all likelihood, would again be unintelligible, he let go the wing of the door, pushed himself through the opening, started to walk toward the chief clerk, who was already ridiculously clinging with both hands to the railing on the landing; but immediately, as he was feeling for a support, he fell down with a little cry upon all his numerous legs. Hardly was he down when he experienced for the first time this morning a sense of physical comfort; his legs had firm ground under them; they were completely obedient, as he noted with joy; they even strove to carry him forward in whatever direction he chose; and he was inclined to believe that a final relief from all his sufferings was at hand. But in the same moment as he found himself on the floor, rocking with suppressed eagerness to move, not far from his mother, indeed just in front of her, she, who had seemed so completely crushed, sprang all at once to her feet, her arms

22. **partial to:** having a special liking for.

WORDS TO KNOW
unintelligible (ŭn′ĭn-tĕl′ĭ-jə-bəl) *adj.* unable to be understood

and fingers outspread, cried: "Help, for God's sake, help!" bent her head down as if to see Gregor better, yet on the contrary kept backing senselessly away; had quite forgotten that the laden table[23] stood behind her; sat upon it hastily, as if in absence of mind, when she bumped into it; and seemed altogether unaware that the big coffeepot beside her was upset and pouring coffee in a flood over the carpet.

"Mother, Mother," said Gregor in a low voice, and looked up at her. The chief clerk, for the moment, had quite slipped from his mind; instead, he could not resist snapping his jaws together at the sight of the streaming coffee. That made his mother scream again, she fled from the table and fell into the arms of his father, who hastened to catch her. But Gregor had now no time to spare for his parents; the chief clerk was already on the stairs; with his chin on the banisters he was taking one last backward look. Gregor made a spring, to be as sure as possible of overtaking him; the chief clerk must have divined his intention, for he leaped down several steps and vanished; he was still yelling "Ugh!" and it echoed throughout the whole staircase.

Unfortunately, the flight of the chief clerk seemed completely to upset Gregor's father, who had remained relatively calm until now, for instead of running after the man himself, or at least not hindering Gregor in his pursuit, he seized in his right hand the walking stick that the chief clerk had left behind on a chair, together with a hat and greatcoat, snatched in his left hand a large newspaper from the table, and began stamping his feet and flourishing the stick and the newspaper to drive Gregor back into his room. No entreaty of Gregor's availed, indeed no entreaty was even understood, however humbly he bent his head his father only stamped on the floor the more loudly. Behind his father his mother had torn open a window, despite the cold weather, and was leaning far out of it with her face in her hands. A strong draught set in from the street to the staircase, the window curtains blew in, the newspapers on

23. **laden table:** table set with plates and food.

NOTES

REREAD the boxed text. Then complete the sentences. **(Infer)**

Gregor probably wishes his father would

Gregor feels

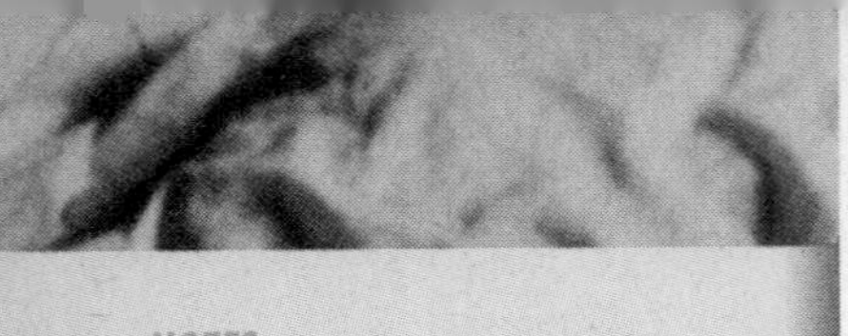

NOTES

READING TIP Visualizing this scene will help you understand why Gregor can't get back into his room. Try picturing these details:

- the narrow doorway
- the broad shape of Gregor's insect body
- how Gregor's body becomes stuck at an angle in the doorway

the table fluttered, stray pages whisked over the floor. Pitilessly Gregor's father drove him back, hissing and crying "Shoo!" like a savage. But Gregor was quite unpracticed in walking backwards, it really was a slow business. If he only had a chance to turn around he could get back to his room at once, but he was afraid of exasperating his father by the slowness of such a rotation and at any moment the stick in his father's hand might hit him a fatal blow on the back or on the head. In the end, however, nothing else was left for him to do since to his horror he observed that in moving backwards he could not even control the direction he took; and so, keeping an anxious eye on his father all the time over his shoulder, he began to turn around as quickly as he could, which was in reality very slowly. Perhaps his father noted his good intentions, for he did not interfere except every now and then to help him in the maneuver from a distance with the point of the stick. If only he would have stopped making that unbearable hissing noise! It made Gregor quite lose his head. He had turned almost completely around when the hissing noise so distracted him that he even turned a little the wrong way again. But when at last his head was fortunately right in front of the doorway, it appeared that his body was too broad simply to get through the opening. His father, of course, in his present mood was far from thinking of such a thing as opening the other half of the door, to let Gregor have enough space. He had merely the fixed idea of driving Gregor back into his room as quickly as possible. He would never have suffered Gregor to make the circumstantial preparations for[24] standing up on end and perhaps slipping his way through the door. Maybe he was now making more noise than ever to urge Gregor forward, as if no obstacle impeded him; to Gregor, anyhow, the noise in his rear sounded no longer like the voice of one single father; this was really no joke, and Gregor thrust himself—come what

24. **make the circumstantial preparations for:** do what he needed to to be able to stand up and maybe slip through the door.

might—into the doorway. One side of his body rose up, he was tilted at an angle in the doorway, his flank was quite bruised, horrid blotches stained the white door, soon he was stuck fast and, left to himself, could not have moved at all, his legs on one side fluttered trembling in the air, those on the other were crushed painfully to the floor—when from behind his father gave him a strong push which was literally a deliverance and he flew far into the room, bleeding freely. The door was slammed behind him with the stick, and then at last there was silence.

Pause & Reflect

II

FOCUS

After the first scare, Gregor's life settles into a new routine. Find out what that routine is.

MARK IT UP Put an *X* next to each detail that shows that Gregor is becoming more and more insect-like.

Not until it was twilight did Gregor awake out of a deep sleep, more like a swoon[25] than a sleep. He would certainly have waked up of his own accord not much later, for he felt himself sufficiently rested and well slept, but it seemed to him as if a fleeting step and a cautious shutting of the door leading into the hall had aroused him. The electric lights in the street cast a pale sheen here and there on the ceiling and the upper surfaces of the furniture, but down below, where he lay, it was dark. Slowly, awkwardly trying out his feelers, which he now first learned to appreciate, he pushed his way to the door to see what

25. **swoon:** fainting spell.

Pause & Reflect

1. **MARK IT UP** Underline Gregor's reason for wanting to keep the chief clerk from leaving. Then think about how Gregor's father interpreted Gregor's actions. Complete this sentence to explain the misunderstanding. **(Draw Conclusions)**

Gregor wanted to keep the chief clerk from leaving because

Gregor's father thought

2. Do you think Gregor's father was justified in driving him back as he did? **(Make Judgments)**

❑ YES ❑ NO

My reason:

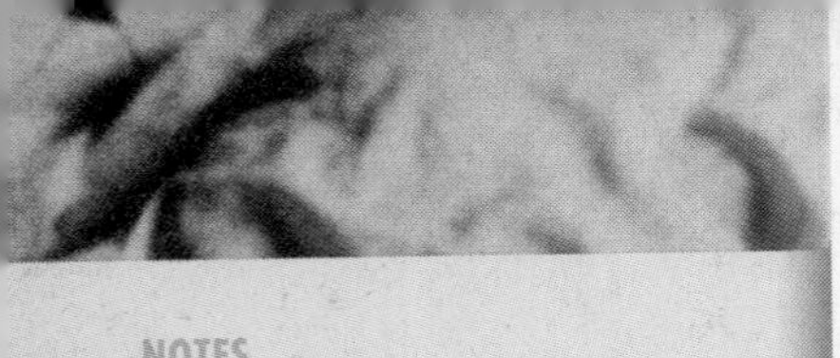

had been happening there. His left side felt like one single long, unpleasantly tense scar, and he had actually to limp on his two rows of legs. One little leg, moreover, had been severely damaged in the course of that morning's events—it was almost a miracle that only one had been damaged—and trailed uselessly behind him.

He had reached the door before he discovered what had really drawn him to it: the smell of food. For there stood a basin filled with fresh milk in which floated little sops of white bread. He could almost have laughed with joy, since he was now still hungrier than in the morning, and he dipped his head almost over the eyes straight into the milk. But soon in disappointment he withdrew it again; not only did he find it difficult to feed because of his tender left side—and he could only feed with the palpitating collaboration[26] of his whole body—he did not like the milk either, although milk had been his favorite drink and that was certainly why his sister had set it there for him, indeed it was almost with repulsion that he turned away from the basin and crawled back to the middle of the room.

He could see through the crack of the door that the gas was turned on in the living room, but while usually at this time his father made a habit of reading the afternoon newspaper in a loud voice to his mother and occasionally to his sister as well, not a sound was now to be heard. Well, perhaps his father had recently given up this habit of reading aloud, which his sister had mentioned so often in conversation and in her letters. But there was the same silence all around, although the flat was certainly not empty of occupants. "What a quiet life our family has been leading," said Gregor to himself, and as he sat there motionless staring into the darkness he felt great pride in the fact that he had been able to provide such a life for his parents and sister in such a fine flat. But what if all the quiet, the comfort, the contentment were now to end in horror? To keep himself from being lost in such thoughts

26. **palpitating collaboration:** working together of all the parts in a trembling way.

NOTES

the boxed text. Then finish these sentences. **(Clarify)**

Gregor is proud of

Gregor is worried about

Gregor took refuge in movement and crawled up and down the room.

Once during the long evening one of the side doors was opened a little and quickly shut again, later the other side door too; someone had apparently wanted to come in and then thought better of it. Gregor now stationed himself immediately before the living-room door, determined to persuade any hesitating visitor to come in or at least to discover who it might be; but the door was not opened again and he waited in vain. In the early morning, when the doors were locked, they had all wanted to come in, now that he had opened one door and the other had apparently been opened during the day, no one came in and even the keys were on the other side of the doors.

It was late at night before the gas went out in the living room, and Gregor could easily tell that his parents and his sister had all stayed awake until then, for he could clearly hear the three of them stealing away on tiptoe. No one was likely to visit him, not until the morning, that was certain; so he had plenty of time to meditate at his leisure on how he was to arrange his life afresh. But the lofty, empty room in which he had to lie flat on the floor filled him with an apprehension he could not account for, since it had been his very own room for the past five years—and with a half-unconscious action, not without a slight feeling of shame, he scuttled under the sofa, where he felt comfortable at once, although his back was a little cramped and he could not lift his head up, and his only regret was that his body was too broad to get the whole of it under the sofa.

He stayed there all night, spending the time partly in a light slumber, from which his hunger kept waking him up with a start, and partly in worrying and sketching vague hopes, which all led to the same conclusion, that he must lie low for the present and, by exercising patience and the utmost consideration, help the family to bear the inconvenience he was bound to cause them in his present condition.

WORDS TO KNOW
refuge (rĕf′yo͞oj) *n.* protection; comfort

NOTES

REREAD the boxed text. What kind of "vague hopes" do you think Gregor has for his future? **(Question)**

MARK IT UP Circle the details on this page that show you how Grete tries to care for Gregor. In the chart below, write some different feelings she has, and list the details that reveal them. **(Analyze)**

How Grete feels	Details that show her feelings

Very early in the morning, it was still almost night, Gregor had the chance to test the strength of his new resolutions, for his sister, nearly fully dressed, opened the door from the hall and peered in. She did not see him at once, yet when she caught sight of him under the sofa—well, he had to be somewhere, he couldn't have flown away, could he?—she was so startled that without being able to help it she slammed the door shut again. But as if regretting her behavior she opened the door again immediately and came in on tiptoe, as if she were visiting an invalid or even a stranger. Gregor had pushed his head forward to the very edge of the sofa and watched her. Would she notice that he had left the milk standing, and not for lack of hunger, and would she bring in some other kind of food more to his taste? If she did not do it of her own accord, he would rather starve than draw her attention to the fact, although he felt a wild impulse to dart out from under the sofa, throw himself at her feet, and beg her for something to eat. But his sister at once noticed, with surprise, that the basin was still full, except for a little milk that had been spilled all around it, she lifted it immediately, not with her bare hands, true, but with a cloth and carried it away. Gregor was wildly curious to know what she would bring instead, and made various speculations about it. Yet what she actually did next, in the goodness of her heart, he could never have guessed at. To find out what he liked she brought him a whole selection of food, all set out on an old newspaper. There were old, half-decayed vegetables, bones from last night's supper covered with a white sauce that had thickened; some raisins and almonds; a piece of cheese Gregor would have called uneatable two days ago; a dry roll of bread, a buttered roll, and a roll both buttered and salted. Besides all that, she set down again the same basin, into which she had poured some water, and which was apparently to be reserved for his exclusive use. And with fine tact, knowing that Gregor would not eat in her presence, she withdrew quickly and even turned the key, to let him understand that he could take his ease as much as he liked. Gregor's legs all whizzed toward the food. His wounds must have healed completely, moreover, for he felt no disability, which amazed him and made him reflect how more than a month ago he had cut one finger a little with a knife and had still suffered pain from the wound only the day before yesterday. Am I less sensitive now? he thought, and sucked greedily at the cheese, which above all the other edibles attracted him at once and strongly. One after another and with tears of satisfaction in his eyes he quickly devoured the cheese, the vegetables, and the sauce; the fresh food, on the other hand, had no charms for him, he could not even stand the smell of it and actually dragged away to some little distance the things he could eat. He had long finished his meal and was only lying lazily on the same spot when his sister turned the key slowly as a sign for him to retreat. That roused him at once, although he was nearly asleep, and he hurried under the sofa again. But it took considerable self-control for him to stay under the sofa, even for the short time his sister was in the room, since the large meal had swollen his body somewhat and he was so cramped he could hardly breathe. Slight attacks of breathlessness afflicted him and his eyes were starting a little out of his head as he watched his unsuspecting sister sweeping together with a broom not only the remains of what he had eaten but even the things he had not touched, as if these were now of no use to anyone, and hastily shoveling it all into a bucket, which she covered with a wooden lid and carried away. Hardly had she turned her back when Gregor came from under the sofa and stretched and puffed himself out.

In this manner Gregor was fed, once in the early morning while his parents and the servant girl were still asleep, and a second time after they had all had their midday dinner, for then his parents took a short nap and the servant girl could be sent out on some errand or other by his sister. Not that they would have wanted him to starve, of course, but perhaps they could not have borne to know more about his

NOTES

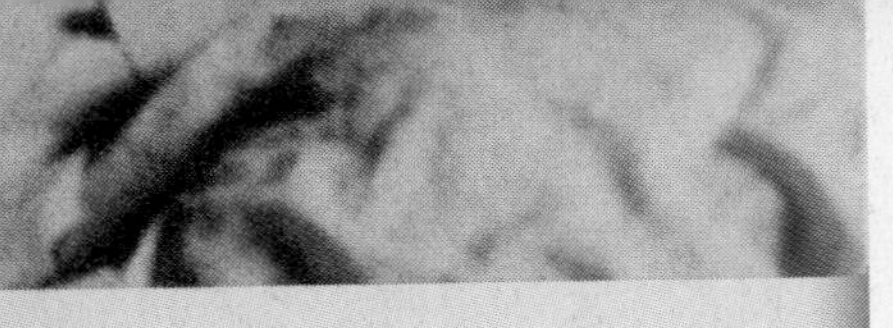

Pause & Reflect

1. Which of the following things happen to Gregor as his metamorphosis continues? Check three. **(Clarify)**

- ❑ He grows more legs.
- ❑ He hides under things.
- ❑ Human food disgusts him.
- ❑ His wounds heal quickly.
- ❑ He learns to fly.

2. How does Gregor's sister try to help him settle into his new life? **(Summarize)**

feeding than from hearsay, perhaps too his sister wanted to spare them such little anxieties whenever possible, since they had quite enough to bear as it was.

Under what pretext[27] the doctor and the locksmith had been got rid of on that first morning Gregor could not discover, for since what he said was not understood by the others it never struck any of them, not even his sister, that he could understand what they said, and so whenever his sister came into his room he had to content himself with hearing her utter only a sigh now and then and an occasional appeal to the saints. Later on, when she had got a little used to the situation—of course she could never get completely used to it—she sometimes threw out a remark which was kindly meant or could be so interpreted. "Well, he liked his dinner today," she would say when Gregor had made a good clearance of his food; and when he had not eaten, which gradually happened more and more often, she would say almost sadly: "Everything's been left standing again."

Pause & Reflect

FOCUS

Read to find out how life changes for the other members of Gregor's family.

MARK IT UP Put a star next to passages that describe how things change.

But although Gregor could get no news directly, he overheard a lot from the neighboring rooms, and as soon as voices were audible, he would run to the door of the room concerned and press his whole body against it. In the first few days especially there was no conversation that did not refer to him somehow, even if only indirectly. For two whole days there were family consultations at every mealtime about what should be done; but also between meals the same subject was discussed, for there were always

27. pretext: excuse.

at least two members of the family at home, since no one wanted to be alone in the flat and to leave it quite empty was unthinkable. And on the very first of these days the household cook—it was not quite clear what and how much she knew of the situation—went down on her knees to his mother and begged leave to go, and when she departed, a quarter of an hour later, gave thanks for her dismissal with tears in her eyes as if for the greatest benefit that could have been conferred on her, and without any prompting swore a solemn oath that she would never say a single word to anyone about what had happened.

Now Gregor's sister had to cook too, helping her mother; true, the cooking did not amount to much, for they ate scarcely anything. Gregor was always hearing one of the family vainly urging another to eat and getting no answer but: "Thanks, I've had all I want," or something similar. Perhaps they drank nothing either. Time and again his sister kept asking his father if he wouldn't like some beer and offered kindly to go and fetch it herself, and when he made no answer suggested that she could ask the concierge[28] to fetch it, so that he need feel no sense of obligation, but then a round "No" came from his father and no more was said about it.

In the course of that very first day Gregor's father explained the family's financial position and prospects to both his mother and his sister. Now and then he rose from the table to get some voucher or memorandum out of the small safe he had rescued from the collapse of his business five years earlier. One could hear him opening the complicated lock and rustling papers out and shutting it again. This statement made by his father was the first cheerful information Gregor had heard since his imprisonment. He had been of the opinion that nothing at all was left over from his father's business, at least his father had never said anything to the contrary, and of course he had not asked

In lines 880–898, the author describes an event that took place five years before the events in this story. Paying attention to verb tenses and time-order words can help you keep track of the shift between present and past.

28. **concierge** (kôN-syârzh′): a person in an apartment complex who serves as a doorkeeper and janitor.

NOTES

him directly. At that time Gregor's sole desire was to do his utmost to help the family to forget as soon as possible the catastrophe that had overwhelmed the business and thrown them all into a state of complete despair. And so he had set to work with unusual ardor[29] and almost overnight had become a commercial traveler instead of a little clerk, with of course much greater chances of earning money, and his success was immediately translated into good round coin which he could lay on the table for his amazed and happy family. These had been fine times, and they had never recurred, at least not with the same sense of glory, although later on Gregor had earned so much money that he was able to meet the expenses of the whole household and did so. They had simply got used to it, both the family and Gregor; the money was gratefully accepted and gladly given, but there was no special uprush of warm feeling. With his sister alone had he remained intimate, and it was a secret plan of his that she, who loved music, unlike himself, and could play movingly on the violin, should be sent next year to study at the Conservatorium,[30] despite the great expense that would entail, which must be made up in some other way. During his brief visits home the Conservatorium was often mentioned in the talks he had with his sister, but always merely as a beautiful dream which could never come true, and his parents discouraged even these innocent references to it; yet Gregor had made up his mind firmly about it and meant to announce the fact with due solemnity on Christmas Day.

Such were the thoughts, completely futile in his present condition, that went through his head as he stood clinging upright to the door and listening. Sometimes out of sheer weariness he had to give up listening and let his head fall negligently against the door, but he always had to pull himself together again at once, for even the slight sound his head made was audible next door and brought all conversation to a stop. "What can he be doing now?" his father

REREAD the boxed text. Why does Gregor think he is being negligent, or careless, when he lets his head fall against the door out of weariness? **(Infer)**

29. ardor: eagerness; enthusiasm.

30. Conservatorium: school of music.

would say after a while, obviously turning toward the door, and only then would the interrupted conversation gradually be set going again.

Gregor was now informed as amply as he could wish—for his father tended to repeat himself in his explanations, partly because it was a long time since he had handled such matters and partly because his mother could not always grasp things at once—that a certain amount of investments, a very small amount it was true, had survived the wreck of their fortunes and had even increased a little because the dividends had not been touched meanwhile. And besides that, the money Gregor brought home every month—he had kept only a few dollars for himself—had never been quite used up and now amounted to a small capital sum. Behind the door Gregor nodded his head eagerly, rejoiced at this evidence of unexpected thrift and foresight. True, he could really have paid off some more of his father's debts to the chief with this extra money, and so brought much nearer the day on which he could quit his job, but doubtless it was better the way his father had arranged it.

Yet this capital was by no means sufficient to let the family live on the interest of it; for one year, perhaps, or at the most two, they could live on the principal, that was all. It was simply a sum that ought not to be touched and should be kept for a rainy day; money for living expenses would have to be earned. Now his father was still hale enough but an old man, and he had done no work for the past five years and could not be expected to do much; during these five years, the first years of leisure in his laborious though unsuccessful life, he had grown rather fat and become sluggish. And Gregor's old mother, how was she to earn a living with her asthma, which troubled her even when she walked through the flat and kept her lying on a sofa every other day panting for breath beside an open window? And was his sister to earn her bread, she who was still a child of seventeen and whose life hitherto had been so pleasant, consisting as it did in dressing herself

Pause & Reflect

1. What new worries do the members of Gregor's family face now? **(Clarify)**

2. Why does Gregor feel "hot with shame and grief"? **(Draw Conclusions)**

3. If you could give Gregor some advice, what would you tell him? **(Connect)**

nicely, sleeping long, helping in the housekeeping, going out to a few modest entertainments, and above all playing the violin? At first whenever the need for earning money was mentioned Gregor let go his hold on the door and threw himself down on the cool leather sofa beside it, he felt so hot with shame and grief.

Pause & Reflect

FOCUS

Read to find out how the family's responses to Gregor gradually change.

Often he just lay there the long nights through without sleeping at all, scrabbling for hours on the leather. Or he nerved himself to the great effort of pushing an armchair to the window, then crawled up over the window sill and, braced against the chair, leaned against the windowpanes, obviously in some recollection of the sense of freedom that looking out of a window always used to give him. For in reality day by day things that were even a little way off were growing dimmer to his sight; the hospital across the street, which he used to execrate[31] for being all too often before his eyes, was now quite beyond his range of vision, and if he had not known that he lived in Charlotte Street, a quiet street but still a city street, he might have believed that his window gave on a desert waste where gray sky and gray land blended indistinguishably into each other. His quick-witted sister only needed to observe twice that the armchair stood by the window; after that whenever she had tidied the room she always pushed the chair back to the same place at the window and even left the inner casements open.

If he could have spoken to her and thanked her for all she had to do for him, he could have borne her ministrations better; as it was, they oppressed him. She certainly tried

31. **execrate** (ĕk′sĭ-krāt′): declare to be hateful.

to make as light as possible of whatever was disagreeable in her task, and as time went on she succeeded, of course, more and more, but time brought more enlightenment to Gregor too. The very way she came in distressed him. Hardly was she in the room when she rushed to the window, without even taking time to shut the door, careful as she was usually to shield the sight of Gregor's room from the others, and as if she were almost suffocating tore the casements open with hasty fingers, standing then in the open draught for a while even in the bitterest cold and drawing deep breaths. This noisy scurry of hers upset Gregor twice a day; he would crouch trembling under the sofa all the time, knowing quite well that she would certainly have spared him such a disturbance had she found it at all possible to stay in his presence without opening the window.

On one occasion, about a month after Gregor's metamorphosis, when there was surely no reason for her to be still startled at his appearance, she came a little earlier than usual and found him gazing out of the window, quite motionless, and thus well placed to look like a bogey.[32] Gregor would not have been surprised had she not come in at all, for she could not immediately open the window while he was there, but not only did she retreat, she jumped back as if in alarm and banged the door shut; a stranger might well have thought that he had been lying in wait for her there meaning to bite her. Of course he hid himself under the sofa at once, but he had to wait until midday before she came again, and she seemed more ill at ease than usual. This made him realize how repulsive the sight of him still was to her, and that it was bound to go on being repulsive, and what an effort it must cost her not to run away even from the sight of the small portion of his body that stuck out from under the sofa. In order to spare her that, therefore, one day he carried a sheet on his back to the sofa—it cost him four hours' labor—and arranged it there in such a way as to hide him completely, so that even if she were to bend down

32. **bogey:** monster.

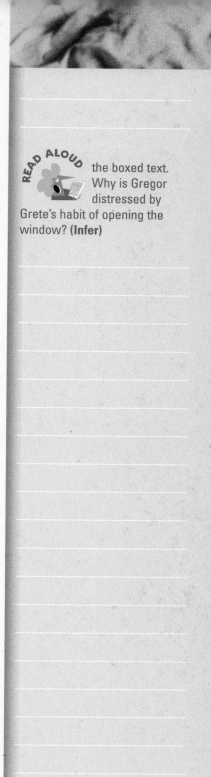

READ ALOUD the boxed text. Why is Gregor distressed by Grete's habit of opening the window? **(Infer)**

Pause & Reflect

1. How does each family member's attitude about Gregor seem to change? Write your answers on the lines. **(Clarify)**

Mother:

Father:

Sister:

2. How have Gregor's feelings toward Grete changed? **(Evaluate)**

she could not see him. Had she considered the sheet unnecessary, she would certainly have stripped it off the sofa again, for it was clear enough that this curtaining and confining of himself was not likely to conduce to Gregor's comfort, but she left it where it was, and Gregor even fancied that he caught a thankful glance from her eye when he lifted the sheet carefully a very little with his head to see how she was taking the new arrangement.

For the first fortnight[33] his parents could not bring themselves to the point of entering his room, and he often heard them expressing their appreciation of his sister's activities, whereas formerly they had frequently scolded her for being as they thought a somewhat useless daughter. But now, both of them often waited outside the door, his father and his mother, while his sister tidied his room, and as soon as she came out she had to tell them exactly how things were in the room, what Gregor had eaten, how he had conducted himself this time, and whether there was not perhaps some slight improvement in his condition. His mother, moreover, began relatively soon to want to visit him, but his father and sister dissuaded her at first with arguments which Gregor listened to very attentively and altogether approved. Later, however, she had to be held back by main force, and when she cried out: "Do let me in to Gregor, he is my unfortunate son! Can't you understand that I must go to him?" Gregor thought that it might be well to have her come in, not every day, of course, but perhaps once a week; she understood things, after all, much better than his sister, who was only a child despite the efforts she was making and had perhaps taken on so difficult a task merely out of childish thoughtlessness.

Pause & Reflect

33. **fortnight:** two weeks.

WORDS TO KNOW
dissuade (dĭ-swād') *v.* to persuade not to; discourage

FOCUS

Gregor's mother enters his room at last. She and Grete start to carry out a plan that irritates Gregor. Find out what happens.

Gregor's desire to see his mother was soon fulfilled. During the daytime he did not want to show himself at the window, out of consideration for his parents, but he could not crawl very far around the few square yards of floor space he had, nor could he bear lying quietly at rest all during the night, while he was fast losing any interest he had ever taken in food, so that for mere recreation he had formed the habit of crawling crisscross over the walls and ceiling. He especially enjoyed hanging suspended from the ceiling; it was much better than lying on the floor; one could breathe more freely; one's body swung and rocked lightly; and in the almost blissful absorption induced by this suspension it could happen to his own surprise that he let go and fell plump on the floor. Yet he now had his body much better under control than formerly, and even such a big fall did him no harm. His sister at once remarked the new distraction Gregor had found for himself—he left traces behind him of the sticky stuff on his soles wherever he crawled—and she got the idea in her head of giving him as wide a field as possible to crawl in and of removing the pieces of furniture that hindered him, above all the chest of drawers and the writing desk. But that was more than she could manage all by herself; she did not dare ask her father to help her; and as for the servant girl, a young creature of sixteen who had had the courage to stay on after the cook's departure, she could not be asked to help, for she had begged as a special favor that she might keep the kitchen door locked and open it only on a definite summons; so there was nothing left but to apply to her mother at an hour when her father was out. And the old lady did come, with exclamations of joyful eagerness, which, however, died away at the door of Gregor's room. Gregor's sister, of course, went in first, to see that everything was in order before letting his mother enter. In great haste Gregor pulled

the sheet lower and rucked it more in folds so that it really looked as if it had been thrown accidentally over the sofa. And this time he did not peer out from under it; he renounced the pleasure of seeing his mother on this occasion and was only glad that she had come at all. "Come in, he's out of sight," said his sister, obviously leading her mother in by the hand. Gregor could now hear the two women struggling to shift the heavy old chest from its place, and his sister claiming the greater part of the labor for herself, without listening to the admonitions of her mother, who feared she might overstrain herself. It took a long time. After at least a quarter of an hour's tugging his mother objected that the chest had better be left where it was, for in the first place it was too heavy and could never be got out before his father came home, and standing in the middle of the room like that it would only hamper Gregor's movements, while in the second place it was not at all certain that moving the furniture would be doing a service to Gregor. She was inclined to think to the contrary; the sight of the naked walls made her own heart heavy, and why shouldn't Gregor have the same feeling, considering that he had been used to his furniture for so long and might feel forlorn without it. "And doesn't it look," she concluded in a low voice—in fact she had been almost whispering all the time as if to avoid letting Gregor, whose exact whereabouts she did not know, hear even the tones of her voice, for she was convinced that he could not understand her words—"doesn't it look as if we were showing him, by taking away his furniture, that we have given up hope of his ever getting better and are just leaving him coldly to himself? I think it would be best to keep his room exactly as it has always been, so that when he comes back to us he will find everything unchanged and be able all the more easily to forget what has happened in between."

On hearing these words from his mother Gregor realized that the lack of all direct human speech for the past two months together with the monotony of family life must

NOTES

MARK IT UP In the boxed text, underline the sentence that shows that Mrs. Samsa, too, believes Gregor's condition is temporary. **(Infer)**

have confused his mind, otherwise he could not account for the fact that he had quite earnestly looked forward to having his room emptied of furnishing. Did he really want his warm room, so comfortably fitted with old family furniture, to be turned into a naked den in which he would certainly be able to crawl unhampered in all directions but at the price of shedding simultaneously all recollection of his human background? He had indeed been so near the brink of forgetfulness that only the voice of his mother, which he had not heard for so long, had drawn him back from it. Nothing should be taken out of his room; everything must stay as it was; he could not dispense with the good influence of the furniture on his state of mind; and even if the furniture did hamper him in his senseless crawling around and around, that was no drawback but a great advantage.

Unfortunately his sister was of the contrary opinion; she had grown accustomed, and not without reason, to consider herself an expert in Gregor's affairs as against her parents, and so her mother's advice was now enough to make her determined on the removal not only of the chest and the writing desk, which had been her first intention, but of all the furniture except the indispensable sofa. This determination was not, of course, merely the outcome of childish recalcitrance[34] and of the self-confidence she had recently developed so unexpectedly and at such cost; she had in fact perceived that Gregor needed a lot of space to crawl about in, while on the other hand he never used the furniture at all, so far as could be seen. Another factor might also have been the enthusiastic temperament of an adolescent girl, which seeks to indulge itself on every opportunity and which now tempted Grete to exaggerate the horror of her brother's circumstances in order that she might do all the more for him. In a room where Gregor lorded it all alone over empty walls no one save herself was likely ever to set foot.

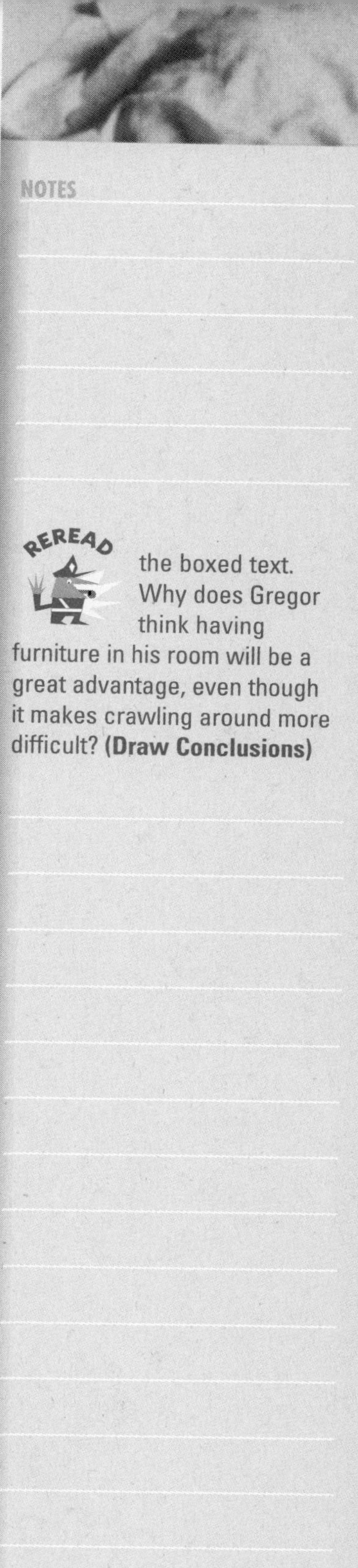

NOTES
REREAD
the boxed text. Why does Gregor think having furniture in his room will be a great advantage, even though it makes crawling around more difficult? **(Draw Conclusions)**

34. recalcitrance (rĭ-kăl′sĭ-trəns): stubborn resistance to authority.

NOTES

READ ALOUD the boxed text. How do you think Mrs. Samsa and Grete will react when Gregor peeks out from under the sofa to "help" them? **(Predict)**

And so she was not to be moved from her resolve by her mother, who seemed moreover to be ill at ease in Gregor's room and therefore unsure of herself, was soon reduced to silence, and helped her daughter as best she could to push the chest outside. Now, Gregor could do without the chest, if need be, but the writing desk he must retain. As soon as the two women had got the chest out of his room, groaning as they pushed it, Gregor stuck his head out from under the sofa to see how he might intervene as kindly and cautiously as possible. But as bad luck would have it, his mother was the first to return, leaving Grete clasping the chest in the room next door where she was trying to shift it all by herself, without of course moving it from the spot. His mother however was not accustomed to the sight of him, it might sicken her and so in alarm Gregor backed quickly to the other end of the sofa, yet could not prevent the sheet from swaying a little in front. That was enough to put her on the alert. She paused, stood still for a moment, and then went back to Grete.

Although Gregor kept reassuring himself that nothing out of the way was happening, but only a few bits of furniture were being changed around, he soon had to admit that all this trotting to and fro of the two women, their little ejaculations,[35] and the scraping of furniture along the floor affected him like a vast disturbance coming from all sides at once, and however much he tucked in his head and legs and cowered to the very floor he was bound to confess that he would not be able to stand it for long. They were clearing his room out; taking away everything he loved; the chest in which he kept his fret saw and other tools was already dragged off; they were now loosening the writing desk which had almost sunk into the floor, the desk at which he had done all his homework when he was at the commercial academy, at the grammar school before that, and, yes, even

35. **ejaculations:** sudden, brief statements or exclamations.

WORDS TO KNOW
intervene (ĭn′tər-vēn′) *v.* to come between; get involved in order to help

at the primary school—he had no more time to waste in weighing the good intentions of the two women, whose existence he had by now almost forgotten, for they were so exhausted that they were laboring in silence and nothing could be heard but the heavy scuffling of their feet.

And so he rushed out—the women were just leaning against the writing desk in the next room to give themselves a breather—and four times changed his direction, since he really did not know what to rescue first, then on the wall opposite, which was already otherwise cleared, he was struck by the picture of the lady muffled in so much fur and quickly crawled up to it and pressed himself to the glass, which was a good surface to hold on to and comforted his hot belly. This picture at least, which was entirely hidden beneath him, was going to be removed by nobody. He turned his head toward the door of the living room so as to observe the women when they came back.

They had not allowed themselves much of a rest and were already coming; Grete had twined her arm around her mother and was almost supporting her. "Well, what shall we take now?" said Grete, looking around. Her eyes met Gregor's from the wall. She kept her composure, presumably because of her mother, bent her head down to her mother, to keep her from looking up, and said, although in a fluttering, unpremeditated voice: "Come, hadn't we better go back to the living room for a moment?" Her intentions were clear enough to Gregor, she wanted to bestow her mother in safety and then chase him down from the wall. Well, just let her try it! He clung to his picture and would not give it up. He would rather fly in Grete's face.

But Grete's words had succeeded in disquieting her mother, who took a step to one side, caught sight of the huge brown mass on the flowered wallpaper, and before she was really conscious that what she saw was Gregor, screamed in a loud, hoarse voice: "Oh God, oh God!" fell with outspread arms over the sofa as if giving up, and did not move. "Gregor!" cried his sister, shaking her fist and

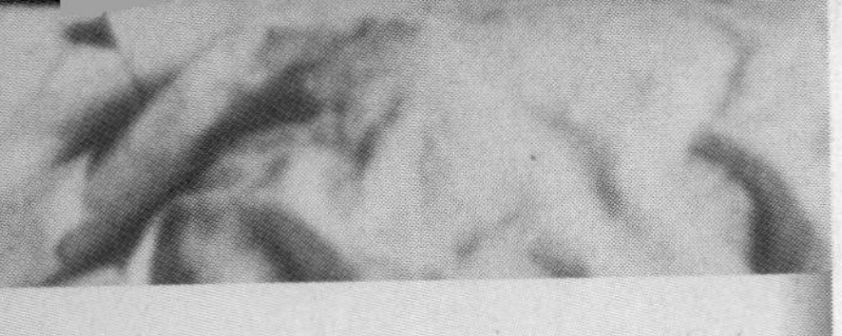

Pause & Reflect

1. How would you describe Mrs. Samsa's first visit to her son's room? **(Summarize)**

2. After his mother faints, Gregor is angry at himself and worried about her. What thoughts might be going through his mind? **(Infer)**

glaring at him. This was the first time she had directly addressed him since his metamorphosis. She ran into the next room for some aromatic essence[36] with which to rouse her mother from her fainting fit. Gregor wanted to help too—there was still time to rescue the picture—but he was stuck fast to the glass and had to tear himself loose; he then ran after his sister into the next room as if he could advise her, as he used to do; but then had to stand helplessly behind her; she meanwhile searched among various small bottles and when she turned around started in alarm at the sight of him; one bottle fell on the floor and broke; a splinter of glass cut Gregor's face and some kind of corrosive[37] medicine splashed him; without pausing a moment longer Grete gathered up all the bottles she could carry and ran to her mother with them; she banged the door shut with her foot. Gregor was now cut off from his mother, who was perhaps nearly dying because of him; he dared not open the door for fear of frightening away his sister, who had to stay with her mother; there was nothing he could do but wait; and harassed by self-reproach and worry he began now to crawl to and fro, over everything, walls, furniture, and ceiling, and finally in his despair, when the whole room seemed to be reeling around him, fell down onto the middle of the big table.

Pause & Reflect

36. **aromatic essence:** strong-smelling solution.

37. **corrosive** (kə-rō′sĭv): capable of eating away solid substances.

FOCUS

Read to find out what Gregor's father does when he learns what happened.

MARK IT UP Underline details that show how Mr. Samsa has changed since Gregor's metamorphosis.

A little while elapsed, Gregor was still lying there feebly and all around was quiet, perhaps that was a good omen. Then the doorbell rang. The servant girl was of course locked in her kitchen, and Grete would have to open the door. It was his father. "What's been happening?" were his first words; Grete's face must have told him everything. Grete answered in a muffled voice, apparently hiding her head on his breast: "Mother has been fainting, but she's better now. Gregor's broken loose." "Just what I expected," said his father, "just what I've been telling you, but you women would never listen." It was clear to Gregor that his father had taken the worst interpretation of Grete's all too brief statement and was assuming that Gregor had been guilty of some violent act. Therefore Gregor must now try to propitiate[38] his father, since he had neither time nor means for an explanation. And so he fled to the door of his own room and crouched against it, to let his father see as soon as he came in from the hall that his son had the good intention of getting back into his room immediately and that it was not necessary to drive him there, but that if only the door were opened he would disappear at once.

Yet his father was not in the mood to perceive such fine[39] distinctions. "Ah!" he cried as soon as he appeared, in a tone that sounded at once angry and exultant. Gregor drew his head back from the door and lifted it to look at his father. Truly, this was not the father he had imagined to himself; admittedly he had been too absorbed of late in his new recreation of crawling over the ceiling to take the same interest as before in what was happening elsewhere in the flat, and he ought really to be prepared for some changes. And yet, and yet, could that be his father? The man who

38. **propitiate** (prō-pĭsh′ē-āt′): calm; soothe.

39. **fine:** subtle; precise.

NOTES

READ ALOUD the boxed text. Write four words below that describe the new Mr. Samsa.

used to lie wearily sunk in bed whenever Gregor set out on a business journey; who welcomed him back of an evening lying in a long chair in a dressing gown; who could not really rise to his feet but only lifted his arms in greeting, and on the rare occasions when he did go out with his family, on one or two Sundays a year and on highest holidays,[40] walked between Gregor and his mother, who were slow walkers anyhow, even more slowly than they did, muffled in his old greatcoat, shuffling laboriously forward with the help of his crook-handled stick which he set down most cautiously at every step and, whenever he wanted to say anything, nearly always came to a full stop and gathered his escort around him? Now he was standing there in fine shape; dressed in a smart blue uniform with gold buttons, such as bank messengers wear; his strong double chin bulged over the stiff high collar of his jacket; from under his bushy eyebrows his black eyes darted fresh and penetrating glances; his onetime tangled white hair had been combed flat on either side of a shining and carefully exact parting.[41] He pitched his cap, which bore a gold monogram, probably the badge of some bank, in a wide sweep across the whole room onto a sofa and with the tail-ends of his jacket thrown back, his hands in his trouser pockets, advanced with a grim visage[42] toward Gregor. Likely enough he did not himself know what he meant to do; at any rate he lifted his feet uncommonly high, and Gregor was dumbfounded at the enormous size of his shoe soles. But Gregor could not risk standing up to him, aware as he had been from the very first day of his new life that his father believed only the severest measures suitable for dealing with him. And so he ran before his father, stopping when he stopped and scuttling forward again when his father made any kind of move. In this way they circled the

40. **highest holidays:** Rosh Hashanah and Yom Kippur, the Jewish New Year and Day of Atonement.

41. **parting:** part.

42. **visage:** face.

room several times without anything decisive happening, indeed the whole operation did not even look like a pursuit because it was carried out so slowly. And so Gregor did not leave the floor, for he feared that his father might take as a piece of peculiar wickedness any excursion of his over the walls or the ceiling. All the same, he could not stay this course much longer, for while his father took one step he had to carry out a whole series of movements. He was already beginning to feel breathless, just as in his former life his lungs had not been very dependable. As he was staggering along, trying to concentrate his energy on running, hardly keeping his eyes open; in his dazed state never even thinking of any other escape than simply going forward; and having almost forgotten that the walls were free to him, which in this room were well provided with finely carved pieces of furniture full of knobs and crevices—suddenly something lightly flung landed close behind him and rolled before him. It was an apple; a second apple followed immediately; Gregor came to a stop in alarm; there was no point in running on, for his father was determined to bombard him. He had filled his pockets with fruit from the dish on the sideboard and was now shying apple after apple, without taking particularly good aim for the moment. The small red apples rolled about the floor as if magnetized and cannoned into each other. An apple thrown without much force grazed Gregor's back and glanced off harmlessly. But another following immediately landed right on his back and sank in; Gregor wanted to drag himself forward, as if this startling, incredible pain could be left behind him; but he felt as if nailed to the spot and flattened himself out in a complete derangement of all his senses. With his last conscious look he saw the door of his room being torn open and his mother rushing out ahead of his screaming sister, in her underbodice, for her daughter had loosened her clothing to let her breathe more freely and recover from her swoon, he saw his mother rushing toward his father, leaving one after another behind her on the floor

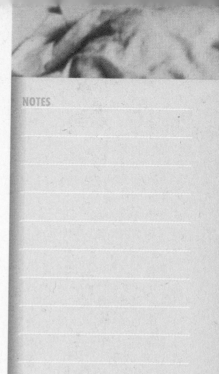

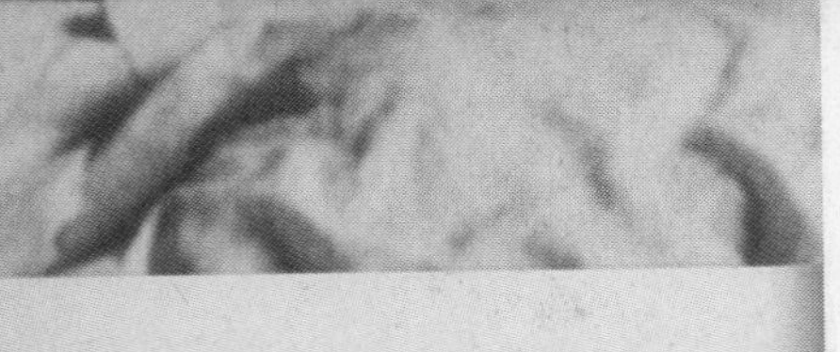

her loosened petticoats, stumbling over her petticoats straight to his father and embracing him, in complete union with him—but here Gregor's sight began to fail—with her hands clasped around his father's neck as she begged for her son's life.

Pause & Reflect

FOCUS

Life becomes more difficult for Gregor and his family. Read to find out what changes take place in the Samsa home.

MARK IT UP Underline details that show how the family has changed.

The serious injury done to Gregor, which disabled him for more than a month—the apple went on sticking in his body as a visible reminder, since no one ventured to remove it—seemed to have made even his father recollect that Gregor was a member of the family, despite his present unfortunate and repulsive shape, and ought not to be treated as an enemy, that, on the contrary, family duty required the suppression[43] of disgust and the exercise of patience, nothing but patience.

And though his injury had impaired, probably forever, his powers of movement, and for the time being it took him long, long minutes to creep across his room like an old invalid—there was no question now of crawling up the wall—yet in his own opinion he was sufficiently compensated for this worsening of his condition by the fact that toward evening the living-room door, which he

43. **suppression** (sə-prĕsh′ən): holding back or keeping in.

Pause & Reflect

1. Number the following events in the sequence in which they happened. **(Sequence)**

___ Mr. Samsa begins to throw apples.

___ Mrs. Samsa runs out of Gregor's room.

___ An apple sinks into Gregor's back.

___ Mrs. Samsa begs for Gregor's life.

___ Grete tells her father that her mother fainted.

2. Do you think the change in Gregor's father is positive or negative? Why? **(Make Judgments)**

used to watch intently for an hour or two beforehand, was always thrown open, so that lying in the darkness of his room, invisible to the family, he could see them all at the lamp-lit table and listen to their talk, by general consent as it were, very different from his earlier eavesdropping.

True, their intercourse lacked the lively character of former times, which he had always called to mind with a certain wistfulness in the small hotel bedrooms where he had been wont to throw himself down, tired out, on damp bedding. They were now mostly very silent. Soon after supper his father would fall asleep in his armchair; his mother and sister would admonish each other to be silent; his mother, bending low over the lamp, stitched at fine sewing for an underwear firm; his sister, who had taken a job as a salesgirl, was learning shorthand and French in the evenings on the chance of bettering herself. Sometimes his father woke up, and as if quite unaware that he had been sleeping said to his mother: "What a lot of sewing you're doing today!" and at once fell asleep again, while the two women exchanged a tired smile.

With a kind of mulishness his father persisted in keeping his uniform on even in the house; his dressing gown hung uselessly on its peg and he slept fully dressed where he sat, as if he were ready for service at any moment and even here only at the beck and call of his superior. As a result, his uniform, which was not brand-new to start with, began to look dirty, despite all the loving care of the mother and sister to keep it clean, and Gregor often spent whole evenings gazing at the many greasy spots on the garment, gleaming with gold buttons always in a high state of polish, in which the old man sat sleeping in extreme discomfort and yet quite peacefully.

As soon as the clock struck ten his mother tried to rouse his father with gentle words and to persuade him after that to get into bed, for sitting there he could not have a proper sleep and that was what he needed most, since he had to go on duty at six. But with the mulishness that had obsessed

NOTES

READ ALOUD the boxed paragraph. Why do you think Gregor's father constantly wears his uniform? **(Draw Conclusions)**

NOTES

the highlighted comment by Gregor's father. Do you think this means he is really happy? Explain. **(Analyze)**

him since he became a bank messenger he always insisted on staying longer at the table, although he regularly fell asleep again and in the end only with the greatest trouble could be got out of his armchair and into his bed. However insistently Gregor's mother and sister kept urging him with gentle reminders, he would go on slowly shaking his head for a quarter of an hour, keeping his eyes shut, and refuse to get to his feet. The mother plucked at his sleeve, whispering endearments in his ear, the sister left her lessons to come to her mother's help, but Gregor's father was not to be caught. He would only sink down deeper in his chair. Not until the two women hoisted him up by the armpits did he open his eyes and look at them both, one after the other, usually with the remark: "This is a life. This is the peace and quiet of my old age." And leaning on the two of them he would heave himself up, with difficulty, as if he were a great burden to himself, suffer them to lead him as far as the door and then wave them off and go on alone, while the mother abandoned her needlework and the sister her pen in order to run after him and help him farther.

Who could find time, in this overworked and tired-out family, to bother about Gregor more than was absolutely needful? The household was reduced more and more; the servant girl was turned off; a gigantic bony charwoman[44] with white hair flying around her head came in morning and evening to do the rough work; everything else was done by Gregor's mother, as well as great piles of sewing. Even various family ornaments, which his mother and sister used to wear with pride at parties and celebrations, had to be sold, as Gregor discovered of an evening from hearing them all discuss the prices obtained. But what they lamented most was the fact that they could not leave the flat which was much too big for their present circumstances, because they could not think of any way to shift Gregor. Yet Gregor saw well enough that consideration for him was not the main difficulty preventing the removal, for they could have easily

---

44. charwoman: cleaning woman.

shifted him in some suitable box with a few air holes in it; what really kept them from moving into another flat was rather their own complete hopelessness and the belief that they had been singled out for a misfortune such as had never happened to any of their relations or acquaintances. They fulfilled to the uttermost all that the world demands of poor people, the father fetched breakfast for the small clerks in the bank, the mother devoted her energy to making underwear for strangers, the sister trotted to and fro behind the counter at the behest of customers,[45] but more than this they had not the strength to do. And the wound in Gregor's back began to nag at him afresh when his mother and sister, after getting his father into bed, came back again, left their work lying, drew close to each other, and sat cheek by cheek; when his mother, pointing toward his room, said: "Shut that door now, Grete," and he was left again in the darkness, while next door the women mingled their tears or perhaps sat dry-eyed staring at the table.

Pause & Reflect

FOCUS

As the family's financial situation worsens, they look for new ways to make money. What happens to Gregor in the meantime?

MARK IT UP Underline details that show Gregor's changing feelings toward his family.

Gregor hardly slept at all by night or by day. He was often haunted by the idea that next time the door opened he would take the family's affairs in hand again just as he used to do; once more, after this long interval, there appeared in his thoughts the figures of the chief and the chief clerk, the commercial travelers and the apprentices, the porter who was so dull-witted, two or three friends in other firms, a chambermaid in one of the rural hotels, a sweet and fleeting memory,

45. **at the behest of customers:** in response to customers' requests.

Pause & Reflect

1. Review the details you underlined on pages 333 and 334. Which changes do you think are good ones? Which changes are not so good? **(Make Judgments)**

Good:

Not so good:

2. Why do you think the women often "mingled their tears" at night? **(Analyze)**

NOTES

a cashier in a milliner's[46] shop, who he had wooed earnestly but too slowly—they all appeared, together with strangers or people he had quite forgotten, but instead of helping him and his family they were one and all unapproachable, and he was glad when they vanished. At other times he would not be in the mood to bother about his family, he was only filled with rage at the way they were neglecting him, and although he had no clear idea of what he might care to eat he would make plans for getting into the larder to take the food that was after all his due, even if he were not hungry. His sister no longer took thought to bring him what might especially please him; but in the morning and at noon before she went to business hurriedly pushed into his room with her foot any food that was available, and in the evening cleared it out again with one sweep of the broom, heedless of whether it had been merely tasted, or—as most frequently happened—left untouched. The cleaning of his room, which she now did always in the evenings, could not have been more hastily done. Streaks of dirt stretched along the walls, here and there lay balls of dust and filth. At first Gregor used to station himself in some particularly filthy corner when his sister arrived, in order to reproach her with it, so to speak. But he could have sat there for weeks without getting her to make any improvement; she could see the dirt as well as he did, but she had simply made up her mind to leave it alone. And yet, with a touchiness that was new to her, which seemed anyhow to have infected the whole family, she jealously guarded her claim to be the sole caretaker of Gregor's room. His mother once subjected his room to a thorough cleaning, which was achieved only by means of several buckets of water—all this dampness of course upset Gregor too and he lay widespread, sulky, and motionless on the sofa—but she was well punished for it. Hardly had his sister noticed the changed aspect of his room that evening than she rushed in high dudgeon[47] into the living room and, despite the implor-

46. **milliner's:** hat maker's.

47. **in high dudgeon:** very angry.

ingly raised hands of her mother, burst into a storm of weeping, while her parents—her father had of course been startled out of his chair—looked on at first in helpless amazement; then they too began to go into action; the father reproached the mother on his right for not having left the cleaning of Gregor's room to his sister; shrieked at the sister on his left that never again was she to be allowed to clean Gregor's room; while the mother tried to pull the father into his bedroom, since he was beyond himself with agitation; the sister, shaken with sobs, then beat upon the table with her small fists; and Gregor hissed loudly with rage because not one of them thought of shutting the door to spare him such a spectacle and so much noise.

Still, even if the sister, exhausted by her daily work, had grown tired of looking after Gregor as she did formerly, there was no need for his mother's intervention or for Gregor's being neglected at all. The charwoman was there. This old widow, whose strong bony frame had enabled her to survive the worst a long life could offer, by no means recoiled from Gregor. Without being in the least curious she had once by chance opened the door of his room and at the sight of Gregor, who, taken by surprise, began to rush to and fro although no one was chasing him, merely stood there with her arms folded. From that time she never failed to open his door a little for a moment, morning and evening, to have a look at him. At first she even used to call him to her, with words which apparently she took to be friendly, such as: "Come along, then, you old dung beetle!" or "Look at the old dung beetle, then!" To such allocutions[48] Gregor made no answer, but stayed motionless where he was, as if the door had never been opened. Instead of being allowed to disturb him so senselessly whenever the whim took her, she should rather have been ordered to clean out his room daily, that charwoman! Once, early in the morning—heavy rain was lashing on the windowpanes, perhaps a sign that

NOTES
REREAD
the boxed text. How does Gregor respond when the charwoman tries to talk to him? Why do you think he responds in this way? **(Analyze)**

48. **allocutions** (ăl′ə-kyo͞o′shənz): formal speeches. (The word is meant ironically here.)

NOTES

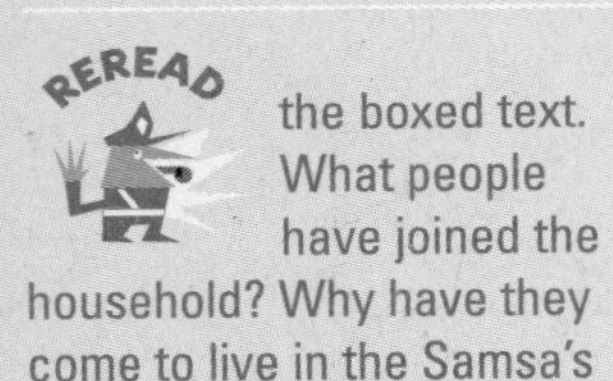

the boxed text. What people have joined the household? Why have they come to live in the Samsa's apartment? **(Clarify)**

spring was on the way—Gregor was so exasperated when she began addressing him again that he ran at her, as if to attack her, although slowly and feebly enough. But the charwoman instead of showing fright merely lifted high a chair that happened to be beside the door, and as she stood there with her mouth wide open it was clear that she meant to shut it only when she brought the chair down on Gregor's back. "So you're not coming any nearer?" she asked, as Gregor turned away again, and quietly put the chair back into the corner.

Gregor was now eating hardly anything. Only when he happened to pass the food laid out for him did he take a bit of something in his mouth as a pastime, kept it there for an hour at a time, and usually spat it out again. At first he thought it was chagrin over the state of his room that prevented him from eating, yet he soon got used to the various changes in his room. It had become a habit in the family to push into his room things there was no room for elsewhere, and there were plenty of these now, since one of the rooms had been let to three lodgers. These serious gentlemen—all three of them with full beards, as Gregor once observed through a crack in the door—had a passion for order, not only in their own room but, since they were now members of the household, in all its arrangements, especially in the kitchen. Superfluous, not to say dirty, objects they could not bear. Besides, they had brought with them most of the furnishings they needed. For this reason many things could be dispensed with that it was no use trying to sell but that should not be thrown away either. All of them found their way into Gregor's room. The ash can likewise and the kitchen garbage can. Anything that was not needed for the moment was simply flung into Gregor's room by the charwoman, who did everything in a hurry; fortunately Gregor usually saw only the object, whatever it was, and the hand that held it. Perhaps she intended to take the things away again as time and opportunity offered, or

WORDS TO KNOW

chagrin (shə-grĭn′) *n.* a feeling of disappointment or humiliation

to collect them until she could throw them all out in a heap, but in fact they just lay wherever she happened to throw them, except when Gregor pushed his way through the junk heap and shifted it somewhat, at first out of necessity, because he had not room enough to crawl, but later with increasing enjoyment, although after such excursions, being sad and weary to death, he would lie motionless for hours. And since the lodgers often ate their supper at home in the common living room, the living-room door stayed shut many an evening, yet Gregor reconciled himself quite easily to the shutting of the door, for often enough on evenings when it was opened he had disregarded it entirely and lain in the darkest corner of his room, quite unnoticed by the family. But on one occasion the charwoman left the door open a little and it stayed ajar even when the lodgers came in for supper and the lamp was lit. They set themselves at the top end of the table where formerly Gregor and his father and mother had eaten their meals, unfolded their napkins, and took knife and fork in hand. At once his mother appeared in the other doorway with a dish of meat and close behind her his sister with a dish of potatoes piled high. The food steamed with a thick vapor. The lodgers bent over the food set before them as if to scrutinize it before eating, in fact the man in the middle, who seemed to pass for an authority with the other two, cut a piece of meat as it lay on the dish, obviously to discover if it were tender or should be sent back to the kitchen. He showed satisfaction, and Gregor's mother and sister, who had been watching anxiously, breathed freely and began to smile.

NOTES
READING TIP
If you come across a word you don't know, try using context clues—the meaning of surrounding words—to help you. The shaded text in lines 1611 and 1612 gives context clues for the meaning of *ajar.* The shaded text in lines 1623 and 1624 gives context clues for the meaning of *scrutinize.*

The family itself took its meals in the kitchen. Nonetheless, Gregor's father came into the living room before going into the kitchen and with one prolonged bow, cap in hand, made a round of the table. The lodgers all stood up and murmured something in their beards. When they were alone again they ate their food in almost complete silence. It seemed remarkable to Gregor that among the various noises coming from the table he could

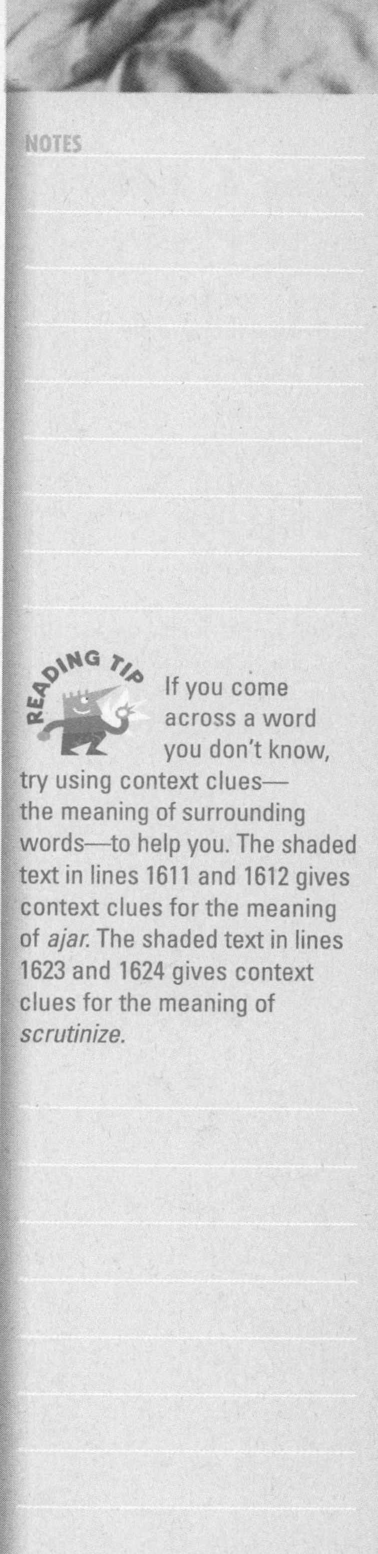

always distinguish the sound of their masticating[49] teeth, as if this were a sign to Gregor that one needed teeth in order to eat, and that with toothless jaws even of the finest make one could do nothing. "I'm hungry enough," said Gregor sadly to himself, "but not for that kind of food. How these lodgers are stuffing themselves, and here I am dying of starvation!"

Pause & Reflect

1. Reread the details you underlined. How does Gregor feel now? **(Draw Conclusions)**
   - ❑ proud
   - ❑ peaceful
   - ❑ neglected
   - ❑ friendly
   - ❑ angry
   - ❑ unimportant

2. What is the family doing with Gregor's room? What does this tell you about their attitude toward Gregor now? **(Analyze)**

FOCUS

One night Gregor's sister is asked to play her violin. Find out what happens when the music draws Gregor out of his room.

On that very evening—during the whole of his time there Gregor could not remember ever having heard the violin—the sound of violin-playing came from the kitchen. The lodgers had already finished their supper, the one in the middle had brought out a newspaper and given the other two a page apiece, and now they were leaning back at ease reading and smoking. When the violin began to play they pricked up their ears, got to their feet, and went on tiptoe to the hall door where they stood huddled together. Their movements must have been heard in the kitchen, for Gregor's father called out: "Is the violin-playing disturbing you, gentlemen? It can be stopped at once." "On the contrary," said the middle lodger, "could not Fräulein[50] Samsa come and play in this room, beside us, where it is much more convenient and comfortable?" "Oh certainly," cried Gregor's father, as if he were the violin-player. The lodgers came back into the living room and waited. Presently Gregor's father arrived with the music stand, his mother carrying the music and his sister with the violin. His sister quietly made everything ready to start playing; his parents, who had never let rooms before and so had an exaggerated idea of the courtesy due

49. **masticating:** chewing.

50. **Fräulein** (froi′līn′): the German equivalent of *Miss*.

to lodgers, did not venture to sit down on their own chairs; his father leaned against the door, the right hand thrust between two buttons of his livery coat, which was formally buttoned up; but his mother was offered a chair by one of the lodgers and, since she left the chair just where he had happened to put it, sat down in a corner to one side.

Gregor's sister began to play; the father and mother, from either side, intently watched the movements of her hands. Gregor, attracted by the playing, ventured to move forward a little until his head was actually inside the living room. He felt hardly any surprise at his growing lack of consideration for the others; there had been a time when he prided himself on being considerate. And yet just on this occasion he had more reason than ever to hide himself, since, owing to the amount of dust that lay thick in his room and rose into the air at the slightest movement, he too was covered with dust; fluff and hair and remnants of food trailed with him, caught on his back and along his sides; his indifference to everything was much too great for him to turn on his back and scrape himself clean on the carpet, as once he had done several times a day. And in spite of his condition, no shame deterred him from advancing a little over the spotless floor of the living room.

To be sure, no one was aware of him. The family was entirely absorbed in the violin-playing; the lodgers, however, who first of all had stationed themselves, hands in pockets, much too close behind the music stand so that they could all have read the music, which must have bothered his sister, had soon retreated to the window, half whispering with downbent heads, and stayed there while his father turned an anxious eye on them. Indeed, they were making it more than obvious that they had been disappointed in their expectation of hearing good or enjoyable violin-playing, that they had had more than enough of the performance and only out of courtesy suffered a continued disturbance of their peace. From the way they all kept blowing the

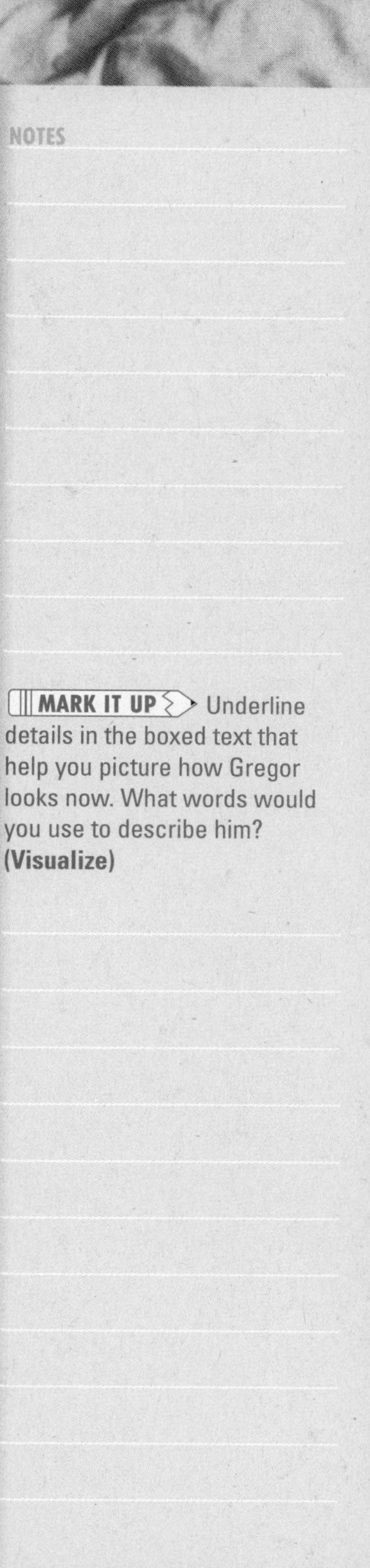

NOTES

MARK IT UP Underline details in the boxed text that help you picture how Gregor looks now. What words would you use to describe him? **(Visualize)**

NOTES

READ ALOUD the boxed text. In what ways does Gregor reveal his human side? In what ways does he reveal his animal side? Write details in the chart. **(Compare and Contrast)**

Gregor's Human Side	Gregor's Animal Side

smoke of their cigars high in the air through nose and mouth one could divine their irritation. And yet Gregor's sister was playing so beautifully. Her face leaned sideways, intently and sadly her eyes followed the notes of music. Gregor crawled a little farther forward and lowered his head to the ground so that it might be possible for his eyes to meet hers. Was he an animal, that music had such an effect upon him? He felt as if the way were opening before him to the unknown nourishment he craved. He was determined to push forward till he reached his sister, to pull at her skirt and so let her know that she was to come into his room with her violin, for no one here appreciated her playing as he would appreciate it. He would never let her out of his room, at least, not so long as he lived; his frightful appearance would become, for the first time, useful to him; he would watch all the doors of his room at once and spit at intruders; but his sister should need no constraint, she should stay with him out of her own free will; she should sit beside him on the sofa, bend down her ear to him, and hear him confide that he had had the firm intention of sending her to the Conservatorium, and that, but for his mishap, last Christmas—surely Christmas was long past?—he would have announced it to everybody without allowing a single objection. After this confession his sister would be so touched that she would burst into tears, and Gregor would then raise himself to her shoulder and kiss her on the neck, which, now that she went to business, she kept free of any ribbon or collar.

"Mr. Samsa!" cried the middle lodger to Gregor's father, and pointed, without wasting any more words, at Gregor, now working himself slowly forward. The violin fell silent, the middle lodger first smiled to his friends with a shake of the head and then looked at Gregor again. Instead of driving Gregor out, his father seemed to think it more needful to begin by soothing down the lodgers, although they were not at all agitated and apparently found Gregor more entertaining than the violin-playing. He hurried toward them and, spreading out his arms, tried to urge them back into their own room and at the same time to block their view of Gregor. They now began to be really a little angry, one could not tell whether because of the old man's behavior or because it had just dawned on them that all unwittingly they had such a neighbor as Gregor next door. They demanded explanations of his father, they waved their arms like him, tugged uneasily at their beards, and only with reluctance backed toward their room. Meanwhile, Gregor's sister, who stood there as if lost when her playing was so abruptly broken off, came to life again, pulled herself together all at once after standing for a while holding violin and bow in nervelessly hanging hands and staring at her music, pushed her violin into the lap of her mother, who was still sitting in her chair fighting asthmatically for breath, and ran into the lodgers' room to which they were now being shepherded by her father rather more quickly than before. One could see the pillows and blankets on the beds flying under her accustomed fingers and being laid in order. Before the lodgers had actually reached their room she had finished making the beds and slipped out.

The old man seemed once more to be so possessed by his mulish self-assertiveness that he was forgetting all the respect he should show to his lodgers. He kept driving them on and driving them on until in the very door of the bedroom the middle lodger stamped his foot loudly on the floor and so brought him to a halt. "I beg to announce," said the lodger, lifting one hand and looking also at Gregor's mother and sister, "that because of the disgusting conditions prevailing in this household and family"—here he spat on the floor with emphatic brevity[51]—"I give you notice on the spot. Naturally I won't pay you a penny for the days I have lived here, on the contrary I shall consider bringing

51. brevity: briefness; abruptness.

NOTES
REREAD
the lodger's words. Do you think he is being fair? Why or why not? **(Make Judgments)**

Pause & Reflect

1. Complete this chart to show what happens when Grete plays the violin. **(Cause and Effect)**

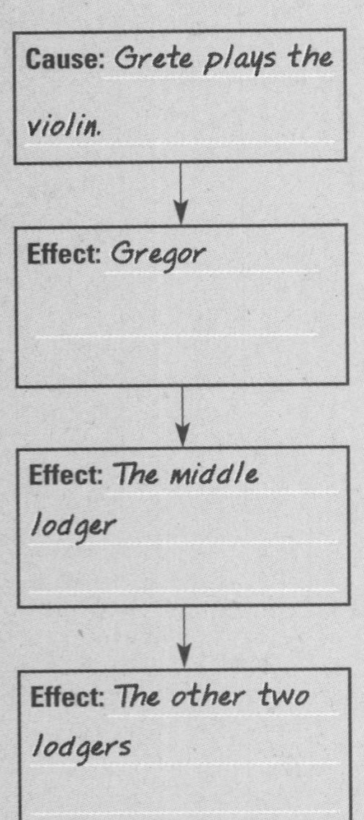

2. What do you think will happen next? **(Predict)**

an action for damages against you, based on claims—believe me—that will be easily susceptible of[52] proof." He ceased and stared straight in front of him, as if he expected something. In fact his two friends at once rushed into the breach[53] with these words: "And we too give notice on the spot." On that he seized the door handle and shut the door with a slam.

Pause & Reflect

FOCUS

Grete comes to a conclusion about Gregor. She decides that this insect isn't really her brother.

MARK IT UP Draw a box around the "proof" Grete gives that the giant bug can't possibly be her brother.

Gregor's father, groping with his hands, staggered forward and fell into his chair; it looked as if he were stretching himself there for his ordinary evening nap, but the marked jerkings of his head, which were as if uncontrollable, showed that he was far from asleep. Gregor had simply stayed quietly all the time on the spot where the lodgers had espied him. Disappointment at the failure of his plan, perhaps also the weakness arising from extreme hunger, made it impossible for him to move. He feared, with a fair degree of certainty, that at any moment the general tension would discharge itself in a combined attack upon him, and he lay waiting. He did not react even to the noise made by the violin as it fell off his mother's lap from under her trembling fingers and gave out a resonant note.

"My dear parents," said his sister, slapping her hand on the table by way of introduction, "things can't go on like this. Perhaps you don't realize that, but I do. I won't utter my brother's name in the presence of this creature, and so

52. **susceptible of:** open to.

53. **breach:** gap; opening.

all I say is: we must try to get rid of it. We've tried to look after it and to put up with it as far as is humanly possible, and I don't think anyone could reproach us in the slightest."

"She is more than right," said Gregor's father to himself. His mother, who was still choking for lack of breath, began to cough hollowly into her hand with a wild look in her eyes.

His sister rushed over to her and held her forehead. His father's thoughts seemed to have lost their vagueness at Grete's words, he sat more upright, fingering his service cap that lay among the plates still lying on the table from the lodgers' supper, and from time to time looked at the still form of Gregor.

"We must try to get rid of it," his sister now said explicitly to her father, since her mother was coughing too much to hear a word, "it will be the death of both of you, I can see that coming. When one has to work as hard as we do, all of us, one can't stand this continual torment at home on top of it. At least I can't stand it any longer." And she burst into such a passion of sobbing that her tears dropped on her mother's face, where she wiped them off mechanically.

"My dear," said the old man sympathetically, and with evident understanding, "but what can we do?"

Gregor's sister merely shrugged her shoulders to indicate the feeling of helplessness that had now overmastered her during her weeping fit, in contrast to her former confidence.

"If he could understand us," said her father, half questioningly; Grete, still sobbing, vehemently waved a hand to show how unthinkable that was.

"If he could understand us," repeated the old man, shutting his eyes to consider his daughter's conviction that understanding was impossible, "then perhaps we might come to some agreement with him. But as it is—"

"He must go," cried Gregor's sister, "that's the only solution, Father. You must just try to get rid of the idea that this is Gregor. The fact that we've believed it for so long is the root of all our trouble. But how can it be Gregor?

MARK IT UP In the boxed text, circle the pronoun that Grete uses to refer to Gregor. Why does she use this pronoun? (Infer)

Pause & Reflect

1. What proof does Grete give that the giant bug is not Gregor? Does her claim make sense? **(Evaluate)**

2. Why do you think Grete tries to convince her parents that the bug is just a vile and mean-spirited insect? **(Draw Conclusions)**

If this were Gregor, he would have realized long ago that human beings can't live with such a creature, and he'd have gone away on his own accord. Then we wouldn't have any brother, but we'd be able to go on living and keep his memory in honor. As it is, this creature persecutes us, drives away our lodgers, obviously wants the whole apartment to himself, and would have us all sleep in the gutter. Just look, Father," she shrieked all at once, "he's at it again!" And in an access[54] of panic that was quite incomprehensible to Gregor she even quitted her mother, literally thrusting the chair from her as if she would rather sacrifice her mother than stay so near to Gregor, and rushed behind her father, who also rose up, being simply upset by her agitation, and half spread his arms out as if to protect her.

Yet Gregor had not the slightest intention of frightening anyone, far less his sister. He had only begun to turn around in order to crawl back to his room, but it was certainly a startling operation to watch, since because of his disabled condition he could not execute the difficult turning movements except by lifting his head and then bracing it against the floor over and over again. He paused and looked around. His good intentions seemed to have been recognized; the alarm had only been momentary. Now they were all watching him in melancholy silence. His mother lay in her chair, her legs stiffly outstretched and pressed together, her eyes almost closing for sheer weariness; his father and his sister were sitting beside each other, his sister's arm around the old man's neck.

Pause & Reflect

54. access: outburst.

FOCUS

Gregor returns to his room one last time. The solution to the family's problem is about to be revealed. Find out what it is.

Perhaps I can go on turning around now, thought Gregor, and began his labors again. He could not stop himself from panting with the effort, and had to pause now and then to take breath. Nor did anyone harass him, he was left entirely to himself. When he had completed the turn-around he began at once to crawl straight back. He was amazed at the distance separating him from his room and could not understand how in his weak state he had managed to accomplish the same journey so recently, almost without remarking it. Intent on crawling as fast as possible, he barely noticed that not a single word, not an ejaculation from his family, interfered with his progress. Only when he was already in the doorway did he turn his head around, not completely, for his neck muscles were getting stiff, but enough to see that nothing had changed behind him except that his sister had risen to her feet. His last glance fell on his mother, who was not quite overcome by sleep.

Hardly was he well inside his room when the door was hastily pushed shut, bolted, and locked. The sudden noise in his rear startled him so much that his little legs gave beneath him. It was his sister who had shown such haste. She had been standing ready waiting and had made a light spring forward, Gregor had not even heard her coming, and she cried "At last!" to her parents as she turned the key in the lock.

"And what now?" said Gregor to himself, looking around in the darkness. Soon he made the discovery that he was now unable to stir a limb. This did not surprise him, rather it seemed unnatural that he should ever actually have been able to move on these feeble little legs. Otherwise he felt relatively comfortable. True, his whole body was aching, but it seemed that the pain was gradually growing less and would finally pass away. The rotting apple in his back and the inflamed area around it, all covered with soft dust,

NOTES
REREAD
the boxed text. What do you think is happening to Gregor? (Analyze)

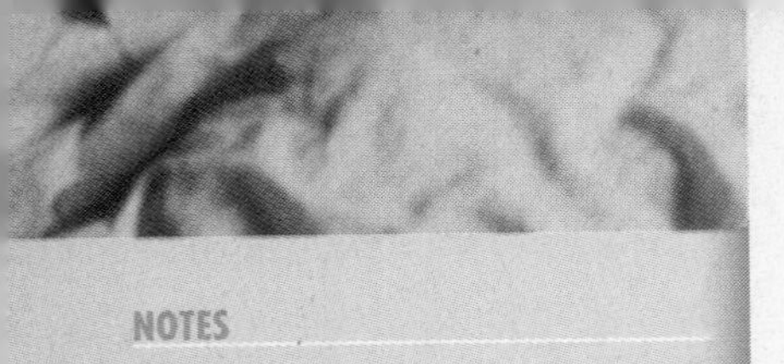

NOTES

already hardly troubled him. He thought of his family with tenderness and love. The decision that he must disappear was one that he held to even more strongly than his sister, if that were possible. In this state of vacant and peaceful meditation he remained until the tower clock struck three in the morning. The first broadening of light in the world outside the window entered his consciousness once more. Then his head sank to the floor of its own accord and from his nostrils came the last faint flicker of his breath.

When the charwoman arrived early in the morning—what between her strength and her impatience she slammed all the doors so loudly, never mind how often she had been begged not to do so, that no one in the whole apartment could enjoy any quiet sleep after her arrival—she noticed nothing unusual as she took her customary peep into Gregor's room. She thought he was lying motionless on purpose, pretending to be in the sulks; she credited him with every kind of intelligence. Since she happened to have the long-handled broom in her hand she tried to tickle him up with it from the doorway. When that too produced no reaction she felt provoked and poked at him a little harder, and only when she had pushed him along the floor without meeting any resistance was her attention aroused. It did not take her long to establish the truth of the matter, and her eyes widened, she let out a whistle, yet did not waste much time over it but tore open the door of the Samsas' bedroom and yelled into the darkness at the top of her voice: "Just look at this, it's dead; it's lying here dead and done for!"

Mr. and Mrs. Samsa started up in their double bed and before they realized the nature of the charwoman's announcement had some difficulty in overcoming the shock of it. But then they got out of bed quickly, one on either side, Mr. Samsa throwing a blanket over his shoulders, Mrs. Samsa in nothing but her nightgown; in this array they entered Gregor's room. Meanwhile the door of the living room opened, too, where Grete had been sleeping since the advent of the lodgers; she was completely dressed as if she had not been to bed, which seemed to be confirmed also by the paleness of her face. "Dead?" said Mrs. Samsa, looking questioningly at the charwoman, although she would have investigated for herself, and the fact was obvious enough without investigation. "I should say so," said the charwoman, proving her words by pushing Gregor's corpse a long way to one side with her broomstick. Mrs. Samsa made a movement as if to stop her, but checked it. "Well," said Mr. Samsa, "now thanks be to God." He crossed himself, and the three women followed his example. Grete, whose eyes never left the corpse, said: "Just see how thin he was. It's such a long time since he's eaten anything. The food came out again just as it went in." Indeed Gregor's body was completely flat and dry, as could only now be seen when it was no longer supported by the legs and nothing prevented one from looking closely at it.

Pause & Reflect

FOCUS

Now that Gregor is gone, his parents and sister take a fresh look at their lives. Find out what they decide to do.

MARK IT UP As you read, put an *X* next to each change the family intends to make.

"Come in beside us, Grete, for a little while," said Mrs. Samsa with a tremulous[55] smile, and Grete, not without looking back at the corpse, followed her parents into their bedroom. The charwoman shut the door and opened the window wide. Although it was so early in the morning a certain softness was perceptible in the fresh air. After all, it was already the end of March.

The three lodgers emerged from their room and were surprised to see no breakfast; they had been forgotten. "Where's our breakfast?" said the middle lodger peevishly

55. **tremulous** (trĕm′yə-ləs): timid or fearful.

Pause & Reflect

1. Explain how the family's problem is solved. Do you think this "solution" was avoidable or not? Explain. **(Evaluate)**

The solution:

❑ Avoidable ❑ Unavoidable

Why or why not?

2. **MARK IT UP** Underline the sentences that suggest that Gregor chose to die.

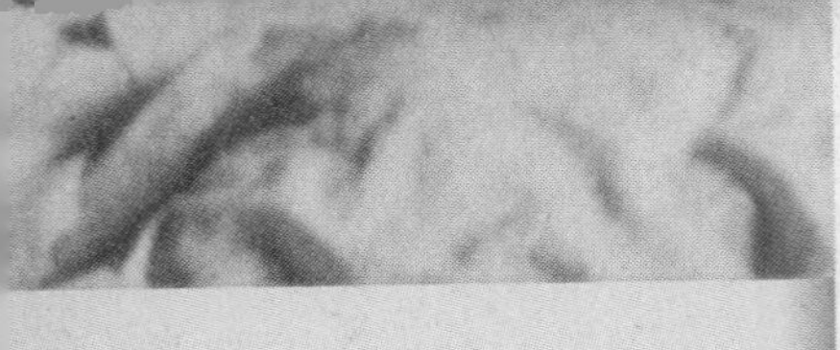

NOTES

to the charwoman. But she put her finger to her lips and hastily, without a word, indicated by gestures that they should go into Gregor's room. They did so and stood, their hands in the pockets of their somewhat shabby coats, around Gregor's corpse in the room where it was now fully light.

At that the door of the Samsas' bedroom opened and Mr. Samsa appeared in his uniform, his wife on one arm, his daughter on the other. They all looked a little as if they had been crying; from time to time Grete hid her face on her father's arm.

"Leave my house at once!" said Mr. Samsa, and pointed to the door without disengaging himself from the women. "What do you mean by that?" said the middle lodger, taken somewhat aback, with a feeble smile. The two others put their hands behind them and kept rubbing them together, as if in gleeful expectation of a fine set-to in which they were bound to come off the winners. "I mean just what I say," answered Mr. Samsa, and advanced in a straight line with his two companions toward the lodger. He stood his ground at first quietly, looking at the floor as if his thoughts were taking a new pattern in his head. "Then let us go, by all means," he said, and looked up at Mr. Samsa as if in a sudden access of humility he were expecting some renewed sanction[56] for this decision. Mr. Samsa merely nodded briefly once or twice with meaning eyes. Upon that the lodger really did go with long strides into the hall, his two friends had been listening and had quite stopped rubbing their hands for some moments and now went scuttling after him as if afraid that Mr. Samsa might get into the hall before them and cut them off from their leader. In the hall they all three took their hats from the rack, their sticks from the umbrella stand, bowed in silence, and quitted the apartment. With a suspiciousness that proved quite unfounded Mr. Samsa and the two women followed them out to the landing; leaning over the banister they watched the three figures slowly but surely going down the long stairs, vanishing from sight at a certain

---

56. sanction (săngk′shən): penalty; punishment.

turn of the staircase on every floor and coming into view again after a moment or so; the more they dwindled,[57] the more the Samsa family's interest in them dwindled, and when a butcher's boy met them and passed them on the stairs coming up proudly with a tray on his head, Mr. Samsa and the two women soon left the landing and as if a burden had been lifted from them went back into their apartment.

They decided to spend this day in resting and going for a stroll; they had not only deserved such a respite from work, but absolutely needed it. And so they sat down at the table and wrote three notes of excuse, Mr. Samsa to his board of management, Mrs. Samsa to her employer, and Grete to the head of her firm. While they were writing, the charwoman came in to say that she was going now, since her morning's work was finished. At first they only nodded without looking up, but as she kept hovering there they eyed her irritably. "Well?" said Mr. Samsa. The charwoman stood grinning in the doorway as if she had good news to impart[58] to the family but meant not to say a word unless properly questioned. The small ostrich feather standing upright on her hat, which had annoyed Mr. Samsa ever since she was engaged, was waving gaily in all directions. "Well, what is it then?" asked Mrs. Samsa, who obtained more respect from the charwoman than the others. "Oh," said the charwoman, giggling so amiably that she could not at once continue, "just this, you don't need to bother about how to get rid of the thing next door. It's been seen to already." Mrs. Samsa and Grete bent over their letters again, as if preoccupied; Mr. Samsa, who perceived that she was eager to begin describing it all in detail, stopped her with a decisive hand. But since she was not allowed to tell her story, she remembered the great hurry she was in, obviously deeply huffed: "Bye, everybody," she said, whirling off violently, and departed with a frightful slamming of doors.

"She'll be given notice tonight," said Mr. Samsa, but neither from his wife nor his daughter did he get any answer,

NOTES
REREAD
the boxed passage. What has the charwoman told the family? How does the family respond? (Infer)

57. **dwindled:** became smaller.

58. **impart:** communicate.

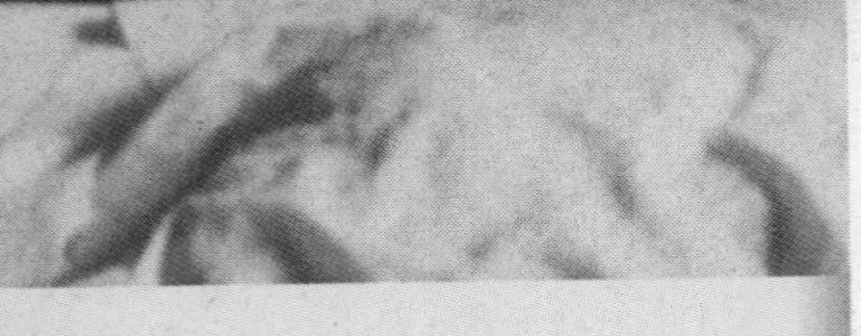

Pause & Reflect

1. Put a *T* next to the statements that are true of the Samsas now that Gregor is gone. Put an *F* next to statements that are not true. **(Draw Conclusions)**

   ___ They mourn Gregor's death.

   ___ They are optimistic about the future.

   ___ They are worried about their prospects.

   ___ They don't want to forget Gregor.

   ___ They feel a sense of freedom.

   ___ They want to leave the past behind.

2. Reread the last sentence. Why do you think the author ends the story this way? **(Evaluate)**

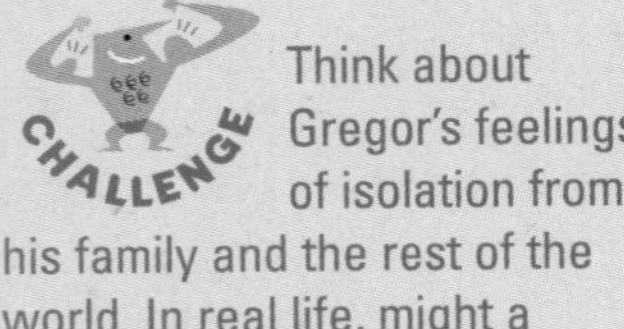

Think about Gregor's feelings of isolation from his family and the rest of the world. In real life, might a person experience similar feelings? Explain. **(Connect)**

for the charwoman seemed to have shattered again the composure they had barely achieved. They rose, went to the window and stayed there, clasping each other tight. Mr. Samsa turned in his chair to look at them and quietly observed them for a little. Then he called out: "Come along, now, do. Let bygones be bygones. And you might have some consideration for me." The two of them complied at once, hastened to him, caressed him, and quickly finished their letters.

Then they all three left the apartment together, which was more than they had done for months, and went by train into the open country outside the town. The tram, in which they were the only passengers, was filled with warm sunshine. Leaning comfortably back in their seats they canvassed[59] their prospects for the future, and it appeared on closer inspection that these were not at all bad, for the jobs they had got, which so far they had never really discussed with each other, were all three admirable and likely to lead to better things later on. The greatest immediate improvement in their condition would of course arise from moving to another house; they wanted to take a smaller and cheaper but also better situated and more easily run apartment than the one they had, which Gregor had selected. While they were thus conversing, it struck both Mr. and Mrs. Samsa, almost at the same moment, as they became aware of their daughter's increasing vivacity, that in spite of all the sorrow of recent times, which had made her cheeks pale, she had bloomed into a pretty girl with a good figure. They grew quieter and half unconsciously exchanged glances of complete agreement, having come to the conclusion that it would soon be time to find a good husband for her. And it was like a confirmation of their new dreams and excellent intentions that at the end of their journey their daughter sprang to her feet first and stretched her young body. ❖

Pause & Reflect

59. canvassed: carefully examined or discussed.

Active Reading SkillBuilder

Visualizing Details

Visualizing is the act of forming mental pictures based upon what you are reading. By paying close attention to the details given by the narrator, you will be able to visualize Gregor's experiences. As you read, notice the details that particularly strike you, those that seem to jump off the page. Jot them down in the chart below. When you have completed the story, go back to the chart and decide what each detail helps you see or understand about the story.

Image from the story	What the image helps you see or understand
1. "He would have needed arms and hands to hoist himself up; instead he had only the numerous little legs which never stopped waving in all directions and which he could not control in the least."	1. Gregor really cannot control his movements at all. It seems he is trapped in this new body and all his movements are limited by its size and shape.

Literary Analysis SkillBuilder

Point of View

Point of view is the method the author uses to narrate a story. In "Metamorphosis," Kafka uses two different points of view–third-person limited, and third-person omniscient. Using the definitions below, find one example of each type of narration in the story. Write them out verbatim, using quotation marks. (Note: third-person omniscient narration is used at the end of the story.) Include page numbers. Two examples have been given.

- Third-person limited: the narrator is "limited" to the thoughts and feelings of only one character, in this case Gregor Samsa.
- Third-person omniscient: perspective in which the narrator is all-knowing and can reveal the thoughts of all the characters.

Point of View	Quotes from the text
Third-person limited	1. *Gregor's eyes turned next to the window, and the overcast day—one could hear the raindrops beating on the window gutter—made him feel quite melancholy. (page 292)* 2. 3.
Third-person omniscient	1. *Then they all three left the apartment together, which was more than they had done for months . . . (page 352)* 2. 3.

Words to Know SkillBuilder

Words to Know

amiably	dissuade	imminent	lavishly	refuge
chagrin	equilibrium	intervene	omission	unintelligible

A. Fill in each set of blanks with the correct word from the word list. The boxed letters will spell out what Gregor Samsa was when he awoke one morning.

1. This describes a message that can not be understood. _ _ _ _ [_] _ _ _ _ _ _ _ _ _
2. You might have this feeling after receiving a piece of bad news. _ _ _ _ [_] _ _
3. If a person has a happy, friendly disposition, he or she acts this way. [_] _ _ _ _ _ _
4. If danger is near or approaching, you might say the danger is this. _ _ _ _ _ _ _ [_] _
5. When a home is decorated richly and abundantly for a celebration, it is decorated this way. _ _ _ _ [_] _ _ _
6. When people seek a safe place to hide or protect themselves, they are seeking this. _ _ [_] _ _ _
7. This is sometimes preceded by the phrase "make an error of," and refers to the act of leaving out. [_] _ _ _ _ _ _ _
8. If you lose your footing or balance, you lose this. _ _ _ _ _ _ _ _ [_] _ _ [_]
9. When it comes to our personal lives, we don't always want our parents to do this. _ _ _ [_] _ _ _ _ _
10. If a friend is about to make a bad decision, you might try to do this in order to change his or her mind. [_] _ _ _ _ _ _ _

B. Write a short essay describing what it might feel like to wake up one morning and have transformed into an animal. Choose a favorite animal. What would your body feel like from the inside, and on the outside? Be specific in your descriptions, and use at least **four** Words to Know.

Before You Read

Connect to Your Life

Think about an important decision you have made. Maybe you had to decide between standing up for a personal belief or going along with the crowd. Why did you decide as you did? What were the consequences of your decision? Write your ideas in the chart below.

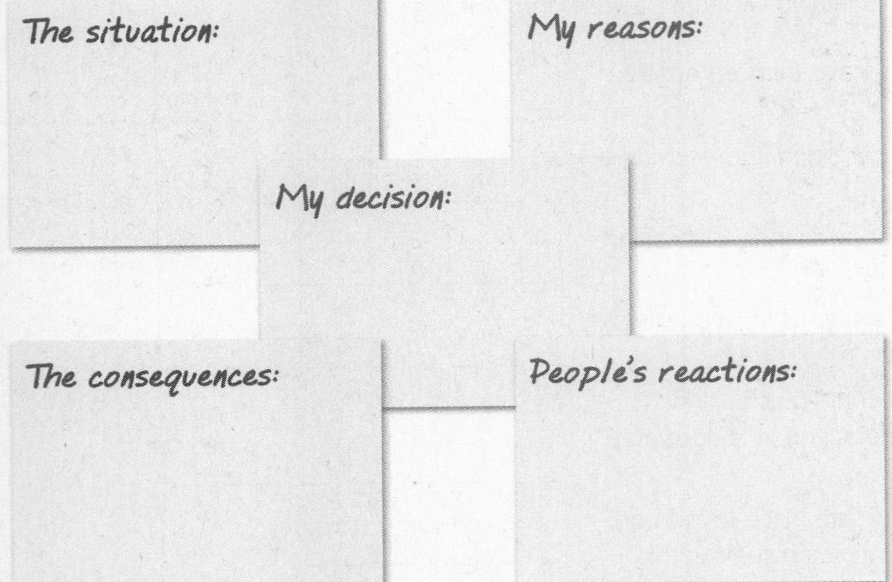

Key to the Story

WHAT YOU NEED TO KNOW Algeria is a country in northwestern Africa. In 1830, France invaded Algeria and set up a colonial government. It took away land and basic rights from the native people, who were mostly Arab Muslims. In 1954, the Arabs started a war to free themselves from French rule. After six years of bloody fighting, Algeria gained its independence. The story you are about to read takes place shortly before the fighting broke out. Albert Camus (äl-bĕr′ kä-mo͞o′), was a French writer who grew up in Algeria.

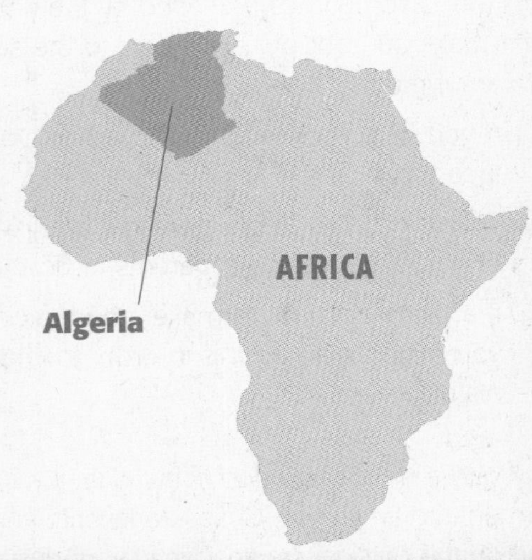

THE Guest

BY ALBERT CAMUS

TRANSLATED BY JUSTIN O'BRIEN

PREVIEW The main character in this story is Daru, a French schoolteacher who lives in the Algerian desert. When two travelers arrive at his school, he is forced to make an important decision—one that will change his life forever.

NOTES

FOCUS

As the story begins, Daru watches two travelers approaching in the distance. Read to find out about Daru and the place where he lives.

MARK IT UP As you read, underline details that help you visualize the landscape. An example is highlighted on this page.

The schoolmaster was watching the two men climb toward him. One was on horseback, the other on foot. They had not yet tackled the abrupt rise leading to the schoolhouse built on the hillside. They were toiling onward, making slow progress in the snow, among the stones, on the vast expanse of the high, deserted plateau.[1] From time to time the horse stumbled. Without hearing anything yet, he could see the breath issuing from the horse's nostrils. One of the men, at least, knew the region. They were following the trail although it had disappeared days ago under a layer of dirty white snow. The schoolmaster calculated that it would take them half an hour to get onto the hill. It was cold; he went back into the school to get a sweater.

He crossed the empty, frigid classroom. On the blackboard the four rivers of France, drawn with four different colored chalks, had been flowing toward their estuaries[2] for the past three days. Snow had suddenly fallen in mid-October after eight months of drought without the transition of rain, and the twenty pupils, more or less, who lived in the villages scattered over the plateau had stopped coming. With fair weather they would return. Daru now heated only the single room that was his lodging, adjoining the classroom and giving also onto the plateau to the east. Like the class windows, his window looked to the south too. On that side the school was a few kilometers from the point where the plateau began to slope toward the south. In clear weather could be seen the

the boxed passage on this page. Daru has drawn the rivers of France on the blackboard. Why do you think he teaches his pupils in Algeria about the rivers of France? **(Infer)**

1. **plateau:** an elevated, relatively level expanse of land.
2. **the four rivers of France . . . estuaries:** France's four major rivers are the Loire (lwär), the Seine (sān), the Marne (märn), and the Rhone (rōn). Their estuaries are the stretches near their mouths, into which ocean tides flow.

purple mass of the mountain range where the gap opened onto the desert.

Somewhat warmed, Daru returned to the window from which he had first seen the two men. They were no longer visible. Hence they must have tackled the rise. The sky was not so dark, for the snow had stopped falling during the night. The morning had opened with a dirty light which had scarcely become brighter as the ceiling of clouds lifted. At two in the afternoon it seemed as if the day were merely beginning. But still this was better than those three days when the thick snow was falling amidst unbroken darkness with little gusts of wind that rattled the double door of the classroom. Then Daru had spent long hours in his room, leaving it only to go to the shed and feed the chickens or get some coal. Fortunately the delivery truck from Tadjid, the nearest village to the north, had brought his supplies two days before the blizzard. It would return in forty-eight hours.

Besides, he had enough to resist a siege, for the little room was cluttered with bags of wheat that the administration left as a stock to distribute to those of his pupils whose families had suffered from the drought. Actually they had all been victims because they were all poor. Every day Daru would distribute a ration to the children. They had missed it, he knew, during these bad days. Possibly one of the fathers or big brothers would come this afternoon and he could supply them with grain. It was just a matter of carrying them over to the next harvest. Now shiploads of wheat were arriving from France and the worst was over. But it would be hard to forget that poverty, that army of ragged ghosts wandering in the sunlight, the plateaus burned to a cinder month after month, the earth shriveled up little by little, literally scorched, every stone bursting into dust under one's foot. The sheep had died then by thousands and even a few men, here and there, sometimes without anyone's knowing.

In contrast with such poverty, he who lived almost like a monk in his remote schoolhouse, nonetheless satisfied with the little he had and with the rough life, had felt like a lord

This story is beautifully written but challenging to read. It has very little action. Instead, the writer explores the main character's inner world. To get the most from your reading, try these strategies:

- Imagine yourself in Daru's place. Ask yourself what you would do in his situation.
- Be ready to **infer,** or read between the lines, to figure out the author's message, or **theme.**
- Use your imagination to picture the **setting** that the author describes through details.

MARK IT UP **KEEP TRACK**
Remember to use these marks to keep track of your reading:

- * This is important.
- ? I have a question about this.
- ! This is a surprise.

Pause & Reflect

1. Look back at the details you underlined. Why is life so difficult for Daru's pupils and their families? **(Infer)**

2. Which two phrases below describe Daru? Check them. **(Clarify)**

- ❑ hides supplies for his own use
- ❑ feels at home in the desert
- ❑ hates France
- ❑ gives wheat to the school children

with his whitewashed walls, his narrow couch, his unpainted shelves, his well, and his weekly provision of water and food. And suddenly this snow, without warning, without the foretaste of rain. This is the way the region was, cruel to live in, even without men—who didn't help matters either. But Daru had been born here. Everywhere else, he felt exiled.

Pause & Reflect

FOCUS

The two travelers arrive at the schoolhouse. One is a gendarme, or a police officer, and the other is an Arab prisoner. Read to find out how Daru reacts to these visitors.

MARK IT UP As you read, underline details that describe Daru's reactions.

He stepped out onto the terrace in front of the schoolhouse. The two men were now halfway up the slope. He recognized the horseman as Balducci,[3] the old gendarme he had known for a long time. Balducci was holding on the end of a rope an Arab who was walking behind him with hands bound and head lowered. The gendarme waved a greeting to which Daru did not reply, lost as he was in contemplation of the Arab dressed in a faded blue jellaba,[4] his feet in sandals but covered with socks of heavy raw wool, his head surmounted by a narrow, short *chèche*.[5] They were approaching. Balducci was holding back his horse in order not to hurt the Arab, and the group was advancing slowly.

Within earshot, Balducci shouted: "One hour to do the three kilometers from El Ameur!"[6] Daru did not answer.

---

3. **Balducci** (bäl-do͞o′chē).
4. **jellaba** (jə-lä′bə): a long, loose, hooded cloak worn by Arab men (usually spelled *djellaba*).
5. ***chèche*** (shĕsh) ***French:*** scarf (here, a type of scarf worn by French troops in Africa).
6. **El Ameur** (ĕl ə-mœr′): a town in northern Algeria, about 150 miles southwest of Algiers.

Short and square in his thick sweater, he watched them climb. Not once had the Arab raised his head. "Hello," said Daru when they got up onto the terrace. "Come in and warm up." Balducci painfully got down from his horse without letting go the rope. From under his bristling mustache he smiled at the schoolmaster. His little dark eyes, deep-set under a tanned forehead, and his mouth surrounded with wrinkles made him look attentive and studious. Daru took the bridle, led the horse to the shed, and came back to the two men, who were now waiting for him in the school. He led them into his room. "I am going to heat up the classroom," he said. "We'll be more comfortable there." When he entered the room again, Balducci was on the couch. He had undone the rope tying him to the Arab, who had squatted near the stove. His hands still bound, the *chèche* pushed back on his head, he was looking toward the window. At first Daru noticed only his huge lips, fat, smooth, almost Negroid; yet his nose was straight, his eyes were dark and full of fever. The *chèche* revealed an obstinate forehead and, under the weathered skin now rather discolored by the cold, the whole face had a restless and rebellious look that struck Daru when the Arab, turning his face toward him, looked him straight in the eyes. "Go into the other room," said the schoolmaster, "and I'll make you some mint tea." "Thanks," Balducci said. "What a chore! How I long for retirement." And addressing his prisoner in Arabic: "Come on, you." The Arab got up and, slowly, holding his bound wrists in front of him, went into the classroom.

With the tea, Daru brought a chair. But Balducci was already enthroned on the nearest pupil's desk and the Arab had squatted against the teacher's platform facing the stove, which stood between the desk and the window. When he held out the glass of tea to the prisoner, Daru hesitated at the sight of his bound hands. "He might perhaps be untied." "Sure," said Balducci. "That was for the trip."

WORDS TO KNOW

obstinate (ŏb′stə-nĭt) *adj.* stubborn

NOTES

REREAD the boxed passage on this page. Daru wants the Arab to be untied. What does this tell you about Daru? **(Infer)**

NOTES

the boxed passage on this page with a partner. If you were in Daru's position, would you agree to deliver the prisoner to the police? Explain. **(Connect)**

He started to get to his feet. But Daru, setting the glass on the floor, had knelt beside the Arab. Without saying anything, the Arab watched him with his feverish eyes. Once his hands were free, he rubbed his swollen wrists against each other, took the glass of tea, and sucked up the burning liquid in swift little sips.

"Good," said Daru. "And where are you headed?"

Balducci withdrew his mustache from the tea. "Here, son."

"Odd pupils! And you're spending the night?"

"No. I'm going back to El Ameur. And you will deliver this fellow to Tinguit. He is expected at police headquarters."

Balducci was looking at Daru with a friendly little smile.

"What's this story?" asked the schoolmaster. "Are you pulling my leg?"[7]

"No, son. Those are the orders."

"The orders? I'm not . . ." Daru hesitated, not wanting to hurt the old Corsican.[8] "I mean, that's not my job."

"What! What's the meaning of that? In wartime people do all kinds of jobs."

"Then I'll wait for the declaration of war!"

Balducci nodded.

"O.K. But the orders exist and they concern you too. Things are brewing, it appears. There is talk of a forthcoming revolt.[9] We are mobilized,[10] in a way."

Daru still had his obstinate look.

"Listen, son," Balducci said. "I like you and you must understand. There's only a dozen of us at El Ameur to patrol throughout the whole territory of a small department and I must get back in a hurry. I was told to hand this guy over to you and return without delay. He couldn't be kept

7. **pulling my leg:** playing a joke on me.

8. **Corsican** (kôr′sĭ-kən): a person from Corsica, an island to the west of Italy.

9. **forthcoming revolt:** The Arabs are preparing to fight the French in order to win their independence.

10. **mobilized:** ready for war.

there. His village was beginning to stir; they wanted to take him back. You must take him to Tinguit tomorrow before the day is over. Twenty kilometers shouldn't faze a husky fellow like you. After that, all will be over. You'll come back to your pupils and your comfortable life."

Behind the wall the horse could be heard snorting and pawing the earth. Daru was looking out the window. Decidedly, the weather was clearing and the light was increasing over the snowy plateau. When all the snow was melted, the sun would take over again and once more would burn the fields of stone. For days, still, the unchanging sky would shed its dry light on the solitary expanse where nothing had any connection with man.

"After all," he said, turning around toward Balducci, "what did he do?" And, before the gendarme had opened his mouth, he asked: "Does he speak French?"

"No, not a word. We had been looking for him for a month, but they were hiding him. He killed his cousin."

"Is he against us?"

"I don't think so. But you can never be sure."

"Why did he kill?"

"A family squabble, I think. One owed the other grain, it seems. It's not at all clear. In short, he killed his cousin with a billhook.[11] You know, like a sheep, *kreezk!*"

Balducci made the gesture of drawing a blade across his throat and the Arab, his attention attracted, watched him with a sort of anxiety. Daru felt a sudden wrath[12] against the man, against all men with their rotten spite,[13] their tireless hates, their blood lust.

But the kettle was singing on the stove. He served Balducci more tea, hesitated, then served the Arab again, who, a second time, drank avidly. His raised arms made

11. billhook: an implement consisting of a curved blade attached to a handle.

12. wrath (răth): great anger.

13. spite (spīt): ill will.

WORDS TO KNOW
avidly (ăv'ĭd-lē) *adv.* eagerly

NOTES

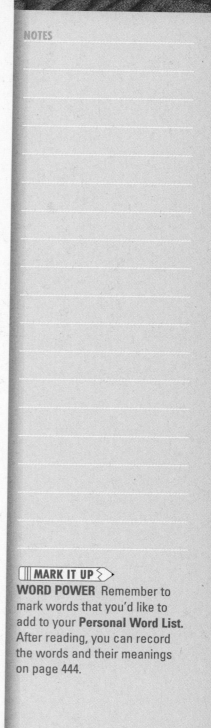

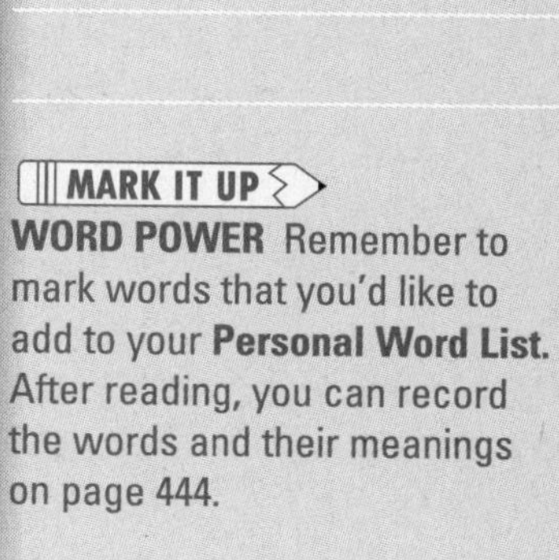

MARK IT UP
WORD POWER Remember to mark words that you'd like to add to your Personal Word List. After reading, you can record the words and their meanings on page 444.

NOTES

the jellaba fall open and the schoolmaster saw his thin, muscular chest.

"Thanks, kid," Balducci said. "And now, I'm off."

He got up and went toward the Arab, taking a small rope from his pocket.

"What are you doing?" Daru asked dryly.

Balducci, disconcerted, showed him the rope.

"Don't bother."

The old gendarme hesitated. "It's up to you. Of course, you are armed?"

"I have my shotgun."

"Where?"

"In the trunk."

"You ought to have it near your bed."

"Why? I have nothing to fear."

"You're crazy, son. If there's an uprising, no one is safe, we're all in the same boat."

"I'll defend myself. I'll have time to see them coming."

Balducci began to laugh, then suddenly the mustache covered the white teeth.

"You'll have time? O.K. That's just what I was saying. You have always been a little cracked. That's why I like you, my son was like that."

At the same time he took out his revolver and put it on the desk.

"Keep it; I don't need two weapons from here to El Ameur."

The revolver shone against the black paint of the table. When the gendarme turned toward him, the schoolmaster caught the smell of leather and horseflesh.

"Listen, Balducci," Daru said suddenly, "every bit of this disgusts me, and first of all your fellow here. But I won't hand him over. Fight, yes, if I have to. But not that."

The old gendarme stood in front of him and looked at him severely.

WORDS TO KNOW
disconcerted (dĭs'kən-sûr'tĭd) *adj.* embarrassed or confused **disconcert** *v.*

"You're being a fool," he said slowly. "I don't like it either. You don't get used to putting a rope on a man even after years of it, and you're even ashamed—yes, ashamed. But you can't let them have their way."

"I won't hand him over," Daru said again.

"It's an order, son, and I repeat it."

"That's right. Repeat to them what I've said to you: I won't hand him over."

Balducci made a visible effort to reflect. He looked at the Arab and at Daru. At last he decided.

"No, I won't tell them anything. If you want to drop us, go ahead; I'll not denounce you. I have an order to deliver the prisoner and I'm doing so. And now you'll just sign this paper for me."

"There's no need. I'll not deny that you left him with me."

"Don't be mean with me. I know you'll tell the truth. You're from hereabouts and you are a man. But you must sign, that's the rule."

Daru opened his drawer, took out a little square bottle of purple ink, the red wooden penholder with the "sergeant-major" pen he used for making models of penmanship, and signed. The gendarme carefully folded the paper and put it into his wallet. Then he moved toward the door.

"I'll see you off," Daru said.

"No," said Balducci. "There's no use being polite. You insulted me."

He looked at the Arab, motionless in the same spot, sniffed peevishly, and turned away toward the door. "Good-by, son," he said. The door shut behind him. Balducci appeared suddenly outside the window and then disappeared. His footsteps were muffled by the snow. The horse stirred on the other side of the wall and several chickens fluttered in fright. A moment later Balducci reappeared outside the window leading the horse by the bridle. He walked toward the little rise without turning around and disappeared from sight with the horse

the boxed passage on this page. Daru insists that he will not hand over the prisoner. Do you think Daru will stick with his decision or change his mind? Explain. **(Predict)**

following him. A big stone could be heard bouncing down. Daru walked back toward the prisoner, who, without stirring, never took his eyes off him. "Wait," the schoolmaster said in Arabic and went toward the bedroom. As he was going through the door, he had a second thought, went to the desk, took the revolver, and stuck it in his pocket. Then, without looking back, he went into his room.

Pause & Reflect

Pause & Reflect

1. Why do you think Daru decides not to hand over the prisoner to the police? **(Infer)**

2. Why does Balducci feel insulted by Daru? **(Infer)**

FOCUS

The Arab prisoner becomes Daru's "guest" for the night. Read to find out how Daru treats him.

MARK IT UP As you read, circle details that show you how Daru treats the prisoner.

For some time he lay on his couch watching the sky gradually close over, listening to the silence. It was this silence that had seemed painful to him during the first days here, after the war. He had requested a post in the little town at the base of the foothills separating the upper plateaus from the desert. There, rocky walls, green and black to the north, pink and lavender to the south, marked the frontier[14] of eternal summer. He had been named to a post farther north, on the plateau itself. In the beginning, the solitude and the silence had been hard for him on these wastelands peopled only by stones. Occasionally, furrows suggested cultivation, but they had been dug to uncover a certain kind of stone good for building. The only plowing here was to harvest rocks. Elsewhere a thin layer of soil accumulated in the hollows would be scraped out to enrich paltry village gardens. This is the way it was: bare rock covered three quarters of the region. Towns sprang up, flourished, then disappeared; men came by, loved one another or fought bitterly, then died. No one in this desert,

14. **frontier:** border.

neither he nor his guest, mattered. And yet, outside this desert neither of them, Daru knew, could have really lived.

When he got up, no noise came from the classroom. He was amazed at the unmixed joy he derived from the mere thought that the Arab might have fled and that he would be alone with no decision to make. But the prisoner was there. He had merely stretched out between the stove and the desk. With eyes open, he was staring at the ceiling. In that position, his thick lips were particularly noticeable, giving him a pouting look. "Come," said Daru. The Arab got up and followed him. In the bedroom, the schoolmaster pointed to a chair near the table under the window. The Arab sat down without taking his eyes off Daru.

"Are you hungry?"

"Yes," the prisoner said.

Daru set the table for two. He took flour and oil, shaped a cake in a frying-pan, and lighted the little stove that functioned on bottled gas. While the cake was cooking, he went out to the shed to get cheese, eggs, dates, and condensed milk. When the cake was done he set it on the window sill to cool, heated some condensed milk diluted with water, and beat up the eggs into an omelette. In one of his motions he knocked against the revolver stuck in his right pocket. He set the bowl down, went into the classroom, and put the revolver in his desk drawer. When he came back to the room, night was falling. He put on the light and served the Arab. "Eat," he said. The Arab took a piece of the cake, lifted it eagerly to his mouth, and stopped short.

"And you?" he asked.

"After you. I'll eat too."

The thick lips opened slightly. The Arab hesitated, then bit into the cake determinedly.

The meal over, the Arab looked at the schoolmaster. "Are you the judge?"

"No, I'm simply keeping you until tomorrow."

"Why do you eat with me?"

the boxed passage on pages 366 and 367. How does Daru feel about the region where he lives and its people? Check two words or phrases to complete each sentence below. **(Infer)**

The region is

- ❑ civilized
- ❑ barely able to support life
- ❑ part of who Daru is
- ❑ fertile

The people in the region are

- ❑ temporary
- ❑ peaceful
- ❑ unimportant
- ❑ wealthy

"I'm hungry."

The Arab fell silent. Daru got up and went out. He brought back a folding bed from the shed, set it up between the table and the stove, perpendicular to his own bed. From a large suitcase which, upright in a corner, served as a shelf for papers, he took two blankets and arranged them on the camp bed. Then he stopped, felt useless, and sat down on his bed. There was nothing more to do or to get ready. He had to look at this man. He looked at him, therefore, trying to imagine his face bursting with rage. He couldn't do so. He could see nothing but the dark yet shining eyes and the animal mouth.

"Why did you kill him?" he asked in a voice whose hostile[15] tone surprised him.

The Arab looked away.

"He ran away. I ran after him."

He raised his eyes to Daru again and they were full of a sort of woeful interrogation.[16] "Now what will they do to me?"

"Are you afraid?"

He stiffened, turning his eyes away.

"Are you sorry?"

The Arab stared at him openmouthed. Obviously he did not understand. Daru's annoyance was growing. At the same time he felt awkward and self-conscious with his big body wedged between the two beds.

"Lie down there," he said impatiently. "That's your bed."

The Arab didn't move. He called to Daru:

"Tell me!"

The schoolmaster looked at him.

"Is the gendarme coming back tomorrow?"

"I don't know."

"Are you coming with us?"

"I don't know. Why?"

15. **hostile** (hŏs′təl): unfriendly.

16. **woeful interrogation:** sad questioning.

NOTES

the boxed passage on this page. What can you tell about the prisoner? Check two phrases below. **(Draw Conclusions)**

- ❑ is sorry for his crime
- ❑ doesn't know what's going on
- ❑ is worried about the future
- ❑ plans to run away

The prisoner got up and stretched out on top of the blankets, his feet toward the window. The light from the electric bulb shone straight into his eyes and he closed them at once.

"Why?" Daru repeated, standing beside the bed.

The Arab opened his eyes under the blinding light and looked at him, trying not to blink.

"Come with us," he said.

In the middle of the night, Daru was still not asleep. He had gone to bed after undressing completely; he generally slept naked. But when he suddenly realized that he had nothing on, he hesitated. He felt vulnerable[17] and the temptation came to him to put his clothes back on. Then he shrugged his shoulders; after all, he wasn't a child and, if need be, he could break his adversary in two. From his bed he could observe him, lying on his back, still motionless with his eyes closed under the harsh light. When Daru turned out the light, the darkness seemed to coagulate[18] all of a sudden. Little by little, the night came back to life in the window where the starless sky was stirring gently. The schoolmaster soon made out the body lying at his feet. The Arab still did not move, but his eyes seemed open. A faint wind was prowling around the schoolhouse. Perhaps it would drive away the clouds and the sun would reappear.

During the night the wind increased. The hens fluttered a little and then were silent. The Arab turned over on his side with his back to Daru, who thought he heard him moan. Then he listened for his guest's breathing, become heavier and more regular. He listened to that breath so close to him and mused without being able to go to sleep. In this room where he had been sleeping alone for a year, this presence bothered him.

the boxed passage on this page. Why do you think the prisoner says to Daru, "Come with us"? **(Infer)**

---

17. **vulnerable** (vŭl′nər-ə-bəl): likely to be hurt.

18. **coagulate:** thicken into a solid mass.

WORDS TO KNOW

adversary (ăd′vər-sĕr′ē) *n.* opponent; enemy

Pause & Reflect

1. Look over the details you circled. How does Daru treat the prisoner? **(Evaluate)**

2. Reread the boxed passage on this page. What does Daru begin to realize about the Arab and himself? Circle one sentence below. **(Draw Conclusions)**

   They will always be bitter enemies.

   They have become like friends or brothers.

But it bothered him also by imposing on him a sort of brotherhood he knew well but refused to accept in the present circumstances. Men who share the same rooms, soldiers or prisoners, develop a strange alliance as if, having cast off their armor with their clothing, they fraternized[19] every evening, over and above their differences, in the ancient community of dream and fatigue. But Daru shook himself; he didn't like such musings, and it was essential to sleep.

A little later, however, when the Arab stirred slightly, the schoolmaster was still not asleep. When the prisoner made a second move, he stiffened, on the alert. The Arab was lifting himself slowly on his arms with almost the motion of a sleepwalker. Seated upright in bed, he waited motionless without turning his head toward Daru, as if he were listening attentively. Daru did not stir; it had just occurred to him that the revolver was still in the drawer of his desk. It was better to act at once. Yet he continued to observe the prisoner, who, with the same slithery motion, put his feet on the ground, waited again, then began to stand up slowly. Daru was about to call out to him when the Arab began to walk, in a quite natural but extraordinarily silent way. He was heading toward the door at the end of the room that opened into the shed. He lifted the latch with precaution and went out, pushing the door behind him but without shutting it. Daru had not stirred. "He is running away," he merely thought. "Good riddance!" Yet he listened attentively. The hens were not fluttering; the guest must be on the plateau. A faint sound of water reached him, and he didn't know what it was until the Arab again stood framed in the doorway, closed the door carefully, and came back to bed without a sound. Then Daru turned his back on him and fell asleep. Still later he seemed, from the depths of his sleep, to hear furtive steps around the schoolhouse. "I'm dreaming! I'm dreaming!" he repeated to himself. And he went on sleeping.

Pause & Reflect

19. **fraternized:** associated in a friendly, brotherly way.

FOCUS

Daru and the Arab set out together on a journey. Each character makes a difficult decision. Read to find out about these decisions.

When he awoke, the sky was clear; the loose window let in a cold, pure air. The Arab was asleep, hunched up under the blankets now, his mouth open, utterly relaxed. But when Daru shook him, he started dreadfully, staring at Daru with wild eyes as if he had never seen him and such a frightened expression that the schoolmaster stepped back. "Don't be afraid. It's me. You must eat." The Arab nodded his head and said yes. Calm had returned to his face, but his expression was vacant and listless.[20]

The coffee was ready. They drank it seated together on the folding bed as they munched their pieces of the cake. Then Daru led the Arab under the shed and showed him the faucet where he washed. He went back into the room, folded the blankets and the bed, made his own bed and put the room in order. Then he went through the classroom and out onto the terrace. The sun was already rising in the blue sky; a soft, bright light was bathing the deserted plateau. On the ridge the snow was melting in spots. The stones were about to reappear. Crouched on the edge of the plateau, the schoolmaster looked at the deserted expanse. He thought of Balducci. He had hurt him, for he had sent him off in a way as if he didn't want to be associated with him. He could still hear the gendarme's farewell and, without knowing why, he felt strangely empty and vulnerable. At that moment, from the other side of the schoolhouse, the prisoner coughed. Daru listened to him almost despite himself and then, furious, threw a pebble that whistled through the air before sinking into the snow. That man's stupid crime revolted him, but to hand him over was contrary to honor. Merely thinking of it made him smart with humiliation. And he cursed at one and the same time his own people who had sent him this Arab and the Arab too who had dared to kill and not managed to get away. Daru got up, walked in a

20. **listless:** lacking energy or enthusiasm.

NOTES

READ ALOUD the boxed passage on this page. What is Daru's state of mind as he thinks about the Arab? Circle two words below. **(Draw Conclusions)**

angry unsure
sympathetic sad

NOTES

circle on the terrace, waited motionless, and then went back into the schoolhouse.

The Arab, leaning over the cement floor of the shed, was washing his teeth with two fingers. Daru looked at him and said: "Come." He went back into the room ahead of the prisoner. He slipped a hunting-jacket on over his sweater and put on walking-shoes. Standing, he waited until the Arab had put on his *chèche* and sandals. They went into the classroom and the schoolmaster pointed to the exit, saying: "Go ahead." The fellow didn't budge. "I'm coming," said Daru. The Arab went out. Daru went back into the room and made a package of pieces of rusk,[21] dates, and sugar. In the classroom, before going out, he hesitated a second in front of his desk, then crossed the threshold and locked the door. "That's the way," he said. He started toward the east, followed by the prisoner. But, a short distance from the schoolhouse, he thought he heard a slight sound behind them. He retraced his steps and examined the surroundings of the house; there was no one there. The Arab watched him without seeming to understand. "Come on," said Daru.

They walked for an hour and rested beside a sharp peak of limestone. The snow was melting faster and faster and the sun was drinking up the puddles at once, rapidly cleaning the plateau, which gradually dried and vibrated like the air itself. When they resumed walking, the ground rang under their feet. From time to time a bird rent the space in front of them with a joyful cry. Daru breathed in deeply the fresh morning light. He felt a sort of rapture[22] before the vast familiar expanse, now almost entirely yellow under its dome of blue sky. They walked an hour more, descending toward the south. They reached a level height made up of crumbly rocks. From there on, the plateau sloped down, eastward, toward a low plain where there were a few spindly trees and, to

---

21. **rusk:** a soft, sweet biscuit.

22. **rapture:** a strong feeling of delight or joy; ecstasy.

the south, toward outcroppings of rock that gave the landscape a chaotic look.

Daru surveyed the two directions. There was nothing but the sky on the horizon. Not a man could be seen. He turned toward the Arab, who was looking at him blankly. Daru held out the package to him. "Take it," he said. "There are dates, bread, and sugar. You can hold out for two days. Here are a thousand francs too." The Arab took the package and the money but kept his full hands at chest level as if he didn't know what to do with what was being given him. "Now look," the schoolmaster said as he pointed in the direction of the east, "there's the way to Tinguit. You have a two-hour walk. At Tinguit you'll find the administration and the police. They are expecting you." The Arab looked toward the east, still holding the package and the money against his chest. Daru took his elbow and turned him rather roughly toward the south. At the foot of the height on which they stood could be seen a faint path. "That's the trail across the plateau. In a day's walk from here you'll find pasturelands and the first nomads.[23] They'll take you in and shelter you according to their law." The Arab had now turned toward Daru and a sort of panic was visible in his expression. "Listen," he said. Daru shook his head: "No, be quiet. Now I'm leaving you." He turned his back on him, took two long steps in the direction of the school, looked hesitantly at the motionless Arab, and started off again. For a few minutes he heard nothing but his own step resounding on the cold ground and did not turn his head. A moment later, however, he turned around. The Arab was still there on the edge of the hill, his arms hanging now, and he was looking at the schoolmaster. Daru felt something rise in his throat. But he swore with impatience, waved vaguely, and started off again. He had

23. nomads (nō′mădz): wandering tribes.

WORDS TO KNOW
chaotic (kā-ŏt′ĭk) *adj.* showing great disorder or confusion

NOTES

REREAD the boxed passage on this page. Daru forces the Arab to choose his own future—either to go to the police or to seek shelter with the nomads. What do you **predict** the Arab will choose to do?

Pause & Reflect

1. What decision do you think Daru wants the Arab to make? **(Infer)**

2. Why do you think the Arab decides to go to the police? **(Analyze)**

3. Reread the boxed passage on this page. Why do the Arab's kinsmen threaten Daru? **(Infer)**

The ending of this story may surprise you. Still, the author foreshadows, or hints at, what will happen. Go back through the story and mark clues that suggest Daru's life is in danger. **(Analyze)**

already gone some distance when he again stopped and looked. There was no longer anyone on the hill.

Daru hesitated. The sun was now rather high in the sky and was beginning to beat down on his head. The schoolmaster retraced his steps, at first somewhat uncertainly, then with decision. When he reached the little hill, he was bathed in sweat. He climbed it as fast as he could and stopped, out of breath, at the top. The rock-fields to the south stood out sharply against the blue sky, but on the plain to the east a steamy heat was already rising. And in that slight haze, Daru, with heavy heart, made out the Arab walking slowly on the road to prison.

A little later, standing before the window of the classroom, the schoolmaster was watching the clear light bathing the whole surface of the plateau, but he hardly saw it. Behind him on the blackboard, among the winding French rivers, sprawled the clumsily chalked-up words he had just read: "You handed over our brother. You will pay for this." Daru looked at the sky, the plateau, and, beyond, the invisible lands stretching all the way to the sea. In this vast landscape he had loved so much, he was alone. ❖

Pause & Reflect

Active Reading SkillBuilder

Making Inferences

Inferences are logical guesses based on clues in the text and on common sense. As you read, you often "read between the lines," or supply information that the author did not directly state. In order to make inferences while you are reading, pay attention to details, especially those that reveal the values and actions of characters, setting, and plot. What do the details add up to? Use the chart below to identify clues about the characters in "The Guest." Then make inferences about the characters based on the clues. An example is shown.

Character	Actions	Inferences
Daru	*He worries about his students being hungry during the blizzard.*	*He is a kind person who cares about his students.*

Literary Analysis SkillBuilder

Theme

The **theme** of a literary work is the central idea or main message of the work. The writer may directly state the theme, but often you must infer it from the events, setting, or characters' actions. To uncover the theme of "The Guest," look back through the story to find phrases, sentences, and events that may provide clues to the author's message about human life. List each clue in the diagram shown below. Use the clues to infer the theme of the story. Then write a sentence stating the theme. An example is shown.

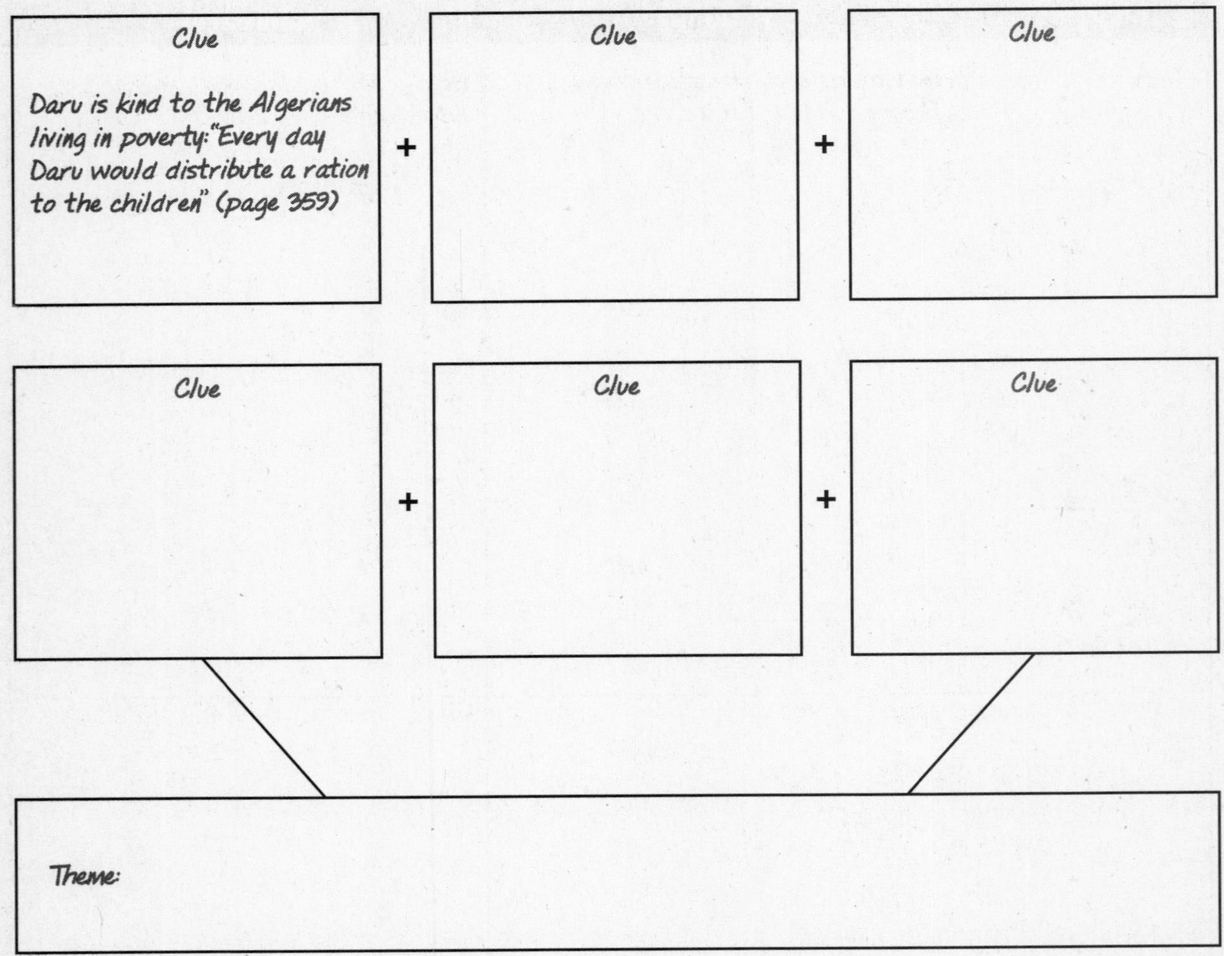

Words to Know SkillBuilder

Words to Know

adversary, avidly, chaotic, disconcerted, obstinate

A. On each blank line, write the word from the word list that the clue describes.

1. This is a word that could be used to describe a stubborn person. ______________
2. This could be another word for enemy. ______________
3. This describes the way that a person conducts a task when they are enthusiastic about it. ______________
4. This word could describe a mob of people which has gotten out of control. ______________
5. You could use this word to describe how you felt in a confusing situation. ______________

B. Fill in each blank with the correct word from the word list.

1. In war, you need to strategically plan your actions in order to outwit your ______________.
2. The commander was ______________ when his first officer suggested his plan wouldn't work.
3. The soldiers ______________ drank from the stream after going without water for two days.
4. After the planes dropped bombs on the city throughout the night, the crowds in the streets were ______________ as residents fled to the country.
5. Even as buildings collapsed into the streets around them, the ______________ little dog wouldn't budge.

C. Imagine what happens to the Arab after he leaves the schoolmaster. Write a letter from the Arab to the schoolmaster describing the events. Use at least **three** of the Words to Know.

Before You Read

Connect to Your Life

What if the person you love most moved far away from you for a long period of time? What would you miss about the person? When the person finally returned home, would you expect your relationship to remain unchanged? Write your ideas in the web below.

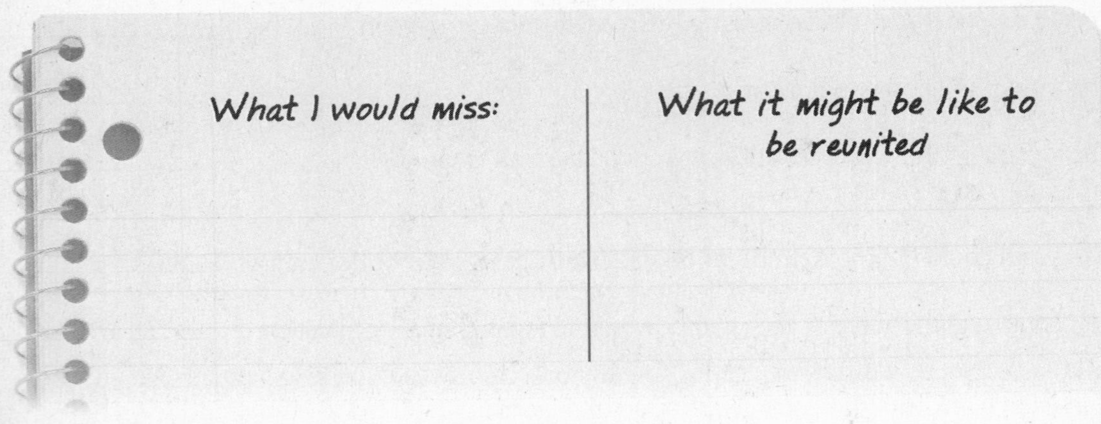

What I would miss:
What it might be like to be reunited

Key to the Story

WHAT YOU NEED TO KNOW "Amnesty" takes place in South Africa during the time of *apartheid.* Under apartheid, white South Africans owned more than 80 percent of the land, although they made up less than 20 percent of the population. Black farm workers struggled to support themselves on small plots of poor farmland. Members of many rural families left home to seek jobs in the cities. Many blacks, as well as some whites, actively opposed apartheid by staging boycotts, demonstrations, and strikes. The government arrested rebel leaders and imprisoned them on Robben Island, off the coast of Cape Town. In 1991 the South African government finally ended apartheid and released the political prisoners. The prisoners were given amnesty, or a formal pardon.

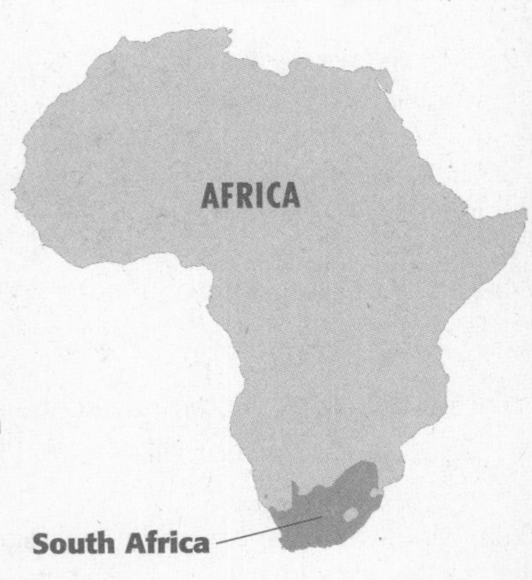

AMNESTY

by Nadine Gordimer

PREVIEW In this story a young woman is separated from her fiancé, whose opposition to apartheid has landed him in prison. She patiently waits for his release, only to discover that he has changed in ways she did not expect.

In this story you will come across words that are written in Afrikaans—a language developed from Dutch colonists, who settled in South Africa. You'll also run into words written in Xhosa, a native South African language. Use the footnotes at the bottom of the page to help you understand the meanings of these words.

NOTES

MARK IT UP KEEP TRACK

As you read, you can use these marks to keep track of your understanding.

- * This is important.
- ? I have a question about this.
- ! This is a surprise.

FOCUS

In the first part of the story, the narrator learns that her fiancé has been released from prison. She describes what her own life has been like while waiting for his return.

MARK IT UP As you read, put a star next to details that help you understand what farm life is like for the narrator.

When we heard he was released I ran all over the farm and through the fence to our people on the next farm to tell everybody. I only saw afterwards I'd torn my dress on the barbed wire, and there was a scratch, with blood, on my shoulder.

He went away from this place nine years ago, signed up to work in town with what they call a construction company—building glass walls up to the sky. For the first two years he came home for the weekend once a month and two weeks at Christmas; that was when he asked my father for me. And he began to pay. He and I thought that in three years he would have paid enough for us to get married. But then he started wearing that T-shirt, he told us he'd joined the union, he told us about the strike, how he was one of the men who went to talk to the bosses because some others had been laid off after the strike. He's always been good at talking, even in English—he was the best at the farm school, he used to read the newspapers the Indian wraps soap and sugar in when you buy at the store.

There was trouble at the hostel where he had a bed, and riots over paying rent in the townships[1] and he told me—just me, not the old ones—that wherever people were fighting against the way we are treated they were doing it for all of us, on the farms as well as the towns, and the unions were with them, he was with them, making speeches, marching. The third year, we heard he was in prison. Instead of getting married. We didn't know where to find him, until he went on trial. The case was heard in a town far away. I couldn't go often to the court because by

1. **townships:** racially segregated areas of South Africa.

that time I had passed my Standard 8[2] and I was working in the farm school. Also my parents were short of money. Two of my brothers who had gone away to work in town didn't send home; I suppose they lived with girl-friends and had to buy things for them. My father and other brother work here for the Boer[3] and the pay is very small, we have two goats, a few cows we're allowed to graze, and a patch of land where my mother can grow vegetables. No cash from that.

When I saw him in the court he looked beautiful in a blue suit with a striped shirt and brown tie. All the accused—his comrades, he said—were well-dressed. The union bought the clothes so that the judge and the prosecutor would know they weren't dealing with stupid *yes-baas*[4] black men who didn't know their rights. These things and everything else about the court and trial he explained to me when I was allowed to visit him in jail. Our little girl was born while the trial went on and when I brought the baby to court the first time to show him, his comrades hugged him and then hugged me across the barrier of the prisoners' dock and they had clubbed together to give me some money as a present for the baby. He chose the name for her, Inkululeko.[5]

Then the trial was over and he got six years. He was sent to the Island.[6] We all knew about the Island. Our leaders had been there so long. But I have never seen the sea except to color it in blue at school, and I couldn't imagine a piece of earth surrounded by it. I could only think of a cake of

NOTES

REREAD the boxed text. Then check four words below that describe the accused. **(Infer)**

- ❑ close-knit
- ❑ smart
- ❑ proud
- ❑ ignorant
- ❑ cowardly
- ❑ courageous

---

2. **Standard 8:** Standards are classes or grades in elementary schools. Standard 8 would have been the top level of elementary school.
3. **Boer:** a descendant of the Dutch colonists of South Africa.
4. ***yes-baas:*** "Yes, boss"—the words of someone who does not question authority.
5. **Inkululeko** (ĭn-ko͞o′lo͞o-lā′kō): a word meaning "freedom" in the Xhosa language of South Africa.
6. **the Island:** Robben Island, the site of a maximum-security prison from the mid-1960s to 1991. Most of its inmates were black political prisoners.

dung, dropped by the cattle, floating in a pool of rain-water they'd crossed, the water showing the sky like a looking-glass, blue. I was ashamed only to think that. He had told me how the glass walls showed the pavement trees and the other buildings in the street and the colors of the cars and the clouds as the crane lifted him on a platform higher and higher through the sky to work at the top of a building.

He was allowed one letter a month. It was my letter because his parents didn't know how to write. I used to go to them where they worked on another farm to ask what message they wanted to send. The mother always cried and put her hands on her head and said nothing, and the old man, who preached to us in the veld[7] every Sunday, said tell my son we are praying. God will make everything all right for him. Once he wrote back. That's the trouble—our people on the farms, they're told God will decide what's good for them so that they won't find the force to do anything to change their lives.

Pause & Reflect

7. **veld:** any open grazing area in southern Africa.

Pause & Reflect

1. Review the details you marked. On the lines below, describe the hardships the narrator and her family endure. **(Summarize)**

2. What opinion does the narrator's fiancé seem to have about "people on the farms"? Check two answers. **(Draw Conclusions)**

   People on the farms are

   - ❑ too accepting
   - ❑ dishonest
   - ❑ unfairly treated
   - ❑ comrades, or allies

FOCUS

The narrator and her fiancé's parents try to visit the fiancé on Robben Island. Find out what prevents them from seeing him.

MARK IT UP As you read, underline details that help you understand how the narrator feels before and after the trip.

After two years had passed, we—his parents and I—had saved up enough money to go to Cape Town[8] to visit him. We went by train and slept on the floor at the station and asked the way, next day, to the ferry. People were kind; they all knew that if you wanted the ferry it was because you had somebody of yours on the Island.

And there it was—there was the sea. It was green *and* blue, climbing and falling, bursting white, all the way to the sky. A terrible wind was slapping it this way and that; it hid the Island, but people like us, also waiting for the ferry, pointed where the Island must be, far out in the sea that I never thought would be like it really was.

There were other boats, and ships as big as buildings that go to other places, all over the world, but the ferry is only for the Island, it doesn't go anywhere else in the world, only to the Island. So everybody waiting there was waiting for the Island, there could be no mistake we were not in the right place. We had sweets and biscuits, trousers and a warm coat for him (a woman standing with us said we wouldn't be allowed to give him the clothes) and I wasn't wearing, any more, the old beret pulled down over my head that farm girls wear, I had bought relaxer cream[9] from the man who comes round the farms selling things out of a box on his bicycle, and my hair was combed up thick under a flowered scarf that didn't cover the gold-colored rings in my ears. His mother had her blanket tied round her waist over her dress, a farm woman, but I looked just as

8. **Cape Town:** the legislative capital of South Africa, in the extreme southeast portion of the country.

9. **relaxer cream:** cream to straighten the hair.

NOTES

READ ALOUD the boxed text. How does the narrator want to look when she sees her fiancé after their long separation? What details help you figure this out? Write your ideas in the chart. **(Draw Conclusions)**

How she wants to look	Details that reveal this

good as any of the other girls there. When the ferry was ready to take us, we stood all pressed together and quiet like the cattle waiting to be let through a gate. One man kept looking round with his chin moving up and down, he was counting, he must have been afraid there were too many to get on and he didn't want to be left behind. We all moved up to the policeman in charge and everyone ahead of us went onto the boat. But when our turn came and he put out his hand for something, I didn't know what.

We didn't have a permit. We didn't know that before you come to Cape Town, before you come to the ferry for the Island, you have to have a police permit to visit a prisoner on the Island. I tried to ask him nicely. The wind blew the voice out of my mouth.

We were turned away. We saw the ferry rock, bumping the landing where we stood, moving, lifted and dropped by all that water, getting smaller and smaller until we didn't know if we were really seeing it or one of the birds that looked black, dipping up and down, out there.

The only good thing was one of the other people took the sweets and biscuits for him. He wrote and said he got them. But it wasn't a good letter. Of course not. He was cross with me; I should have found out, I should have known about the permit. He was right—I bought the train tickets, I asked where to go for the ferry, I should have known about the permit. I have passed Standard 8. There was an advice office to go to in town, the churches ran it, he wrote. But the farm is so far from town, we on the farms don't know about these things. It was as he said; our ignorance is the way we are kept down, this ignorance must go.

We took the train back and we never went to the Island—never saw him in the three more years he was there. Not once. We couldn't find the money for the train. His father died and I had to help his mother from my pay. For our people the worry is always money, I wrote. When will we ever have money? Then he sent such a good letter.

NOTES

the boxed text. What realization does the narrator have as she thinks about her failure to get the permits? **(Cause and Effect)**

That's what I'm on the Island for, far away from you, I'm here so that one day our people will have the things they need, land, food, the end of ignorance. There was something else—I could just read the word "power" the prison had blacked out. All his letters were not just for me; the prison officer read them before I could.

Pause & Reflect

FOCUS

After five years the fiancé finally returns home. How easy will it be for the couple to resume their relationship?

MARK IT UP As you read, underline the details that show how the relationship has changed.

He was coming home after only five years!

That's what it seemed to me, when I heard—the five years were suddenly disappeared—nothing!—there was no whole year still to wait. I showed my—our—little girl his photo again. That's your daddy, he's coming, you're going to see him. She told the other children at school, I've got a daddy, just as she showed off about the kid goat she had at home.

We wanted him to come at once, and at the same time we wanted time to prepare. His mother lived with one of his uncles; now that his father was dead there was no house of his father for him to take me to as soon as we married. If there had been time, my father would have cut poles, my mother and I would have baked bricks, cut thatch,[10] and built a house for him and me and the child.

We were not sure what day he would arrive. We only heard on my radio his name and the names of some others who were released. Then at the Indian's store I noticed the newspaper, *The Nation,* written by black people, and on

10. thatch: plant stalks or leaves used to make roofs.

Pause & Reflect

1. The narrator and her fiancé's parents are unable to visit the prisoner because

   (Clarify)

2. How do you think the narrator felt when she got the first letter from her fiancé? the second letter? Explain. **(Infer)**

   After the first letter she felt

   After the second letter she felt

3. Why do you suppose the word power had been blacked out by the prison guards? **(Infer)**

NOTES

the boxed text. How do the details about the characters help show the contrast between them now? **(Compare and Contrast)**

Details about him:

Details about her:

How they are different now:

the front a picture of a lot of people dancing and waving—I saw at once it was at that ferry. Some men were being carried on other men's shoulders. I couldn't see which one was him. We were waiting. The ferry had brought him from the Island but we remembered Cape Town is a long way from us. Then he did come. On a Saturday, no school, so I was working with my mother, hoeing and weeding round the pumpkins and mealies,[11] my hair, that I meant to keep nice, tied in an old *doek*.[12] A combi came over the veld and his comrades had brought him. I wanted to run away and wash but he stood there stretching his legs, calling, hey! hey! with his comrades making a noise around him, and my mother started shrieking in the old style aie! aie! and my father was clapping and stamping towards him. He held his arms open to us, this big man in town clothes, polished shoes, and all the time while he hugged me I was holding my dirty hands, full of mud, away from him behind his back. His teeth hit me hard through his lips, he grabbed at my mother and she struggled to hold the child up to him. I thought we would all fall down! Then everyone was quiet. The child hid behind my mother. He picked her up but she turned her head away to her shoulder. He spoke to her gently but she wouldn't speak to him. She's nearly six years old! I told her not to be a baby. She said, That's not him.

The comrades all laughed, we laughed, she ran off and he said, She has to have time to get used to me.

He has put on weight, yes; a lot. You couldn't believe it. He used to be so thin his feet looked too big for him. I used to feel his bones but now—that night—when he lay on me he was so heavy, I didn't remember it was like that. Such a long time. It's strange to get stronger in prison; I thought he wouldn't have enough to eat and would come out weak. Everyone said, Look at him!—he's a man, now. He laughed

11. **mealies:** corn.

12. ***doek*** (dŏŏk) . . . **combi:** A *doek* is a headscarf worn like a turban. A combi is a vehicle that can serve various functions.

and banged his fist on his chest, told them how the comrades exercised in their cells, he would run three miles a day, stepping up and down on one place on the floor of that small cell where he was kept. After we were together at night we used to whisper a long time but now I can feel he's thinking of some things I don't know and I can't worry him with talk. Also I don't know what to say. To ask him what it was like, five years shut away there; or to tell him something about school or about the child. What else has happened, here? Nothing. Just waiting. Sometimes in the daytime I do try to tell him what it was like for me, here at home on the farm, five years. He listens, he's interested, just like he's interested when people from the other farms come to visit and talk to him about little things that happened to them while he was away all that time on the Island. He smiles and nods, asks a couple of questions and then stands up and stretches. I see it's to show them it's enough, his mind is going back to something he was busy with before they came. And we farm people are very slow; we tell things slowly, he used to, too.

Pause & Reflect

1. Look over the details you underlined. How does the narrator seem to feel about her fiancé now? **(Clarify)**

2. Compare the narrator's life on the farm with her husband's life as an anti-apartheid leader. **(Compare and Contrast)**

her life	his life

3. Reread the boxed text on page 387. What is the narrator saying in the last sentence? **(Paraphrase)**

NOTES

FOCUS

The narrator's fiancé tells her about his work in the anti-apartheid movement. Find out how she feels about the choices he has made.

MARK IT UP As you read, underline details that show that the narrator is beginning to understand what her fiancé is fighting for.

He hasn't signed on for another job. But he can't stay at home with us; we thought, after five years over there in the middle of that green and blue sea, so far, he would rest with us a little while. The combi or some car comes to fetch him and he says don't worry, I don't know what day I'll be back. At first I asked, what week, next week? He tried to explain to me: in the Movement it's not like it was in the union, where you do your work every day and after that you are busy with meetings; in the Movement you never know where you will have to go and what is going to come up next. And the same with money. In the Movement, it's not like a job, with regular pay—I know that, he doesn't have to tell me—it's like it was going to the Island, you do it for all our people who suffer because we haven't got money, we haven't got land—look, he said, speaking of my parents', my home, the home that has been waiting for him, with his child: look at this place where the white man owns the ground and lets you squat in mud and tin huts here only as long as you work for him—*Baba*[13] and your brother planting his crops and looking after his cattle, Mama cleaning his house and you in the school without even having the chance to train properly as a teacher. The farmer owns us, he says.

I've been thinking we haven't got a home because there wasn't time to build a house before he came from the Island; but we haven't got a home at all. Now I've understood that.

I'm not stupid. When the comrades come to this place in the combi to talk to him here I don't go away with my

13. ***Baba***: a title of respect for an aged man, here indicating the narrator's father.

mother after we've brought them tea or (if she's made it for the weekend) beer. They like her beer, they talk about our culture and there's one of them who makes a point of putting his arm around my mother, calling her the mama of all of them, the mama of Africa. Sometimes they please her very much by telling her how they used to sing on the Island and getting her to sing an old song we all know from our grandmothers. Then they join in with their strong voices. My father doesn't like this noise traveling across the veld; he's afraid that if the Boer finds out my man is a political, from the Island, and he's holding meetings on the Boer's land, he'll tell my father to go, and take his family with him. But my brother says if the Boer asks anything just tell him it's a prayer meeting. Then the singing is over; my mother knows she must go away into the house.

I stay, and listen. He forgets I'm there when he's talking and arguing about something I can see is important, more important than anything we could ever have to say to each other when we're alone. But now and then, when one of the other comrades is speaking I see him look at me for a moment the way I will look up at one of my favorite children in school to encourage the child to understand. The men don't speak to me and I don't speak. One of the things they talk about is organizing the people on the farms—the workers, like my father and brother, and like his parents used to be. I learn what all these things are: minimum wage, limitation of working hours, the right to strike, annual leave, accident compensation,[14] pensions, sick and even maternity leave. I am pregnant, at last I have another child inside me, but that's women's business. When they talk about the Big Man, the Old Men,[15] I know who these are: our leaders are also back from prison. I told him about the child coming; he said, And this one belongs to a

14. **accident compensation:** money or medical benefits paid to someone who has been injured on a job.

15. **the Big Man, the Old Men:** Nelson Mandela and several of his elderly associates were freed from prison in the early 1990s.

NOTES

REREAD the boxed passage. What can you tell about the fiancé's opinion of the narrator? Check one. **(Infer)**

The fiancé thinks the narrator is

- ❑ foolish for staying on the farm.
- ❑ an important freedom fighter.
- ❑ capable of understanding big ideas.

NOTES

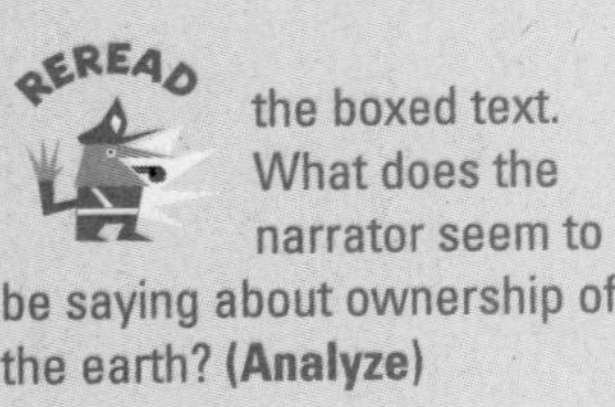

the boxed text. What does the narrator seem to be saying about ownership of the earth? **(Analyze)**

new country, he'll build the freedom we've fought for! I know he wants to get married but there's no time for that at present. There was hardly time for him to make the child. He comes to me just like he comes here to eat a meal or put on clean clothes. Then he picks up the little girl and swings her round and there!—it's done, he's getting into the combi, he's already turning to his comrade that face of his that knows only what's inside his head, those eyes that move quickly as if he's chasing something you can't see. The little girl hasn't had time to get used to this man. But I know she'll be proud of him, one day!

How can you tell that to a child six years old? But I tell her about the Big Man and the Old Men, our leaders, so she'll know that her father was with them on the Island, this man is a great man, too.

On Saturday, no school and I plant and weed with my mother, she sings but I don't; I think. On Sunday there's no work, only prayer meetings out of the farmer's way under the trees, and beer drinks at the mud and tin huts where the farmers allow us to squat on their land. I go off on my own as I used to do when I was a child, making up games and talking to myself where no one would hear me or look for me. I sit on a warm stone in the late afternoon, high up, and the whole valley is a path between the hills, leading away from my feet. It's the Boer's farm but that's not true, it belongs to nobody. The cattle don't know that anyone says he owns it, the sheep—they are grey stones, and then they become a thick grey snake moving—don't know. Our huts and the old mulberry tree and the little brown mat of earth that my mother dug over yesterday, way down there, and way over there the clump of trees round the chimneys and the shiny thing that is the TV mast of the farmhouse—they are nothing, on the back of this earth. It could twitch them away like a dog does a fly.

I am up with the clouds. The sun behind me is changing the colors of the sky and the clouds are changing themselves, slowly, slowly. Some are pink, some are white, swelling like bubbles. Underneath is a bar of grey, not enough to make rain. It gets longer and darker, it grows a thin snout and long body and then the end of it is a tail. There's a huge grey rat moving across the sky, eating the sky.

The child remembered the photo; she said *That's not him.* I'm sitting here where I came often when he was on the Island. I came to get away from the others, to wait by myself.

I'm watching the rat, it's losing itself, its shape, eating the sky, and I'm waiting. Waiting for him to come back.

Waiting.

I'm waiting to come back home. ❖

Pause & Reflect

Pause & Reflect

1. Review the details you marked. How does the narrator seem to view her fiancé's work now that she knows more about it? **(Draw Conclusions)**

2. MARK IT UP How can you tell that the anti-apartheid fighters value the traditions of their culture? Put a star next to the passage that shows this. **(Draw Conclusions)**

3. What do you think the narrator is saying in the last line of the story? **(Analyze)**

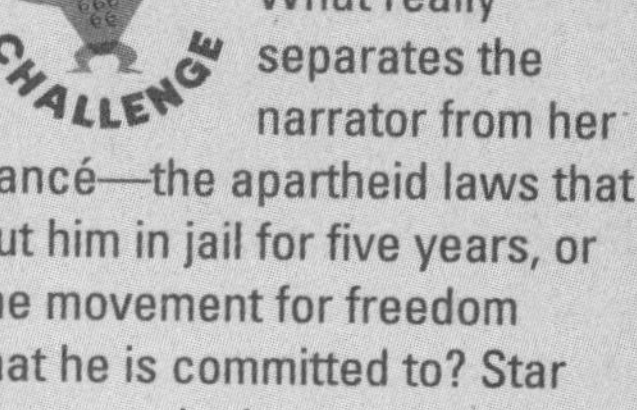

What really separates the narrator from her fiancé—the apartheid laws that put him in jail for five years, or the movement for freedom that he is committed to? Star passages in the story to support your view. **(Analyze)**

Active Reading SkillBuilder

Making Inferences

An **inference** is a logical guess based on evidence and clues. Often readers need to make inferences to figure out what is unstated yet implied in a literary work. For example, clues provided by the writer can be used to infer—simply from the way a character acts—that the character is lonely, self-conscious, or disappointed. As you read "Amnesty," pause to make inferences about the customs and conditions in South Africa and about the main characters and their relationship. Use the chart below to record your inferences and the story details that helped you make them. An example has been done for you.

Inferences	Story Details
The fiancé is better educated and more ambitious than the narrator.	*The narrator says that her fiancé is good at talking, even in English, and that he used to read newspapers used as wrappers for soap and sugar.*

Literary Analysis SkillBuilder

First-Person Point of View

In the **first-person point of view,** the narrator is a character in the story who describes the story action as he or she perceives and understands it. Using the first-person point of view usually ensures that readers will feel close to the narrator, but it also restricts readers to knowing only what the narrator understands and tells them, and no more. In "Amnesty," for example, readers don't know what the narrator's fiancé feels each time he leaves his family. In the chart below, list some events and incidents that the narrator of this selection describes. Then briefly explain the narrator's thoughts and feelings about them. An example has been done for you.

Story Events	Narrator's Thoughts and Feelings
The fiancé goes to trial.	*The narrator is proud of the way her fiancé is dressed and she admires him. She does not know exactly what is going on except for what her fiancé tells her.*

Follow Up: How would this story be different if it were told from a third-person omniscient point of view? (In this point of view, the narrator is all-knowing and can see into the mind of more than one character.)

Connect to Your Life

Have you ever met or heard of someone who made you want to live your life differently? What did that person make you wish for? Write your ideas in the chart. One example has been given.

This person	might make me wish . . .
an adventurer	I could travel to exotic places

Key to the Story

WHAT'S THE BIG IDEA? Gabriel García Márquez writes in a style known as **magical realism.** In this type of fiction, writers use realistic details to describe strange or unrealistic events. These events often happen in realistic settings, and the characters accept them without question. As a result, the line between fantasy and reality can be a little blurry. Read the following two examples. The first contains an example of a realistic event, and the second adds a bit of fantasy.

> Annelisse's eyes shone with pride.

> Annelisse's eyes shone so brightly that they lit up the whole street. People began to notice her from great distances and were drawn to her burning gaze. Before long, a crowd had gathered around her.

THE Handsomest Drowned Man in the World

BY GABRIEL GARCÍA MÁRQUEZ

TRANSLATED BY GREGORY RABASSA

PREVIEW In this story, the people who live in an isolated village by the sea discover the body of a drowned man. This event changes their lives.

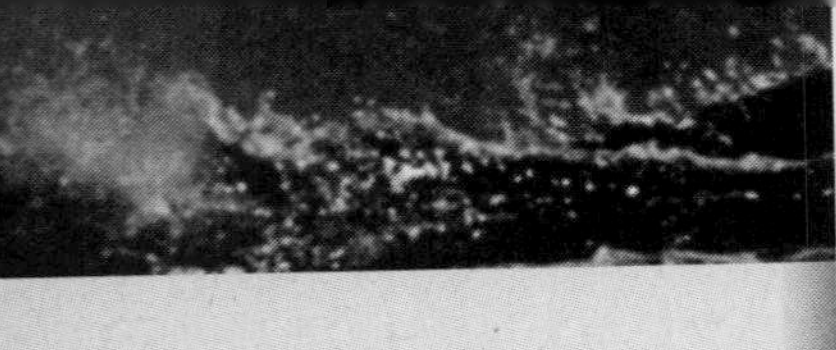

NOTES

the boxed text. Underline the explanations the villagers give for the drowned man's great weight and size. What do these explanations reveal about the villagers? **(Evaluate)**

FOCUS

One day a group of children discover a drowned man on the beach. Read to find out what is so remarkable about him.

The first children who saw the dark and slinky bulge approaching through the sea let themselves think it was an enemy ship. Then they saw it had no flags or masts and they thought it was a whale. But when it washed up on the beach, they removed the clumps of seaweed, the jellyfish tentacles, and the remains of fish and flotsam,[1] and only then did they see that it was a drowned man.

They had been playing with him all afternoon, burying him in the sand and digging him up again, when someone chanced to see them and spread the alarm in the village. The men who carried him to the nearest house noticed that he weighed more than any dead man they had ever known, almost as much as a horse, and they said to each other that maybe he'd been floating too long and the water had got into his bones. When they laid him on the floor they said he'd been taller than all other men because there was barely enough room for him in the house, but they thought that maybe the ability to keep on growing after death was part of the nature of certain drowned men. He had the smell of the sea about him and only his shape gave one to suppose that it was the corpse of a human being, because the skin was covered with a crust of mud and scales.

They did not even have to clean off his face to know that the dead man was a stranger. The village was made up of only twenty-odd wooden houses that had stone courtyards with no flowers and which were spread about on the end of a desertlike cape. There was so little land that mothers always went about with the fear that the wind would carry off their children and the few dead that the years had caused among them had to be thrown off the cliffs. But the sea was calm and bountiful and all the men

1. **flotsam:** wreckage or debris floating in the water.

fit into seven boats. So when they found the drowned man they simply had to look at one another to see that they were all there.

Pause & Reflect

FOCUS

The women of the village prepare the drowned man for burial. Find out how they react to him once they remove the mud and scales from his body.

MARK IT UP As you read, underline the comparisons the women make between the dead stranger and the men in their own village.

That night they did not go out to work at sea. While the men went to find out if anyone was missing in neighboring villages, the women stayed behind to care for the drowned man. They took the mud off with grass swabs, they removed the underwater stones entangled in his hair, and they scraped the crust off with tools used for scaling fish. As they were doing that they noticed that the vegetation on him came from faraway oceans and deep water and that his clothes were in tatters, as if he had sailed through labyrinths of coral. They noticed too that he bore his death with pride, for he did not have the lonely look of other drowned men who came out of the sea or that haggard, needy look of men who drowned in rivers. But only when they finished cleaning him off did they become aware of the kind of man he was and it left them breathless. Not only was he the tallest, strongest, most virile, and best built man they had ever seen, but even though they were looking at him there was no room for him in their imagination.

WORDS TO KNOW

labyrinth (lăb′ə-rĭnth′) *n.* a confusing network of passages; maze
haggard (hăg′ərd) *adj.* looking worn and exhausted
virile (vîr′əl) *adj.* masculine; full of manly strength

Pause & Reflect

1. What is unusual about the drowned man? **(Clarify)**

2. How would you describe the town that the drowned man landed in? Check three adjectives. **(Visualize)**

- ❑ simple
- ❑ bustling
- ❑ crowded
- ❑ prosperous
- ❑ quiet
- ❑ desolate

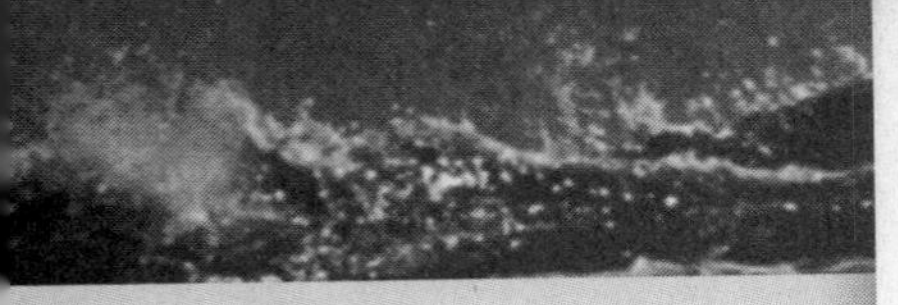

NOTES

MARK IT UP

WORD POWER Mark words that you'd like to add to your **Personal Word List.** After reading, you can record the words and their meanings beginning on page 444.

They could not find a bed in the village large enough to lay him on nor was there a table solid enough to use for his wake. The tallest men's holiday pants would not fit him, nor the fattest ones' Sunday shirts, nor the shoes of the one with the biggest feet. Fascinated by his huge size and his beauty, the women then decided to make him some pants from a large piece of sail and a shirt from some bridal brabant linen[2] so that he could continue through his death with dignity. As they sewed, sitting in a circle and gazing at the corpse between stitches, it seemed to them that the wind had never been so steady nor the sea so restless as on that night and they supposed that the change had something to do with the dead man. They thought that if that magnificent man had lived in the village, his house would have had the widest doors, the highest ceiling, and the strongest floor, his bedstead would have been made from a midship frame held together by iron bolts, and his wife would have been the happiest woman. They thought that he would have had so much authority that he could have drawn fish out of the sea simply by calling their names and that he would have put so much work into his land that springs would have burst forth from among the rocks so that he would have been able to plant flowers on the cliffs. They secretly compared him to their own men, thinking that for all their lives theirs were incapable of doing what he could do in one night, and they ended up dismissing them deep in their hearts as the weakest, meanest, and most useless creatures on earth. They were wandering through that maze of fantasy when the oldest woman, who as the oldest had looked upon the drowned man with more compassion than passion, sighed:

"He has the face of someone called Esteban."[3]

It was true. Most of them had only to take another look at him to see that he could not have any other name.

---

2. **brabant linen:** cloth from a particular region of Belgium.

3. **Esteban** (ĕ-stĕ′bän).

The more stubborn among them, who were the youngest, still lived for a few hours with the illusion that when they put his clothes on and he lay among the flowers in patent leather shoes his name might be Lautaro.[4] But it was a vain illusion. There had not been enough canvas, the poorly cut and worse sewn pants were too tight, and the hidden strength of his heart popped the buttons on his shirt. After midnight the whistling of the wind died down and the sea fell into its Wednesday drowsiness. The silence put an end to any last doubts: he was Esteban. The women who had dressed him, who had combed his hair, had cut his nails and shaved him were unable to hold back a shudder of pity when they had to resign themselves to his being dragged along the ground. It was then that they understood how unhappy he must have been with that huge body since it bothered him even after death. They could see him in life, condemned to going through doors sideways, cracking his head on crossbeams, remaining on his feet during visits, not knowing what to do with his soft, pink, sea lion hands while the lady of the house looked for her most resistant chair and begged him, frightened to death, sit here, Esteban, please, and he, leaning against the wall, smiling, don't bother, ma'am, I'm fine where I am, his heels raw and his back roasted from having done the same thing so many times whenever he paid a visit, don't bother, ma'am, I'm fine where I am, just to avoid the embarrassment of breaking up the chair, and never knowing perhaps that the ones who said don't go, Esteban, at least wait till the coffee's ready, were the ones who later on would whisper the big boob finally left, how nice, the handsome fool has gone. That was what the women were thinking beside the body a little before dawn. Later, when they covered his face with a handkerchief so that the light would not bother him, he looked so forever dead, so defenseless, so much like their men that the first

4. **Lautaro** (lou-tä'rô).

NOTES

READING TIP This story contains some very long sentences, like the one that starts on line 112 and ends on line 126. In this sentence, the author uses the voices of several different speakers—Esteban and several other imagined people. The shaded text gives an example of two of these voices. Read this sentence slowly. Try underlining the different speakers' exact words.

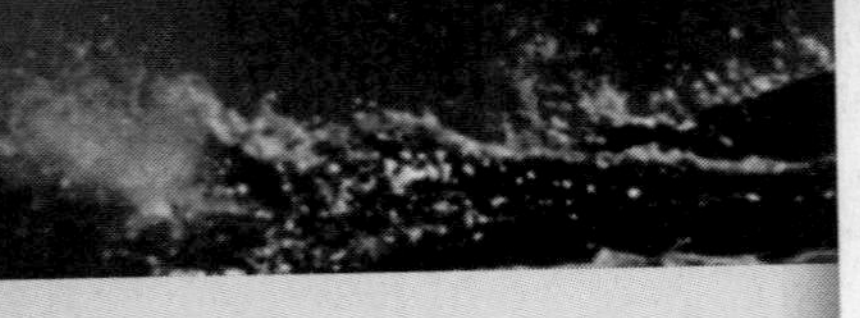

Pause & Reflect

1. After Esteban's body has been cleaned, what effect does it have on the women? **(Clarify)**

2. According to the women, how is Esteban different from and similar to the men of their village? Write your responses in the chart. **(Compare and Contrast)**

How is he like the men?	How is he different?

3. Why do the women begin to cry? **(Clarify)**

furrows of tears opened in their hearts. It was one of the younger ones who began the weeping. The others, coming to, went from sighs to wails, and the more they sobbed the more they felt like weeping, because the drowned man was becoming all the more Esteban for them, and so they wept so much, for he was the most destitute, most peaceful, and most obliging man on earth, poor Esteban. So when the men returned with the news that the drowned man was not from the neighboring villages either, the women felt an opening of jubilation in the midst of their tears.

"Praise the Lord," they sighed, "he's ours!"

Pause & Reflect

FOCUS

The women become more and more fascinated by the drowned stranger, and even find ways to postpone his burial. Find out how the men feel about all the attention the dead man is getting.

The men thought the fuss was only womanish frivolity. Fatigued because of the difficult nighttime inquiries, all they wanted was to get rid of the bother of the newcomer once and for all before the sun grew strong on that arid, windless day. They improvised a litter with the remains of foremasts and gaffs,[5] tying it together with rigging so that it would bear the weight of the body until they reached the cliffs. They wanted to tie the anchor from a cargo ship to him so that he would sink easily into the deepest waves, where fish are blind and divers die of

5. **gaffs:** hooks attached to poles, used for pulling fish out of the water.

WORDS TO KNOW

arid (ăr′ĭd) *adj.* dry

improvise (ĭm′prə-vīz′) *v.* to make on the spur of the moment, using any resources available

nostalgia, and bad currents would not bring him back to shore, as had happened with other bodies. But the more they hurried, the more the women thought of ways to waste time. They walked about like startled hens, pecking with the sea charms on their breasts, some interfering on one side to put a scapular[6] of the good wind on the drowned man, some on the other side to put a wrist compass on him, and after a great deal of get away from there, woman, stay out of the way, look, you almost made me fall on top of the dead man, the men began to feel mistrust in their livers and started grumbling about why so many main-altar decorations for a stranger, because no matter how many nails and holy-water jars he had on him, the sharks would chew him all the same, but the women kept piling on their junk relics,[7] running back and forth, stumbling, while they released in sighs what they did not in tears, so that the men finally exploded with since when has there ever been such a fuss over a drifting corpse, a drowned nobody, a piece of cold Wednesday meat. One of the women, mortified by so much lack of care, then removed the handkerchief from the dead man's face and the men were left breathless too.

He was Esteban. It was not necessary to repeat it for them to recognize him. If they had been told Sir Walter Raleigh,[8] even they might have been impressed with his gringo accent, the macaw on his shoulder, his cannibal-killing blunderbuss, but there could be only one Esteban in the world and there he was, stretched out like a sperm whale, shoeless, wearing the pants of an undersized child, and with those stony nails that had to be cut with a knife.

the boxed text on the left. Compare the way the men feel about Esteban with how the women feel. Write your observations in the chart. **(Compare and Contrast)**

The men feel . . .	The women feel . . .

6. **scapular:** a religious badge consisting of two pieces of cloth worn over the shoulders.

7. **relics:** objects that once belonged to a holy person.

8. **Sir Walter Raleigh . . . blunderbuss:** Sir Walter Raleigh (1552?–1618) was an English explorer. A macaw is a parrot, and a blunderbuss is a type of gun—short and not very accurate—that was used from the 1600s to the 1800s.

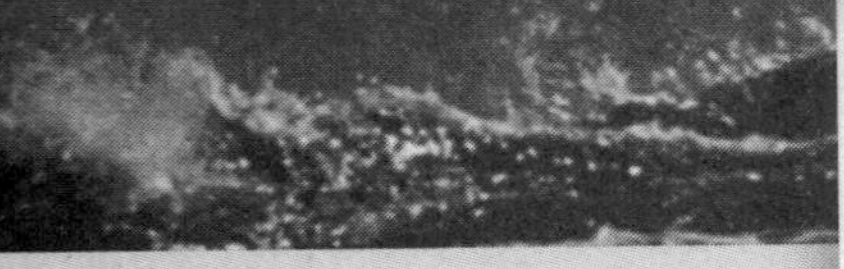

Pause & Reflect

1. How do the men change their view of Esteban? Why? Write your ideas below. **(Infer)**

At first the men feel

Then they feel

Reason:

2. Apart from his size, what do the villagers find remarkable about Esteban? **(Clarify)**

Why is it strange that he should have these qualities? **(Evaluate)**

They only had to take the handkerchief off his face to see that he was ashamed, that it was not his fault that he was so big or so heavy or so handsome, and if he had known that this was going to happen, he would have looked for a more discreet place to drown in, seriously, I even would have tied the anchor off a galleon[9] around my neck and staggered off a cliff like someone who doesn't like things in order not to be upsetting people now with this Wednesday dead body, as you people say, in order not to be bothering anyone with this filthy piece of cold meat that doesn't have anything to do with me. There was so much truth in his manner that even the most mistrustful men, the ones who felt the bitterness of endless nights at sea fearing that their women would tire of dreaming about them and begin to dream of drowned men, even they and others who were harder still shuddered in the marrow of their bones at Esteban's sincerity.

Pause & Reflect

FOCUS

The villagers bury Esteban at sea. Read to find out how Esteban has changed their vision of the future.

That was how they came to hold the most splendid funeral they could conceive of for an abandoned drowned man. Some women who had gone to get flowers in the neighboring villages returned with other women who could not believe what they had been told, and those women went back for more flowers when they saw the dead man, and they brought more and more until there were so many flowers and so many people that it was hard to walk about. At the

9. **galleon:** a type of large sailing ship in use from the 1400s through the 1600s, with three masts and two or more decks.

final moment it pained them to return him to the waters as an orphan and they chose a father and mother from among the best people, and aunts and uncles and cousins, so that through him all the inhabitants of the village became kinsmen. Some sailors who heard the weeping from a distance went off course and people heard of one who had himself tied to the mainmast, remembering ancient fables about sirens.[10] While they fought for the privilege of carrying him on their shoulders along the steep escarpment[11] by the cliffs, men and women became aware for the first time of the desolation of their streets, the dryness of their courtyards, the narrowness of their dreams as they faced the splendor and beauty of their drowned man. They let him go without an anchor so that he could come back if he wished and whenever he wished, and they all held their breath for the fraction of centuries the body took to fall into the abyss. They did not need to look at one another to realize that they were no longer all present, that they would never be. But they also knew that everything would be different from then on, that their houses would have wider doors, higher ceilings, and stronger floors so that Esteban's memory could go everywhere without bumping into beams and so that no one in the future would dare whisper the big boob finally died, too bad, the handsome fool has finally died, because they were going to paint their house fronts gay colors to make Esteban's memory eternal and they were going to break their backs digging for springs among the stones and planting flowers on the cliffs so that in future years at dawn the passengers on great liners would awaken, suffocated by the smell of gardens

NOTES

10. **ancient fables about sirens:** In the *Odyssey,* an ancient Greek epic, the hero Odysseus has himself tied to the mast of his ship to resist the Sirens, sweet-voiced nymphs who lure sailors to their destruction on the rocks.

11. **escarpment:** a steep slope or long cliff.

Pause & Reflect

1. The villagers imagine that their lives will change because of Esteban. How? **(Cause and Effect)**

2. Do you think the village will really change as the people imagine? Why or why not? **(Evaluate)**

CHALLENGE The author of this story mixes realistic descriptions with episodes of pure imagination to create a fantasy that almost seems believable. Underline two examples of realism. Put a star by two examples of fantasy. Compare your findings with a partner. Then discuss your opinions of this style of writing. **(Evaluate)**

on the high seas, and the captain would have to come down from the bridge in his dress uniform, with his astrolabe, his pole star,[12] and his row of war medals and, pointing to the promontory of roses on the horizon, he would say in fourteen languages, look there, where the wind is so peaceful now that it's gone to sleep beneath the beds, over there, where the sun's so bright that the sunflowers don't know which way to turn, yes, over there, that's Esteban's village. ❖

Pause & Reflect

12. **astrolabe** (ăs′trə-lāb′) . . . **pole star:** An astrolabe is an instrument formerly used to measure the altitude of stars, including the North Star, or pole star.

Active Reading SkillBuilder

Understanding Cause and Effect

Events in a story are often related by **cause and effect,** which means that one event is the reason that another event happens. The first event is the cause; the events produced by the cause are the effects. In a story, as in real life, a single cause may have more than one effect. In "The Handsomest Drowned Man in the World," the discovery of a drowned man has many effects on the people in a small village. Use the chart below to record three effects. An example has been done for you.

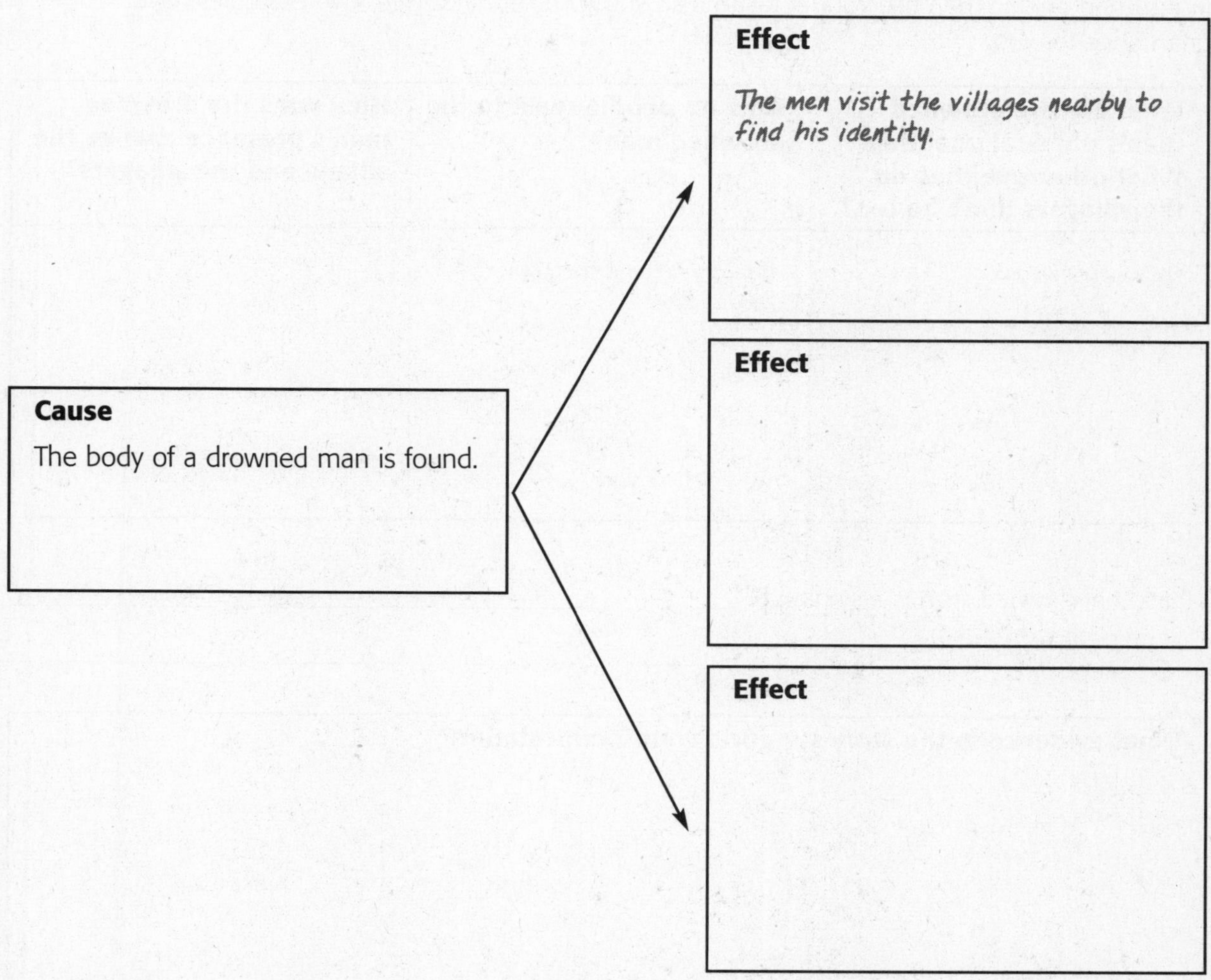
Effect
The men visit the villages nearby to find his identity.
Effect
Effect
Cause
The body of a drowned man is found.

Follow Up: Can you think of any other effects? Write them on the back of this sheet.

Literary Analysis SkillBuilder

Symbol

A **symbol** is a person, place, or object that represents something beyond itself, such as an idea or a feeling. For example, a dove is a symbol of peace, and a national flag is the symbol of a country. Such visual symbols have standard interpretations. In a literary work, however, you have to figure out a symbol's meaning by thinking about the ideas the symbol represents. In this selection, the drowned man is an important symbol. What ideas or feelings does the drowned man represent? Use the activities on this page to help you figure this out. Take notes in the chart below. Then use your notes to help you complete the page. Two examples have been done for you.

What are the drowned man's physical qualities? What other qualities do the villagers think he has?	How do people react to the drowned man?	How does the drowned man's presence change the village and the villagers?
He is very large.	*The children treat him like a toy.*	

I think the drowned man is a symbol of ______________________________

____

What evidence in the story supports your interpretation?

Words to Know SkillBuilder

Words to Know

arid haggard improvise labyrinth virile

A. On each blank line, write the word from the word list that seems to go with each clue.

1. This describes the way you look if you stay awake for 48 hours. ______________________
2. You might use this word to describe a male bodybuilder. ______________________
3. A place that gets very little rain might be described as this. ______________________
4. This is something you might get lost in. ______________________
5. If you can do this, you are a problem-solver. ______________________

B. Fill in the blank in each sentence with the correct Word to Know.

1. Andy looked ______________________ after being lost in the woods for three days and having almost nothing to eat.
2. Mitch doesn't have a tent, so he will have to ______________________ one by leaning some branches against a tree trunk and then covering the branches with leaves.
3. The big old house had many rooms and hallways, and Emma was always getting lost in its ______________________.
4. The quarterback of the university football team was tall, strong, and ______________________.
5. Val lives in the desert where there is little rainfall and the air is ______________________.

C. Write a diary entry from the point of view of one of the inhabitants of the town. In your entry, describe the arrival of the drowned man and your reactions to him. Use at least **two** of the Words to Know in your diary entry.

Academic and Informational Reading

In this section you'll find strategies to help you read all kinds of informational materials. The examples here range from magazines you read for fun to textbooks and television schedules. Applying these simple and effective techniques will help you be a successful reader of the many texts you encounter every day.

Reading a Magazine Article

A magazine article is designed to catch and hold your interest. Learning how to recognize the items on a magazine page will help you read even the most complicated articles. Look at the sample magazine article as you read each strategy below.

A Read the **title** and other **headings** to get an idea of what the article is about. Frequently, the title presents the article's main topic. Smaller headings may introduce subtopics related to the main topic.

B Note introductory text that is set off in some way, such as an **indented paragraph** or a passage in a **different typeface.** This text often summarizes the article.

C Pay attention to terms in **italics** or **boldface.** Look for definitions or explanations before or after these terms.

D Study **visuals**—photos, pictures, or maps. Visuals help bring the topic to life and enrich the text.

E Look for **special features,** such as charts, tables, or graphs, that provide more detailed information on the topic or on a subtopic.

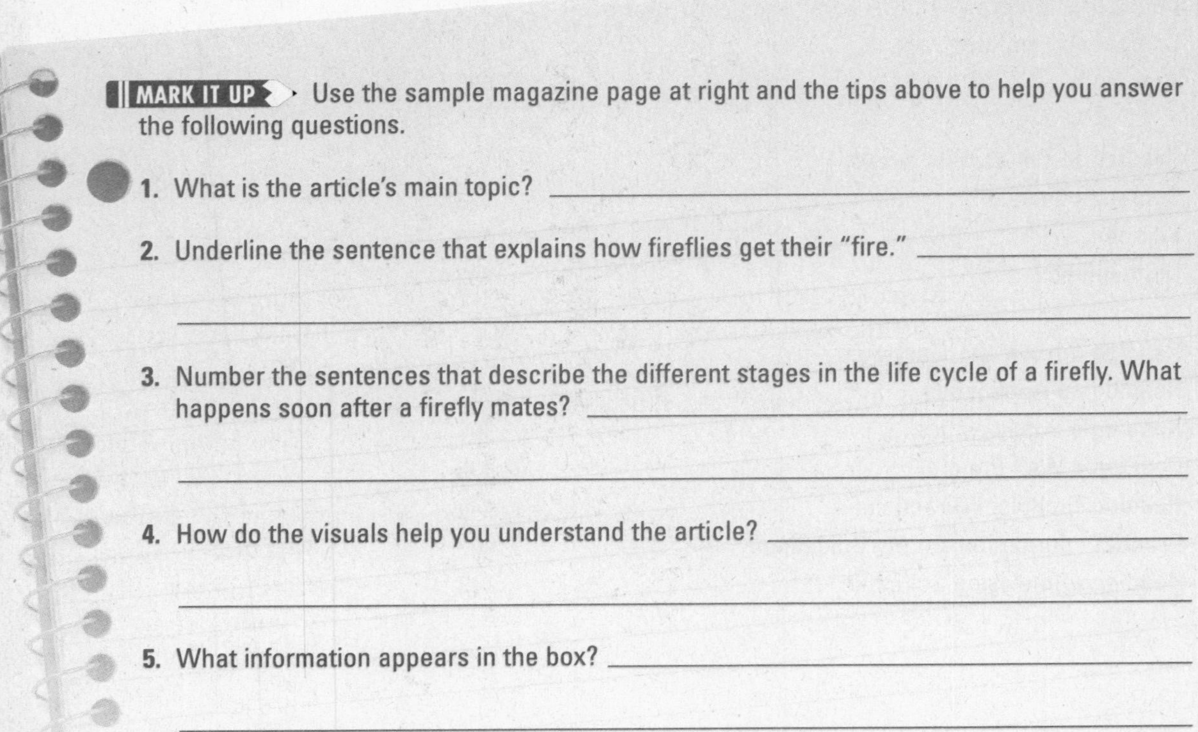

MARK IT UP Use the sample magazine page at right and the tips above to help you answer the following questions.

1. What is the article's main topic? ____________________

2. Underline the sentence that explains how fireflies get their "fire." ____________________

____

3. Number the sentences that describe the different stages in the life cycle of a firefly. What happens soon after a firefly mates? ____________________

____

4. How do the visuals help you understand the article? ____________________

____

5. What information appears in the box? ____________________

____

A

The Lure of Light

B

For humans, cosmic showers are awe-inspiring.
For fireflies, lights closer to home mean it's time to mate.

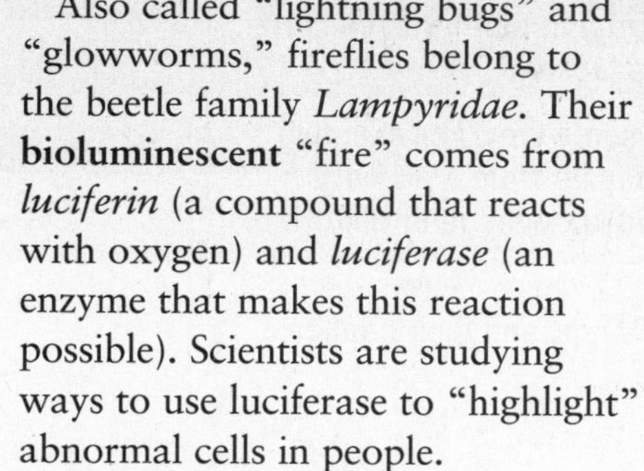

Also called "lightning bugs" and "glowworms," fireflies belong to the beetle family *Lampyridae.* Their C **bioluminescent** "fire" comes from *luciferin* (a compound that reacts with oxygen) and *luciferase* (an enzyme that makes this reaction possible). Scientists are studying ways to use luciferase to "highlight" abnormal cells in people.

Most fireflies look for mates on warm summer evenings. Each species seems to have its own light signal. The male firefly flies around flashing his light signal. When the flightless female, perched on a plant, sees the appropriate signal, she responds by flashing her light. Then the male flies toward her, repeating his signal. . . .

D

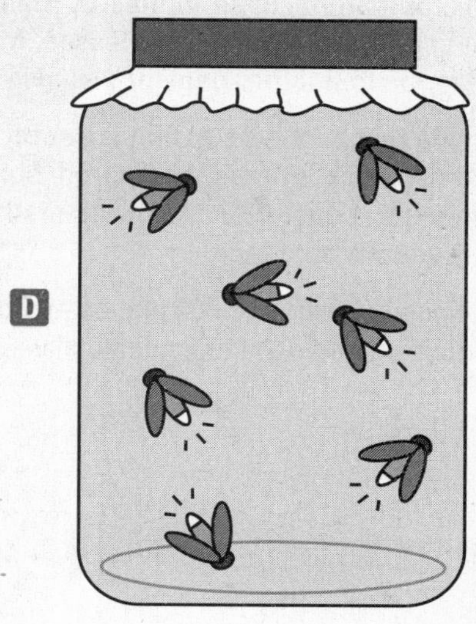

Fireflies die within days after mating. Their young hatch as wormlike larvae. They hide (on land or underwater), eat, grow, **molt,** and grow some more. After several months, each larva buries itself in an underground chamber, where it transforms into an adult firefly. The adult then chews through its chamber wall, pushes up to the surface, and searches for a mate.

The lure of light begins again.

E

> **bioluminescent:** emitting visible light (in a living organism)
> **molt:** to shed a body covering

Reading a Textbook

The first page of a textbook lesson introduces you to a particular topic. The page also provides important information that will guide you through the rest of the lesson. Look at the sample textbook page as you read each strategy below.

A Preview the **title** and other **headings** to find out the lesson's main topic and related subtopics.

B Look for a list of terms or **vocabulary words.** These words will be identified and defined throughout the lesson.

C Read the **main idea, objectives,** or **focus.** These items summarize the lesson and establish a purpose for your reading.

D Find words set in special type, such as **italics** or **boldface.** Also look for material in **parentheses.** Boldface is often used to identify the vocabulary terms in the lesson. Material in parentheses may refer you to another page or visual in the lesson.

E Notice text on the page that is set off in some way. For example, text placed in a tinted, or colored, box may be from a **primary source** or a **quotation** that gives firsthand knowledge or historical perspective on a topic.

F Examine **visuals,** such as photos and drawings, and their captions. Visuals can help the topic come alive.

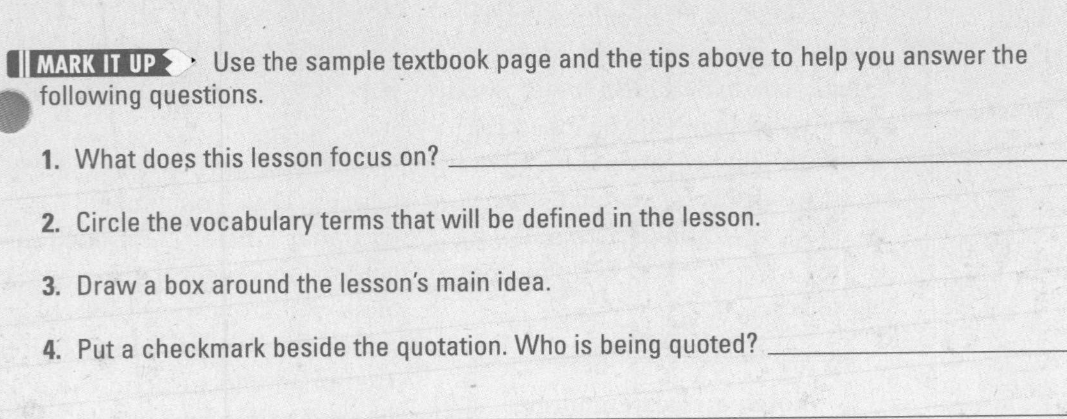

MARK IT UP Use the sample textbook page and the tips above to help you answer the following questions.

1. What does this lesson focus on? ____________________

2. Circle the vocabulary terms that will be defined in the lesson.

3. Draw a box around the lesson's main idea.

4. Put a checkmark beside the quotation. Who is being quoted? ____________________

____

5. Where did the Assyrians come from? ____________________

____

A **2**

Assyria Dominates the Fertile Crescent

B TERMS & NAMES
- Assyria
- Sennacherib
- Nineveh
- Ashurbanipal
- Medes
- Chaldeans
- Nebuchadnezzar

C

MAIN IDEA	WHY IT MATTERS NOW
Assyria developed a military machine, conquered an empire, and established imperial administration.	Some leaders still use military force to extend their rule, stamp out opposition, and gain wealth and power.

SETTING THE STAGE For more than two centuries, the Assyrian army advanced across Southwest Asia. It overwhelmed foes with its military strength. After the Assyrians seized control of Egypt, the Assyrian king Esarhaddon proclaimed, "I tore up the root of Kush, and not one therein escaped to submit to me." The last Kushite pharaoh retreated to Napata, Kush's capital city.

F

This detail of a sandstone relief shows an Assyrian soldier with a shield and iron-tipped spear.

A Mighty Military Machine

Beginning around 850 B.C., **Assyria** (uh·SEER·ee·uh) acquired a large empire. It accomplished this by means of a sophisticated military organization and state-of-the-art weaponry. For a time, this campaign of conquest made Assyria the greatest power in Southwest Asia.

The Rise of a Warrior People The Assyrians came from the northern part of Mesopotamia. Their flat, exposed farmland made them easy to attack. Invaders swept down from the nearby mountains. The Assyrians may have developed their warlike behavior in response to these invasions. Lacking natural barriers such as mountains or deserts, they repelled invaders by developing a strong army. Through constant warfare, Assyrian kings built an empire that stretched from east and north of the Tigris River all the way to central Egypt.

One of these Assyrian kings, **Sennacherib** (sih·NAK·uhr·ihb), bragged that he had sacked 89 cities and 820 villages, burned Babylon, and ordered most of its inhabitants killed. Centuries later, in the 1800s, the English poet George Gordon, Lord Byron, romanticized the Assyrians' bloody exploits in a poem:

A VOICE ABOUT THE PAST

The Assyrian came down like a wolf on the fold,
And his cohorts were gleaming in purple and gold;
And the sheen of their spears was like stars on the sea,
When the blue wave rolls nightly on deep Galilee.

GEORGE GORDON, LORD BYRON, "The Destruction of Sennacherib"

E

THINK THROUGH HISTORY
A. Analyzing Causes What caused the Assyrians to develop a strong army and large empire?
A. Possible Answer No natural barriers to invasion; needed strong army to repel invaders; constant warfare produced large empire.

D

Military Organization and Conquest Assyria was a society which glorified military strength. Its soldiers were well equipped for conquering an empire. Making use of the iron-working technology of the time, the soldiers covered themselves in stiff leather and metal armor. They wore copper or iron helmets, padded loincloths, and leather skirts layered with metal scales. Their weapons were iron swords and iron-pointed spears. Infantry, archers, and spear throwers protected themselves with huge shields.

Advance planning and technical skill allowed the Assyrians to lay siege to enemy cities. When deep water blocked their passage, engineers would bridge the rivers with pontoons, or floating structures used to support a bridge. Tying inflated animal skins

B

Vocabulary
siege: a military blockade to force a city to surrender.

Reading a Table

Tables hold a lot of information in an organized way. These tips can help you read a table quickly and accurately. Look at the example as you read each strategy in this list.

A Read the **title** to find out the content of the table.

B Read the **introduction** to get a general overview of the information included in the table.

C Look at the **heading** of each row and column. To find specific information, find the place where a row and column intersect.

D Check the **credit** to see if the information is up-to-date and from a respected source.

A **Planets of the Solar System**

B Each planet in our solar system is unique. As the table shows, these differing traits include mass, mean distance from the sun, revolution period, and surface gravity.

C	**Mass (kg)**	**Mean Distance from the Sun (km)**	**Revolution Period (Earth time)**	**Surface Gravity (m/s^2)**
Mercury	3.3×10^{23}	57,909,175	87.97 days	3.69
Venus	4.87×10^{24}	108,208,930	224.7 days	8.86
Earth	5.9742×10^{24}	149,597,890	365.26 days	9.81
Mars	6.42×10^{23}	227,936,640	686.98 days	3.73
Jupiter	1.9×10^{27}	778,412,010	11.86 years	22.96
Saturn	5.69×10^{26}	1,426,725,400	29.46 years	11.38
Uranus	8.68×10^{25}	2,870,972,200	83.75 years	11.28
Neptune	1.02×10^{26}	4,498,252,900	163.72 years	11.67
Pluto	1.29×10^{22}	5,906,376,200	248 years	0.65

Source: National Aeronautics and Space Administration Jet Propulsion Laboratory Web site: *http://www.jpl.nasa.gov/solar_system/planets/planets_index.html* **D**

MARK IT UP Answer the following questions using the table of information and tips.

1. Which planet has the strongest surface gravity? Circle the answer on the table.
2. Which planet is about ten times farther from the Sun than Earth? ____________
3. Which planet is more massive: Earth or Venus? ____________

Reading a Map

To read a map correctly, you have to identify and understand its elements. Look at the example below as you read each strategy in this list.

A Scan the **title** to understand the content of the map.

B Study the **key,** or **legend,** to find out what the symbols and colors on the map stand for.

C Study **geographic labels** to understand specific places on the map.

D Look at the **pointer,** or **compass rose,** to determine direction.

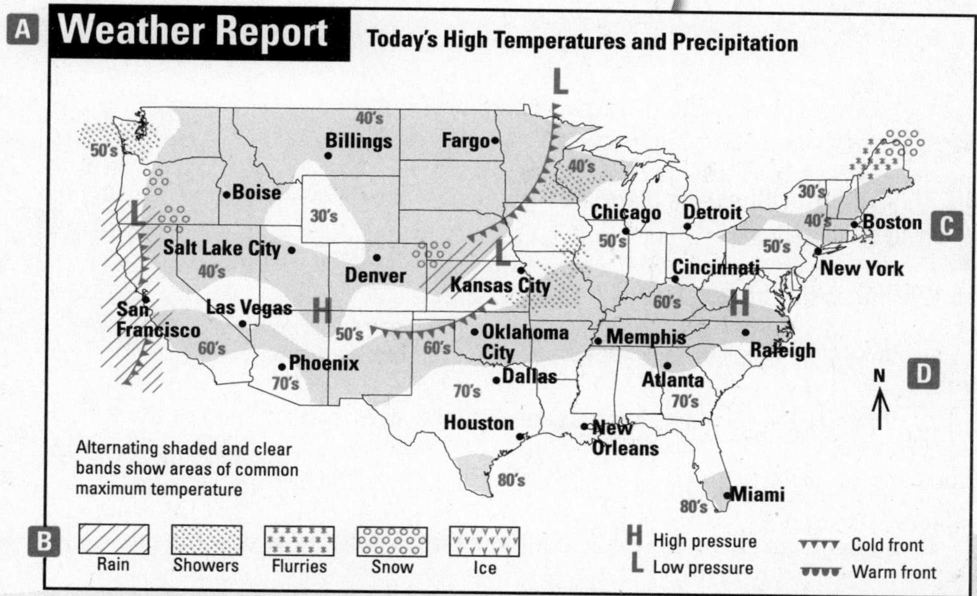

MARK IT UP Use the map to answer the following questions.

1. What is the purpose of this map? ______

2. What does the symbol ▾▾▾▾ mean?

3. Circle the cities where rain is indicated.

4. What seems to be the relationship between rain and cold fronts?

______

5. Draw a star next to the names of the coldest cities in the country.

Reading a Diagram

Diagrams combine pictures with a few words to provide a lot of information. Look at the example on the opposite page as you read each of the following strategies.

A Look at the **title** to get a quick idea of what the diagram is about.

B Study the **images** closely to understand each part of the diagram.

C Look at the **captions** and the **labels** for more information.

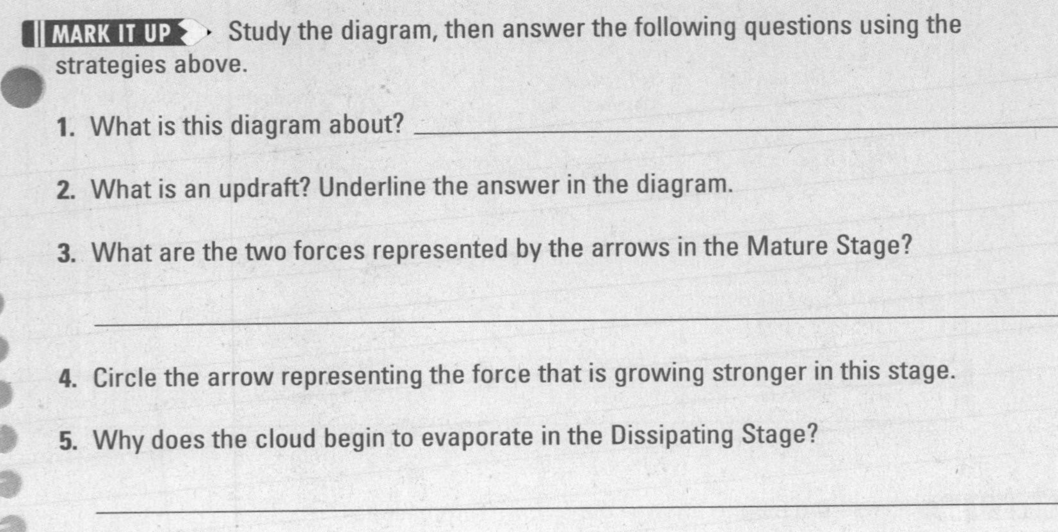

MARK IT UP Study the diagram, then answer the following questions using the strategies above.

1. What is this diagram about? ______________________________

2. What is an updraft? Underline the answer in the diagram.

3. What are the two forces represented by the arrows in the Mature Stage?

   ____

4. Circle the arrow representing the force that is growing stronger in this stage.

5. Why does the cloud begin to evaporate in the Dissipating Stage?

   ____

   ____

A

Life Cycle of a Thunderstorm

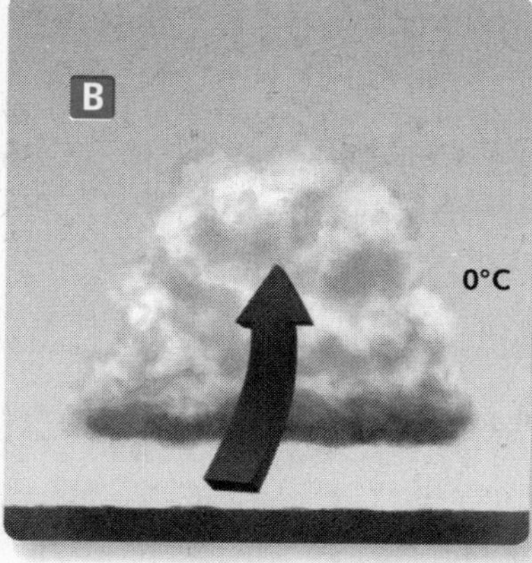

1

C **CUMULUS STAGE** Air rises and a cumulus cloud forms. The rising air is called an updraft. The updraft prevents precipitation from reaching the ground.

2

MATURE STAGE The precipitation becomes heavy enough to fall through the updraft and reach the ground. The falling precipitation creates a downdraft.

3

DISSIPATING STAGE
The downdraft weakens the updraft, eventually cutting off the supply of moist air rising to the cloud. The cloud begins to evaporate.

Main Idea and Supporting Details

The *main idea* in a paragraph is its most important point. *Details* in the paragraph support the main idea. Identifying the main idea will help you focus on the main message the writer wants to communicate. Use the following strategies to help you identify a paragraph's main idea and supporting details.

- Look for the **main idea,** which is often the first sentence in a paragraph.
- Use the main idea to help you **summarize** the point of the paragraph.
- Identify specific **details,** including facts and examples, that **support** the main idea.

Creatures of the Night

Main idea — Bats are nocturnal animals—animals that

Details — are awake during the night and sleep during the day. Just before dusk, bats wake from their slumber. At dusk they begin their search for food; most eat insects, but some also eat fruit, pollen, or nectar. After feeding, bats rest, and then may eat again. Before dawn, they return to their roost for a good day's sleep.

MARK IT UP Read the following paragraph. Circle its main idea. Then underline three of the paragraph's supporting details, numbering each one.

When a volcano erupts, it produces a molten rock called lava. Lava is extremely hot when it first escapes but hardens as it cools. There are two kinds of lava; one kind is fast and fluid, while the other is slow and sticky.

Problem and Solution

Does the proposed solution to a problem make sense? In order to decide, you need to look at each part of the text. Use the following strategies to read the text below.

- Look at the beginning or middle of a paragraph to find the **statement of the problem.**
- Find **details** that explain the problem and tell why it is important.
- Look for the **proposed solution.**
- Identify the **supporting details** for the proposed solution.
- Think about whether the solution is a good one.

Safer Streets *by Wanda Briggs*

Statement of problem

Explanation of problem

The intersection at Fourth and D streets, two blocks from our school, is an accident waiting to happen. Cars speed down the street while students stand at the crosswalk. Every day there are a few drivers who barely slow down, creating a dangerous situation.

Currently there is no stop sign at this intersection. Although the intersection is two blocks away from the school, many students use it because D Street connects the school with the subway station. Every morning and afternoon, hundreds of students and teachers cross the intersection at Fourth and D Streets.

The city should put a stop sign at this intersection and station adult crossing guards there. The presence of a stop sign will be a signal to motorists, and the crossing guard will make sure that students know when it is safe to cross. These safety measures would make the streets safer for students and teachers as well as drivers.

MARK IT UP Read the text above. Then answer these questions.

1. Underline the proposed solution in the third paragraph.
2. Circle at least one detail that supports the solution.
3. Do you think the solution is a good one? Explain why or why not. ______________________

____

Sequence

It's important to understand the *sequence,* or order of events, in what you read. It helps you know what happens and why. Read the tips below to make sure a sequence is clear to you. Then look at the example on the opposite page.

- Read through the passage and think about what its **main steps,** or stages, are.
- Look for **words and phrases that signal time:** such as *today, Friday, that night, later,* or *at 3 o'clock.*
- Look for **words and phrases that signal order:** such as *first, second, now, after that,* or *finally.*

MARK IT UP Read the article on the next page, which describes how to make your own photographic print. Use the information from the article and the tips above to answer the questions.

1. Circle words or phrases that signal time.
2. Underline the phrases in the article that signal order.
3. A flow chart can help you understand a sequence of events. Use the information from the article to complete this flow chart.

1. Load and focus the image.

Put the *negative* in the enlarger.

Adjust the ____________________ knob.

2. Load and expose the paper.

Put the paper on the ______________.

Set the ______________ and push start.

3. Develop and fix the paper.

a. ______________________________

b. ______________________________

c. ______________________________

How to Develop a Photograph

To make a black-and-white photographic print, you will need a photographic negative and a darkroom with an enlarger, photo paper, a printing easel to hold the paper, a clock or watch, and four trays with tongs. Each tray will contain one of four solutions: (1) developer; (2) a stop bath, or "stop"; (3) a fixing solution, or "fix"; and (4) water.

First, put the negative in the negative carrier of the enlarger. Switch the bulb on and adjust the size of the image on the easel. Then turn the focus knob until the image is sharp. Now, without moving the easel, turn off the bulb and place a sheet of photo paper on the easel. Set the timer on the enlarger on five seconds and expose the paper by pressing *start*.

After the paper has been exposed, remove it and place it in the developer tray for one minute. When the minute is up, remove the paper with tongs and place it in the stop bath for five seconds. Then move the paper to the fix tray and leave it there for three to five minutes. Once this time is up, the print has been "fixed" and you may view it in the light.

Look at the print to see whether it is too light or too dark. You may need to start again and adjust the time of exposure. Place the print in the water tray and start over with a new sheet of paper. If your first print was too dark, cut the time of exposure in half. If it was too light, double the time of exposure. Then repeat the remaining steps.

Cause and Effect

A *cause* is an event that brings about another event. An *effect* is something that happens as a result of the first event. Identifying causes and effects helps you understand how events are related. The tips below can help you find causes and effects in any reading.

- Look for an action or event that answers the question "What happened?" This is the **effect.**
- Look for an action or event that answers the question "Why did it happen?" This is the **cause.**
- Identify words or phrases that **signal** causes and effects, such as *because, as a result, therefore, thus, consequently, since,* and *led to.*

MARK IT UP Read the cause-and-effect passage on the next page. Then answer the following questions. Notice that the first cause and effect in the passage are labeled.

1. Circle words in the passage that signal causes and effects. The first one is done for you.
2. Sometimes a cause has more than one effect. Underline the two problems that result when acid rain destroys the waxy coating on a plant's leaves.
3. Use three of the causes and effects in the third paragraph to complete the following diagram.

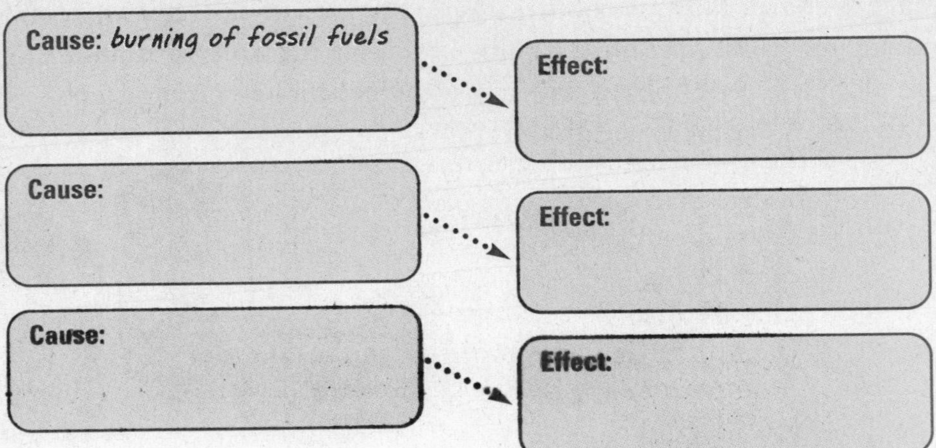

Acid Rain

One of the more serious threats to our environment is acid rain. This term refers to polluted precipitation such as rain, sleet, snow, or fog. The acid in acid rain comes from sulfur dioxide and nitrogen oxides. The presence of sulfur dioxide and nitrogen oxides in the air is caused by the burning of fossil fuels by automobiles, factories, and energy plants. Once released into the atmosphere, sulfur dioxide and nitrogen oxides react with the moisture in the air, producing nitric acid and sulfuric acid. In the last fifty years, taller smokestacks in urban areas have allowed acid pollutants to be blown great distances by the wind. For this reason acid rain has become a problem in rural as well as industrialized areas.

Effect

Signal word

Cause

Acid rain can hinder a plant's growth and reproduction by damaging the roots, destroying nutrients in the soil, or inhibiting the plant's processing of nutrients. Acid rain also damages the protective waxy coating on a plant's leaves, thus making plants more vulnerable to disease and adverse weather conditions such as strong wind, heavy rain, or drought.

Another harmful effect of acid rain is that the water in rivers, lakes, and streams can become more acidic, threatening fish and other aquatic life. It also dissolves metals such as mercury and aluminum, which are found in the surrounding soil and rocks; these toxic elements are then carried into the water supply, where they can poison plants and wildlife. Acid rain can lead to serious health problems if people drink water contaminated with aluminum or eat fish tainted with mercury.

There are certain ways to counteract the effects of acid rain, such as adding lime to lakes and rivers, which temporarily reduces their acidity. However, this may have its own harmful side effects. It may be more effective to reduce the pollution at its source by removing sulfur and nitrogen compounds from fuel, or by burning less fossil fuel altogether.

Comparison and Contrast

Comparing **two things means showing how they are the same.** ***Contrasting*** **two things means showing how they are different. Comparisons and contrasts are often used in science and history books to make a subject clearer. Use these tips to help you understand comparison and contrast in reading assignments, such as the article on the opposite page.**

- Look for **direct statements** of comparison and contrast: "These things are similar because . . . " or "One major difference is. . . ."
- Pay attention to **words and phrases that signal comparisons,** such as *also, both, is the same as,* and *in the same way.*
- Notice **words and phrases that signal contrasts.** Some of these are *however, still, but,* and *on the other hand.*

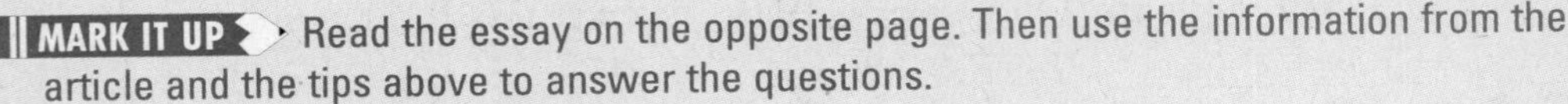

MARK IT UP Read the essay on the opposite page. Then use the information from the article and the tips above to answer the questions.

1. Circle the words and phrases that signal comparisons. A sample has been done for you.
2. Underline the words and phrases that signal contrasts. A sample has been done for you.
3. A Venn diagram shows how two subjects are similar and how they are different. Complete this diagram, which uses information from the essay to compare and contrast emotional and irritant tears. Add at least one similarity to the middle part of the diagram. Add at least one difference in each outer circle.

EMOTIONAL TEARS
caused by strong feelings

BOTH
come from the lacrimal glands

IRRITANT TEARS
caused by smoke, onion vapors, foreign substances

What Are Tears?

Humans shed two kinds of tears. Irritant tears occur in response to irritating physical stimuli, while emotional tears occur in response to sadness, anger, joy, or other intense emotions.

Comparison

Both kinds of tears come from glands above the eyes called lacrimal glands. The fluid from the lacrimal glands moistens the eyes and keeps them clear of foreign particles. With each blink, a little bit of fluid is secreted from the glands. Tears form when the lacrimal glands produce more fluid than can drain through the available ducts.

Emotional tears occur when a strong feeling, such as grief, anger, or joy, causes the muscles around the lacrimal glands to tighten up and squeeze out excess fluid. These emotional tears differ from irritant tears, which occur in response to irritants such as smoke, onion vapors, or bits of dirt in the eye.

Contrast

Irritant tears have a clear purpose—to wash the eye and keep it moist. What is the purpose of emotional tears? Scientist William Frey suspects that emotional tears might help relieve the body of chemicals that build up during stress.

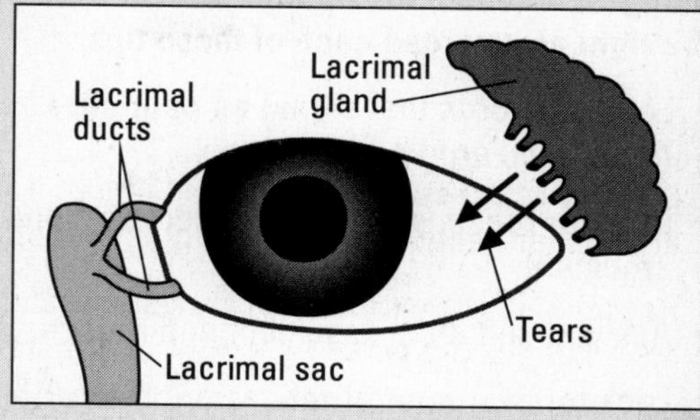

He conducted a study in which he compared irritant tears with emotional tears. To produce irritant tears, he exposed people to grated onions and collected the resulting tears. Producing emotional tears was a little bit more complicated—what is the best way to make people cry without being mean to them? He finally decided to show them sad movies.

Frey found that emotional tears were in fact different from irritant tears. For one thing, people tended to shed many more emotional tears than irritant tears. And while both kinds of tears contained the element manganese, emotional tears had a much higher concentration of protein. However, the reason for this difference was not clear.

The mysterious causes and functions of tears are still being researched, but if you want to avoid shedding tears, stay away from onions and sad movies—at least that much is clear.

Argument

An *argument* is an opinion backed up with reasons and facts. Examining an opinion and the reasons and facts that back it up will help you decide if the opinion makes sense. Look at the argument on the right as you read each of these tips.

- Look for words that **signal an opinion:** *I believe; I think; in my view; they claim, argue,* or *disagree.*
- Look for reasons, facts, or expert opinions that **support** the argument.
- Ask yourself if the argument and reasons **make sense.**
- Look for overgeneralizations or other **errors in reasoning** that may affect the argument.

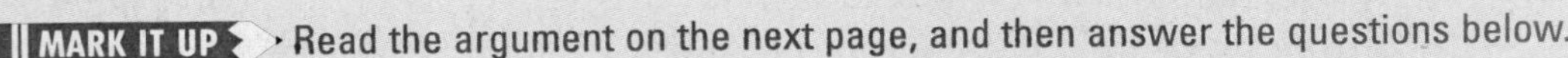

MARK IT UP Read the argument on the next page, and then answer the questions below.

1. Circle any words that signal an opinion.
2. Underline the words or phrases that give the writer's opinion.
3. The writer presents both sides of the argument. Fill in the chart below to show the two sides. One reason has been provided for you.

Reasons for	Reasons Against
1. Bicycles produce less air pollution than cars.	

More Rights for Bikes

By Maxine Fujita

I believe bicyclists should have as much claim to city streets as automobiles. In my view, it is time to encourage bicycle riding by increasing the number of bike lanes and by changing motorists' attitudes toward bicycle riders.

The advantages of riding a bicycle rather than driving a car are clear. For one thing, automobile exhaust adds to already grave air pollution problems in our cities. By choosing to ride a bike instead of drive, we help keep our air clean. We also keep our streets quiet. Although we often forget about noise pollution, few people would miss the constant revving of car engines and honking of horns if our streets were filled with bicycles. Cycling also provides great exercise. If more people rode bikes, our population would have healthier hearts, lungs, and legs.

There are those who oppose bicycle traffic. They say the streets were made for cars, so cars have more right to be on the streets. They claim that cyclists are a nuisance and a danger because they interfere with auto traffic and are hard to see. They themselves don't want to cycle because it's too strenuous, too cold, too wet, too far, or too dangerous.

I'm not saying that bicycling is for everyone, but I am saying it's a safer, healthier, environmentally friendly alternative to driving. So join me in supporting more bike lanes and increased respect for the people who use them.

Social Studies

Social studies class becomes easier when you understand how your textbook's words, pictures, and maps work together to give you information. Following these tips can make you a better reader of social studies lessons. As you read the tips, look at the sample lesson on the right-hand page.

A First, look at any **headlines** or **subheads** on the page. These give you an idea of what each section covers.

B Make sure you know the meaning of any boldfaced or underlined **vocabulary terms.** These terms often appear on tests.

C Carefully read the text and think about **ways the information is organized.** Social studies books are full of sequence, comparison and contrast, and organization by geographic location.

D Look closely at **maps** and **map titles.** Think about how the map and the text are related.

E Read any **study tips** in the margins or at the bottom of the page. These let you check your understanding as you read.

MARK IT UP Carefully read the textbook page at right. Use the information from the page and from the tips above to answer these questions.

1. What are the two main subjects covered on this page? ______________________

   What secondary subject is covered? ______________________

2. Circle the three vocabulary terms. Then underline the parts of the text that define those terms.

3. Give three examples of uplands. ______________________

   ____

4. On the map, circle the river that empties into the North Sea. Draw a star at the river's mouth.

5. Read the "Geographic Thinking" question in the left margin. Circle the paragraph in the text that contains the answer to this question.

off the Balkan Peninsula from the rest of Europe. Historically, they also have isolated the peninsula's various ethnic groups from each other.

A B **UPLANDS** Mountains and uplands differ from each other in their elevation. **Uplands** are hills or very low mountains that may also contain mesas and high plateaus. Some uplands of Europe are eroded remains of ancient mountain ranges. Examples of uplands include the Kjølen (CHUR•luhn) Mountains of Scandinavia, the Scottish highlands, the low mountain areas of Brittany in France, and the central plateau of Spain called the ***Meseta*** (meh•SEH•tah). Other uplands border mountainous areas, such as the Central Uplands of Germany, which are at the base of the Alps. About one-sixth of French lands are located in the uplands called the ***Massif Central*** (ma•SEEF sahn•TRAHL).

BACKGROUND
Brittany is a region located on a peninsula in northwest France.

A Rivers: Europe's Links

Traversing Europe is a network of rivers that bring people and goods together. These rivers are used to transport goods between coastal harbors and the inland region, aiding economic growth. Historically, the rivers also have aided the movement of ideas.

C Two major castle-lined rivers—the Danube and the Rhine—have served as watery highways for centuries. The Rhine flows 820 miles from the interior of Europe north to the North Sea. The Danube cuts through the heart of Europe from west to east. Touching 9 countries over its 1,771-mile length, the Danube River links Europeans to the Black Sea.

Many other European rivers flow from the interior to the sea and are large enough for ships to traverse. Through history, these rivers helped connect Europeans to the rest of the world, encouraging both trade and travel. Europeans have explored and migrated to many other world regions. B

E

Seeing Patterns
B How does the direction in which European rivers flow aid in linking Europeans to the world?

B. Answer
Because they flow toward seas, the rivers help Europeans to travel to other regions.

D

Rivers of Europe

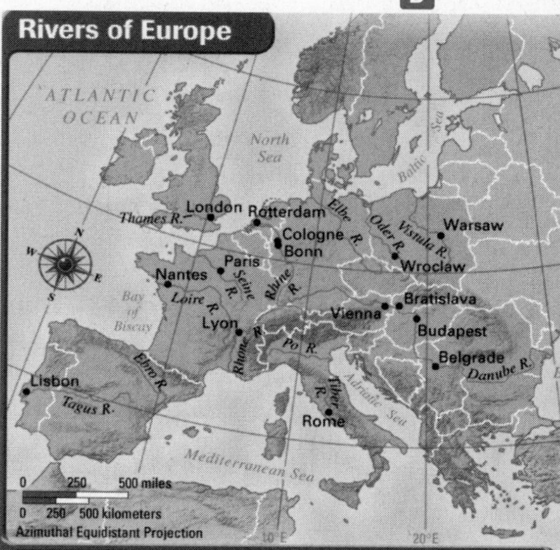

SKILLBUILDER: Interpreting Maps

1. **MOVEMENT** Which rivers empty into the North Sea? Into the Mediterranean Sea?
2. **PLACE** What port is at the mouth of the Rhine?

Science

Reading a science textbook becomes easier when you understand how the explanations, drawings, and special terms work together. Use the strategies below to help you better understand your science textbook. Look at the examples on the opposite page as you read each strategy in this list.

A Preview the **title** and **headings** on the page to see what scientific concepts will be covered.

B Read the **key idea, objectives,** or **focus.** These items summarize the lesson and establish a purpose for your reading.

C Look for **boldfaced** and **italicized** words that appear in the text. Look for **definitions** of those words.

D Carefully examine any **pictures** or **diagrams.** Read the **captions** and evaluate how the graphics help to illustrate and explain the text.

E Many science textbooks discuss **scientific concepts** in terms of **everyday events** or **experiences.** Look for these places and consider how they improve your understanding.

MARK IT UP Use the sample science page and the tips above to help you answer the following questions.

1. What scientific concepts will be covered in this lesson? Where on the page did you find this information? ______________________________

   ____

2. Circle the key term *fault* and underline its definition.

3. Why do you think the earthquake model described in the third paragraph is called the *elastic-rebound theory?* ______________________________

   ____

4. What are two things the diagram tells you about earthquakes? ______________________________

   ____

5. Put a star next to the image that shows the visible result of an earthquake.

10.1

A How and Where Earthquakes Occur

B **KEY IDEA**

Most earthquakes result from the strain that builds up at plate boundaries.

KEY VOCABULARY

- earthquake
- fault
- focus
- epicenter
- body waves
- P waves
- S waves
- surface waves

More than 3 million earthquakes occur each year, or about one earthquake every ten seconds. Most of these are too small to be noticeable. Each year, however, a number of powerful earthquakes occur. Because such earthquakes are among the most destructive of natural disasters, it is important to understand how and where earthquakes occur in order to prevent the loss of lives and property.

Causes of Earthquakes

C An **earthquake** is a shaking of Earth's crust caused by a release of energy. Earthquakes can occur for many reasons. The ground may shake as a result of the eruption of a volcano, the collapse of a cavern, or even the impact of a meteor. The cause of most major earthquakes is the strain that builds up along faults at or near boundaries between lithospheric plates. A **fault** is a break in the lithosphere along which movement has occurred.

Most of the time, friction prevents the plates from moving, so strain builds up, causing the plates to deform, or change shape. Eventually, the strain becomes great enough to overcome the friction, and the plates move suddenly, causing an earthquake. The plates then snap back to the shapes they had before they were deformed, but at new locations relative to each other. This model of an earthquake is called the elastic-rebound theory.

The point at which the first movement occurs during an earthquake is called the **focus** of the earthquake. The focus is the point at which rock begins to move or break. It is where the earthquake originates and is usually many kilometers beneath the surface. The point on Earth's surface directly above the focus is the **epicenter** of the earthquake. News reports about earthquakes usually give the location of the epicenters.

E **EARTHQUAKE** These rows of lettuce were displaced by an earthquake in California in 1979.

Focus and Epicenter of an Earthquake D

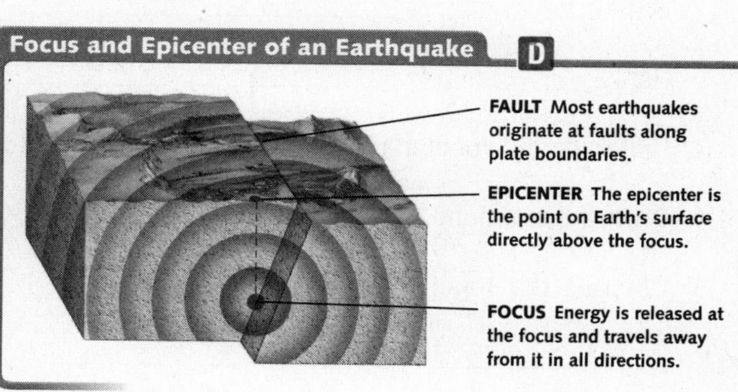

FAULT Most earthquakes originate at faults along plate boundaries.

EPICENTER The epicenter is the point on Earth's surface directly above the focus.

FOCUS Energy is released at the focus and travels away from it in all directions.

The depth at which an earthquake originates depends upon the type of plate boundary involved. At divergent boundaries, such as the Mid-Atlantic Ridge, earthquakes tend to occur within 30 kilometers of the surface. Earthquakes also tend to occur at shallow depths along transform boundaries. At subduction boundaries, however, where plates plunge beneath other plates, the focus of an earthquake can be located as far as

Mathematics

Reading in mathematics is different from reading in history, literature, or science. Use the strategies below to help you better understand your mathematics textbook. Look at the examples on the opposite page as you read each strategy in the list.

A Preview the **title** and **headings** on the page to see what math concepts will be covered.

B Find and read the **goals** or **objectives** for the lesson. These will tell you the most important points to know.

C Read **explanations** carefully. Sometimes a concept is explained in more than one way to make sure you understand it.

D Look for **special features,** such as study or vocabulary tips. They provide more help or information.

E Study any **worked-out solutions** to sample problems. These are the key to understanding how to do the homework assignment.

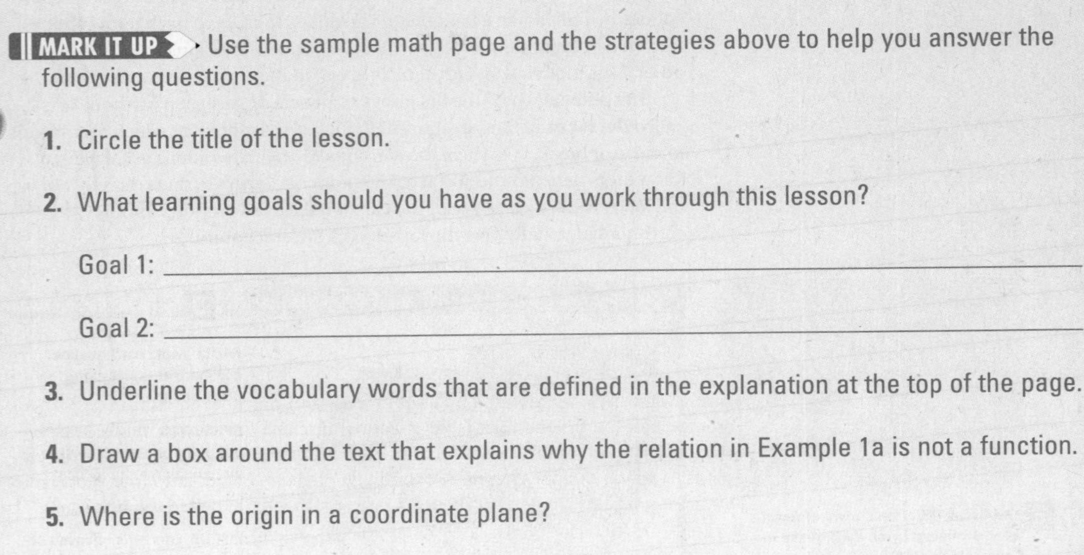

MARK IT UP Use the sample math page and the strategies above to help you answer the following questions.

1. Circle the title of the lesson.

2. What learning goals should you have as you work through this lesson?

   Goal 1: ______________________________

   Goal 2: ______________________________

3. Underline the vocabulary words that are defined in the explanation at the top of the page.

4. Draw a box around the text that explains why the relation in Example 1a is not a function.

5. Where is the origin in a coordinate plane?

   ____

6. Draw a box around the name that is given to the first number in an ordered pair.

A

2.1 Functions and Their Graphs

What you should learn

B **GOAL 1** Represent relations and functions.

GOAL 2 Graph and evaluate linear functions, as applied in **Exs. 55 and 56.**

Why you should learn it

▼ To model **real-life** quantities, such as the distance a hot air balloon travels in **Example 6.**

A **GOAL 2** **REPRESENTING RELATIONS AND FUNCTIONS**

C A **relation** is a *mapping*, or pairing, of input values with output values. The set of input values is the **domain**, and the set of output values is the **range**. A relation is a **function** provided there is exactly one output for each input. It is not a function if at least one input has more than one output.

Relations (and functions) between two quantities can be represented in many ways, including mapping diagrams, tables, graphs, equations, and verbal descriptions.

A **EXAMPLE 1** ***Identifying Functions***

Identify the domain and range. Then tell whether the relation is a function.

a. Input Output

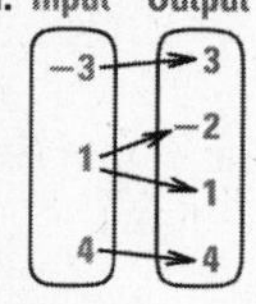

b. Input Output

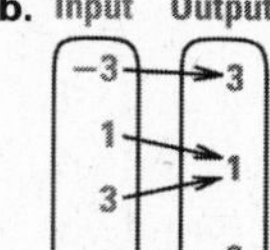

E **SOLUTION**

a. The domain consists of −3, 1, and 4, and the range consists of −2, 1, 3, and 4. The relation is not a function because the input 1 is mapped onto both −2 and 1.

b. The domain consists of −3, 1, 3, and 4, and the range consists of −2, 1, and 3. The relation is a function because each input in the domain is mapped onto exactly one output in the range.

....

A relation can be represented by a set of **ordered pairs** of the form (x, y). In an ordered pair the first number is the ***x*-coordinate** and the second number is the ***y*-coordinate**. To graph a relation, plot each of its ordered pairs in a **coordinate plane,** such as the one shown. A coordinate plane is divided into four **quadrants** by the ***x*-axis** and the ***y*-axis**. The axes intersect at a point called the **origin**.

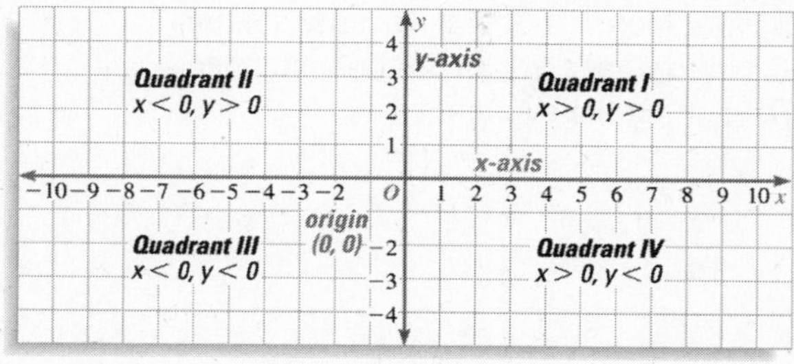

D 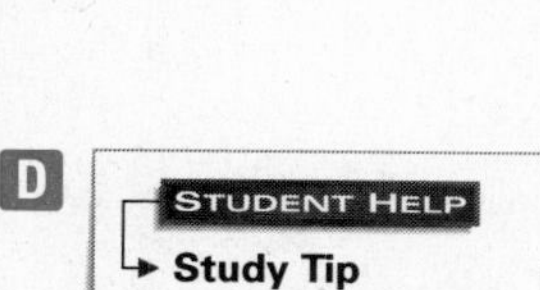

STUDENT HELP

Study Tip

Although the origin *O* is not usually labeled, it is understood to be the point (0, 0).

Reading an Application

Reading and understanding an application will help you fill it out correctly and avoid mistakes. Use the following strategies to help you understand any application. Look at the example on the next page as you read each strategy.

A **Begin at the top.** Scan the application to understand the different sections.

B Look for special **instructions for filling out** the application.

C Note any **request for materials** that must be attached to the application.

D Watch for **sections you don't have to fill in** or **questions you don't have to answer.**

E Look for difficult or confusing words or abbreviations. Look them up in a dictionary or ask someone what they mean.

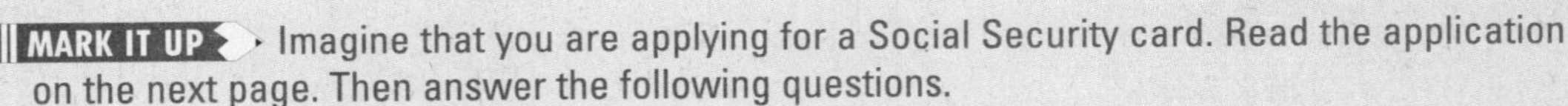

MARK IT UP Imagine that you are applying for a Social Security card. Read the application on the next page. Then answer the following questions.

1. Underline the part of the application that tells you where to send the completed form.

2. Which questions can you skip if you have never before applied for or received a Social Security card? ______________________________

3. Circle the section of the application where your phone number should be entered.

4. Put a star next to the portion of the application that describes the penalty for deliberately giving false information.

5. **ASSESSMENT PRACTICE** What should be written in section 8B of the application?
   A. your father's name
   B. your mother's Social Security number
   C. your father's Social Security number
   D. your mother's name

A # SOCIAL SECURITY ADMINISTRATION
Application for a Social Security Card

Form Approved
OMB No. 0960-0066

B **STEP 1** Complete and sign the application using BLUE or BLACK ink. Do not use pencil or other colors of ink. Please print legibly.

C **STEP 2** Submit the completed and signed application with all required original documents to any Social Security office. To find out what documents are needed, please visit www.ssa.gov/online.

1	**NAME** → TO BE SHOWN ON CARD	First / Full Middle Name / Last
	FULL NAME AT BIRTH IF OTHER THAN ABOVE	First / Full Middle Name / Last
	OTHER NAMES USED	
2	**MAILING ADDRESS** → Do Not Abbreviate	Street Address, Apt. No., PO Box, Rural Route No. / City / State / Zip Code
3	**CITIZENSHIP** (Check One) →	☐ U.S. Citizen ☐ Legal Alien Allowed To Work ☐ Legal Alien **Not** Allowed To Work (See Instructions On Page 1) ☐ Other (See Instructions On Page 1)
4	**SEX** →	☐ Male ☐ Female
5	**RACE/ETHNIC DESCRIPTION** (Check One Only - Voluntary) →	☐ Asian, Asian-American or Pacific Islander ☐ Hispanic ☐ Black (Not Hispanic) ☐ North American Indian or Alaskan Native ☐ White (Not Hispanic)
6	**DATE OF BIRTH** Month, Day, Year	**7** **PLACE OF BIRTH** (Do Not Abbreviate) City / State or Foreign Country / FCI / Office Use Only
8	A. **MOTHER'S MAIDEN NAME** →	First / Full Middle Name / Last Name At Her Birth
	B. **MOTHER'S SOCIAL SECURITY NUMBER** →	☐☐☐—☐☐—☐☐☐☐
9	A. **FATHER'S NAME** →	First / Full Middle Name / Last
	B. **FATHER'S SOCIAL SECURITY NUMBER** →	☐☐☐—☐☐—☐☐☐☐
10	Has the applicant or anyone acting on his/her behalf ever filed for or received a Social Security number card before? ☐ Yes (If "yes", answer questions 11-13.) ☐ No (If "no", go on to question 14.) ☐ Don't Know (If "don't know", go on to question 14.)	
11	Enter the Social Security number previously assigned to the person listed in item 1. →	☐☐☐—☐☐—☐☐☐☐
12	Enter the name shown on the most recent Social Security card issued for the person listed in item 1. →	First / Middle Name / Last
13	Enter any different date of birth if used on an earlier application for a card. →	Month, Day, Year
14	**TODAY'S DATE** Month, Day, Year	**15** **DAYTIME PHONE NUMBER** ( ) Area Code / Number

E DELIBERATELY FURNISHING (OR CAUSING TO BE FURNISHED) FALSE INFORMATION ON THIS APPLICATION IS A CRIME PUNISHABLE BY FINE OR IMPRISONMENT, OR BOTH.

16	**YOUR SIGNATURE** ▶	**17** **YOUR RELATIONSHIP TO THE PERSON IN ITEM 1 IS:** ☐ Self ☐ Natural Or Adoptive Parent ☐ Legal Guardian ☐ Other (Specify)

D DO NOT WRITE BELOW THIS LINE (FOR SSA USE ONLY)

EVIDENCE SUBMITTED	SIGNATURE AND TITLE OF EMPLOYEE(S) REVIEWING EVIDENCE AND/OR CONDUCTING INTERVIEW
	DCL / DATE

Reading a Public Notice

Public notices can tell you about events in your community and give you valuable information about safety. When you read a public notice, follow these tips. Each tip relates to a specific part of the notice on the opposite page.

A Read the notice's **title,** if it has one. The title often gives the main idea or purpose of the notice.

B See if there is a logo, credit, or other way of telling **who created the notice.**

C Ask yourself, **"Who should read this notice?"** If the information in it might be important to you or someone you know, then you should pay attention to it.

D Look for **instructions**—things the notice is asking or telling you to do.

E See if there are details that tell you how you can **find out more** about the topic.

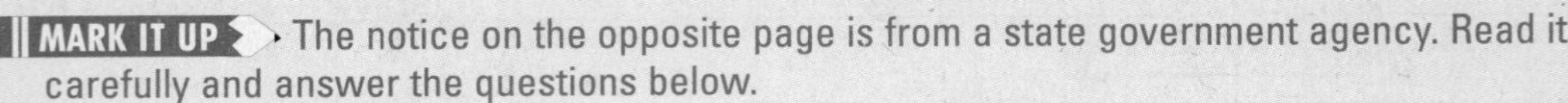

MARK IT UP The notice on the opposite page is from a state government agency. Read it carefully and answer the questions below.

1. Who is the notice from? ______________________________

2. Who is the notice for? ______________________________

3. What does the notice ask readers to do? ______________________________

____

4. Put a star next to the portion of the notice that explains where proposals should be sent.

5. Underline the text that explains what will be done with the proposals.

6. **ASSESSMENT PRACTICE** According to the notice, the state is looking to enact projects that will
   A. help manage the governor's Web site.
   B. offer assistance to families in need.
   C. reduce coastal beach contamination.
   D provide scholarships for college-bound students.

B **STATE WATER CONTROL BOARD**

The energy challenge facing our state is real. Every citizen needs to take immediate action to reduce energy consumption. For a list of simple ways you can reduce demand and cut your energy costs, see our website at www.stategovxyz.gov.

A PUBLIC NOTICE REQUESTING PROJECT PROPOSALS FOR THE BEACH CLEANUP ACT (BCA)

C **ATTENTION:** COASTAL BIOLOGISTS, VOLUNTEER BEACH MONITORS, AND CONCERNED CITIZENS

The State's coastal beach monitoring programs indicate that beach pollution is widespread and too often exceeds acceptable levels, resulting in beach postings and closures. The major goal of the BCA is to reduce health risks and increase the public's access to clean beaches.

D **The State wants your proposals.** The State Water Control Board (SWCB) is in the process of identifying traditional and innovative projects that will result in a reduction of coastal beach contamination. These projects will be located in the areas of the state where beach postings and closures have been most prevalent. Project proposals that are submitted to the SWCB will be placed on a list and will be eligible for loans and grants, as they become available. During the fiscal year 2001–2002, loan moneys will be available through the State Fund for:

- development and implementation of programs to control pollution from nonpoint sources and stormwater drainage;
- publicly-owned capital improvement projects that benefit water quality;
- implementation of estuary enhancement programs.

Additionally, it is possible that a grant program may become available for local diversions, catch basins, filtration systems, and other projects that will reduce untreated runoff from reaching coastal waters. However, the SWCB will continue to seek funding for projects that will result in significant and steady decreases in beach postings and closures.

D In preparing this list, we are seeking information on viable projects that will help us attain our goal of providing clean and healthy coastal beaches for all that reside in and visit our state. Enclosed is a list of items and considerations that will be necessary for a timely review of all projects submitted. Priority will be given to projects that can be in place and in operation by July 2004. With your assistance, we plan to have an initial list of projects compiled by mid-April, 2003. Projects will be reviewed as they are received by staff for concurrence with the BCA's intent and completeness of information. We will post more information on our website at www.swcb.xyz.gov as it becomes available.

Project Proposals should be sent to:

State Water Control Board
Loans & Grants Branch
P.O. Box 1234
San Pedro, CA 90202

E If you have any questions, please contact Dr. John Smith, Clean Beaches Coordinator for the SWCB at (555) 555-1111 or jsmith@exec.swcb.xyz.gov.

Reading a Web Page

If you need information for a report, project, or hobby, the World Wide Web can probably help you. The tips below will help you understand the Web pages you read. As you look at the tips, notice where they match up to the sample Web page on the right.

A Notice the page's **Web address,** or URL. You may want to write it down in case you need to access the same page at another time.

B Look for **menu bars** along the top, bottom, or side of the page. These guide you to other parts of the site that may be useful.

C Look for **links** to other parts of the site or to related pages. Links are often shown as underlined words.

D Use a **search** feature to quickly find out whether a certain kind of information is contained anywhere on the site.

E Many sites have a link that allows you to **contact** the creators with questions or feedback.

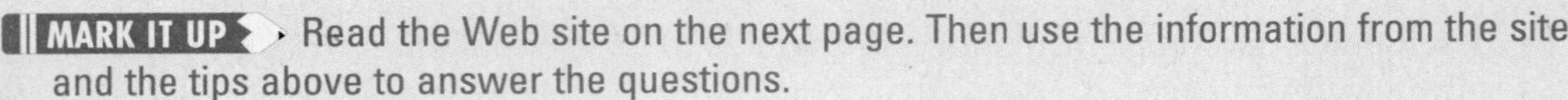

MARK IT UP Read the Web site on the next page. Then use the information from the site and the tips above to answer the questions.

1. Circle the Web address.

2. If you wanted to know whether the ClassZone site contained any information about adjective clauses, how would you go about finding out? ____________________

   ____

3. Read the paragraph under "Topic." Then look at the thought bubbles below. What would you expect to find if you clicked on "Write About It"? ____________________

   ____

4. Circle the links that would take you to different sites where you might publish your work.

5. **ASSESSMENT PRACTICE** Choose the sentence that best summarizes this site.
   A. It encourages Americans to exercise.
   B. It assigns a research report about physical fitness.
   C. It describes the problem of Americans' lack of exercise and asks students to respond in writing.
   D. none of the above

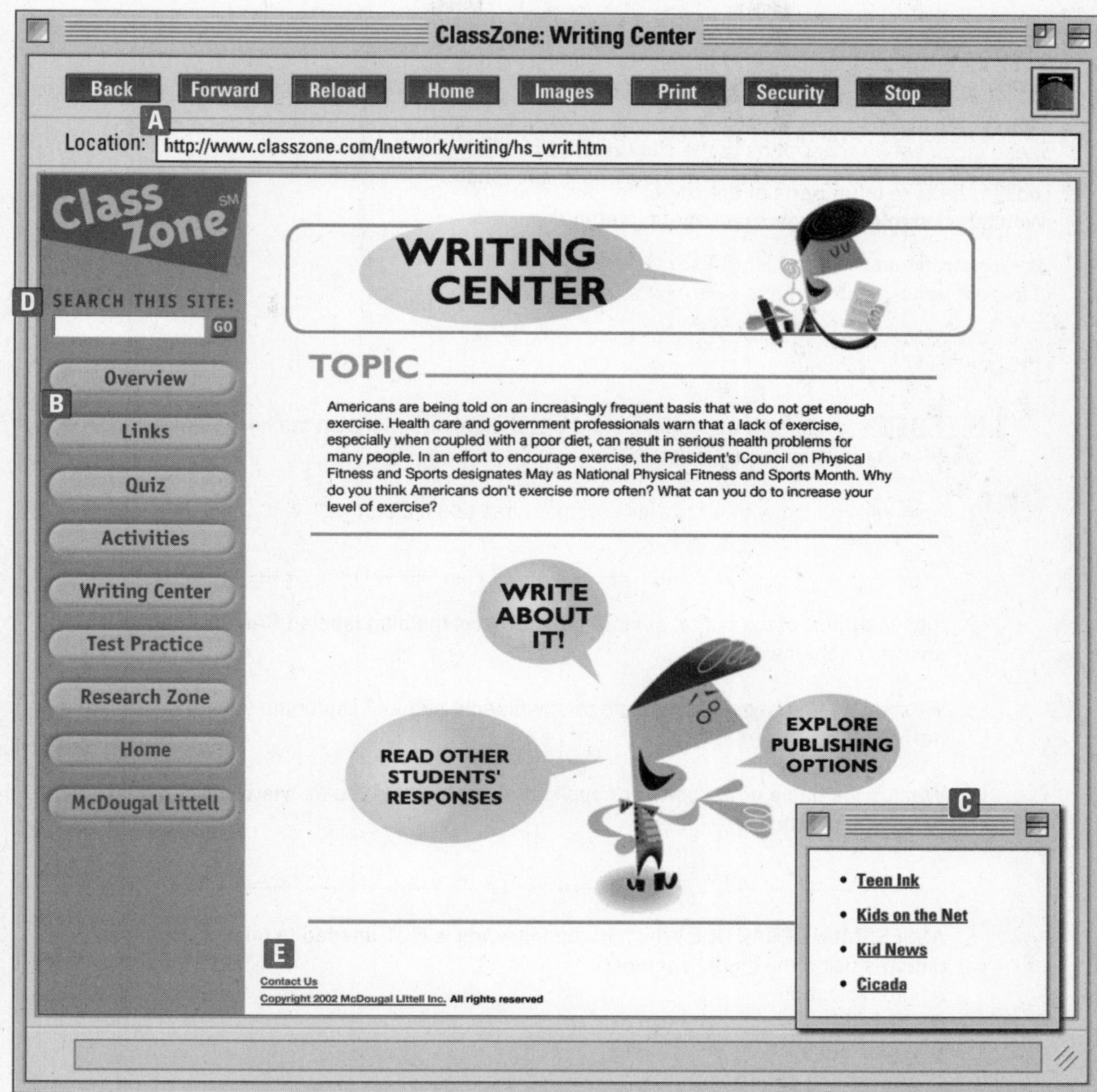
ClassZone: Writing Center
Back
Forward
Reload
Home
Images
Print
Security
Stop
A
Location: http://www.classzone.com/lnetwork/writing/hs_writ.htm
Class Zone SM
D SEARCH THIS SITE:
GO
Overview
B
Links
Quiz
Activities
Writing Center
Test Practice
Research Zone
Home
McDougal Littell
WRITING CENTER
TOPIC
Americans are being told on an increasingly frequent basis that we do not get enough exercise. Health care and government professionals warn that a lack of exercise, especially when coupled with a poor diet, can result in serious health problems for many people. In an effort to encourage exercise, the President's Council on Physical Fitness and Sports designates May as National Physical Fitness and Sports Month. Why do you think Americans don't exercise more often? What can you do to increase your level of exercise?
WRITE ABOUT IT!
READ OTHER STUDENTS' RESPONSES
EXPLORE PUBLISHING OPTIONS
C
• Teen Ink
• Kids on the Net
• Kid News
• Cicada
E
Contact Us
Copyright 2002 McDougal Littell Inc. All rights reserved

Reading Technical Directions

Reading technical directions will help you understand how to use the products you buy. Use the following tips to help you read a variety of technical directions.

A Look carefully at any **diagrams** or **other images** of the product.

B **Read all the directions** carefully at least once before using the product.

C Notice **headings** or **rules** that separate one section from another.

D Look for **numbers** or **letters** that give the steps in sequence.

E Watch for **warnings** or **notes** with more information.

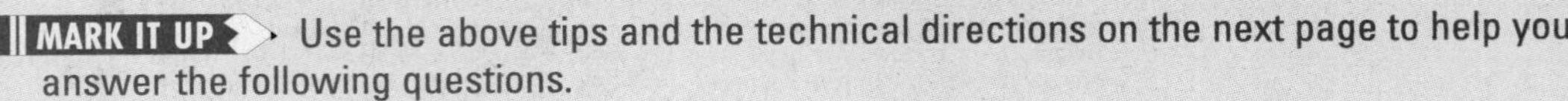

MARK IT UP Use the above tips and the technical directions on the next page to help you answer the following questions.

1. How will you know that the digital camera has taken a picture?

____

2. Into what part of the digital camera do you insert the plug labeled CAM? Circle your answer on the next page.

3. What is the first thing you must do to download a picture? Underline your answer on the next page.

4. What is the name of the software application that allows you to "view" and "get" images on your computer?

____

5. **ASSESSMENT PRACTICE** Which of the following is NOT needed to take or download pictures using the digital camera?
   A. shutter button
   B. CD-ROM
   C. e-mail account
   D. connecting cable

Digital Camera Instructions

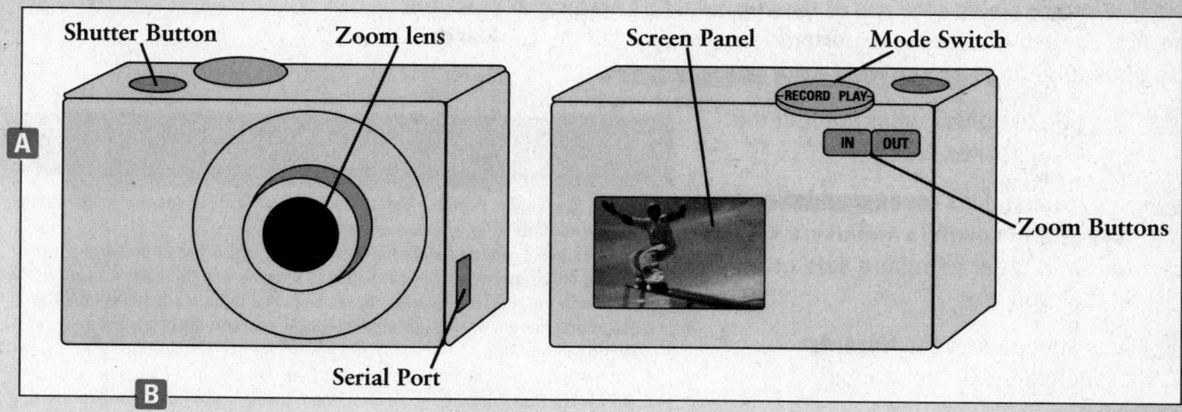

C **A. Taking Pictures**

1. Turn the Mode Switch to RECORD.

D 2. Compose the image on the Screen Panel using the Zoom Buttons.

3. Press the Shutter Button halfway. This will freeze the image on the Screen Panel.

E **NOTE:** You will feel the button settle into a notch when it is halfway depressed.

4. If satisfied with the frozen image, press the Shutter Button fully to take the picture. **NOTE:** The camera will emit a beep to show that the picture has been taken.

B. Connecting to Your Computer

1. Locate the provided connecting cable.
2. Insert the plug labeled CAM into the camera's Serial Port.
3. Insert the plug labeled CPU into the serial port labeled CAM1 at the rear of your computer.

C. Installing Software

1. Locate the provided CD-ROM.
2. Insert the CD-ROM into your computer's CD-ROM drive and double-click on the INSTALL icon when it appears on your desktop.
3. The CD-ROM will install the necessary digital camera software over a period of up to five minutes.

D. Downloading Pictures

1. Turn the Mode Switch to PLAY.
2. Start the CamPics software by double-clicking the CamPics application icon.
3. Once the CamPics application has launched, select View Image from the Camera menu.
4. Select an image by either double-clicking on the individual image or clicking on the Get Images icon.
5. When an image has finished downloading, you may print, edit, organize, or transfer it to another host. The images are in JPEG format making them accessible to many applications.

Product Information: Safety Guidelines

Safety guidelines are facts and recommendations provided by government agencies or product manufacturers offering instructions and warnings about safe use of these products. Learning to read and follow such guidelines is important for your own safety. Look at the sample guidelines as you read each strategy below.

A The **title** identifies what product the safety guidelines focus on.

B This section lists **recommendations** that product owners and users should follow in order to ensure safe usage of the product.

C This section lists the **hazards** associated with the product.

D This section includes phone number and e-mail address where dangerous products or product-related injuries can be reported.

A Spa Safety Information

The U.S. Consumer Product Safety Commission (CPSC) recommends these safety precautions for spa owners and users.

B
1. Always use a locked safety cover when the spa is not in use and keep young children away from spas unless there is constant adult supervision.
2. Maintain the dual drains and covers required by current safety standards.
3. Regularly have a professional check your spa and make sure it is in safe working condition.
4. Locate the cut-off switch for your pump so you can turn it off in an emergency.
5. Be aware that consuming alcohol while using a spa could lead to drowning.
6. Keep the temperature of the water in the spa at 104° Fahrenheit or below.

C CPSC warns about these **hazards** related to spas, hot tubs, and whirlpools:
Drownings—Since 1980, the CPSC has reports of 700 deaths in spas and hot tubs. About one-third of those were drownings by children under age five.
Hair Entanglement—Since 1978, CPSC has reports of 49 incidents (including 13 deaths) in which people's hair was sucked into the suction fitting (drain) of a spa, hot tub, or whirlpool, causing the victim's head to be held under water.
Hot Tub Temperatures—CPSC knows of several deaths from extremely hot water (approximately 110 degrees Fahrenheit) in a spa. High temperatures can lead to unconsciousness.

D To report a dangerous product or a product-related injury, please contact info@cpsc.gov, or call the CPSC's hotline at (800) 638-2772.

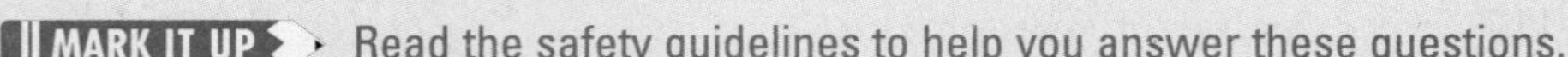

Read the safety guidelines to help you answer these questions.

1. Circle the major cause of spa deaths.
2. What should you always do when a spa is not in use? Circle the answer on the guidelines.
3. Why does the CPSC recommend that water temperature in a spa should be kept at 104 degrees Fahrenheit or below? ______________________________
4. Circle the e-mail address you can write to about a dangerous spa or a spa-related injury.
5. **ASSESSMENT PRACTICE** What temperature should the water in a spa be kept at?
   A. below 110° F
   B. above 104° F
   C. above 700° F
   D. below 104° F

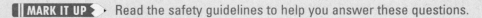

Reading a Television Schedule

Knowing how to read a television schedule accurately will help you figure out the times of your favorite programs. Look at the example as you read each strategy on this list.

- **A** Scan the **title** to know what the schedule covers.
- **B** Look for **labels** that show **dates** or **days of the week** to help you understand how the weekly or daily schedule works.
- **C** Look for **expressions of time** to know what hours or minutes are listed on the schedule.
- **D** Study the **labels** identifying the different channels listed on the schedule.
- **E** Look at **program titles** to see what shows are playing at a given time on a given channel.

A **Afternoon Programming Schedule** **B** **July 19, 2002**

C	**1:00 P.M.**	**1:30 P.M.**	**2:00 P.M.**	**2:30 P.M.**	**3:00 P.M.**	**3:30 P.M.**	**4:00 P.M.**
2 NMXX	Antique Timezone		Trixie Bear	Ken Marx	Who's That Head?		News
D 6 NPRR	Judge Gus	Judge Edna	The Stanleys		Town Noise		News
7 NABQ	Foot Sore (cont.) **E**		U.S. Shot Put Finals		Infomercial	Space Time	Starmix
8 NHH	Movie: Condor's Revenge				Movie: The Road to Ruin		
11 EPS	Too Many Tomatoes		Cook Karl	Fast Times	Travel Log	Travel Log	Mexican Cuisine
13 MP&Z	Soapy	Mush	Tears	Infomercial	News	News	Carrie C
18 WOW	Kids Kraft		Movie: KeeKee and Sammy				Kids News
19 PBJ	Jam City	Keevo	Behind the…	Behind the…	Storyback	Storyback	Dance Party
Pay Channels listed in **BOLD**							

MARK IT UP Answer the following questions using the television schedule and the strategies on this page.

1. What time span is covered by this schedule? ______________________
2. Circle the pay channels.
3. How many movies are listed on this schedule? ______________________
4. **ASSESSMENT PRACTICE** If you watched channel 6 from 1:30 to 2:00 and then watched channel 11 from 2:00 to 2:30, what two programs did you view?
   A. *Too Many Tomatoes* and *The Stanleys*
   B. *Judge Gus* and *Tears*
   C. *Judge Edna* and *Cook Karl*
   D. *Herbs and Gardens* and *Fast Times*

Personal Word List

Use these pages to build your personal vocabulary. As you read the selections, take time to mark unfamiliar words. These should be words that seem interesting or important enough to add to your permanent vocabulary. After reading, look up the meanings of these words and record the information below. For each word, write a sentence that shows its correct use.

Review your list from time to time. Try to put these words into use in your writing and and conversation.

Word: ____________________

Selection: ____________________

Page/Line: __________ / __________

Part of Speech: ____________________

Definition: ____________________

____

____

Sentence: ____________________

____

____

____

Word: ____________________

Selection: ____________________

Page/Line: __________ / __________

Part of Speech: ____________________

Definition: ____________________

____

____

Sentence: ____________________

____

____

____

Word: ____________________

Selection: ____________________

Page/Line: __________ / __________

Part of Speech: ____________________

Definition: ____________________

____

____

Sentence: ____________________

____

____

____

Word: ______________________

Selection: ______________________

Page/Line: __________ / __________

Part of Speech: ______________________

Definition: ______________________

____

____

Sentence: ______________________

____

____

____

Word: ______________________

Selection: ______________________

Page/Line: __________ / __________

Part of Speech: ______________________

Definition: ______________________

____

____

Sentence: ______________________

____

____

____

Word: ______________________

Selection: ______________________

Page/Line: __________ / __________

Part of Speech: ______________________

Definition: ______________________

____

____

Sentence: ______________________

____

____

____

Word: ______________________

Selection: ______________________

Page/Line: __________ / __________

Part of Speech: ______________________

Definition: ______________________

____

____

Sentence: ______________________

____

____

____

Personal Word List

Word: ______________________

Selection: ______________________

Page/Line: __________ / __________

Part of Speech: ______________________

Definition: ______________________

____

____

Sentence: ______________________

____

____

____

Word: ______________________

Selection: ______________________

Page/Line: __________ / __________

Part of Speech: ______________________

Definition: ______________________

____

____

Sentence: ______________________

____

____

____

Word: ______________________

Selection: ______________________

Page/Line: __________ / __________

Part of Speech: ______________________

Definition: ______________________

____

____

Sentence: ______________________

____

____

____

Word: ______________________

Selection: ______________________

Page/Line: __________ / __________

Part of Speech: ______________________

Definition: ______________________

____

____

Sentence: ______________________

____

____

____

Word: ______________________

Selection: ______________________

Page/Line: __________ / __________

Part of Speech: ______________________

Definition: ______________________

____

____

Sentence: ______________________

____

____

____

Word: ______________________

Selection: ______________________

Page/Line: __________ / __________

Part of Speech: ______________________

Definition: ______________________

____

____

Sentence: ______________________

____

____

____

Word: ______________________

Selection: ______________________

Page/Line: __________ / __________

Part of Speech: ______________________

Definition: ______________________

____

____

Sentence: ______________________

____

____

____

Word: ______________________

Selection: ______________________

Page/Line: __________ / __________

Part of Speech: ______________________

Definition: ______________________

____

____

Sentence: ______________________

____

____

____

Personal Word List

Word: ____________________

Selection: ____________________

Page/Line: __________ / __________

Part of Speech: ____________________

Definition: ____________________

____

____

Sentence: ____________________

____

____

____

Word: ____________________

Selection: ____________________

Page/Line: __________ / __________

Part of Speech: ____________________

Definition: ____________________

____

____

Sentence: ____________________

____

____

____

Word: ____________________

Selection: ____________________

Page/Line: __________ / __________

Part of Speech: ____________________

Definition: ____________________

____

____

Sentence: ____________________

____

____

____

Word: ____________________

Selection: ____________________

Page/Line: __________ / __________

Part of Speech: ____________________

Definition: ____________________

____

____

Sentence: ____________________

____

____

____

Word: ______________________________

Selection: ______________________________

Page/Line: ______________ / ______________

Part of Speech: ______________________________

Definition: ______________________________

____

____

Sentence: ______________________________

____

____

____

Word: ______________________________

Selection: ______________________________

Page/Line: ______________ / ______________

Part of Speech: ______________________________

Definition: ______________________________

____

____

Sentence: ______________________________

____

____

____

Word: ______________________________

Selection: ______________________________

Page/Line: ______________ / ______________

Part of Speech: ______________________________

Definition: ______________________________

____

____

Sentence: ______________________________

____

____

____

Word: ______________________________

Selection: ______________________________

Page/Line: ______________ / ______________

Part of Speech: ______________________________

Definition: ______________________________

____

____

Sentence: ______________________________

____

____

____

Personal Word List

Word: ______________________

Selection: ______________________

Page/Line: __________ / __________

Part of Speech: ______________________

Definition: ______________________

____

____

Sentence: ______________________

____

____

____

Word: ______________________

Selection: ______________________

Page/Line: __________ / __________

Part of Speech: ______________________

Definition: ______________________

____

____

Sentence: ______________________

____

____

____

Word: ______________________

Selection: ______________________

Page/Line: __________ / __________

Part of Speech: ______________________

Definition: ______________________

____

____

Sentence: ______________________

____

____

____

Word: ______________________

Selection: ______________________

Page/Line: __________ / __________

Part of Speech: ______________________

Definition: ______________________

____

____

Sentence: ______________________

____

____

____

Acknowledgments

(Continued from page ii)

Excerpts from *The Iliad* by Homer, translated by Robert Fagles. Copyright © 1990 by Robert Fagles. Used by permission of Viking Penguin, a division of Penguin Putnam Inc.

Oedipus the King, from *Three Theban Plays* by Sophocles, translated by Robert Fagles. Copyright © 1982 by Robert Fagles. Used by permission of Viking Penguin, a division of Penguin Putnam Inc.

Random House: Excerpts from the *Aeneid* by Virgil, translated by Robert Fitzgerald. Copyright 1980, 1982, 1983 by Robert Fitzgerald. Used by permission of Random House, Inc.

New Directions Publishing Corp.: "The River-Merchant's Wife: A Letter" by Li Po, translated by Ezra Pound, from *Personae: The Collected Shorter Poems of Ezra Pound.* Copyright © 1926 by Ezra Pound. Reprinted by permission of New Directions Publishing Corp.

"Gazing at the Lu Mountain Waterfall" by Li Po, from *The Selected Poems of Li Po,* translated by David Hinton. Copyright © 1996 by David Hinton. Reprinted by permission of New Directions Publishing Corp.

Columbia University Press: "Still Night Thoughts" by Li Po, translated by Burton Watson, from *The Columbia Anthology of Traditional Chinese Literature,* edited by Victor H. Mair. Copyright © 1994 by Columbia University Press. Reprinted by permission of the publisher.

Pearson Education: Excerpt from *Sundiata: An Epic of Old Mali* by D. T. Niane, translated by G. D. Pickett. Copyright © 1965 by Longman Group Limited. Reprinted by permission of Pearson Education Limited.

Farrar, Straus & Giroux: "Canto I" and "Canto III," from *The Inferno of Dante: A New Verse Translation* by Robert Pinsky. Translation copyright © 1994 by Robert Pinsky. Reprinted by permission of Farrar, Straus and Giroux, LLC.

Viking Penguin: Excerpts from *Don Quixote* by Miguel de Cervantes Saavedra, translated by Samuel Putnam. Copyright © 1949 by The Viking Press, Inc. Used by permission of Viking Penguin, a division of Penguin Putnam Inc.

Doubleday: Excerpts from *Goethe's Faust,* translated by Walter Kaufmann. Copyright © 1961 by Walter Kaufmann. Used by permission of Doubleday, a division of Random House, Inc.

Schocken Books: "The Metamorphosis" by Franz Kafka, translated by Willa and Edwin Muir, from *Franz Kafka: The Complete Stories,* edited by Nahum N. Glatzer. Copyright © 1946, 1947, 1948, 1949, 1954, 1958, 1971 by Schocken Books. Used by permission of Schocken Books, a division of Random House, Inc.

Alfred A. Knopf: "The Guest," from *Exile and the Kingdom* by Albert Camus, translated by Justin O'Brien. Copyright © 1957, 1958 by Alfred A. Knopf, a division of Random House, Inc. Used by permission of Alfred A. Knopf, a division of Random House, Inc.

Farrar, Straus & Giroux: "Amnesty," from *Jump and Other Stories* by Nadine Gordimer. Copyright © 1991 by Felix Licensing, B. V. Reprinted by permission of Farrar, Straus and Giroux, LLC, and Penguin Books Canada Limited.

HarperCollins Publishers: "The Handsomest Drowned Man in the World," from *Leaf Storm and Other Stories* by Gabriel Garcia Marquez. Copyright © 1971 by Gabriel Garcia Marquez. Reprinted by permission of HarperCollins Publishers Inc.

Cobblestone Publishing Company: Excerpt and adaptation from "The Lure of Light" by Ruth Tenzer Feldman, *Odyssey,* October 1999. Reprinted by permission of Cobblestone Publishing Company.

Art Credits

2 Statue of a hero, possibly Gilgamesh, taming a lion (722–705 B.C.). Musée du Louvre, Paris. Photograph copyright © Erich Lessing/Art Resource, New York; **3** Musée du Louvre, Paris. Photograph copyright © Erich Lessing/Art Resource, New York; **27** Detail of illustration of Rama fighting Ravana. Courtesy of the Trustees of the Victoria & Albert Museum, London; **159** Copyright © Clive Druett/Papilio/Corbis; **166–167, 209** Copyright © Corbis; **259** Mark Douet/Stone/Getty Images; **291** Michael Wilson/The Image Bank/Getty Images.

Cover

Illustration copyright © 2002 Glenn Harrington.